EDIBLE MEMORY

Edible Memory

The Lure of Heirloom Tomatoes & Other Forgotten Foods

Jennifer A. Jordan

The University of Chicago Press · Chicago and London

Jennifer A. Jordan is associate professor of sociology
at the University of Wisconsin, Milwaukee. She is also
the author of *Structures of Memory: Understanding
Urban Change in Berlin and Beyond.*

The University of Chicago Press, Chicago 60637
The University of Chicago Press, Ltd., London
© 2015 by The University of Chicago
All rights reserved. Published 2015.
Printed in the United States of America

24 23 22 21 20 19 18 17 16 15   1 2 3 4 5

ISBN-13: 978-0-226-22810-5 (cloth)
ISBN-13: 978-0-226-22824-2 (e-book)
DOI: 10.7208/chicago/9780226228242.001.0001

Library of Congress Cataloging-in-Publication Data
Jordan, Jennifer A., 1970– author.
Edible memory: the lure of heirloom tomatoes &
other forgotten foods / Jennifer A. Jordan.
pages; cm
Includes bibliographical references and index.
ISBN 978-0-226-22810-5 (cloth: alk. paper) —
ISBN 978-0-226-22824-2 (e-book)
1. Heirloom varieties (Plants) 2. Food—social aspects. I. Title.
SB453.5.J67 2015
634—dc23   2014035972

♾ This paper meets the requirements of ANSI/NISO
Z39.48-1992 (Permanence of Paper).

For Clyde Carlos

Contents

Acknowledgments

I ALWAYS READ a book's acknowledgments in search of networks and connections, but also as an insight into the conditions under which a book was produced. In my experience a book takes twice as long to write as I originally expect, and this one has undergone dramatic transformations over the years of its slow creation. Many, many people have helped me along the way, and some may already have forgotten the role they played at critical early stages. So much of this book was a learning experience for me, and it is deeply pleasurable and immensely humbling to realize how little I knew when I began and how much I had to learn from the people I spoke with and read about. I very much appreciate the patience of so many people, both with my questions and with the time that has elapsed between our conversations in fields, orchards, or gardens and the appearance of this book.

The first people to thank are those who funded various stages of the research. A Fulbright fellowship to the International Research Center for Cultural Studies (IFK) in Vienna in 2007 afforded the first opportunity to really throw myself into this research (quite literally at one point). The remarkable collection of people at the IFK played a crucial role in developing my thinking about this subject. The opportunity to read, write, talk, and eat with such an energetic group of graduate students, midcareer faculty like myself, and bright stars in the academic skies was invaluable.

A subsequent and much longer fellowship from the Austrian Research Fund (FWF) for a position as a senior scientist at the Austrian Academy of Sciences took place in the welcoming context of the Institute for Cultural Studies (IKT), led first by Moritz Csáky and then by Michael Rössner. While much of this time was spent working on a different book, discussing my research with these wonderful colleagues was invaluable for *Edible Memory* as well as for the book I was writing then (a book about gardens that will someday see the light of day). This position also gave me the opportunity to meet with a diverse array of colleagues from many disciplines, who would bring me newspaper clippings about heirloom vegetable fairs and generously critique my work. Moritz Csáky in particular contributed great enthusiasm and extremely fruitful conversations, most often within the welcoming walls of the Altes Café. Special thanks in this era are also due to Aleida Assmann, Kurt Farasin, Lutz Musner, Reinhard Puntigam, Herwig Pucher, Oliver Rathkolb, and especially Beate Koller and Dirk Rupnow. Other stages of the research were helped tremendously by the gardeners, curators, monks, and public relations people who answered my e-mails and showed me around. Marcia Carmichael, Andy Mariani, and Andy Griffin were extremely helpful, as were Chris Braithwaite and Ulrike Nehiba.

I was able to take advantage of external funding only because of the patience and forbearance of my colleagues at the University of Wisconsin–Milwaukee, who recognized the once-in-a-lifetime chance these fellowships afforded me. They tolerated my lengthy absence, welcomed me back home and (as so many others have done) passed along recipes and tales of fabulous tomatoes. The colleagues who read my work include Nancy Mathiowetz, Bill Mayrl, Stacey Oliker, and Kent Redding. It would have taken considerably more than seven years to write this book without the help of Deb Ritchie Kolberg, Alexander Taylor, Heather Durant, Mary O'Bryan, and Diana Jaskierny, who oversaw hours of scanning and searching for everything from articles about peaches to statistics about supermarkets. I am so grateful for their help and their good cheer! Deb Ritchie Kolberg in particular provided not only support but also inspiration, in our many conversations about the world in general and food in particular. Ashkan Rezvani Naraghi also deserves many thanks for his tireless work in the final stages of editing, as well as his assistance with the next project.

My students over the many years of my career also deserve many thanks. I have only once taught a class on food, but I manage to work the topic into seminars on the history of sociological theory or urban change nonetheless. My students have followed the progress of the book, waited patiently for comments on their work when I was trying to meet a deadline, brought me articles and stories and bits of trivia, and inspired me with their curiosity and enthusiasm for the subject. I have learned more from them than they will probably ever know, and their imprint is definitely on the pages of this book. I hesitate to name names because I would no doubt leave out someone important, so suffice it to say that I am grateful to you all.

Several professionals in the world of words lent a hand at various points in the arduous task of writing, including Shari Caudron, Peter Dreyer, and Alice Bennett, cogent readers whose efforts helped clarify the manuscript at crucial moments. In the world of sociology and neighboring disciplines, Wendy Griswold, Chandra Mukerji, Jeff Olick, Julie Guthman, Michael Carolan, and Rick Biernacki, among many others, offered valuable insight and support across the many years of writing. The talks I gave at widely different stages of research, writing, and thinking also shaped the final product, including talks at Northwestern University, the University of California, Santa Cruz, Ohio State University, the Chicago Rarities Orchard Project, Slow Food/Terra Madre Austria, University College Dublin, and the Chicago Columbia Society. Speaking to such a range of audiences honed my thinking about food and memory, and I also appreciate the stories and examples that people happily shared at every one of these events.

When it takes seven years to write a book, the debts of gratitude to friends and family and colleagues pile up considerably. Many, many thanks are due to the people who have read and commented on portions of the manuscript over the years. Particular thanks are due to Jim Jordan, Sandy Jordan, and Dick Archer for generously reading the entire manuscript at a late stage. My mother, Sandy Jordan, deserves special thanks for the steady stream of newspaper clippings and recipes, and for her careful perusal of *British Country Living* for any information about antique pigs or heirloom beans. How lucky I am to have parents who understand why their daughter might set out to write a book about tomatoes, and who have been unwavering in their support from the moment it became clear that much of my life would be wrapped up in words and books and classrooms. Much love and many thanks are also due to some of my favorite people on this earth, Carl Jordan, Carrie Diaz, and Clyde Jordan, for their support and patience with the project, and for their gentle encouragement to wrap it up.

Jasmine Alinder, Aims McGuinness, Alice McGuinness, Eliza Mae McGuinness, Rob Smith, Nakia Gordon, Marcus Filippello, Lisa Silverman, David Divalerio, Tami Williams, Elena Gorfinkel, Jennifer Johung, Andy Noble, Kennan Ferguson, Carolyn Eichner, Jocelyn Szczepaniak-

Gillece, Richard Leson, Philip Minehan, Oriol Mirosa, Gordon Gauchat, Tasha Oren, Stewart Ikeda, Gary Steinhafel, Jocelyn Servick, Isabella Winkler, Andrew Zimmerman, Johanna Bockman, Laura Avedisian, Andre Venter, Anne Basting, Dan Vyleta, Lauren Fox, Chantal Wright, Josh Dunsby, Rebecca Wittman, Christine Evans, Karolina May, Nick Fleischer, Brad Lichtenstein, Debbie Jordan, Ian Dunhill, Hadley Northrop, Anne Bramley, Eric Beck, Amanda Seligman, Dirk Rupnow, Steve McKay, Megan Baumann, Chris Henke, Carolyn Hsu, Doug Hartmann, Laura Miller, Winson Chu, Dan Kern, Brigitte Gretner, Rolf Göder, Colleen Foley, and many other dear friends and colleagues here in Milwaukee and beyond offered beautiful meals and nights out, great conversations, and the pleasant sociability necessary (to me) for productive writing. All of these kind and generous people have been grounding and comforting, a perfect antidote to the solitude of writing. Jasmine Alinder in particular offered so many meals and pep talks and encouraging text messages—I'm so grateful for the happy accident of finding an old friend just down the block, thousands of miles from home. Ana Acena, Kam Shapiro, Jason Frank, and Jerry Johnson all influenced this book in various ways, and certainly through the many meals and conversations we've had together, often within sight of a shoreline. And I'm pretty sure the title of the book came about in Kam and Ana's living room. Thanks are also due to Margaret Kaye Curtis, whose strength and resilience continue to inspire me, in good times and hard times alike. Alexander Kaesbohrer deserves thanks as well, even if we didn't get to spend as much time together in the writing of this book as in the last one. Jeremie Ruby-Strauss may not be accustomed to having his name associated with such a subdued topic as heirloom vegetables, but his friendship and editorial acumen have also played an important role in getting this book out of my brain and into the world.

Much of this book came about while I was living in Austria, a country of passionate eaters and remarkably good food. Dominik Göbel, Lena Göbel, Maria Moser, and Heinz Göbel (rest his soul) deserve many thanks for their hospitality and friendship. I am so fortunate to have been taken in by all of them, and I hope they know how much I appreciate their kindness and warmth. Heinz left this world too soon, just as this book was being completed, and he leaves an imprint on the manuscript. I have such clear images in my mind of talking with him at the kitchen table, or watching him work quietly in his studio or gather windfall fruit in the meadow out back. My thinking about tomatoes, apples, turnips, and so much else was forged in the crucible created by his son, Dominik Göbel, who long understood this project better than I did, and who engaged in years of conversations and excursions with me, talking through these ideas year after year, even when we went down different paths.

Toward the end of the long period of writing, I received a boost of enthusiasm from wonderful people in Chicago. Conversations with Dave Snyder of the Chicago Rarities Orchard Project, with Alex Poltorak of the Urban Canopy, and with LaManda Joy of the Peterson Garden Project, among many others, helped me see the end of the book on the horizon, in addition to providing some of the most delightful moments of the writing process in their farms and gardens, and in their company.

Many, many thanks are also due to Doug Mitchell of the University of Chicago Press, whose enthusiasm for the project energized me the moment we met, in a fateful and pleasurable conversation in a San Francisco Hilton, reminding me that people outside my own head might also find heirloom tomatoes interesting. Our correspondence is peppered less with discussions of prose than with thoughts about cherries and apples, and with recollections of past meals and plans for future ones. I look forward to many more good meals with Doug and am very grateful to be in his orbit. Tim McGovern, Erin DeWitt, and Carrie Adams have also been immensely helpful, and the anonymous readers of the manuscript offered invaluable suggestions with generous and careful readings. The book is vastly improved by their selfless and anonymous work. At the same time, even though I could not have written this book without the small army of people mentioned above, any mistakes and omissions are entirely my own.

Prologue

I BEGAN THIS BOOK several years ago in a third-floor walkup in Chicago, pondering what path to take after finishing my first book. I was living with no hint of a garden, but with a decent kitchen and a willing consumer for my cooking. It was a classic Chicago kitchen, with the original primitive icebox—a cupboard built into the wall so the back was more or less open to the elements. There was the obligatory back door, originally for the milkman and other deliveries up the rickety back stairs. The kitchen was shoehorned into a space not designed to hold modern conveniences like a refrigerator and stove, but I loved its worn wood floor and its high windows showing nothing but sky and a few treetops. Because there wasn't quite enough room for a chair, the man I happily shared this space with would perch on a footstool while I cooked what I'd found at the farmers' market. In turn, I would perch there while he taught me to make the dumplings, crepes, and stews of his homeland and his mother's kitchen.

As high summer slowly turned to autumn, the city itself played an important role in my thinking about heirloom food. In particular, my visits to the Green City Market in Lincoln Park introduced me to a range of edible biodiversity I'd never seen before. Like many people who may read this book, my connection to heirloom fruits and vegetables developed less in the misty recesses of childhood than in the throes of urban adulthood. I didn't grow up eating many of the fruits and vegetables understood today as heirloom varieties—I was well into my thirties before I really started to notice heirloom tomatoes. Even though I'd been going to farmers' markets for years, I found the biodiversity at the Green City Market remarkable. The market offered great bins of so many varieties of tomatoes, potatoes, and apples, trucked in from Chicago's agricultural hinterlands—rural Illinois, southern Michigan, and a growing number of farms right in the city. It was full of foods I'd never seen before, foods that cried out to be cooked and eaten.

When I could swing it, I'd go to the Lincoln Park farmers' market on Wednesday mornings, which were quieter than the bustling Saturdays when the market filled with happy weekenders. The main competition early on Wednesdays came from the men and women in chefs' whites, dragging coolers and wheeled carts. The market itself was pleasantly informal. Each stand was different in both content and style of display, and my shopping bags quickly filled. However, I went to the market not only as an eager consumer, but also as a sociologist, and cooking, shopping, and research were difficult to separate as the seeds of a new book began to germinate.

But why should the edible biodiversity I found at the market become a subject for a book by a sociologist and not just ingredients for a pleasurable dinner? Particularly given that my first book treated what was seemingly a very different topic—urban change after the Berlin Wall fell, and especially how people understood the past in the fabric of that city. But that book, and indeed most of my writing and research, addressed a question similar to the one at the heart of this current book: How does memory shape materiality—how do the stories we tell each other about the past shape the material world? In the context of the farmers' market, the questions guiding this book emerged. How does a tomato become an heirloom, how does an apple become an antique? And what are the implications of this transformation, for society, for biodiversity, and for the world around us? In answering these questions, as later chapters will show, I uncovered the phenomenon I have come to call edible memory, the infusing of food, heirloom and otherwise, with connections to the past in ways both deeply personal and inherently social.

That fall I started to work on a new manuscript, wanting to write about my great-great-aunt's kitchen—so different from my own up high in that apartment, which was a perfect vantage point for watching thunderstorms move across the city and out over the lake and airplanes heading the opposite way. My aunt's kitchen, on the other hand, looked out over the sparsely populated foothills of California's Gold Country, and housed a cast-iron woodstove and lace curtains in the heart of an old homestead. I wanted to delve into this mythical family realm, to see what lessons I could learn and to follow these personal stories back out to the broader realm of sociology.

We called my aunt Budder. As a child, my grandmother rechristened just about every member of the family with a new name, and somehow her Aunt Annabelle became Budder. Budder was born on the border between Mexico and Arizona, the last surviving daughter of my gun-toting, colonizing, Spanish-speaking Anglo, silver-mining, stagecoach-driving great-great-grandmother, Mae. At nineteen, Budder married a man my grandmother named Uncle Mutts, and they moved to a tiny homestead on a sprawling Northern California ranch, where she spent more than fifty years as a cattle rancher. She lived a long life, and three generations of nieces (including me) and one nephew spent important parts of our childhood at the ranch. My mother spent every summer there with another of Budder's grand-nieces, running wild with the calves, spending hours in the swimming pool fed by an ice-cold mountain spring, and hiding in the garden full of hefty beefsteak tomatoes and dahlias the size of dinner plates until, at the end of the summer, Budder would take them into town to buy back-to-school clothes, a portent of the inevitable end of a summer at the ranch. My mother would return to Los Angeles and her cousin would return to Marin County, leaving the sun-warmed tomatoes and peaches behind.

In my Chicago kitchen, and at my Chicago desk, I kept thinking about Budder's kitchen, and about her garden. Poring over old photographs, asking my mother endless questions, I originally sketched out a memoir of that time and place, moving inward through that mythical kitchen and its garden. Remnants of that kitchen still circulate in my family—damask linens from Budder's surprisingly well-dressed table, our beloved stainless-steel steam table pans, and an inordinate number of gelatin molds we can't seem to part with despite the diminished significance of Jell-O in our culinary lives. In my memory, perhaps combined with my imagination, I would wander through Budder's house, always coming back to the kitchen dominated by an enormous cast-iron woodstove, enameled in the creamy white and mint green ubiquitous at the ranch. On winter mornings, when I was a little girl, some family member would bundle me and my little brother downstairs from the chilly attic or back bedroom into the kitchen, to get dressed in front of the stove, already giving off substantial warmth because

Budder was an early riser. One of my most powerful memories is the sound and smell of Budder starting the fire at dawn—the strike of the sturdy wooden match, the acrid smell of newspaper catching fire, and the clank of a burner as she popped it open to feed more kindling into the stove's belly.

For decades, Budder baked untold numbers of pies made from scratch, filling the homemade crusts with the fruits of her garden to feed the hungry ranch hands. The pies made a fine breakfast for a long day of riding through the foothills. Like many people in the rural United States at the time, she lived without electricity until sometime in the second half of the twentieth century, and for much of her life she drew her water from the cool, silvery hand pump in the middle of her screened-in porch. Budder put up much of what they ate, grown in her expansive and orderly garden. Town was a long drive away in their old Buick, and even longer in their beat-up farm truck, so a quick trip to the grocery store was not an option. They supplied their own beef, milk, chicken, eggs, fruit, and vegetables—a level of self-sufficiency many people now aspire to in the current trend toward local and artisanal production. But Budder was not operating as some heir to an unbroken chain of agricultural production. She spent her first years on the Mexican border, in a very different ecosystem with a necessarily different approach to food production, facing scorching heat and fluctuations between monsoons and a lengthy dry season.[1] The rest of her childhood and young adulthood she spent mostly in Burbank, California, in a vast Victorian boardinghouse where her mother traded in her pearl-handled pistol for a life as a local matriarch, a translator in the courts, and countless other pursuits that led to fame, if not fortune. At her funeral hundreds of people lined up to pay their respects. The family kept no livestock at the boardinghouse, to the best of my knowledge, and their milk came from the milkman. Fruit and vegetables came from truck farms in the surrounding valley, farms that have long since given way to subdivisions and freeways.

Although my great-great-aunt came from a generation many of us might associate with old-fashioned food, she had to teach herself many of the skills of gardening, preserving, and cooking. As unconventional as her mother was, she did follow the basics of white middle-class Victorian femininity, including hiring a family cook. This means that Budder would likely not have learned many of these skills hands-on before she and her new husband moved to their isolated ranch. Budder also (like so many of her generation) was fascinated by non-heirloom foods, the results of an early era of industrialized food production. Hybrid tomatoes, Jell-O, and store-bought cake mix all captured her imagination and appetite. In my family (and no doubt in many others), many of our edible heirlooms have little to do with rare genes, and this is important to remember. While this book focuses on the heirloom food movement, I argue that edible memory is far more expansive than simply the way people treat old-fashioned tomatoes or apples. Based on my observations, edible memory is something people enact with regard to a whole range of foods—including some of the most highly processed foods around. The heirloom varieties I focus on in most of this book are a particularly charged site of the intersections of food, memory, and meaning, but they serve as one rich example of a much bigger process.

One of the treasured recipes passed down through at least four generations of my family is seafoam salad—green Jell-O with mayonnaise, pineapple, cottage cheese, and horseradish. I'm not making this up! Other folks list very different ingredients under the same name: Cool Whip, maraschino cherries, pear juice, and all kinds of other delicacies that never made their way into *our* ancestral salad. Our version of seafoam salad is especially appetizing when chilled in a massive copper mold shaped like a curved fish and served on a big platter in all its jiggling opaque green glory, chunks of pineapple and curds of cottage cheese poking through the glossy surface. As far as we can tell, Budder initiated our seafoam salad tradition, clearly wowed by one of the free full-color recipe booklets that used to tempt homemakers in the early days of such novel foods.

My great-great-aunt embodies a paradox in the family trees of many people in the United States. She possessed old-fashioned self-reliance and housekeeping talent combined with a love of the new and an enthusiasm for precisely the processed foods and narrow gene pool that emerged from the mechanization of agriculture in the middle of the twentieth century, which shrank the genetic diversity in our food supply (something I will come back to in chapter 1). She was a talented gardener who coaxed an incredible bounty out of the red soil of California's Gold Country (the soil of her vegetable garden was a deep, rich brown, built up over many years), and she loved hybrid beefsteak tomatoes above all others. Bushels of them ripened under her care. She owned pickle crocks as big as dishwashers to preserve her bumper crops of cucumbers, and once she did have electricity, she kept in her freezer cuts of meat that most of us today would have no clue what to do with. Yet for all her self-reliance and culinary skill without conveniences like running water and electricity, my aunt was also bewitched by the modern innovations of lime Jell-O and hybrid tomato seed, and she embraced many foods worlds away from the heirloom plants described in the rest of this book.

Budder fed legions of friends and family, hosting parties that lasted for days, with guests waking up on the lawn or the front porch. The garden, the kitchen, a house full of perfectly made twin guest beds and so many nooks and crannies, drew us all into her orbit. So too did the tremendous meals she cooked for the gathered generations at Thanksgiving and Easter. For reasons that will soon become clear, Christmas fell off the roster of family holidays for nearly a decade. Every gathering had the same culinary starting point—the pot of ranch beans simmering on the woodstove as relatives trickled in after their long, dusty drives from Los Angeles or Marin County or the Central Coast. The family ate the beans with homemade Parker House rolls and of course butter from Budder's beloved Jersey cows (she usually kept two at a time). As the family readied for their long drive home after a holiday, Budder would pack what she called a *liacha*, a term from her childhood in Arizona: a parcel of delicious things to take on the road. Every *liacha* included her homemade butter, rock hard, grooved with the imprint of her butter paddles and engraved with her initials, a deft A.M. (for Annabelle McNutt), and wrapped tightly in an insulating layer of the local newspaper. All this love, her warm, capable arms, and her stainless-steel catering pans full of the season's food kept us close and adoring until the end of her life.

But a shadow of excruciating loss hung over the ranch, barely perceptible in the glow of my aunt's love for her generations of nieces (and a single nephew later in her life, my little brother), of the kitchen and garden that nourished so many, and of every *liacha* carefully packed with butter and the garden's current crop of corn or peaches or tomatoes. Budder and Uncle Mutts had only one child, a daughter named

Bobby who grew up in the rough-and-tumble life of the ranch hands. Starting as a very young girl, she would ride her horse out into the foothills with her father and the ranch hands, helping with the dusty hard work of cattle ranching. She kept up with ranch life as she got ready to go to Stanford University, an unusual step for a sixteen-year-old girl in 1942. One morning Bobby and Uncle Mutts were heading to one of the pastures to look after some of their Herefords. Bobby rode out ahead, and Uncle Mutts planned to meet her there. As he rode over a ridge, he caught sight of her riderless horse and soon found her nearly lifeless body. The horse must have been spooked, perhaps by a snake, and threw Bobby, who hit her head on a rock. Uncle Mutts carried her back to the ranch house with an anguish and desperation I thankfully cannot begin to imagine. She never regained consciousness, and over the following days the life slipped out of her. Family stories tell of Budder's curly brown hair, so similar to mine and my mother's, turning white and falling out in handfuls in the wake of Bobby's death. When I knew Budder, she always wore a wig or a little turban over the sparse white strands.

Cooking can be a way of expressing love. Not always, and not for everyone, but at times a shared meal can be warmth in a cold world, a focal point, a literal or metaphorical hearth to gather around. Budder gathered us around her, with a broad hospitality that included the fruits of her garden and the products of her kitchen, to fill a cavernous space in a broken heart, to bring life into a tragically empty house. Ten years after Bobby died, she and Uncle Mutts felt they could have a Christmas tree in the house again and began inviting the family for Christmas dinner too. In some form this book began in her kitchen, in that focal point of joy and sadness, love and loss, reaching for those lost memories, for that sweet space framed by incongruous lacy curtains, the clank of the woodstove, and the love of this matriarch.

When I was a little girl, one of my favorite things was making a spice cake with Budder from a store-bought mix. This cake was worlds away from the homemade pies she'd baked for decades, and from the heirloom fruits and vegetables discussed in the rest of this book. Everything we needed for the cake came straight out of the box, including the foil cake pan. I can still see myself standing with her in the little kitchen of the house she lived in during the late 1970s, after she'd moved into town. In her eighties by then, she had left her ranch and her wood-stove and the homemade pies behind, along with most of the people who'd accompanied her through her long life. Whenever my family came to visit, she'd have bought the cake mix so she and I could spend time together in the kitchen. Even today it brings tears to my eyes to think of her making the arduous journey to the grocery store and carefully putting that box of cake mix in the shopping cart, knowing I was coming for a visit soon.

We'd open the package, add water, and mix it up directly in that aluminum pan. Later we'd ice it with the foil packet of bright white frosting that also came in the package. An important part of the whole experience was the time spent in the kitchen together, mixing up the cake, then eating it washed down with glasses of milk, catching up on the important events in the lives of a nine-year-old and an eighty-year-old. The milk, too, was modern—homogenized whole milk in plastic jugs. This was worlds away from the metal pans of fresh milk she'd once set out in her pantry day after day. She'd pour the milk carefully from a big dented milk can brought in from the dairy barn by one of the ranch hands, then leave it to sit so the cream would float to the top. She skimmed off the cream to make butter, churned it, and formed blocks in oily wooden molds, then she pasteurized the milk herself by heating it on the stove.

For me, no antique apple or heirloom tomato—foods I knowingly encountered only as an adult—will ever evoke the same emotions as that highly processed cake mix.[2] There's no denying the meaning a cardboard box of artificially flavored spice cake held for both of us, the way it became a ritual we both looked forward to, a way to bring us even closer. To me this cake mix is emblematic of one of the ways edible memory can operate. As sociologist Michael Carolan recalls, "Mr. Freeze Freeze Pops . . . Push-ups, Chef Boyardee canned food, and Little Debbie snack cakes . . . take me back in a very visceral, positive way [to] my childhood," even though these foods play no real role in his appetites or eating habits today.[3] This book focuses in particular on fruits and vegetables, and mostly on what would be widely understood as heirloom varieties. But these foods are by no means the exclusive domain of edible memory, something I've found in restaurants and markets, among people with little money and those with more than enough, in popular food writing and scholarly articles. Rather, heirloom fruits and vegetables are a particularly illustrative case of the much broader construct of edible memory.

These memories sit deep. That spice cake is etched into my memory and evokes emotions difficult for me to re-create with the most old-fashioned of heirloom produce. The mix itself no longer exists, discontinued long ago and visible only in fleeting images on the Internet. Our memories of food defy easy categorization. Something happens when we eat: the transformation, even transubstantiation, of these molecules into energy and strength—and sometimes into love handles, spare tires, or what in German is called a "life preserver" (*Rettungsring*). But it can also transform into social bonds and memories, connections within families and communities and larger social groups—as well as stark divisions and distinctions, ways of resisting or oppressing, controlling and rebelling. Food—its production, consumption, and distribution—shapes and transforms a range of places as well: kitchens and dining tables, fields and forests.

At the same time that I was revisiting Budder's kitchen in my memory, I was making the rounds of Chicago's farmers' markets, tracking down flavors, colors, and textures brand-new to me but deeply familiar to people for whom these were true heirlooms, for whom a particular apple or tomato was as deeply etched into memory as that store-bought cake mix was for me. I am a sociologist, after all, and part of our job is to look beyond the individual, to identify social patterns and their connections to larger forces, these dynamic relationships between the individual and the broader world. I began to search, not for a single kitchen, but for patterns, for a multitude of kitchens—and gardens and farms and markets—set in a framework of laws and regulations, cultures and habits, landscapes and technologies. I have long been interested in the connections between memory and materiality, between the stories we tell about the past and the material world around us, whether urban space or tomatoes and apples.

The season changed in Chicago, the snow came, and I left for a research grant in Vienna. There, since spring comes far earlier than it comes to Chicago, I soon set out to explore living history museums, which seemed like another good place to look for powerful connections between memory and materiality, as well as kitchens and culture.

The markets of Chicago had planted a seed, so to speak, that bore fruit when I was standing in the garden of one of these museums. One day I took the train out to a living history museum on the eastern edge of Austria, near the border with Slovakia—a place where a two-car train runs along a single track, its horn blaring as it hurtles across country roads. The ride offers a vivid picture of people's abundant gardens, aboveground swimming pools, and elaborate clotheslines on this hot, sunny plain. The museum itself was made up of farmhouses typical of the region that had been painstakingly moved from their original locations to this patch of land. The houses were used to exhibit old ways of farm and village life—traditional furniture, clothing, and farm implements. But the buildings were nestled among flourishing gardens and thriving fruit trees, living landscapes also meant to convey elements of daily life from long ago.

In an unexpected epiphany, I was standing in front of a small espaliered apple tree alongside one of the old farmhouses at this museum, reading the little sign identifying its name and origins. I began to think how strange it was to have a sign in front of an apple tree, to connect a living tree to daily life a century or two ago. In fact, when I interviewed the gardener several months later, she explained that they had stopped putting signs in front of trees, because visitors would quickly strip all the fruit off a marked tree as soon as it was even close to being ripe, whereas the unmarked trees—equally "historical" or traditional but simply lacking signs—kept their fruit until it was ripe. Singling out a little apple tree, labeling it in a way that connects it to the past, that makes these small apples conduits to past ways of life, struck me as both very odd and very familiar. I realized I had seen this over and over in similar museums, this infusion of particular fruits and vegetables (and their genotypes) with this deep connection to the past. I had seen this linking of food, history, and memory in the gardens and kitchens of Mount Vernon and Monticello, in Stockholm's vast open-air folk museum, Skansen, and in Monterey's well-preserved adobes. I had also encountered these connections in the pages of the *New York Times* and seen Martha Stewart champion old-fashioned tomatoes and chickens to millions of readers and viewers.

I moved from the highly personal story of my great-great-aunt, this journey through my own memory with the help of my mother's stories and a few precious photographs and my own hazy recollections, to something bigger and more sociological. As I began to conduct research, talking to farmers and gardeners, reading for hours, days, and months, visiting urban farms and historical gardens, the contours of edible memory began to take shape. In its broadest sense, this concept encompasses both my own highly processed spice cake and someone else's grandmother's tomatoes—deeply individual and personal memories, shaped by and shaping the social and material world. So I set out to investigate not just my own memories of a particularly meaningful kitchen, but rather a society's memories, practices, and habits. I wanted to understand the way stories of the past attach to particular seeds and genotypes and get passed not just from one generation to the next but also to people who do not experience these memories on their own biographical paths but consume, in essence, other people's memories—a process I describe in more detail below.[4]

I began to think about edible memory not only in terms of this Proustian spice cake (recalling the madeleine that transported Marcel Proust to deep memories of his childhood) or memorable tomatoes, but also as a force driving so much social activity. In particular, members of the heirloom food movement—ranging from the hardworking seed savers who preserved this biodiversity through decades of obscurity to the diners shelling out exorbitant sums for a plate of sliced heirloom tomatoes in the nation's fanciest restaurants—were also engaged in edible memory. Edible memory encompasses ways of talking about the world, but also ways of acting on and moving through the world. I found edible memory propelling people into action—to save seeds, to plant gardens, to eat meals and tell stories. The search for edible memory took this book far afield from Budder's great cast-iron stove and her tomato patch. But it was in thinking about Budder that I began to think about edible memory—about this way that food is not just physical sustenance but also fundamentally social. Both the production and the consumption of food take place in rich layers of history and politics, economics and science, memory and materiality. Chicago's farmers' markets, Budder's kitchen, and an Austrian apple tree began to coalesce into a set of sociological questions: How did a tomato become an heirloom, and what are the causes and consequences of this change? How do the stories we tell each other about the past shape the material and social world? How do tastes in foods change over time, and how do these tastes alter landscapes, affect biodiversity, and feed into shared understandings of ourselves?

· 1 ·

Edible Memory

ONE SUMMER, on the hottest day Chicago had experienced since the 1930s, I found myself standing on the roof of a former meatpacking plant. Watching the sun set over the flat western reaches of the city, listening to the hum of bees in their rooftop hives, watching the swallows give way to bats in the evening hunt for insects, I stood in the scorching heat surrounded by the quiet foliage of tomatoes, squash, sunchokes, and potatoes growing in repurposed pickle buckets, burlap sacks, and crooked PVC pipes. The farmer had planted a mix of fruits and vegetables that he hoped could handle the unique demands of a rooftop farm, but that would also appeal to his customers' palates.[1] He had also planted seeds from a stock of family heirlooms, familiar flavors from his childhood. He transformed cast-off pulp from a local juice bar into the rich, loamy foundation for his farm, thanks in part to his hardworking interns and earthworms. Thus new flavors and familiar memories, fruits and vegetables that form the simple components of someone's lunch, yet also represent vast networks of global trade and world history, momentarily came to rest in this unlikely place. Rare fruits and vegetables that preserve flavors of the past are to be found on rooftops like this and farms, gardens, and vacant lots in many parts of the world.

For many of us, food shapes our sense of who we are. From backyard tomato patches in the United States to the potato parks of Peru, from the cornfields of Iowa to the rice paddies of Thailand, the world is crisscrossed with powerful connections among memory, food, and the places we inhabit. With the mid-twentieth-century rise of industrial farming, the genetic makeup of our food supply—the root of these memories and meanings, and of our survival—changed dramatically, more in some parts of the world than in others. In particular, the cornucopia of grains, fruit, vegetables, and livestock that the agricultural peoples of the world have relied on for millennia shrank over the century. In the United States and Europe, where industrialized agriculture is the norm, this reliance on a small fraction of the available edibles has meant a superabundance of identical corn plants in the fields of Iowa and lean white pigs populating the hog factories of South Carolina, but it leaves out an array of genetic and culinary diversity. This change came about in the face of a declining market for the plants and animals that were not well-suited to industrial agriculture. Large old apple trees are just one example. Orchards full of standard apple trees (as opposed to dwarf and semi-dwarf) that grow to twenty-five feet once containing tremendous biodiversity were felled by the thousands as developers subdivided farms and orchards, built houses, and carved roads and freeways into the changing landscape.[2] Apple production became more standardized and centralized, shifting from tall trees in backyards and farms and small orchards to short trees in large orchards growing only a few varieties. Laws and farming practices and subsidies changed in this era, as did tastes and habits.[3] This change has occurred not only in the United States but also around the world, as great swaths of land have been covered in monocultures of Cavendish bananas, pineapples, and corn and soybeans that are nearly identical genetically.

Numerous apple varieties have vanished permanently from the face of the earth[4] and cattle breeds that numbered in the tens of thousands in the 1920s are now gone forever, but in many parts of the world people are working hard to preserve the biodiversity and genetic heritage not only of rare panda bears or singular orchids, but also of barnyard animals and the backyard vegetable garden.[5] A major consequence of this work in the United States has been the revival of neglected varieties of fruits, vegetables, grains, and livestock.

All my senses were engaged in my search for the connections among food, memory, and the earth around us, discovering rich, living landscapes of old-fashioned plants and animals and delicious meals of locally grown and home-cooked food. I came upon the links between a simple midday meal and the complex webs of history and geography in which we dwell. I learned the ways a tomato can evoke the past and an apple can offer hope for the future. These memories and meanings matter not only to the menus of fancy restaurants or well-stocked organic grocery stores, but also to subsistence gardeners and to agricultural biodiversity and the future of the food supply.[6] This is a story that comes about from watching people do their thing—from observing individual farmers and eaters and whole populations pursuing their habits and appetites across time and space, the ways people experience and work on and narrate the world.[7]

One of the last trips I took before finishing the final draft of this book was to the Seed Savers Exchange Conference and Campout in Decorah, Iowa. In one of the show gardens, seeds are grown out that have been sent in by members across the country, with little signs that recount their particular stories. These plants thus contribute to both a thriving seed bank and a garden full of visitors learning about varieties of edible plants once doomed to either obscurity or extinction. The seeds themselves then also become available through the Seed Savers Exchange catalog and website, filling gardens across the country and even around the world—when I visited a seed savers' garden in Austria, for example, I found that some of their seeds had been ordered from Decorah. The 2013 Seed Savers Exchange Yearbook offered sixteen varieties of collards (*Brassica oleracea*), for example, listing them with details like "Grown in Eastern N[orth] C[arolina] for 100 years," "Creole, old southern favorite," "Good texture, from Ralph Blackwell, Jasper, AL, 1989, passed down in the Blackwell family . . . grown by Ralph's aunt Ila (Blackwell) Spoker as early as the 1930s."[8]

When not walking down garden paths and reading about some long-forgotten (but now remembered) variety of collard greens or carrots during that conference in Iowa, I attended workshops on cider making and seed saving and urban gardens. I listened in as earnest newlyweds embarking on their own heirloom farming careers talked with grizzled farmers in well-worn Dickies overalls.[9] On the conference's main evening, a few hundred people sat together to hear the keynote lecture in the natural amphitheater created by this beautiful valley. Multiple generations of us, coming from many different places, stretched out on the grass in the fading daylight, mesmerized by the buttermilk sky. This little valley and farm have been crucial to a nationwide (and indeed international) movement, but this group is only one of many players at many levels. A host of similar groups across the country and the world, made up of people doing what they love, what comes naturally, what they're passionate about, help to stem the tide of disappearing genes and genotypes. This shared passion for seeds, for vegetables, for botany, for nourishment, repeated in private rural gardens and public seed archives, changes the world in important ways.

After I roused myself from the grassy hill, and before the barn dance, I climbed into the cramped backseat of an old truck packed with farm tools and went for a ride along a bumpy trail in the growing dusk through a landscape profoundly affected by human hands, and that harbors rare genetic codes in the cattle and the vegetables and the fruit trees. Ancient White Park cattle, a rare breed being preserved here at the Heritage Farm, were lowing in the twilight, and a sliver of a moon rose above the ridge. We drove through valleys, forests, meadows, and pastures, past beaver dams and streams with an evening mist rising as the heat of the day dissipated. Notwithstanding the understandable worry and urgency about issues of health and hunger, and their connections to politics and economics,[10] there is something joyful about food. Even in this strange year of terrible drought, this valley overflowed with exuberant vegetables and exuberant people.

Such gardens and seed banks dot the globe. Some are large scale and well funded; others are at risk and scraping by. They include the Millennium Seed Bank in Britain's Royal Botanical Gardens (with 10 percent of the world's plant species); Navdanya in Uttrakhand, India, with 5,000 varieties of crop plants; Svalbard Global Seed Vault in Norway (the so-called "Doomsday" Vault) with space for 4.5 million seeds; the National Center for Genetic Resources in Fort Collins, Colorado, with more than 8,000 species of seeds; and the Vavilov Research Institute in Russia, with 60,000 seed varieties.[11] Others are on a much smaller scale, including seed banks in war-torn regions like Iraq and Syria, or those exposed to tsunamis, floods, and other cataclysmic events.[12]

Many of the people running these seed banks—including the Iowa seed savers and many other people I spoke with or came across in my reading of thousands of newspaper articles and books—connect memory with seeds. At the 2013 Conference and Campout, for example, there was a bean giveaway—the massive bean archive of a woman who had died that year. She had carefully saved beans, cataloging them in plastic soda bottles. This highly personal archive, the result of tremendous work, could have been forgotten, thrown away, or lost. Instead, these beans found their way into the pockets and gardens of countless gardeners and farmers. Conference attendees who wanted to take beans home were asked to leave their names and the varieties they took, and to report back on how the beans grew out. Some bottles contained just a few seeds; others were filled to the cap with more seeds than one person could possibly plant. The bottles were labeled with the variety names (like Turkey Craw) and hints about flavor, texture, and use. The beans themselves recalled not only this ardent seed saver, but also the growers and eaters of those beans over decades and centuries, across continents and oceans.

There are many motivations for seeking out heirloom varieties: not only for flavor, novelty, resilience, and the preservation of biodiversity, but because of childhood memories of eating particular fruits and vegetables, or shared stories of a specific seed, tuber, or graft. Many seed savers see themselves as stewards, not only of their own family memories but of the shared stories and genetic codes contained within these plants. This kind of recollection works against collective forgetting and the widespread disappearance of so many agricultural plants and animals. Old localized, traditional varieties of plants and animals fell (or were pushed) out of everyday use as agriculture became increasingly large scale, industrialized, and standardized, relying on ever fewer varieties in order to achieve the high levels of uniformity and predictability expected not only by stockholders but also by grocery store shoppers. The loss of biodiversity also means a broader form of forgetting. These genes connect many people to the past, to the ways people gardened, farmed, and raised livestock in their own families or in far-off places. The genotypes of heirloom varieties—of Tennessee fainting goats or of the Abraham Lincoln or Arkansas Traveler tomatoes—speak both to particular genetic arrangements and to specific times and places, as responses to short growing seasons or rocky soil.

Genetic Memory

At the heart of all food are the genes that form its essence and the work that goes into its production: the towering pastries in the windows of Parisian patisseries have their origins in wheat grown in Canadian fields and shipped across the Atlantic;[13] the butter my great-great-aunt churned came from the doe-eyed Jersey cows in her barn in Northern California; the high-fructose corn syrup in so much of the food on supermarket shelves and fast-food menus comes mostly from fields of genetically modified corn stretched across the center of the United States. Each of these raw materials receives its shape from particular genes and genotypes. The genes and especially the genotype (the particular combination of genes in a given variety of plant or breed of animal) guide the growth of wheat and cows and corn—of everything we eat. This tiny code gives commands that pull together the right proteins to end up with kernels of wheat and tubs of butter. Genes and genotypes ultimately give food (or the raw materials of fruits, vegetables, grains, and animals) its particular form—whether heirloom tomatoes in a garden in Kentucky, potatoes in the high, rocky fields of Peru, or the highly processed wheat that goes into boxed cake mixes. The results of these genetic raw materials are in turn shaped by planting, harvesting, and processing—milking the cow, crafting the pastry, milling the corn into corn syrup and then processing it into other foods. On top of these genes, the particular plants and animals they produce, and the work of processing, we humans add layers of meaning and memory, as well as politics and economy, that prefer some genes over others.

Wheat offers just one example.[14] A small range of closely related genotypes produces wheat kernels that most of us would have trouble distinguishing from one another. *Triticum aestivum* or *Triticum durum* and other domesticated *Triticum* varieties have been layered with culture and politics for millennia. Wheat served as the basis for the breads so essential to medieval European culinary traditions (whether low-status dark bread or high-status white bread). Rachel Laudan, for example, cites many instances of the seemingly ever-changing meanings of white bread and whole-wheat bread.[15] Yet advocates of many alternative diets today see modern wheat as one of the most unhealthful foods modern humans can eat. The raw genetic material's expression, the phenotype, gets processed by a multitude of technologies: hand-held scythes and giant mechanized threshers, water-powered grinding stones and monumental flour mills. These foods contain particular nutrients and have direct effects on our bodies' chemistry. They become cultural objects, embedded in physiological, political, and economic systems, but also in systems of meaning, memory, and identity. These close relatives of the wheat family become many different things: the bread that was so scarce in France in the late eighteenth century, the ubiquitous baguettes of contemporary Vietnam (edible remnants of the French colonial presence), the Roman Meal bread my mother used to make our peanut butter and jelly sandwiches, or the coveted loaves produced by Tartine Bakery in San Francisco, where the bread is sold once a day (after 4:30 p.m.) to those at the head of the long line that forms outside the store. A single plant species, *Triticum*, here acts as an almost-blank canvas for human meaning. Particular farmers and living history museums now plant long-neglected heirloom varieties of wheat, like Red Fife or Turkey Hard Red Winter wheat, re-creating the flavors and the landscape of Canadian pioneers or fleeing Mennonites. But these heirloom wheats occupy only a tiny percentage of global wheat acreage, and it often takes a fair amount of effort or expense to actually get to eat them.

Many heirloom plants (including these old-fashioned forms of *Triticum*) and animals carry traits not especially well suited to large-scale and industrial agriculture, which goes a long way toward explaining their decline in the twentieth century. As nitrogen fertilizers, cross-country transportation, and refrigeration greatly increased, so too did ways of producing food that strongly favor uniformity, durability, longevity, and transportability. As early as 1929, Edward Bunyard (an eloquent and opinionated fruit connoisseur) was already complaining in England about the sacrifice of flavor for transportability.[16]

Uniformity, whether of corncobs or wheat kernels, is more conducive to large-scale industrial production, processing, and distribution than is heterogeneity. A mechanized slaughterhouse is not geared to a range of sizes and shapes of animals, and combines and other large agricultural equipment work best with crops that are uniform in height and harvest date. Much of this change originated in boardrooms and regulatory bodies as agribusiness developed; consumers in many parts of the world also contributed to these changes by reaching for the shiniest apple or the leanest pork chop, expecting (and getting) consistency, predictability, and plenty. Home gardeners and small-scale farmers, however, often choose other genetic blueprints. The Tuxer Rind, for example, is a cow that makes a wonderful mother for small-scale dairy farming on a lonely Alpine hillside, but her willingness to defend her calf with her tremendous horns makes her less suited to larger-scale dairy operations. When I visited one in her stall at the Vienna zoo, I was warned to keep clear of her and her tiny calf and to avoid any sudden movements in her direction. But the speckled cow in the stall next to her, the color of chocolate-chip ice cream, nuzzling a similarly tiny calf, perceived no threat in the sociologist leaning on the wooden slats of her stall—she had a different blueprint guiding her attitude about mothering and thus a different set of qualities for a particular farmer. These traits in cattle are in large part genetic, not simply the quirks of individual personalities, and are part of the collection of traits that animal breeders have long sought to control.

Consumer demand certainly is partially responsible for the uniformity found on the supermarket shelves—and for the plentiful parking out front. An appetite for chickens we don't have to slaughter ourselves, or for produce we can't grow because we lack the time and space (or interest), and tastes for very standardized food—no wormholes in our apples, no scrawny chicken breasts—alter the landscape of both supermarket produce sections and farmers' fields. And many foods have simply fallen out of fashion: cider apples and salsify, for example, not to mention fatty pork, can be hard to come by outside well-stocked farmers' markets or boutique grocery stores. Precisely these foods used to sustain people of modest means, but today they are often accessible only at comparatively high prices and with some effort. Some fruits and vegetables are thus acutely endangered, while others are doing fine but still are hard to find in supermarkets. There are also limits to the variety and bounty at the supermarket. First, access to such produce sections, and such supermarkets, is not evenly distributed around this country, not to mention the world. Second, even in the best-stocked produce sections, the fruits and vegetables regularly sold represent only a small proportion of the edible biodiversity out there. The standardization that allows for such uniform, plentiful, and predictable produce is part of what has moved much agricultural biodiversity off our plates and out of cultivation. This rarity comes about not from objective bad taste or a lack of Darwinian fitness, but because they are not well suited to large-scale farming and food-processing techniques and to modern tastes. One of the consequences is that we are actively eating (as a population, not necessarily as individuals) from a narrower range of biodiversity.

The genetic foundations of heirloom food are far more heterogeneous and essentially impossible to replace when lost. They are of great importance for the future, when changing climatic, economic, or political conditions may require plants and animals better suited to altered circumstances. No amount of genetic engineering could supply this diversity of genotypes; there are limits, of both cost and science, to what these technologies can do. These old genotypes might offer resistance to heat and drought or be impervious to specific strains of future blights or insects. With the loss of old or traditional varieties of edible plants, we also face the loss of possibility, variety, insurance against future failure, and in many cases of cultural heritage, identity, and autonomy.[17] While much of the danger for many varieties has receded in the United States, there are still grave threats to agricultural biodiversity around the world. Many heirloom plants and animals lend themselves to small-scale and independent farming, as well as situations where (as is currently the case in many parts of the world) the global markets in staple foods break down and people try to fight rising prices by increasing smaller-scale and local farming.[18]

The turn to heirloom food in more privileged regions of the world is also in part a response to the alienation or monotony some people experience in the face of mass-produced produce. Chefs make decisions based on what they want to end up on diners' plates. The search for novelty may lead them not only to molecular gastronomy but also to smaller farms where they can work with farmers to plan what gets planted, and served, in the coming growing season. Many chefs go in both directions simultaneously, pushing the limits of both innovation and tradition (like Noma in Denmark, the now-defunct El Bulli in Spain, or Alinea and Elizabeth in Chicago). The quest for heirloom food, combined with the search for local and seasonal food, can also be a response to the dangers posed by a system so massive that it is nearly impossible to trace any given bag of spinach or pound of ground beef back to a specific farm, so that a single bit of *E. coli* from a single farm may find its way into a shocking number of grocery stores, kitchens, and bellies.[19]

Making Heirlooms

How could anything as perishable as fruits and vegetables become an heirloom? Many things that are heirlooms today were once simple everyday objects. A quilt made of fabric scraps, a wooden bowl used in the last stages of making butter, both become heirlooms only as time increases between now and the era of their everyday use. Likewise, the Montafoner Braunvieh—a tawny, gorgeously crooked-horned cow that roams a handful of pastures and zoos in Europe, a tuft of hair like bangs above her big brown eyes—or the Ossabaw pigs that scurry around on spindly legs at Mount Vernon were not always "heirlooms." Nor were the piles of multicolored tomatoes that periodically grace the cover of *Martha Stewart Living* magazine or the food pages of daily newspapers. What happened to change these plants and animals from everyday objects into something rare and precious, imbued with stories of the past? In fact, food has always been an heirloom in the sense of saving seeds, of passing down the food you eat to your children and your children's children, in a mixture of the genetic code of a given food (a cow, a variety of wheat, a tomato), and also in handing down the techniques of cultivation, preservation, preparation, and even a taste for particular foods.[20] It is only with the rise of industrial agriculture that this *practice* of treating food as a literal heirloom has disappeared in many parts of the world—and that is precisely when the heirloom label emerges. The chain is broken for many people as they flock to the cities and the number of farmers and gardeners declines. So the concept of an heirloom becomes possible only in the context of the loss of actual heirloom varieties, of increased urbanization and industrialization as fewer people grow their own food, or at least know the people who grow their food. These are global issues, relevant to hunger and security *and* to cultural memory, community, and place. This book addresses one aspect of the much larger spectrum of issues around culture and agricultural biodiversity, focusing on these old seeds and trees.

In some ways heirlooms become possible (as a concept) only because of the industrialization and standardization of agriculture. They went away, there was a cultural and agricultural break, placing temporal and practical distance between current generations and past foods. In the meantime, gardeners and farmers quietly saved seeds for their own use. And then, as I discuss in much greater detail below, these heirloom foods began, tomato by tomato, apple by apple, to return to some degree of popularity.

In the United States, newspaper article after article, activist after activist, describes heirloom varieties as something one's grandmother might have eaten. The implication is that there has been a significant break—that the current generation and their parents lost touch with these fruits, vegetables, and animals but that their grandparents might not have. "Heirlooms are major-league hot," a reporter marveled in 1995. "As we become more of a technological society, people are reaching into the garden to get back that simple life, the simple life of their grandparents."[21] Concepts like "old-fashioned," "just like Grandma ate," and even "heirloom" can feel very American. But this is a mythical grandmother. The grandmothers of today's United States are a diverse crew whose cooking habits are just one of the ways they differ. Gender is also obviously a vital element of the study of food production and consumption. Women are perceived as (and often are) the primary cooks and shoppers, and there are many gendered understandings of our relationships to food.[22] Many people, men and women alike, have little time to cook, despite recent exhortations to engage in more home cooking.[23] My own grandmother (the niece of my great-great-aunt Budder whom I write about in the prologue) smoked cigarettes and drank martinis with gusto, and for her, making Christmas cookies consisted of melting peanut butter and butterscotch chips, stirring in cornflakes, and forming the mixture into little clumps that would harden as they cooled. I loved them as a child, and when I make them today, I am invoking my grandmother just as much as other people may when serving up a platter of ancestral heirloom tomatoes.

In the context of food, however, the word "heirloom" also has a genetic connotation.[24] The object itself is not handed down. Heirloom tomatoes are either eaten or they rot. Old-fashioned breeds of pigs are slaughtered and end up as pork chops; they rarely live a long life like Wilbur in *Charlotte's Web*, without the help of a literate spider and a film career. The "heirloom," then, what is handed down, is the genetic code. Heirloom foods are products of human intervention, ranging from selecting what seeds to save for the next growing season to deciding which tom turkey should father poults with which hen.

The genetic heirloom takes on a physical expression in the form of a pig or a tomato, for example, to which people may then attach all kinds of meanings—not only the physical appetite for the flavor of a particular tomato or pork chop, but also the sense that edible heirlooms connect us to something many people see as more authentic than supermarket fare.[25] Over and over, in conversations and newspaper articles, orchards and public lectures, I have heard people articulating a search for a connection to the past, even as they also sought out appealing flavors, colors, and textures. The appetite for an heirloom food commonly leads, of course, to the destruction of its embodiment—in a Caprese salad, say, or an apple pie—but it is precisely the consumption of its phenotype that ensures the survival of the genetic code that gave rise to it.

A guide to heirloom vegetables describes heirloom status (of tomatoes and other produce) in three ways:

1. The variety must be able to reproduce itself from seed [except those propagated through roots or cuttings]. . . .
2. The variety must have been introduced more than 50 years ago. Fifty years, is, admittedly, an arbitrary cutoff date, and different people use different dates. . . . A few people use an even stricter definition, considering heirlooms to be only those varieties developed and preserved outside the commercial seed trade. . . .
3. The variety must have a history of its own.[26]

The term "heirloom" itself generally applies to varieties that are capable of being pollen fertilized and that existed before the 1940s, when industrial farming spread in North America and the variety of species grown commercially was significantly reduced. Generally speaking, an heirloom can reproduce itself from seed, meaning seed saved from the previous year. When growing hybrids, you have to buy new seed each year (for plants that reproduce true to seed; apples, potatoes, and some other fruits and vegetables are preserved and propagated through grafts or cuttings rather than seeds). In other words, if you save the seeds of a hybrid tomato and plant them the next year, you more than likely won't be pleased with what you get, if you get anything at all. Furthermore, simply because they are "heirloom" tomatoes does not mean they are native. In fact, tomatoes are native not to the United States, but to South and Central America, and many heirloom varieties such as the Caspian Pink were developed in Russia and other far-off places.[27] People also use the term "heirloom" to describe old varieties of roses, ornamental plants, fruit trees (reproduced by grafting rather than from seed), potatoes, and even livestock.

As the US Department of Agriculture's heirloom vegetable guide explains, "Dating to the early 20th C. and before, many [heirloom varieties] originated during a very different agricultural age—when localized and subsistence-based food economies flourished, when waves of immigrant farmers and gardeners brought cherished seeds and plants to this country, and before seed saving had dwindled to a 'lost art' among most North American farmers and gardeners." Fashions, tastes, and technology changed, but "since the 1970s, an expanding popular movement dedicated to perpetuating and distributing these garden classics has emerged among home gardeners and small-scale growers, with interest and endorsement from scientists, historians, environmentalists, and consumers."[28] In Germany they speak of *alte Sorten*, "old varieties," but this phrasing does not carry the same symbolic, nostalgic weight as the homey word "heirloom." In French heirloom varieties may be called *légumes oubliés*, "forgotten vegetables," or *légumes anciennes*.[29] Of course, once vegetables are labeled forgotten, they're not really forgotten anymore. In general, the United States has a different relationship to its past than European countries do. Thus there are regional gardening and cooking traditions in the United States, as well as a particular form of nostalgia that allows the term "heirloom" to apply to fruits, vegetables, and animals in the first place. The idea of an heirloom object can be very homespun. Certainly an heirloom can be something of great monetary value, but it can also be a threadbare quilt, a grandfather's toolbox, or in my case the worn and mismatched paddles my great-great-aunt used in the last stages of making butter. The word "heirloom" can be a way to preserve biodiversity, but it can also be inaccurate and misused, a label slapped on an overpriced tomato. There is always the danger that dishonest grocers and restaurateurs will exploit the desire for local, seasonal, and heirloom food.[30]

Heirlooms of all sorts are often wrapped up in nostalgic ideas about the past. Patchwork quilts and butter churns evoke not only idyllic images of yesteryear, but often difficult lives circumscribed by poverty and dire necessity as much as by simplicity and self-sufficiency. They speak of times (and, when we think globally, of places) when life may have been (or may still be) not only technologically simpler but also much, much harder. Old-fashioned farm implements in the front yards of rural Wisconsin, or in living history museums, evoke nostalgic feelings. But there's a reason they're in museums or front yards and not hitched to a team of horses or in the hands of a farmer, at least in Wisconsin. These are backbreaking tools whose functions have wherever possible been transferred to machines.

Even today, while it may surprise people who pick up a book like this, when I first tell someone about my work, I routinely have to explain what an heirloom tomato is. On a recent trip to a Milwaukee farmers' market, I heard an older man say to his female companion, "Heirloom tomatoes? Never heard of 'em." He's not alone. While some food writers and restaurant reviewers may feel that heirloom tomatoes are yesterday's news, plenty of consumers are still encountering them for the first time.

Heirloom varieties are just one form of edible memory, but they offer a unique opportunity to understand the powerful ways memory and materiality interact, and how the stories we tell one another about the past shape the world we inhabit. I write about heirlooms not because I think they're the only way to go, but because they present an intriguing sociological puzzle (How can something as perishable as a tomato become an heirloom?) and because they are the subject of so much activity by so many different people. These efforts, all this work, are also just the latest turn in the twisting path of fruit and vegetable trends, of the relationship of these plants to human communities. This book recounts my search for endangered squashes, nearly forgotten plums, and other rare genes surviving in barnyards, gardens, and orchards, this intertwining of botanical, social, and edible worlds.

Investigating Heirlooms

I relish the moments I have spent with the old-fashioned farm animals at the Vienna zoo, standing in the stall with the zookeeper to scratch the fluffy head of a newborn lamb or the vast forehead of that speckled black-and-white cow, one of only a few of her breed remaining on the planet, who had just dutifully produced a calf that looked exactly like her. I also relish the meals I've prepared from multicolored potatoes or tomatoes; and, given a free Saturday, I can spend hours at farmers' markets, contemplating what I can do with a bucket of almost overripe peaches (freeze them for my winter oatmeal) or a pile of striped squash (a spectacularly failed attempt at whole wheat squash gnocchi, which may still be lurking in the back of my freezer). And I have my own history of deep attachment to processed spice cake and the unctuous taste of a rare glass of whole milk—a reminder that "edible memory" goes far beyond the relatively narrow confines of heirloom food.

But I am also a sociologist, so in this book, while I am fond of many of the places, people, and foods I discuss, I also aim, ultimately, to tell a sociological story. I did not, like Barbara Kingsolver in *Animal, Vegetable, Miracle*, try to raise turkeys or can a heroic quantity of heirloom tomatoes.[31] Unlike Michael Pollan in the journey he undertook for *The Omnivore's Dilemma*, I did not try to shoot anything or make my own salt. Along the way, however, I *did* get involved; I immersed myself in these rich landscapes, markets, and texts and in conversations with diverse groups and individuals who often, unknown to anyone else, managed to hold on to vital and beautiful collections of genes in the form of old apple trees or tomato seeds, turnips or taro. I set out not to grow these plants and raise these animals myself, but to talk with and observe the diverse and committed gardeners, farmers, curators, seed savers, animal breeders, and other people who make possible the persistence of these plants and animals on this planet. I set out to understand in particular where these plants have come from, the threats they face, the kinds of places that are created in the attempt to save them, and the stories they tell us about the past and about ourselves, as well as how they figure in the broader patterns of human appetites, trends and fashions, habits and intentions.

The research for this book comprised seven years of observation and analysis. In my efforts to understand how tomatoes became heirlooms and apples became antiques, I set out on multiple journeys, of varying sorts. I drove down Lake Shore Drive to the Green City Market and urban farms and gardens in Chicago, traveled across town in Milwaukee to Growing Power[32] and other urban growers, flew across the Atlantic to Vienna, took a streetcar over the bridges of Stockholm to get to the barnyards and gardens of the Swedish national open-air folk museum, and got lost on the tangle of bridges and highways between Washington, DC, and rural Virginia in search of Thomas Jefferson's vegetable garden and George Washington's turkeys. I also took more philosophical journeys: literary and archival travels through the pages of government reports, scholarly periodicals, and popular and scientific books. I traveled through recipe collections and the glossy pages of food magazines, through the digital universe of online databases, and through correspondence with colleagues and informants in far-off places. The collection of these journeys, of this movement through gardens, barnyards, orchards, and markets, as well as thickets of printed and digital information, accounts for the story I tell here.

This book emerged in part from solitary hours in front of the computer, taking notes, with stacks of books at my side, reading newspaper articles and academic journal articles on everything from apple grafting to patent law. I analyzed thousands of newspaper articles, charting the emergence of the term "heirloom" in popular food writing and looking for changes in the quantity and quality of the discussion over time as well as differences and similarities across different kinds of foods. Much of this book is based on the ways heirloom varieties register in public discussions, especially the media, and the ways they get taken up by organizations and individuals, both in and out of the limelight. Blogs and other food writing have also figured centrally in my analysis of the heirloom food movement as markers of popular discussions, and I have relied on hundreds of secondary sources (see the bibliography) for historical information about specific foods. I read encyclopedias and fascinating scholarly and popular books, charting the rise and fall of particular foods and their historical transformations. And I drew on the insights of my colleagues in sociology and neighboring academic disciplines and the ways they think about things like culture, memory, and food.

Occasionally I would take a break and cook one of the recipes I came across, and I also left my desk and set out to visit the farms and gardens, camera and notebook in hand. I scratched the noses of wiry old pigs, walked through fragrant herb gardens, and tasted hard cider and fresh bread, the hems of my jeans coated in mud and my nose sunburned from a long day in an Alpine valley or at a midwestern heirloom seed festival. I spoke formally and informally with gardeners, farmers, and chefs, activists, seed savers, academics, and all kinds of people devoted to food. I visited farms and gardens and living history museums and farmers' markets, and I attended conferences and public lectures and delivered some of my own to smart crowds full of eager gardeners, eaters, and thinkers. I also spoke with the gardeners of less well-known historical kitchen gardens across Europe and the United States, quiet conversations about their enthusiasm for their work and about their assessments of the changing public perceptions of edible biodiversity over recent decades. Many of these farmers and gardeners became good friends, and our late-night conversations over good meals in my dining room or cheap beer at a rooftop farm in Chicago's Back of the Yards also came to shape my sociological understanding of these trends. Sifting through the stacks of papers on my desk in the depths of winter, and wandering through gardens, barnyards, and farmers' markets in the heat of summer, I wanted to see what patterns I might find.

Finding Edible Memory

What I found was something I came to call "edible memory." And I want to emphasize that I did not expect to find it. Edible memory emerged out of these documents, landscapes, and conversations. This book focuses largely on the contemporary United States, with occasional examples drawn from elsewhere. But the fundamental ideas and questions can help us to think about other times and places as well. For sociologists, the study of human behavior—of what people actually do, and do in large enough numbers to register as visible patterns—is at the heart of our work. Many of us are studying what happens when people are highly motivated, when they are so passionate about something that the passion provokes action. That said, many of us are also deeply interested in the small actions of habit, the little steps we take every day that add up to this big thing called society. What we eat for breakfast, who we spend time with and how, what we buy, even what we ignore—these are all crucial to understanding how and why things are as they are. This book is about the fervent devotees, the people who can't *not* plant orchards full of apple trees or spend countless hours saving turnip seeds. But it is also about the ways millions (perhaps even billions) of people make small decisions every day about what to serve their families, about how to feed themselves.

When I began to look in scholarly and popular writing, and in kitchens, gardens, farms, and markets, I saw more and more evidence of edible memory: in the rice described by geographer Judith Carney, in the gardens of Hmong refugees in Minnesota, in the hard-won community gardens of New York's Lower East Side, and in the appetites and memories of friends and strangers alike.[33] Edible memory appears in the reverberations of African foods in a range of North American culinary traditions, in the efforts to cultivate Native American foods today, in the shifting appetites of immigrant populations and ardently trendy folks in Brooklyn or Portland.[34] It goes far beyond the heirloom, but heirlooms were my way in, a way to narrow, at least temporarily, the scope of the investigation and to explore one particularly potent intersection of food, biodiversity, and tales of past ways of being. Edible memory is a widely applicable concept, and I hope it will resonate well beyond the boundaries of the examples I have included in this book.

Edible memory is also in no way the sole province of elites. Much of what people understand as heirloom food today is expensive and out of reach, justifying the pretensions sometimes assigned to heirloom tomatoes, farmers' markets, or the pedigreed chicken in the television show *Portlandia*. Food deserts, double shifts, cumbersome or expensive transportation, and straight-up poverty greatly reduce access to a wide range of foods, heirlooms included.[35] But to assume that edible memory is strictly connected to privilege ignores the vital connections people have to food at a range of locations on the socioeconomic scale. Poverty, and even hunger, does not preclude (and indeed may intensify) the meanings and memories surrounding food. As many researchers have discussed, the various alternative approaches to food—heirlooms, but also farmers' markets, organic and local foods, and artisanal foods—tend to be expensive, eaten largely by elites—well-off and often white.[36] However, while that may characterize what we might call mainstream alternative, both edible biodiversity and edible memory happen across the socioeconomic spectrum. There are vibrant, successful projects in which people worlds away from expensive restaurants and farmers' markets grow and eat many of the same kinds of memorable vegetables, in rural backyards, small urban allotments, and school gardens.[37] Chicago alone is home to many farms and gardens supplying food and often employment and other projects in low-income communities, projects like the Chicago Farmworks,[38] Growing Home,[39] Gingko Gardens, or the Chicago location of Growing Power, which is even selling its produce in local Walgreens, trying to improve access to locally grown produce in predominantly low-income and African American neighborhoods.[40] The numerous farms and gardens profiled on Natasha Bowen's blog and multimedia project, *The Color of Food*, also offer examples across the country of farmers and gardeners with a deep commitment to many of the same foods that find their way into high-priced grocery stores or expensive restaurant dinners.[41]

At the same time, I do not want to argue that edible memory is a universal concept. We can ask where and how it appears and matters, but we should not assume that it is everywhere either present or significant. It is certainly widespread, based on the research I have conducted, but it is not universal. For some people food may be a way to imagine communities, to understand their place in the world and connect to other people, but for others it is simply physical sustenance or transitory pleasure.

Tickling Nerves

What do people look for in heirloom foods? Often they are searching for flavor and texture, familiarity or originality. Sociologists Josée Johnston and Shyon Baumann describe the pursuit of both the exotic and the purportedly authentic among the readers of gourmet food magazines, and I think something similar takes place in the realm of heirloom food.[42] These foods can evoke nostalgia and novelty alike. Many people are motivated by their own memories, while others are driven by the combined promise of unfamiliarity and a rich narrative, some kind of connection to the past, even if it's in a food they've never tasted.

Some of the interest in heirlooms is related to what in German is called a *Nervenkitzel*, a "tickling of the nerves," the excitement of the exotic. It's what some people might feel if they happen on a pile of some unfamiliar but enticing vegetable at a farmers' market or bite into an unknown apple variety. That novelty can be highly pleasurable for some but unpleasant or even unnerving for others.

People are also engaged in preserving food security through edible memory—holding on to old, familiar seeds that are also genetic resources for the future. I have seen this kind of preservation matter very much to people, watched people dedicated to their tomato patches, or electrified by the discovery of a new taste or texture that actually is old. There is bountiful evidence of the ways tastes can change over time, either by accident or through intentional efforts. Drawing on the work of historian Martin Bruegel, Michael Carolan describes "tuning" people to buy canned food (for soldiers in World War I), which even led to the creation "of new memories for this otherwise non-memorable food item" in France, where there had been more resistance to canned food than in the United States, England, and Germany. Carolan also cites Bruno Latour's discussion of the perfume industry, and the importance (and possibility) of training noses over time, as relevant to taste because so much of what we experience as taste is perceived through our olfactory sense rather than on our tongues. People acquire and change tastes over time and through the body, and they can learn (either through their own efforts or through concerted campaigns) to have tastes for new things.[43] Likewise, Lizzie Collingham finds that "American and Australian tastes in vegetables also differed greatly [during World War II]. The Americans preferred tinned tomatoes, peas, corn, string beans and asparagus, and they hated the canned beets, carrots, cabbage, parsnips and pumpkins that prevailed in Australia."[44]

What accounts for such widely variant tastes among these young men? Their Australian and American childhoods tuned them to have such different reactions to cans of parsnips or pumpkin. There is a whole realm of inquiry into edible memory that takes a more neurological, physiological, and chemical approach. Indeed, Shepherd tells us that "what we call the *taste* of our food beyond these simple sensations [of sweet, salt, sour, bitter, and umami] should be called *flavor* and is mostly due to retronasal smell [those smells perceived not as air is breathed in, but as it is breathed back out, in the process of chewing and swallowing]. . . . Simple tastes are hardwired from birth, whereas retronasal smells are learned and thus open to individual differences."[45] What we understand as taste is acutely connected to smell. The olfactory receptors connect smell, memory, and the brain in ancient and immediate ways. The brain's centers for processing smell and those for creating memories are adjacent to each other, and, unlike the other senses, smell does not get routed through the thalamus. The olfactory sense is also far more responsible for what we perceive as flavor than is the tongue, and is also the oldest sense.[46]

Much of edible memory definitely has to do with the senses. Taste of course, but all the others as well. Smell occupies a special place—in part because of the direct physical connection to sensors in the brain triggering deep, bodily memory. The nose, perhaps a bit like the soul, tends to grow used to things. Both may become somewhat impervious to the familiar and the everyday. But the nose (and, let's hope, the soul) can be shocked back to life, back to awareness—by a completely unfamiliar scent or an emotionally familiar one. How often do we smell something truly new? In the routine of everyday life, rarely. The decaying leaves at my great-great-aunt's ranch are one of my clearest memories from childhood, so different from the pine needles and sea air I breathed on other days of my life. Some people seek out new smells, tastes, and other sensory experiences with reckless abandon or relentless thoroughness. Others much prefer the compact and familiar universe of tastes and smells where they reside, maintaining a comforting continuity within their kitchens and dining rooms, not to mention their hearts.

As superficial as much of the treatment of heirlooms may be (in many restaurant reviews, for example), for many people I have observed there is also something highly grounding about heirloom foods. People find their calling, find a connection to the earth and to others, not just through heirlooms, but also through gardening and cooking together, through imagining a past that came before they were born and a future where people will continue to eat the descendants of these fruits and vegetables long after they themselves have passed on. A very important part of this effort is the people who save seeds and trees off the grid. They are the origins and heart of the heirloom food movement. A wide-ranging collection of groups and individuals has ensured the genetic basis for the future and preserved these edible connections to the past.

People become zealous, even fanatic about the heirloom objects of their affections. I know a zookeeper who keeps ninety varieties of tomatoes in his garden, and a banker who tends his heirloom apple orchard while his colleagues tend their yachts. There are heirloom chicken farmers whose lives revolve around their poultry and melon enthusiasts who carefully wrap the blossoms in netting at a crucial fertile moment to prevent insects and breezes from cross-pollinating the purebred melon patch. I visited an heirloom orchard in California where Andy Mariani preserves dozens of varieties of stone fruits as a living archive in one of his orchard plots, while not far away he tinkers expertly with brand-new varieties of nectarines and pluots, apricots and plums. Mariani and countless others, like the off-the-grid seed savers described by the anthropologist Virginia Nazarea, are essential to the survival and preservation of heirloom plants and animals.

On a much larger scale, there are massive cryogenic seed banks aimed at preserving some of this biodiversity, most notably the "Doomsday Vault," the Svalbard Global Seed Vault in a distant Norwegian archipelago.[47] There are also projects like the Potato Park in Peru, working to preserve potato biodiversity in the high-altitude fields where these potatoes developed.[48] Ancient Peruvian pottery reflects the cultural significance of the potato, with awkward clay tubers mounted to ceremonial jugs and statues of deities. In many parts of the world such "old" seeds, tubers, and animals are still essential to survival, even if they also carry memory and a connection to the past—to childhood or to ancestors. In many places bitter battles are now fought, and more loom on the horizon, over who possesses the rights to the very fundamental DNA floating in the nuclei of these cells, who has the right to save seeds and plant them the following year, and whether imported livestock and seeds will eliminate local and indigenous breeds and varieties.[49]

Making Edible Memory

Edible memory does not exist in a vacuum, nor does it operate alone. In conversations, the concept of edible memory has resonated deeply with some people but puzzled others for whom the connections between food and memory are less obvious. Very often, even before I can finish explaining this project, someone will launch into a story that perfectly explains what I mean by edible memory. How do we acquire collective memory, edible and otherwise, with these layers of culture, attachment, meaning, and habit?

Alison Landsberg's concept of "prosthetic memory" is a very useful way of thinking about memory in the broadest sense. She uses the term to describe how people watching movies, visiting museums, and otherwise being exposed in very visceral ways to "memories" that are not their own, come to be familiar with them and to feel they have some sense of the experience themselves.[50] Thus when people eat an heirloom tomato, they may be eating the memory of a relative, or they may be eating a more inclusive and less personal sense of collective memory—the heirloom being handed down not just within a family but within a society, accessible far beyond the private realm.[51]

I use the term "edible memory" in several ways. One refers to the particular experience of eating heirloom food, food that carries a cultural story along with its genetic code, rare varieties of tomatoes or apples that faded out of view in the twentieth century, but now increasingly find their way onto menus and into popular awareness. But I also mean the emotions and habits evoked by the memory of sitting at the kitchen table with my great-great-aunt, eating a highly processed spice cake that could not have meant more to us if it had been made of heritage grain we had grown ourselves. There are foods we collectively grow attached to as societies and communities, or personally attached to through individual experience and as members of families.[52] Literature and film are full of powerful symbolic images of food, and most of us have lasting memories of culinary high points like holidays or birthdays, or low points like perilously empty cupboards. Foods of all sorts are laden with memories, whether our own recollections of our childhood, recipes handed down in families, or collective national attachments to particular foodstuffs.

That is, edible memory reveals humans' remarkable capacity to invest objects with personal and social meaning, and the unique qualities of food as a carrier of such meanings. The term can describe a range of attitudes about food and—more important—*actions* regarding food that have important consequences. I also firmly believe that edible memory can help us understand not only the meteoric rise in popularity of the heirloom tomato but also essential issues of hunger, famine, and survival.[53] Edible memory is less a theoretical concept than a way of describing the behavior I saw in the legions of people whose actions I studied, in the pages of newspapers or in the shade of their fruit trees.

The concept and practice of edible memory can incorporate seafoam salad or spice cake as well as landraces of millet in the highlands of India or varieties of corn brought to West Africa in the sixteenth century by Portuguese seafarers and slave ships. Food becomes incorporated into our personal memories, identities, and daily practices and also into the collective identities of communities, diasporas, and nations. Memory, culture, and tradition need to be taken very seriously. Part of taking them seriously, however, is realizing that they can be both stable and dynamic. At one end of this spectrum is a painful poignancy, the threat of hunger, the unsolvable longing for a lost flavor, aroma, or texture from childhood, from a homeland, or from a fruit tree long since felled to make way for a freeway or housing development or cornfield. At the same time, certain flavors, textures, and aromas can provide comfort and pleasure hard to find from any other source, and often serendipitous, even fleeting.

Edible memory is not simply a luxury of a comparatively affluent society. People who are receiving sufficient calories will still report feeling achingly hungry when they are forced, for a variety of reasons, to eat foods devoid of meaning or, more accurately, are deprived of the staples of their home.[54] Elizabeth Dunn writes of displaced people suffering from being given the wrong food and even refusing to eat. In this case it was Georgian refugees refusing to eat the unfamiliar macaroni supplied at the refugee camp because "in the context of Georgian cuisine, which is highly elaborate and full of spices, walnuts, pomegranates, fresh vegetables, and meats, macaroni is hardly food at all."[55] The refugees' elaborate, palpable memories of their orchards and gardens were often recounted in this desolate refugee camp, along with a deep sense of loss not only of the food but also of the act of making food, even the jars used for canning the bounty of gardens and orchards.

Anthropologist Elizabeth Saleh also sees connections between memory and sensory experience. In her work in Lebanon, she finds that the *karam* ("an olive grove, a fig tree orchard or a vineyard" in Lebanese Arabic) is a place where people produce food and eat it, but also root themselves in place, connecting themselves not only to each other and the past but to the future as well. Thus memory and practice are rooted in and produce both a landscape and a community. "The knowledge of waiting (to pick), knowing what and where to pick, as well as knowing how to eat it draws upon layers of embodied experiences; an engendered form of knowledge as it is increasingly transmitted and reproduced through time by grandmothers, mothers, and daughters."[56] People enter the *karam* and feel the presence of ancestors, and also feel a sense of responsibility for feeding future generations. Seed saver and author Janisse Ray conveys some of this sense of edible memory as well: "My garden brims with storied varieties, plants linked to anecdote and legend. Whippoorwill Field pea, mentioned by Edmund Ruffin (the Virginian fabled to have fired the first shot of the Civil War) in his 1855 homage to cowpeas.... Aunt Ruby's German Green Tomato came from Ruby Arnold of Greeneville, Tennessee, who passed away in 1997."[57]

And one of the early readers of this manuscript was immediately reminded of his own memories of highly processed sweets that he would be unlikely to eat today but that still evoke powerful, pleasant memories capable of transporting him back to childhood. In other words, these connections between food and both personal and collective memory are by no means the sole province of old-fashioned tomatoes or historical apples but can (and do) attach to the vast range of foods that humans eat, from Big Macs to wild greens foraged at the edge of a forest.[58]

Eating Other People's Memories

Edible memory can describe our personal memories of things eaten at formative moments in our lives, the tomatoes or peas or greens of one's own childhood. But what I saw as I observed the rise of the heirloom food movement was also an entirely different way of eating memory: eating other people's memories, eating food that is presented with a story about someone else's past.[59] Heirloom produce is frequently eaten by people who have no past experience with these particular foods. There is personal memory of a lifetime of experiences, of food that we ourselves ate at formative moments in our lives—in childhood, certainly, but also the experiences as we grow up and expand our palates. For me, in my twenties, I realized there was a whole world of untouched flavors and textures out there. On the other hand, a second meaning of edible memory (as I use the term), is less direct and personal, more collective and cultural. In this case, edible memory is a way to approach stories about the past, and in particular stories about a past that you or I have not experienced for ourselves. People eat other people's memories in many settings. Urbanites eat rural dwellers' memories of the food grown by generations past, or the memories of other generations, immigrant groups, and countries.[60] And if you eat someone else's memories long enough, they may eventually become your own (or your children's). This is partly how culture works: it is changeable over time, but also sturdy and plodding, personal and social.

I once gave a lecture to a group of fruit aficionados at a fieldhouse in Chicago. I talked about heirloom apples, forgotten orchards, and homemade hard cider, illustrating my lecture with dozens of images of shiny apples, hazy orchards, and jugs of cider. A few weeks later, leaving a gathering of some of those same people at a Chicago brewery, a young man stood in my path as I headed toward the door. He asked if I was who I am, and when I said yes, he told me he'd been at my lecture—and that I'd made him nostalgic for things he'd never even known existed. Indeed, this experience—of heirloom foods that don't actually inhabit the memories of the people eating them—is a widespread factor in popularizing heirloom fruits and vegetables. Heirloom fruits and vegetables are eaten both by people who literally inherited seeds and saplings from green-thumbed relatives and by the growing number of people who seek in heirlooms both a new culinary experience and a connection to a more generalized past.

On the one hand, food, heirloom and otherwise, is very private. What we eat—what we actually put in our mouths—and our childhood memories of food are very personal.[61] At the same time, food is very public, from the transnational systems of food production and distribution, to the brightly lit aisles of the supermarket, to the collective meanings of food in a given community or society: the cheerfulness of a birthday cake with candles or the millions of people in the United States who see family and national identity embodied in a twenty-pound Thanksgiving turkey.[62] A mix of culture, economics, marketing, habit, nostalgia, psychology, and physiology influences what we reach for when we're hungry.[63] This is a story of what people actually do, the choices they make and the habits they form. This book is about not just food, but what food represents, from a cultural, sociological, and individual standpoint.

At the same time, the heirloom food movement turns out to be simply the latest change over centuries, even millennia, of changing tastes, habits, and practices with respect to food. Fruits and vegetables have come and gone across thousands of years of human cultivation. There is a mobility in meanings of food, and a fair amount of shapeshifting. These are the particular convulsions of recent trends, but they also connect to a bigger scope of changes in meanings, uses, practices, habits, appetites, culture, and territory. We can learn a lot by observing the changing fates of fruits and vegetables over time.[64] And we can take nostalgia seriously as a social force.

Edible memory makes heirloom foods, but it also makes other things, including landscapes and connections between people and places.[65] The symbolic qualities of these heirloom foods have undoubtedly contributed to their resurgence. A paradox of heirloom food is that, unlike what happens to bluefin tuna or beluga caviar, whose skyrocketing popularity leads to overfishing and near-extinction (and very high prices), the popularity of heirloom foods leads to preservation and availability.[66] Even as heirloom tomatoes developed an elitist reputation, and prices for heritage turkeys run well over a hundred dollars, this trend has succeeded both in helping to prevent extinctions and in making more of such varieties available to more people. Heirloom popularity ultimately means, in some respects, more rather than less for everyone. For activists, seed savers, and consumers alike, growing, buying, cooking, and eating heirloom food is also a concrete way to help preserve agricultural biodiversity. Community gardens, urban farms, and suburban, rural, and even urban private vegetable gardens, orchards, chicken coops, and turkey runs all can find a much wider variety of plants and animals than they would have a decade or two ago.

Ideas translate into action, and the desire for these old foods (including their flavors, colors, and textures, as well as their stories) becomes tangible preservation. The plants I investigate inhabit often beautiful, always thought-provoking, and sometimes bittersweet landscapes of food and recollection, holding the mysteries of something we all experience and cannot afford to ignore: edible memory.

· 2 ·

A Short History of Heirloom Tomatoes

WALKING THROUGH Chicago's Green City farmers' market in the heat of August, it's hard to overlook the abundance of heirloom tomatoes, in colors ranging from near black to pink or green, filling plastic bins and laid out on tables.[1] Some are small as marbles, others large and lobed, almost like bell peppers. Their skins are often fragile, prone to splitting and poorly suited to lengthy journeys in refrigerated trucks. Depending on the point in the growing season, prices can be high, but they come down as the summer wears on and the tomatoes ripen. Other produce on sale—peaches, berries, corn, squash, potatoes, and some of the first apples of the season—cries out for attention as well. This is a moment that cannot occur at any other time of the year. No amount of greenhouse growing or refrigerated trucking can summon the array of flavors offered here. But the tomatoes are especially precious, and I can't resist the Black Krims or the enormous red-and-yellow Hillbillys. The whole range of "paste" tomatoes is not necessarily ideal in a summer salad, but they are well suited to cooking down into sauces and pastes, as the name suggests. The enormous Brandywines can be sliced in thick slabs, a meal in themselves. The traveler's tomato, or *Reisetomate*, is so deeply lobed that you can break the lobes off individually and carry the rest of the tomato in your pocket for later.

For old fans and new converts alike, heirloom tomatoes can be a revelation, a delightful encounter with marvelous flavor and with a striking array of shapes, sizes, colors, and uses. For some people heirloom tomatoes are a symbol of wealth and taste. For others they are a way to carry on a family tradition, flavors loved by past generations. The actual flavors vary widely, but the fans of such tomatoes hail them for actually tasting like tomatoes, in contrast to the perceived blandness of the mass-produced hybrids bred to resemble projectiles, designed for the big rig transport system and the supermarket produce section.[2] Indeed, university labs were instructed to imagine the tomato as a projectile in their efforts to develop hybrids that could withstand long journeys and extended refrigeration.[3]

Once upon a time what we call heirloom tomatoes were simply tomatoes. This chapter seeks to understand how a tomato becomes an heirloom, as well as the consequences of this transformation. The heirloom tomato has shifted from being a food produced and eaten in an entirely private way (in gardens, at home) to a food also bought and eaten in very public ways by more affluent consumers, at restaurants in particular, but also at farmers' markets and high-end grocery stores. The tomato supply hasn't always been like this, with heirloom varieties for sale at most farmers' markets and even in many supermarkets. For decades it was nearly impossible to buy an heirloom tomato, and in many places it still is.[4] In my local supermarket, on a good day, I can choose from five or six varieties of hybrid tomatoes, and I spent most of my life completely unaware that I was missing out on thousands of other varieties. Not long ago I would have had to work a lot harder to put an heirloom tomato on my plate. I would have had to grow it myself, or seek out one of a handful of cutting-edge restaurants serving up local and seasonal food, or befriend a gifted home gardener. And even if I were ready to grow them myself—if I had a little earth, a little time, a little gardening skill—I still would have had to search far and wide just to track down the seeds.

Today I can order hundreds of varieties from dozens of websites, page through stacks of catalogs, visit heirloom vegetable fairs, and even buy heirloom tomato seedlings at a local nursery. I can then save my own tomato seeds. Gardeners, shoppers, diners, and chefs clamor for heirloom tomatoes, in urban allotments and Michelin-starred restaurants, on back porches and at upscale grocery stores. Even Martha

Stewart jumped on (and helped propel) the heirloom bandwagon, with the heritage turkeys she has taken to serving for Thanksgiving and her magazine covers overflowing with multicolored ripe heirloom tomatoes.[5] The past decade has seen a notable increase in the popularity of heirloom tomatoes in the United States. They have made their way not only into backyard gardens, but also into grocery stores, restaurant kitchens, cookbooks, and the pages of popular newspapers and magazines as well as the fields of organic and conventional small farmers (and, increasingly, agribusiness farms). Tomatoes first piqued my interest in the late 2000s in part because by that time they had become ubiquitous—but it took a lot of work to get them to that point.

In his memoir about becoming an accidental tomato farmer, Tim Stark describes in great detail the sheer physical effort required to get his rainbow of heirloom tomatoes to the New York Greenmarket and into Manhattan restaurant kitchens every week.[6] He recounts the struggle to prepare the fields, getting thousands of fragile seedlings into the ground, fighting off deer and other hungry mammals (not to mention hungry invertebrates like aphids, cabbage looper, Colorado potato beetle, fall army worm, corn earworm, leaf miners, thrips, and tomato pinworm that plague many growers of tomatoes), the endless weeding, the rush to pick the tomatoes as they suddenly begin to ripen.[7] And once the tomatoes are picked, new problems appear: loading inadequate delivery trucks, fighting city traffic and unsympathetic parking regulations, muscling boxes of tender tomatoes down the narrow stairwells of Manhattan's restaurant basements. And all this was taking place because of the voracious appetite for heirloom tomatoes that had developed among New Yorkers who could afford these markets and restaurants. But similar tomatoes were growing nearby in the thriving community gardens of Alphabet City and other neighborhoods across New York City and farther afield.[8] Even as heirloom tomatoes rocketed to fame and became status symbols in some settings, not only did they continue to be grown by people who could never afford them either at the Greenmarket or in restaurants, they became *more* accessible to a wider range of people.

Stark's stories of getting his tomatoes to market reminded me of the opening of French novelist Émile Zola's tale of market life in nineteenth-century Paris in *The Belly of Paris*: a resolute vegetable seller guiding her rickety horse-drawn wagon full of just-picked vegetables the long twelve kilometers from Nanterre to Les Halles, the then brand-new market hall of soaring iron and glass, today vanished and replaced by a massive and largely underground shopping mall.[9] Madame François, the ruddy-cheeked vegetable seller, struggled with many of the same issues Stark faces: the race to get highly perishable produce to market before it disintegrates into compost, the relentless routine of waking in the middle of the night to make it to the market in time, the physical work of unloading the wagon or van box by box, basket by basket, the hours of back-and-forth with customers in search of impossible deals or just looking for someone to talk to, the countryside feeding the cavernous appetites of the city—all so similar in twenty-first-century New York and nineteenth-century Paris.

Even when I visited his stand at Union Square, Stark was knee deep in tomatoes, hoisting cartons out of the back of his truck. Union Square, early on a Saturday, was also full of people in chefs' whites pushing or dragging carts of produce back to nearby trucks (or nearby restaurants). I walked through the market with two good friends and their two splendid Labradors, Jack and Diane, who get star treatment and are offered cheese and organic dog treats. On that same trip to New York, every heirloom tomato I ate in a restaurant was underwhelming and overpriced, the result of the hollowing out of the heirloom label into a fad—something I'll discuss later in this chapter. Only when we conjured up our own tomato brunch with a rainbow of Stark's tomatoes did I finally have a satisfying mouthful. At the same time, back home in the Midwest, my green-thumbed friends and neighbors were drowning in the riches of their delicious tomato crops at that glorious moment in high summer when everything seems to ripen before your eyes, when you can almost hear your garden growing in the brilliant sunlight.

The Rise of the Heirloom

That single adjective, "heirloom," marks the rupture of the mid-twentieth century, when a historically unprecedented change in the quality and scale of agricultural production in the United States changed the ways that many of us produce and consume food. Beginning in the 1990s, tomatoes went from being the work of unknown green thumbs in out-of-the-way places to being essential ingredients on the summer menu of any self-respecting expensive restaurant and to the well-set picnic tables and benefit galas of elites across the country. They came to be in such demand that it is worthwhile for Tim Stark and so many others to haul their delicate produce into the metaphorical belly of the city.

Starting in the late 1980s and early 1990s, heirloom tomatoes moved from backyards, kitchen tables, and the barns and garden sheds of a few seed-saving projects to farmers' markets, commercial nurseries, school gardens, urban farms, and upscale restaurants.[10] Soon they appeared in the culinary discourse of restaurant reviews and cookbooks as well. So how did they get here? How can there now be dozens, even hundreds of tomato varieties to choose from in the middle of Chicago? As *Sunset Magazine* once asked, "Where have they been all our lives?"[11] The heirloom tomato made a quantum leap out of the backyards of tomato fanatics and solitary seed savers and into the pages of the *New York Times* and beyond.[12] The continuum that is edible memory played a role in this resurgence. At one end are people with their personal edible memories of cherished family heirloom tomatoes (and other fruits and vegetables) whose seeds, grafts, and tubers were handed down from one generation to the next, fed to hungry toddlers and family elders alike. At the other end of the continuum are newcomers who seek out heirloom tomatoes as part of a broader pursuit of local, seasonal, or novel cuisine.[13]

Yesterday's Tomatoes

The origins of the tomato lie somewhere in the Andes, in a wild plant with tiny berries that no one seemed to have been especially interested in eating.[14] Tomatoes were later cultivated and eaten in Central America, and they were well known to the Aztecs, though reportedly less beloved than tomatillos.[15] As they did with so many other foods (turkeys, potatoes, squash, corn, etc.), the first European explorers and conquistadors returned to Europe with tomatoes (or tomato seeds) in the holds of their ships. Tomatoes (and turkeys and other New World plants and animals) touched European soil in the early years of the New World conquerors, taking root here and there. But many of these foods also appear to have found their way to European popularity by a different route—from Portuguese explorers and traders through India and into Turkey and the Ottoman Empire, coming from the east rather than the west.[16] The tomato, not unlike the potato, crept rather slowly across the European continent and into European cuisine, not really taking off in many places until the nineteenth century, when it went from being a largely ornamental and medicinal plant to being a fundamental component of much of world cuisine.

In his wonderful book *The Tomato in America*, Andrew Smith dates the first European mention of tomatoes to 1544, but it took more than two hundred years for the tomato to become a regular part of European cooking and to break from its image of being either poisonous or purely medicinal. Many people found the smell of its foliage unpleasant, although for many of us today this pungent aroma is a harbinger of summer. This is a stunning change—showing how a food's image and popularity can be so radically and fundamentally altered, from poison to the intensely familiar flavor and colors of regional European cooking, the taste of home and childhood. The transformation of apples into something American (discussed in chapter 3), and of tomatoes into something Italian, is a long process.

The story of the tomato's movement, not only from its wild origins in South America to its cultivated form in Central America, but also from Central America to all corners of the globe, is still something of a mystery to many researchers.[17] *The Cambridge World History of Food* asserts that "the sudden introduction of several American foods had left Europeans a bit confused about where all of these new items were coming from. As a rule, new foods had arrived from across the Mediterranean with the Moors."[18] Multiple sources pinpoint the likely place of arrival of the tomato in Europe as Seville, "the only port for Spanish ships returning from the New World."[19] References to tomatoes do appear here and there in Italian and Dutch herbalists' accounts and other sources in the early sixteenth century, and they are more frequently described thereafter, also appearing in the occasional cookbook and painting, like Murillo's *The Angels' Kitchen* in 1646.[20] The tomato made faster headway in Spain and Italy than elsewhere, although it still did not achieve its status as a staple in Italy until the nineteenth century.[21] There are accounts of tomatoes being planted in Britain starting in the sixteenth century, although often as botanical curiosities. Italian gardeners also bred tomatoes that grew larger, smoother, and more thick-skinned.[22] By the eighteenth century, tomatoes had found their way into British soups, but it took until the early nineteenth century for them to appear more widely in French recipes, and they still met with much suspicion in Britain and France alike.[23] In India, the Bengali name for tomato is *biliti begun*, meaning "English [or foreign] aubergine [eggplant]," indicating a colonial-era introduction of the tomato into Indian cooking by the British.[24] Tomatoes came to Africa via some combination of "invaders, explorers, missionaries, and traders" and were found throughout the continent by the late nineteenth century.[25] As Alan Davidson, the erudite food enthusiast behind *The Oxford Companion to Food*, proclaims, "For a foodstuff which has come up to the front from almost nowhere in under two centuries, the tomato has proved to have astonishingly vigorous penetrative qualities, so that it is as close to being ubiquitous in the kitchens of the world as any plant food."[26]

Spanish colonists brought tomatoes to Florida and the Southwest, and English colonists brought them to South and North Carolina as early as the eighteenth century.[27] In the 1820s (at a time when the United States was pretty much the East Coast), the tomato began to take hold in cooking here, creeping into cookbooks and onto greengrocers' shelves and being planted in gardens. Smith explains that part of the impetus behind the increasing popularity of the tomato in the early nineteenth century came from farm periodicals and agricultural and horticultural societies, leading to more widespread cultivation in the 1830s and 1840s.[28] The rising acceptance of tomatoes is also visible in their increasing frequency in cookbooks and on restaurant menus. Canning too became popular around the country, and tomatoes lent themselves especially well to being preserved this way. Housekeeping manuals and cookbooks taught housewives how to incorporate tomatoes into their families' meals, and fresh (and, later, commercially canned) tomatoes became more widely available. Italian immigrants are also credited with increasing the popularity and availability of tomatoes in the Northeast in the late nineteenth century, as well as the burgeoning supply of canned tomatoes imported from Italy to the United States.[29]

The nineteenth century was also a time of widespread interest in breeding fruits and vegetables, including tomatoes, in both Europe and the United States. Breeders like Alexander W. Livingston sought the perfect combination of uniformity, productivity, and attractiveness, creating tomatoes like Acme and Favorite.[30] Much of what we today label "heirloom" was developed during this era. The pasts reached for by the consumers of heirloom tomatoes today are often relatively new, generally from the nineteenth century, a particular moment in the history of breeding domesticated plants and animals. That is, a large number of the foods now in vogue as heirlooms—in restaurant reviews and food writing—were not even bred until the mid-nineteenth century. So the memory bound up in heirloom foods in the United States is in part from a relatively limited and recent period.

Across Germany, France, the Netherlands, England, and the United States (among other places), biologists and botanists, but also gentleman farmers and hobby breeders, engaged in the widespread categorizing and supposed perfecting of everything from gooseberries to cattle, and this certainly included tomatoes. For example, breed books still used today were established for livestock, and competitive breeding of all sorts led to fairs and competitions. In the nineteenth century, fruit and vegetable breeding moved beyond the glasshouses and potager gardens of the aristocracy and into the nurseries, backyards, and allotment gardens of the middle and working classes. Gooseberry societies, for example, spread across England, bringing together across class lines people (mostly men) obsessed with growing the biggest possible gooseberry.[31] Similarly, pigeon breeding became a competitive passion in imperial Vienna, and indeed throughout Europe. This was part of a broader European mania for collecting and categorizing the plant and animal kingdoms.

Tomatoes, too, become the object of serious dedication from hobby breeders and market farmers, and local production and distribution continued for decades (at least of fresh tomatoes—canned tomatoes could obviously be transported far greater distances).[32] Markets for tomatoes did grow, and more gardeners planted them, but without refrigerated distribution or large-scale industrial farming, most fresh tomato production and consumption was still local, seasonal, and relatively heterogeneous. Most of the tomato varieties available before the Civil War have long since disappeared, although a few have been preserved at places like the Oliver Kelley Farm in Minnesota, while other living history museums and seed saver groups offer seeds from later in the nineteenth century.

Tomatoes like Black Prince or Black from Tula, which could thrive in northern latitudes with long summer days and short growing seasons, appeared in Russia and neighboring countries. Meanwhile farmers and gardeners in the American Midwest went in search of record-breaking varieties meant to tip the scales competitively at county fairs. Some of these varieties remain, but others have disappeared. It is difficult to calculate how much agricultural biodiversity has been lost, in part because of similarities between varieties, in part because of name changes and because few systematic records have been kept.[33]

In the United States in the 1930s and 1940s, agriculture turned away from a wider array of crops based on open pollination toward a narrower range of hybrid crops, in conjunction with a substantial increase in the scale of farming, the widespread application of synthetic fertilizers, and the growth of agribusiness.[34] The case of corn is just one illustration of this rapid change. Partly in response to Stewart's bacterial wilt, according to Janisse Ray, "in 1935, less than 10 percent of Iowa corn was hybrid. Four years later, 90 percent of it was—specifically Golden Cross Bantam [resistant to this wilt]. . . . Trusting the advertisements, not knowing long-term consequences, not understanding the loss, and wanting to survive, farmers stuck canisters of homegrown seed-corn on back shelves and went to town for Golden Cross Bantam."[35] Those forgotten canisters of corn contained open-pollinated seeds rather than hybrids. Open pollination means that a grower can save the seeds from one season's plants, plant them, and have them breed true in the next growing season. Hybrids involve the intentional (and often commercial) crossing of two distinct varieties in order to select for particular qualities. It is possible to stabilize a hybrid over seven generations or so, and natural hybridization regularly takes place. Ray notes that "folk growers have been producing happenchance hybrids for centuries, hence all the agricultural diversity to start with."[36] Hybrids often have what is called "hybrid vigor," particular levels of disease resistance or high yields, but they frequently are not fertile—that is, generally their seeds will not germinate, so that anyone growing hybrids needs to buy new seeds each year rather than saving seeds themselves from one year to the next. If the hybrid seeds are fertile, they can produce an unpredictable result, drawn from the genes of their significantly different parent plants. Thus people wanting to save seeds need to plant open-pollinated seeds rather than hybrids, and then they need to pay attention to the particular reproductive habits of the plant in question so as to keep unwanted pollen from fertilizing the desired plant (via a gust of wind or insect visitors) and thus creating an unintended hybrid.[37]

Another issue with hybrids is plant breeders' rights. Not only is it generally impossible to carry hybrids on to the next generation in a satisfactory way, but in many cases the rights to a hybrid are owned by the person or corporation that developed (and registered) the particular variety.[38] A further step is creating genetically modified organisms (GMO), a different process entirely where genes from unrelated organisms (such as bacteria) are spliced into the DNA of other organisms such as corn. In 2013, 90 percent of corn and 93 percent of soybeans planted in the United States was genetically engineered.[39] Like hybrids, these are proprietary—owned by the person or company that developed and registered or patented them. But they are quite different, and utterly new in human and natural history, in bringing together genes that would never meet in nature (given the difficulty of bacteria breeding with corn, for starters).[40] Two of the most common genetic modifications are corn modified to contain a bacillus that resists pest infestations, and an herbicide tolerance that allows glyphosate to be sprayed on fields, killing weeds without killing the corn plants. Today most corn—along with most canola, soy, papaya, and sugar beets—is genetically modified. There are no genetically engineered tomatoes on the market today—the Flavr Savr tomato was launched in 1994 but taken off the market in 1997.

The industrialization of agriculture that has led to more reliance on hybrids and genetically modified crops also led to a decrease in the overall number of tomato varieties available to consumers through standard commercial channels and to breeding for qualities sought by grocery customers. Standing in the produce sections of the nation's grocery stores, shoppers sought (and still generally seek) a uniform red color, spherical shape, smooth skin, and perhaps most important, a tomato that was intact—so transporting the produce without much damage became essential. This kind of durability also allowed consumers access to produce even when it was not in season locally.[41] They became available out of season and non-locally, shipped from the temperate climates of Mexico or California and from Dutch hothouses. The tomato varieties available in the grocery store represent only a tiny portion of the thousands of tomato varieties that still exist. When people walk into grocery stores in more affluent parts of the world, they invariably face a contradiction—an unprecedented variety of products to buy, from acorn squash to eggplants to mangoes, and a diminishing diversity in their genetic makeup.

In 2011, there were 373,500 acres of tomatoes planted in the United States (100,400 fresh and 273,100 for processing into tomato paste, etc.).[42] The same year per capita consumption of tomatoes was more than eighty-five pounds.[43] More than nine thousand of those acres of tomato production were organic, a little over 2.5 percent of the total production.[44] Today in the United States approximately 12 million tons of tomatoes are eaten each year, and between 25 and 40 million Americans grow their own tomatoes.[45] The reduction in the varieties of a given food grown commercially (accompanied by the increased predictability of the market and quality, as well as often lower prices but loss of flavor) affected far more than tomatoes—everything from apples and corn to chickens and pigs.[46]

Saving Tomatoes

Cryogenic seed banks are in a sense a form of collective memory, but they are inherently limited because what seeds are saved depends on who controls or has access to the bank. Moreover, seeds are not indefinitely viable, and if they are not being grown out, people forget both how to grow them and how to cook and process the vegetables. On an airplane I once sat next to an investment banker who assumed it was natural that certain varieties of plants would go extinct if there was no demand for them and wondered aloud why anyone would need a seed bank. I quickly convinced him that the heavy reliance on monoculture—the genetic uniformity of most of our food supply—means that changes in climate or disease or even consumer taste might prompt breeders to go back to the traits available in less popular and even endangered varieties, which is the reason we need the seeds. Resistance to drought or excess rain or particular blights might not be necessary for Kansas corn in 2015, but what about 2020? Or 2200?[47]

Taylor's Guide to Heirloom Vegetables finds that "the real danger [of modern monoculture] lies not so much in planting hybrids for large-scale cash crops but in losing or neglecting the broad genetic base of both wild and cultivated plants that have made these productive hybrids possible."[48] It is both private and organized seed savers who hold on to this genetic base and the well-developed taste for the produce that comes from these seeds.[49] In what the *Wall Street Journal* has called "seed wars," access to, control over, and preservation of plant genetic resources have now emerged as a field of international concern and conflict: "The principal arena for this conflict is the Food and Agriculture Organization (FAO) of the United Nations. . . . [T]he plant germplasm controversy [the question of who has the rights to the genetic code in a given seed] finds the advanced industrial nations of the North ranged against the less-developed countries of the South."[50] Questions surrounding biodiversity as well as genetically modified foods continue to be highly contentious. Biodiversity itself began to capture more widespread attention in the 1980s, an awareness that coalesced in events like the 1986 National Forum on Biodiversity organized by the National Academy of Sciences and the Smithsonian Institution and extensive discussions at the 1992 Rio Earth Summit, cementing global understandings of biodiversity (both wild and domesticated).[51] Discussions of biodiversity seem simultaneously to invoke notions of biological and cultural heritage, along with genotypes and phenotypes lasting through generations, both as fondly remembered old-style produce and as material for future genetic diversity. Biodiversity (and the systems of classification it is closely related to) is itself a concept worthy of deeper sociological inquiry, albeit elsewhere.

As documented in important books like Barry Estabrook's *Tomatoland* and Seth M. Holmes's *Fresh Fruit, Broken Bodies*, the mass production of tomatoes and other produce often depends on large quantities of toxic chemicals and what amounts to slave labor.[52] Groups engaged in fighting against these conditions include the Coalition of Immokalee Workers (CIW), which has been successful in implementing a Fair Food Program (including buyers paying an additional penny per pound of tomatoes harvested, which tomato growers pass on to workers), as well as improved health and safety regulations and better protection against forced labor and sexual assault, on a growing number of farms.[53] As Holmes says, today "it is likely that the last hands to hold the blueberries, strawberries, peaches, asparagus, or lettuce before you pick them up in your local grocery store belong to Latin American migrant laborers,"[54] whose labor is often invisible.

Following the development of these standardized commercial tomatoes—generally picked green and then reddened with ethylene gas, as well as the labor and agricultural practices that accompany these tomatoes, backyard gardeners and small farmers increasingly turned to heirloom tomatoes.

As this standardization of agriculture grew, so did a grassroots movement to preserve edible biodiversity, to hold on to the flavors, colors, and genes at risk of being lost.[55] As long ago as 1984, a journalist could already write, "When it comes to taste, the future is the past, some gardeners say. That means 'heirloom' seeds, not modern hybrids."[56] That is, the attention to heirlooms, and the habit of infusing them with this connection to the past, was already happening decades ago, but that awareness was far less widespread than it is today. From the 1940s until the 1980s, the producers and consumers of heirloom tomatoes were mostly the same. People ate what they grew in their backyards or community garden plots, sharing both seeds and tomatoes with friends and neighbors, but heirloom tomatoes were unavailable in supermarkets and even many farmers' markets, which were also far fewer than today. As hybrid tomatoes were conquering the commercial market, individual gardeners and seed savers were continuing to propagate a much broader variety of tomatoes (as well as other crops) out of their own devotion to the characteristics and traditions of particular varieties and because these heirlooms offered far more flavor and variation than the bland supermarket tomatoes.

Anthropologist Virginia Nazarea writes of the seed savers (not only in the United States but around the world) who preserve biodiversity in what she finds to be beautifully haphazard ways: "With their heirloom plants, seedsavers embroider the landscape with memories that awaken connections to past and place in many of us. Through an informal network of exchange, ritual and celebration, they embellish a countermemory that helps us dig in rather than fade out."[57] Many of the diverse groups of people who worked to preserve biodiversity through seed saving began out of some self-interest—the pleasure of particular plums or green beans, grown for personal consumption. But satisfying one's own appetites in the garden and the orchard also meant saving seeds and particular fruit trees, as well as carefully selecting the best plants year after year. These tiny private reserves of genetic material form part of the foundation of what we have available today.

People have saved seeds for millennia, although this practice is now much less widespread. In the 1970s and 1980s, most seed savers operated locally, exchanging seeds with friends and neighbors. Here and there slightly larger networks developed. Seed savers let each other know by mail or in mimeographed lists what seeds they had available. Many of these networks have turned into well-established organizations with their own seed libraries and gardens where they can regularly grow out the seeds (important for keeping them viable over the years). Carolyn Jabs, one of the first to mention heirloom food in popular media, wrote an article for the *New York Times*, followed by a book in 1984, detailing the procedure of seed saving and describing various people involved in this work.[58] Jabs found that collectors usually started for varyingly individual reasons, including nostalgia and family tradition, but often got caught up in the larger mission of preserving biodiversity.[59] An even earlier instance of the word "heirloom" being applied to seeds came from J. R. Hepler, an avid plant breeder and seed collector: "We call those beans which have been grown for many years in one neighborhood, but which have never found their way into commerce, 'Heirloom Beans.'"[60] Hepler's son Bill founded a seed company as a teenager, titling his catalog "Novelties, Specialties, and Heirloom Beans."

Native Seeds/SEARCH, Seed Savers Exchange, Southern Seed Legacy, and many other groups collect not only seeds, but also stories, growing instructions, and cooking techniques. One of the earliest seed-saving efforts to become a larger network developed in the 1970s and 1980s: Ken and Diane Ott Whealy's Seed Savers Exchange. The Whealys had planted a few seeds obtained from a Bavarian relative, and soon afterward they started a group of like-minded seed savers, an undertaking Diane Ott Whealy describes in compelling detail in *Gathering: Memoir of a Seed Saver*.[61] In 1975 the Whealys had a six-page list of available heirloom seeds, including tomatoes, beans, and squash, and a group of twenty-nine corresponding gardeners. By the early 1980s the seed list had grown to two hundred pages. At that point, Ken Whealy estimated, the group had led to the planting of three thousand old-fashioned rarities, including tomatoes.[62] Today Seed Savers Exchange operates a well-developed website with hundreds of varieties of seeds available, as well as sponsoring other fund-raising ventures and an on-line gift shop. And they still operate as an extensive clearinghouse for seed savers across the country, who list the seeds they have available in an annual catalog.[63] As the Seed Savers Exchange proclaims today:

> When people grow and save seeds, they join an ancient tradition as stewards, nurturing our diverse, fragile, genetic and cultural heritage. Our organization is saving the world's diverse, but endangered, garden heritage for future generations by building a network of people committed to collecting, conserving and sharing heirloom seeds and plants, while educating people about the value of genetic and cultural diversity. Few gardeners comprehend the true scope of their garden heritage or how much is in immediate danger of being lost forever.[64]

In his intriguing study of Seed Savers Exchange (as well as CSA [community-supported agriculture] farms and chicken coops), Michael Carolan found that Seed Savers Exchange was focused on both the past and the future. It also functioned as a site of resistance to monoculture and industrial agriculture.

In addition, he found plentiful evidence of edible memory. One of his interview subjects states, "'There is something special about the fact that I can grow something in my garden that my dad and his dad grew. I see what they saw, taste what they tasted, smell what they smelled.'"[65] Native Seeds/SEARCH is another well-established group of seed savers that "conserves, distributes and documents the adapted and diverse varieties of agricultural seeds, their wild relatives and the role these seeds play in cultures of the American Southwest and northwest Mexico. We promote the use of these ancient crops and their wild relatives by gathering, safeguarding, and distributing their seeds to farming and gardening communities." The origins of the group date back to the work of Gary Nabhan and Mahina Drees in the early 1980s. The group maintains a seed bank with more than two thousand varieties of seeds well adapted to the dry conditions of the Southwest, and they have also developed a Cultural Memory Bank, collecting in various ways the stories of the seeds as well as growers' firsthand knowledge of techniques of cultivation, preparation, and preservation. They explain, "Our story began in 1983 following a profound realization. While working on a Meals for Millions project to assist the Tohono O'odham Nation with establishing gardens, NS/S co-founders Gary Nabhan and Mahina Drees presented tribal elders with broccoli and radish seeds. *'What we are really looking for,'* the elders replied, *'are the seeds for the foods our grandparents used to grow.'* This revelatory remark inspired the formation of Native Seeds/SEARCH as a collector and preserver of these endangered traditional seeds."[66]

Janisse Ray's 2012 account of the world of seed saving profiles key, but often relatively unknown, figures on the front lines of preserving edible biodiversity. They are not doing this as a flash-in-the pan lifestyle choice or to catch the latest trend. This kind of farming and gardening can be a rewarding way to live, but can also be very challenging—not particularly lucrative, and not easy on the body.[67] She finds that "the work of seed savers counters loss of memory, identity, and sense of place—and this is especially true for those immigrant gardeners who bring their own food crops with them."[68] She is also concerned, as many people are, about the loss of knowledge and skill that accompanies the loss of seeds.[69]

Reading the stories collected by the Southern Seed Legacy, Native Seeds/SEARCH, or Seed Savers Exchange, it is easy to be drawn into these other worlds, other times and places. A space opens up—a memory of lost loved ones, of hard times, of beautiful summer days in gardens and farms. It is often the memory of an elderly man or woman, recalling his or her childhood or youth. The stories are necessarily tinged with loss, even if they also mean that the seed itself (and its story) is now being preserved. Many of these stories (and seeds) also recall hard times—Jim Crow and the Depression, wars and political violence, or the global slave trade. The history of seeds moving around the world also involves the movement of people, sometimes voluntarily, sometimes as refugees.[70]

Today many groups make it relatively easy to get an array of seeds that it would have been impossible to acquire so easily less than a generation ago.[71] The Seed Savers Exchange website offers about seventy-five varieties of tomatoes, not to mention Cherokee Trail of Tears beans and Oxheart carrots. There are twelve hundred tomato seed varieties in the Kendall-Jackson seed collection in California.[72] In conjunction with his project TomatoFest in Carmel, California, Gary Ibsen offers six hundred varieties of organic tomato seeds and an annual tasting. At Chicago's Green City Market, the Nichols Farm offers more than thirty tomato varieties in the course of a growing season. In southeastern Austria, the "tomato emperor" Erich Stekovics plants hundreds of varieties each year.[73] Stekovics, like many other tomato enthusiasts, has an infectious entrepreneurial and even evangelical spirit, spreading the good word about tomato biodiversity and personally leading groups of visitors on tours through his fields. Fancy stores in Vienna carry black-labeled jars of his pickled tomatoes (some looking like red, green, and yellow gumballs), heirloom tomato preserves, and pale yellow apple peppers stuffed with sauerkraut.

Baker Creek is another source for heirloom seeds today, starting in 1998 and now selling a few million seed packets annually including fourteen hundred seed varieties from approximately seventy countries.[74] They define an heirloom in the following ways: "nonhybrid and open-pollinated," "heirlooms taste great," "heirlooms come with history."[75] Anne Raver offers a list of places to find heirloom seeds, including the American Horticultural Society, the Garden State Heirloom Society, the New England Wildflower Society, Seed Savers Exchange, and the Thomas Jefferson Center for Historic Plants.[76] The Southern Seed Legacy has also been an important resource, both regionally and nationally, providing connections between existing local seed exchanges, and focusing on the preservation and distribution of both seeds and the cultural knowledge surrounding them.[77]

Slow Food is another organization playing an important role in the preservation of various foods. The group started in Italy but is now in dozens of countries, with projects ranging from visits to beehives in the heart of Chicago to efforts to preserve the tradition of *chuño blanco*, a traditional method of freeze-drying potatoes long used in the highlands of Peru.[78] Its efforts focus on specific animal breeds and plant varieties, as well as on processing techniques and skills and the knowledge necessary to make certain kinds of sausage or cheese, for example. Central to these efforts are the farmers and artisans who create these foods, as well as the landscapes and communities where they arise, and the human and cultural knowledge and skills just as much at risk of disappearing as the genes. Slow Food has projects focusing on both endangered agricultural animals and endangered crops. It is committed not only to particular techniques of food processing and production, but also to the genes that create particular kinds of food, and thus to traditional seeds and agricultural animals. Slow Food has been accused of commercializing local, handmade food, critics pointing to recurring tension in the world of local and heirloom food: tracing authenticity, balancing consumer demand with small-scale techniques of production, and walking the fine line between supporting local products and hyping them so much that consumers lose interest. Overall, however, there seems to be a trend among well-off consumers to seek out authentic, rustic food and exclusive culinary experiences.[79]

Slow Food USA's Ark of Taste[80] seeks to preserve heirloom fruits, vegetables, grains, and farm animals that have a history and tradition in North America, even if they are not native. It is a more recent participant in seed-saving efforts and worked with Seed Savers Exchange, Chefs Collaborative, and the American Livestock Breeds Conservancy, among other groups, in the RAFT (Renewing America's Food Traditions) project.[81] By 2008, more than five hundred growers had joined in the work of growing out the seeds inducted into the RAFT program. While the original partners of RAFT, like Chefs Collaborative and the American Livestock Breeds Conservancy, are still going strong, RAFT itself is no longer funded. When it was active, RAFT was "explicitly working toward renewing nothing less than the diverse, multicultural food traditions of the North American continent, accepting all of the social, technical, ethical, economic, and ecological challenges that task may entail."[82] It was especially interested in using the unique qualities of heirloom varieties to strengthen local and regional "foodsheds," cutting down the distances food has to be transported and connecting local growers with local consumers. Tomatoes adopted into the RAFT project included Amish Paste, Aunt Molly's Husk, Aunt Ruby's German Green, Burbank, Chalk's Early Jewel, Cherokee Purple, Djena Lee's Golden Girl, German Pink, Livingston's Globe, Livingston's Golden

Queen, Orange Oxheart, Radiator Charlie's Mortgage Lifter, Red Fig, Sheboygan, Valencia, and the Sudduth Strain Brandywine.[83]

The interest in heirloom food affects more than tomatoes, and it also takes place far beyond the United States. A growing market for local, traditional, and artisanal food has emerged in Europe as well, connected in part to the Slow Food movement. In Japan there is a robust interest in heirloom vegetables, particularly in Kyoto, where they are called *kyo yasai*.[84]

Tomato biodiversity gives us an amazing range of both colors and flavors, some accidents of nature, others the products of careful breeding by nineteenth-century hobby botanists, twentieth-century Russian scientists, and all sorts of home gardeners.[85] I think, for example, of the great Hillbilly tomatoes, yellow on the outside, but revealing a splash of bright red flesh when sliced, and the lemony flavors of some yellow and green tomatoes. But tomato (and other edible) biodiversity is about more than just flavor and looks. It is also about all kinds of traits that may be invisible to the eye but fundamental to future tomato crops. While some heirloom tomatoes are especially susceptible to particular diseases or adverse conditions, others carry the genes of resistance to both sickness and hard times (botanically speaking). Losing tomato biodiversity means losing not only the pleasure of the different flavors and colors and the memory of relatives or communities that might once have grown such tomatoes, but also this treasure trove of genetic possibilities for future environmental challenges, and for future appetites and dinner tables.

Writing and Reading about Tomatoes

To understand the emergence of heirloom tomatoes as a concept and as a commodity, I observed the changing ways of treating them in popular food writing, beginning with the first mentions of heirloom tomatoes and charting their rise in popularity. Taking the *New York Times* and the *San Francisco Chronicle* as tastemakers both responding to particular trends and fanning the flames, I coded every article from 1989 to 2013 that mentions heirloom tomatoes, searching for the emergence and persistence of recurrent themes. I also searched for the same term in the Lexis-Nexis newspaper database, yielding 2,258 articles over a twenty-five-year period dating from the first mention of heirloom tomatoes.[86] These newspapers mention heirloom tomatoes over and over in hundreds of restaurant reviews (significantly increasing in number over time), as well as in discussions of farmers' markets, public lectures, recipes, and gardening tips, both reflecting and creating attitudes about heirloom tomatoes and other such produce. The newspaper analysis I conducted reveals a changing discourse as discussions of gardening or biodiversity became overshadowed by restaurant reviews as well as (but to a lesser extent) accounts of elite consumption. This analysis also reveals the changing locations of heirloom tomatoes, including the creation of markets and other physical sites (restaurants, farmers' markets, supermarkets) where heirloom tomatoes become commodities.[87]

Seed-saving activists, who not only saved seeds themselves but also sought to spread awareness of the importance of preserving biodiversity, were key in the transition from growing heirloom tomatoes in one's home garden to ordering them in restaurants. Early on, chefs like Alice Waters at Chez Panisse in Berkeley, Nora Pouillon at Nora's in Washington, DC, and Thomas Keller at the French Laundry in Yountville, California, also championed using local and seasonal foods and fostering lasting relationships between farmers and restaurants. Hundreds of other chefs—including Bryant Terry, Rick Bayless, Dan Barber, and the late Judy Rodgers—encouraged this change in tastes by introducing diners to unfamiliar and/or locally sourced foods.[88]

Backyard, non-activist seed savers have also contributed to the preservation of seeds but generally have not figured prominently in the widespread cultivation of a taste for heirloom tomatoes. The seed savers described by Jabs and, two decades later, by Nazarea, by and large operate worlds apart from these trends. They are carrying on family traditions and family seeds, preserving their personal memories of the tastes of fruits and vegetables and the techniques for cultivating them. Food writers in the *New York Times*, the *San Francisco Chronicle*, and other newspapers necessarily influenced the coverage of heirloom tomatoes. There are sporadic references in the press during this period to biodiversity and steady (if somewhat scanty) references to gardening and seed saving. However, the heirloom tomato was steadily emerging as something of a status symbol, now sold not only at farmers' markets but also at upscale stores like Whole Foods, Zabar's, Dean and Deluca, and Fairway. Articles refer to heirloom tomatoes' being served at the White House and the exclusive Four Seasons Hotel.[89]

Tomatoes as Status Symbols

As I read through hundreds of newspaper articles, a category appeared that I hadn't initially sought—the invocation of the heirloom tomato as an explicit badge of an elite lifestyle. By the late 1990s, reviewers and journalists heaped praise on the colorful tomato salads and dishes that seemed to be exploding from every restaurant menu, while others complained about a chef's willingness to serve up mealy, out-of-season heirloom tomatoes just to be sure to include them. Heirloom tomatoes as a further marker of status appeared in a wave of associations with fancy events and famous people. The actor Vincent Gallo received a complimentary heirloom tomato salad from a chef while being interviewed at a restaurant in Los Angeles, for example; and at an opera patrons' dinner in San Francisco, an heirloom tomato salad was served to wealthy donors.

At times these references are also critical, as when food writer Frank Bruni wearily described how "a thousand heirloom tomato salads bloomed."[90] One restaurant reviewer puzzled over how the menu could promise an heirloom tomato salad containing more varieties of tomato than there were tomato slices on his plate. Supermarkets offer baskets of multicolored "heirloom tomatoes"—some very large and some a little cracked—that make no mention of the actual varieties. Farmers, and increasingly agribusiness, may also charge a premium for unusual tomatoes or heritage turkeys. On many restaurant menus, the term "heirloom" may have little to do with flavor. Part of the heirloom food movement does involve creating a market for these foods, especially among people who can afford higher prices. At one end of the spectrum, the label may become a relatively hollow marketing tool. But it is a spectrum, and the other end is occupied by committed gardeners, farmers, and seed savers who curate their own collections of their favorite tomatoes over years and decades. The celebration of heirloom tomatoes in the *New York Times* and other elite venues does not decrease the traditional backyard gardener's access to them. In fact, the greater demand for seeds and seedlings makes them more available.

Tomatoes are only one part of a much larger movement to save seeds in order to preserve both biodiversity and the pleasure of eating so many varieties of food, such as beans, tomatoes, squashes, and other produce (and increasingly the breeding of traditional livestock as well). For many diners, chefs, and gardeners, the appeal of heirloom tomatoes and other heirloom foods is in part the feeling of authenticity they convey.[91] Nazarea finds that modernity intensifies the impulse to save seeds, to seek out "old" forms of produce and thus traces of the past: "In many instances, heirloom plants play a central role in the restoration of landscapes of remembrance. Some of the reasons for the resurgence of interest in garden staples from another time are distinct flavor, beauty, aroma, novelty and whimsy, evocativeness and familiarity, carefree productivity, and drought and insect tolerance."[92] Indeed, it is difficult to separate the motivations for seed saving from one another—memory and tradition are intertwined with commitment to biodiversity, as *Taylor's Guide to Heirloom Vegetables* proclaims: "Delving into the histories of specific varieties is another part of our modern fascination with heirloom gardening. The search can lead us to a deeper understanding of our own traditions and to a greater appreciation of other cultures. . . . To many people, the true value of heirloom vegetables transcends the simple pleasures of growing and eating them. The seeds become living windows to the past."[93]

The marked increase in the heirloom tomato's popularity and ensuing commodification over recent decades resulted from a convergence of distinct but interdependent factors. Without the solitary seed savers there might not be the biological resources necessary for such a change. Without the more vocal activist seed savers and their networks, there would be both fewer seeds and fewer people growing these plants. Without tastemakers like Alice Waters and Chez Panisse and so many others, as well as *New York Times* and other food writers, there would not be the same collective turn to seasonal eating and local ingredients. Regardless of your feelings about Martha Stewart, she and her colleagues deserve some credit for raising awareness of, and encouraging a liking for, heirloom varieties. Perhaps without modernization and industrial farming there would be less of a taste for unusual, unfamiliar, but also "old," "heritage," and "authentic" foods.

Heirloom tomatoes, with their crevices and unfamiliar colors, even stripes, offer the sensation of something new. But they also offer something pleasantly old, with folksy names like Aunt Ginny's Purple or Mortgage Lifter. People eat them for a range of reasons—flavor, familiarity and personal memory, exoticism coupled with a sense of a connection to the past. By the early twenty-first century, however, they had also come to signify elite status.

But people who can't (or don't want to) pay the premium placed on heirloom tomatoes in restaurants, grocery stores, and farmers' markets can, if they are gardeners (or friends of gardeners) enjoy them homegrown.[94] And this happens everywhere—tiny patches of reclaimed urban land, secret rooftops, sprawling rural backyards, and even schoolyards and the occasional baseball stadium (in 2014 an edible garden opened in the San Francisco Giants' AT&T Park). But these do-it-yourself tomato patches have a very different botanical and historical heritage from supermarket tomatoes.

Elite tastes and grassroots labor alike function to preserve biodiversity and increase the availability of heirloom varieties. Its new status does not bar the seed savers and backyard gardeners from continuing to enjoy the pleasures of the heirloom tomato.[95] Moreover, as sociologist Gary Alan Fine notes, "It has become commonplace to suggest that you are what you eat. However, it is equally appropriate to suggest that you are *where* you eat."[96] The growing taste for heirloom tomatoes among elites opens up new spaces of consumption (high-end restaurants, farmers' markets, and upscale grocery stores) and production (whether small organic farms in the Midwest or large industrial greenhouses in northern Mexico). Tastes shape landscapes, and changing landscapes also shape tastes, in conjunction with marketing campaigns, agricultural subsidies, transnational trade agreements, and so forth.[97]

In the 1980s there emerged steady, generally behind-the-scenes activity like gardening, cooking, sharing seeds, and networking, along with activists (primarily chefs and seed savers) whose campaigns for local, seasonal food and biodiversity contributed to the appearance of the heirloom tomato in more popular media and in new spatial settings.

Long before heirloom tomatoes had gone mainstream, Alice Waters and other avant-garde restaurateurs put them on their menus.[98]

As grassroots interest in heirloom produce blossomed, other changes were afoot. The growing popularity and availability of organic food, and movements like Slow Food—a turn to what people perceived as healthier and more authentic or artisanal food—all played a role in the popularity of the heirloom tomato. Today it is much easier for gardeners, restaurant patrons, and home cooks to get their hands on quite a variety of heirloom tomatoes.[99]

Farmers' markets have also played a part in this resurgence. There were many farmers' markets in the United States in the first half of the twentieth century, but they became less widespread as mass production and national distribution of farm produce increased.[100] In the 1960s there were as few as 100 farmers' markets nationwide, but by 2000 there were more than 2,800, and by 2013 there were more than 8,100, with estimated sales of about a billion dollars.[101] Sociologist Clare Hinrichs and her colleagues attribute the newfound popularity of farmers' markets to "producers' renewed search for more profitable alternatives to wholesale commodity markets, consumers' rising interest in farm-fresh and regional specialty foods, and also the cachet of colorful open-air markets as trendy arenas for consumption."[102] The more than eight thousand farmers' markets in the United States also convey messages about sustainability, local and seasonal eating, and biodiversity.[103] The exponentially increased demand for heirloom tomatoes among elites at restaurants and farmers' markets took advantage of, and created further demand for, the biodiversity that had been preserved by out-of-the-way gardeners and devoted seed savers in decades of quiet work.[104]

These changing tastes have consequences for producers as well. In Chicago, for example, local restaurant patrons' taste for heirloom tomatoes were satisfied in part by the fruits of an urban farm at the site of Cabrini-Green, where Ken Dunn, a committed urban farmer and activist, began this project in his decades-long effort to turn Chicago into a more environmentally sound city. The Cabrini Green housing complex has since been demolished, but there is still a robust urban farm in the neighborhood, the Chicago Lights Urban Farm.[105] Dunn says of the less-than-one-acre farm: "This is not a hobby. . . . This is a real product, and part of that is that it must make money. To make a permanent change in society, it has to function in the existing economy, being able to bring its benefits while paying its bills." The farm earned $45,000 in one year. This, then, is one of the ways elite tastes for local produce can feed back into an urban ecosystem, creating both green space and income in neighborhoods short of both.

It can be a good thing for biodiversity to have a turkey or tomato become a status symbol. Unlike the symbolic goods that sociologist Max Weber saw monopolized by certain status groups (an insight carried over into the work of Pierre Bourdieu), the heirloom tomato does not decrease in availability when it becomes a symbol of elite status and good taste.[106]

Taste and Place

French sociologist Pierre Bourdieu calls on us to take breakfast (and other meals) seriously as sites of cultural practice and sociological inquiry.[107] A meal as intimate as breakfast can reveal the depth of the habitus: unspoken, automatic, a driver of desires, appetites, and deepset habits. Appetites and tastes are handed down in families, but as with other cultural practices, great changes or slight adjustments may take place, the workings of both continuity and change. Heirloom status, for example, is just the most recent phase in centuries, even millennia, of changes in the uses and meanings of tomatoes.[108] As geographer Julie Guthman and other scholars contend, a sound understanding of the social qualities of taste is essential to any study of the cultural economy of food.[109] In sociological work on culture, researchers have tracked how certain cultural objects—a Beethoven sonata or a light Italian song, foie gras or grilled cheese sandwiches, Marcel Duchamp's infamous urinal or the *Mona Lisa*—move in and out of being considered tasteful. They are also interested in how "good" taste and "bad" taste feel very natural to many of us—yet tastes vary widely across time and space and become ways that groups of people actively distinguish themselves from other groups. Thus the tastes for certain aesthetic objects indicate (and indeed maintain) pronounced distinctions between groups.[110] Investigations of such changes in the conceptions of beautiful and high-status objects have followed the way tastes change over time, how obscure things become normal, and how experts and elites emerge. At the heart of this work are objects and practices that offer the consumer a supposedly superior and inherently sensory experience. Their popularity changes over time (so that objects once considered ugly become beautiful and food once seen as inedible becomes delicious), as at first only some people "recognize" such beauty or flavor. In the research conducted by Bourdieu and others, the ability to see beauty in an abstract painting or taste deliciousness in something like foie gras overlaps with class position and serves not only as a source of pleasure, but also as a technique of marking one's distinction, rarely intentionally. Part of Bourdieu's approach is to recognize how naturally and viscerally we experience our own tastes for food, art, or clothes—and how naturally and viscerally we may judge or disparage other people's tastes.[111] Presumably many of the heirloom tomato varieties have always tasted especially good, but once technological and corporate changes sent them into obscurity, extensive cultural and agricultural work has been necessary to bring them back into more mouths and markets.[112]

As Guthman and others find, everything we eat has a corresponding geography, a place where it was grown, distance covered from field to processing plant to market to table, and the individual people whose labor is essential to food production. Guthman rightly reminds people that many current books on food may offer in-depth critiques of the political and economic background of our food, but ultimately they place the lion's share of the work of improving our culinary lives on individuals as consumers—not on individuals as people actively engaged in politics.[113] The journey of food from farm to table might involve a short ride in the back of a truck from a farm to a farmers' market or CSA drop-off point, or it might involve a long sea voyage and going through customs and fumigation in the Port of Long Beach. Despite the comparative popularity of local and seasonal foods, I have been at numerous supermarkets in August (peak tomato season in much of the United States) and found only tomatoes from Mexico and the Netherlands, when I knew tomatoes were happily ripening just a few miles away. Even the way supermarkets are integrated into landscapes is not accidental. The big-box architectural style is a part of a larger set of social habits and zoning regulations. This style leaves three sides of the building more or less blank and encourages shoppers to come in their cars rather than on foot. This layout in turn makes it possible for customers with cars to buy far more than if they came on foot or on public transportation. Food is always about place. It is made, transported, and eaten in real places, in factories and kitchens and school cafeterias. It is also always about work, the labor of innumerable human hands, bodies, and minds at all the different steps in the supply chain—all the different ways to proceed from farm to table.

The smaller unit of social space, we could argue, is the human body. (Or perhaps the stomach?) The growing popularity of heirloom foods reveals new sites of production and consumption of these tomatoes. Community-supported agriculture (CSA) also developed during the heirloom tomato's emergence, forging direct links between farmers and communities by having customers buy shares in a farm for an entire growing season, in return receiving boxes of produce every week or two. (A list of CSA farms is available from Local Harvest.)[114] I recently found a CSA near my parents' house, and my mother became a loyal supporter. The CSA box my parents subscribed to cost twenty-five dollars a week for very satisfying quantities of tiny new potatoes, tubby squashes, dense, sweet strawberries, and much more. My mother now encourages her friends and relatives to join as well, and they are abuzz about the contents of their weekly boxes. Despite more than six decades of living in California, my mother was surprised every week by a new herb or vegetable in her CSA box, and the box changed how and what she cooks and eats. The people who run the two farms that formed this particular CSA at the time were also very good at providing their customers with recipes and other information, adding to people's interest in the produce itself and their loyalty to the farmers who grow it.

Of course, if my mother relied solely on her CSA box for her tomato supply, she'd lead a tomato-less life for much of the year. These two coastal farms start producing tomatoes only very late in the season, and then only for a brief window. She may get squash and lettuces and greens of all sorts, spinach and carrots and months of strawberries, but tomatoes are late bloomers on the foggy parts of the California coast.

When visiting one August, I went with my mother to pick up her box. Someone from the farm would drop the boxes off in the side yard of a pretty Victorian house a few blocks from my parents' house. The stack of boxes waits in the shade as one by one people come to pick up their boxes and cross their names off the list tacked to the wall above them. The drill is to open a box, pull out the plastic bag nearly overflowing with vegetables, then fold up the box, leaving it for next week's shipment. As we got into the car, the bag of vegetables was nearly too heavy to hold on my lap and smelled deliciously of leeks. I peeked into a tiny paper bag tucked among the baby leeks, fat orange carrots, slender white eggplants, and jumbo pattypan squash. The bag held orange tomatoes the size of gumballs—the first tomatoes of the season, well into August. We ate as many as we could on their own, then had the rest in a tian, or vegetable gratin, of thinly sliced vegetables: a bed of sautéed baby leeks covered in layers of very thinly sliced red and blue potatoes and thin wedges of pale green pattypan squash, baked with the tomatoes halved and scattered over the top, along with thyme from the garden. Roasted and melted into the other vegetables, the tomatoes created a succulent, caramelized connection between the other ingredients, all from the same box.

A few days before that box arrived, I visited the farm itself on a summer morning that started out cool and foggy until suddenly the fog vanished in the heat of the late morning sun. (The farm appears again in chapter 4.) Walking through the fields of chili peppers, Italian greens, artichokes, carrots, beets, leeks, and much more, I saw row after row of green tomatoes hanging from the well-staked plants. Andy Griffin, the farmer kind enough to show me around his fields, plants very few heirloom tomatoes. Having experimented with different varieties, he has found those that strike the proper balance between resistance to disease and pests and satisfying his subscribers' expectations, so he is happy to plant hybrids and more modern varieties if they are better at warding off pests and thriving in this particular climate. At any rate, if my parents want tomatoes outside the narrow window when Griffin's coastal tomatoes ripen, they have to resort to supermarket hybrids or the vagaries of the farmers' market, where a few stands offer tomatoes from farms deeper in the inland valleys, farther from the coastal fog and its cold summer winds.

There is a tomato-by-tomato resurgence involving the preservation of biodiversity through taste-making. While CSAs often require a seasonal commitment—paying up front for a season's worth of produce deliveries—farmers' markets offer the convenience of just showing up on market day. Most farmers' markets in the United States are geared to letting farmers sell their own products rather than providing space for non-farmers to mark produce up and sell it. While prices at farmers' markets may sometimes be higher than at the supermarket, the quality, especially the flavor, is often much better. And there is no guarantee that my urban chain supermarket has the cheaper prices, and a great certainty that it does not have the fresher produce.

I get excited when I walk away with a bag full of great deals—three ears of fresh organic corn for a dollar, pounds of tomatoes, potatoes, and apples for just a few dollars, peaches in their prime, great butternut squashes weighing down my shopping bag, and handfuls of herbs. I look forward to that delightful moment in late August when there are peaches labeled "slightly bruised" for two dollars for a big bucket. Slightly bruised is no matter at all if the peaches are going straight into the freezer or into a peach cobbler. Likewise, when the raspberry price suddenly drops a bit, it's a good time to buy more than I need and lay the berries out on wax paper on a cookie sheet, freeze them solid, then put the loose berries in a container to go back in the freezer. When I get up on dark winter mornings, once I put the kettle on for my coffee, I toss a handful of raspberries into the bottom of my oatmeal bowl. By the time I'm a bit more awake and my oatmeal is ready, the berries will have started to thaw, and the hot oatmeal will take care of the rest. When I stir it all up the oatmeal turns a beautiful magenta.

Some farmers' markets are the expensive domain of well-off urbanites, but others are set up—often with great success, like the Fondy Farmers' Market in Milwaukee—for far less affluent groups and neighborhoods. And in some places and at particular moments, heirloom tomatoes and other local, seasonal produce do become available to people without that kind of money. Many markets now accept WIC and SNAP and have agreements with nearby food pantries and shelters. To characterize either farmers' markets or this kind of food as strictly for privileged consumption does a disservice to the robust farm stands, markets, community gardens, urban farms, and other projects and locations created, tended, and frequented by people with less money than the stereotypical patrons. That said, access to food (as noted in the previous chapter) continues to be a significant problem for far too many people, and the vibrancy and popularity of these success stories should not eclipse the challenges that continue to face so many people in accessing food.

At farmers' markets, the supply really does affect the price. So the first tomatoes of the season are going to be expensive because the demand is high and the supply is fairly thin. Indeed, farmers have competed for centuries to produce the earliest tomatoes (or apricots or rhubarb or peaches) of the season. People's mouths water for the first ripe tomato, and the early rising chefs of local restaurants show up at ungodly hours to buy as many tomatoes as they think they can serve. By August, however, prices come down, and shopping baskets and canvas bags fill with the bounty. The biodiversity so many farmers and gardeners have been working so hard to preserve in recent decades finds its way into shopping bags, freezers, and soup pots.

Naturally there is a limit to how many tomatoes I can use before they get a little overripe on the countertop, but I can dry them or cook sauces and store them for the winter. I have little experience with canning, and I confess to being somewhat intimidated by it, but I'm very good at freezing things in containers. Homemade sauce, as Nigella Lawson or Barbara Kingsolver or a whole host of other cooks and writers like to tell us, is very easy to make—though not so easy if you try to do it in the narrow time slot between getting home from work and facing the distress of your family, friends, or roommates when dinner is late and people are starting to get what my family calls the "whim-whams." A sauce made entirely of yellow or green tomatoes, for example, can be a pleasant diversion from a lifetime of red spaghetti sauce, but a sauce I made by mixing different colors of heirloom tomatoes turned an unappetizing murky gold-brown. I had more success drying tomatoes. The dried sections of yellow tomato were sweet and caramelized, and halved black plum tomatoes dry deliciously as well, with an intense berry flavor.[115]

In much of the writing, and work, around heirloom tomatoes and other heirloom produce, there is no mistaking the mixture of memory and agriculture, the powerful idea of "garden heritage," and the close connections between plants, food, culture, and the past. The renewed commitment to biodiversity (linked to memory) creates concrete places—in backyard gardens, but also in the seed-saving projects I mentioned above, and in the gardens of living history museums or historic houses like George Washington's Mount Vernon or Thomas Jefferson's Monticello.[116] People develop literal appetites for the past. Edible heirlooms become part of our molecular structure, absorbed into the body. What are people seeking in this moment? An unreachable past and self, perhaps—a past that many of us never experienced firsthand. People are also seeking new sensory experiences—even though these are "traditional" vegetables, for many people they are brand-new experiences. If heirloom tomatoes tasted uniformly bad (or even just uniform!) no amount of compelling narrative would have brought them into the mainstream.[117] But the story plays a crucial role, with lasting effects captured in the word "heirloom" itself, which then comes to stand in for other things.[118]

The heirloom tomato illuminates the intersection of macro-level changes: industrial agriculture, species loss, the development of GMOs, efforts to preserve biodiversity, the Slow Food movement and a broader turn to organic, local, and seasonal foods; and micro-level practices: dining out, gardening, shopping, cooking, and newspaper reading.[119] These factors contribute to taste-making, but taste in turn leaves its mark on social and physical landscapes. If we want to understand the problems and possibilities of the food supply today (including heirloom food), turning to the ways most of us actually get that food is enlightening and surprising. The changing ways of getting food from the countryside to legions of gardenless urbanites reveal the alterations in everything from the genetic basis of our food supply to the differences in the way many of us eat today as opposed to how our grandparents or great-grandparents acquired, prepared, and ate food. The truck farms that supplied much of Los Angeles with fresh produce in the early twentieth century, the great covered market halls of European capitals, like Les Halles in Paris, many of them now gone forever, or the supermarket chains that dominate food distribution today all help us understand the changes in our food supply—and in edible memory—over the course of the twentieth century.

These tomatoes break out of the highly individualized realm of the private seed saver into a much more collective arena of consumption and meaning, widely available both as a natural resource and as a symbolic resource. Gardeners far out of the mainstream and people following their hearts, habits, and appetites preserve the tomato and carry it forward. That work provides the raw material for the trend that developed in the 1990s as heirlooms soared to popularity in fancy restaurants and food writing. The tomato can harbor memories of the past and hopes for the future. Tomatoes were in the vanguard of the heirloom food movement, and they continue to be the most prevalent and popular heirloom produce. Although tomatoes were the first food to experience the heirloom resurgence, they are not alone, and their sweeping popularity paved the way for other heirloom plants.

· 3 ·

Remembering Apples

AS I MADE my way through a Milwaukee farmers' market early in a recent autumn, I experienced a mild epiphany. Among the busy rows of stalls, people bustled about stocking up on the cheap, plentiful produce of the season—multicolored towers of crispy bell peppers, squashes in all sorts of shapes, potatoes in many colors, and possibly more beets than even this hungry city could eat. A diverse crowd of Milwaukeeans navigated the narrow concrete paths between the wooden tables, pulling laden shopping carts or pushing strollers so loaded with produce that there was little room for babies. This farmers' market has a long history in Milwaukee, and I regularly see droves of my fellow Wisconsinites trudging back to their cars carrying great stalks of dill and enormous bags of cucumbers, ready to diligently put up their own pickles, just as my great-great-aunt used to do.

I slowed in front of a wooden crate of apples: Wolf River, one I'd never heard of. They were very large red apples that felt too light for their size and turned out to be nearly inedible raw. Wolf River is an apple so regional that it is named for a river in northern Wisconsin, well adapted to the particularities of the local growing season.[1] Not long after I bought several pounds of them, my brother and sister-in-law were visiting during Wisconsin's glorious autumn. I came home one afternoon to find a Wolf River sitting on the kitchen counter with a single large bite taken out of it. My sister-in-law had brought it along on an excursion as sustenance, taken one bite, and been sorely disappointed, wondering why

I'd keep such a bland, dry apple in the house. But Wolf River is at its best as a baking apple, and it proved its mettle that fall in countless crisps and crumbles and pies, retaining its shape during cooking (one of its major virtues) and proving delicious when mixed with a few juicier apples of other varieties.

I took home more than Wolf River from the farmers' market that day. As I began to look more closely at the apple sellers' tables, I realized I was seeing apples I'd only read about in books. Most of these apples had become rather rare as, tree by tree, they disappeared or faded into obscurity, eclipsed by acres and acres of Gala and Red Delicious. Many old apple varieties were rendered irrelevant by inexpensive supermarket apples, or by improvements in the water supply, so that people can safely drink water and don't have to resort to hard cider as they once did across the United States.[2] One particular stand at that farmers' market caught my eye. It was especially rich in elegantly named apples that I'd seen only as dusty wax models in museums or portrayed in colorful plates in old books. Esopus Spitzenberg, Cornish Gilliflower, Ashmead's Kernel, Hubbardston Nonesuch, and my very favorite, Calville Blanc d'Hiver, all leaped out at me from the crates of apples from Weston Orchards, an apple seller I later came to know well. I returned to that stand each week to see an ever-changing collection of apples as different varieties ripened and then faded. This is a scene repeated in some form across the country every fall, judging by the growing popularity of heirlooms in general and apples in particular and on their increase in farmers' markets, living history museums, apple festivals, pick-your-own orchards, and even the occasional grocery store.[3]

The apple I now love above all others, the Calville Blanc d'Hiver, is shaped more like a bell pepper than like a conventional apple. It has a translucent pale yellow-green skin and crisp white flesh, with a scattering of red pointillist freckles and an occasional pink blush. My students make fun of me for (among other things) loving such a clearly obscure (and to some, elitist) apple. My case is not aided when one author recalls that the "Calville Blanc d'Hiver . . . was grown over 300 years ago in the garden of King Louis XIII. It is still served in the finest Parisian restaurants."[4] Is it snobbery that makes me eagerly anticipate the brief autumnal weeks of the Calville's season and leaves me unsatisfied by so many supermarket apples? I would say perhaps in part, and some of my friends say that's definitely the entire reason, claiming that my recent and thorough fascination with rare produce clouds my judgment. Indeed, writing this book has forever changed how I think about food, and while I don't adhere to a strict obscurist diet, I much appreciate the privilege and pleasure of finding apples and plums, greens or tomatoes I've never tasted before. This book has definitely involved the education of this particular sociologist, learning about things previously unknown to me. But does the Calville possess an objectively better flavor and texture? Is it the novelty these apples afford? Or is it an accident of genetics that shapes my taste in apples and gives me a visceral appreciation of the crisp flesh and clear flavor? In my case I'm sure novelty is part of the appeal, but novelty is not sufficient to make me love Esopus Spitzenberg as much as I love the Calville. Esopus may have been Thomas Jefferson's favorite apple, but it isn't mine.

Apple taste itself is personal and individual. Many people (Americans in particular) prefer sweetness, as Michael Pollan notes, and many of us have lost (or never acquired) the taste for tart or tannic apples. I find the slightest hint of mealiness in an apple off-putting, but I know people far more tolerant of the textural spectrum. Fred Lape, author of the very informative *Apples and Man*, prizes the Northern Spy above all others—but would I? And the same variety of apple can taste very different depending on the weather, even the apple's location in relation to the sun. In general, more sun means more sugar. The variety of flavors available in apples is striking. Harold McGee, an expert on the science of the kitchen, discovered in various apple varieties "the distinct taste of anise or fennel. . . . Flowers and spices and nuts, including coconut. Lots of other fruits: orange peel and lemon, strawberry, pineapple, green banana. Rhubarb. Occasionally, popcorn and potatoes."[5] Is it snobbery that prompts Lape and others to disparage the Red Delicious and the Golden Delicious as predictable and pedestrian? Are commercially available apples really as insipid as so many apple fanatics find them to be, or does their easy availability simply make them less fashionable or perhaps less intriguing to people who spend a lot of time thinking and writing about food? Does sheer availability, even more than their purported blandness, doom these varieties to criticism from the purveyors of apple taste? Or, as with the tomato so eloquently described by Estabrook,[6] have the decades of breeding for a mass market and the rigors of cross-country trucking and transoceanic shipping led to a watering down of flavor and texture?

As with tomatoes, differing opinions about apples can also be influenced by the particular growing season or even the apple's location on the tree, since both can affect texture and taste. Pockets of weather and soil can have positive or negative consequences for apple flavors and looks. Valleys and hilltops may be blessed with particularly advantageous growing conditions, like the microclimate around Blenheim Palace (Churchill's boyhood home) in Oxfordshire, a trove of delicious English fruit varieties. The influence of weather goes a step beyond terroir (briefly understood as the sense of a given wine, apple, cheese, or other food being distinctly influenced by its location of origin), and, as any gardener knows, a bad summer can render the advantages of soil or terrain irrelevant.[7] Ill-timed rain or a windy year can wreak havoc on an apple harvest. As an example of the consequences of weather for flavor, Edward Bunyard, in his lovely book *Anatomy of Dessert*, describes the finicky Allington Pippin: "Particular as to soil, demanding sun and open exposure, it must not be judged by the products of a dull and cold summer; the unhappy results of such seasons should pass to the kitchen, as its quince-like flavour is enhanced by cooking, and it makes a pie full of subtle memories."[8]

The year 2012, for example, was very difficult for midwestern fruit. An early warm spell brought the cherry, peach, and apple trees into bud, followed by a cruel frost that killed off these nascent blossoms, and this misfortune was topped off by one of the driest and hottest summers since the 1930s, leaving little fruit even for baking pies full of Bunyard's "subtle memories."[9] The Westons, the apple growers who sold me my first Calville Blanc d'Hiver, lost much of their crop: I saw no Calvilles that year and little of the usual variety of apples. One week there was almost nothing but a big crateful of beautiful Arkansas Black apples—a deep, dark red, with crisp white flesh. And they were delicious. The Arkansas Black thrived in this difficult year, a clear example of the value of diversifying an orchard.

I bought my first Calville Blanc d'Hiver from Genevieve Weston, the proprietor of that farmers' market stand, a nonagenarian apple grower from New Berlin, Wisconsin, with a sweet, high voice and an acute knowledge of apples. She and her equally long-lived brother oversee a treasure chest of an orchard, where I visited a few weeks after I first came across their stand. In the summertime the Westons sell little cardboard baskets of red, yellow, and black cherries, berries, and the earliest summer apples. But their real season is the fall. And they have nearly ruined me for other apples. I bought up bags of fruit from Genevieve and her colleague Tammy, taking pictures of the apples next to their labels so I'd know what I was eating when I got home. Since then Tammy has guided me through the surprisingly variable apple season. Until the difficult year of 2012 when prices went up to $3 a pound, apples at one end of the table cost $2 a pound while at the other end they were a mere $1.50, and each week there was a different array depending on what had begun to ripen and what trees were already stripped bare and settling in for the coming winter. The Westons also supply apples to local restaurants, part of the current (and still growing) trend toward local sourcing.

I returned to the market a few weeks after that first visit, this time with my parents, and when we had bagged our purchases and I had replenished my supply of Calvilles, Tammy slipped into my hand three tiny apples, each with a deep red blush. She explained that they were snow apples, and that they would make me sleepy. I promptly forgot this detail. When we got home I ate one (with a slice of deliciously elderly Wisconsin cheddar) and uncharacteristically fell asleep for an hour— only afterward recalling what Tammy had told me. Did this apple really bring on my unplanned nap?

Like the Calville, this was a French apple, also known as the Fameuse. What are French apples doing in New Berlin, Wisconsin—and how did an apple become French in the first place? These botanical objects move about the earth, but they can also become deeply rooted, physically and symbolically. Over time, apples become intertwined with local, regional, and national identities: French or English, southern or midwestern. I wanted to find out where these apples come from and what meanings people attach to them. I went to the Westons' wizened, hilly orchard on a gorgeous fall day and saw the gnarled trees with Calville Blanc d'Hiver still hanging from their branches. I've always had an idealized fondness for old orchards, but the research for this book has taken this fondness to a new level, even if it has stripped me of my more romantic visions. I still love the feeling of walking into this three-dimensional space of edible memory, settled in over decades. And I have an increased appreciation for an orchard like the Westons', full of trees of widely varying shapes, sizes, and ages, planted across an idyllic hillside, the autumn light slanting through the branches.[10]

The Westons' trees have been here a long time, and it shows. Their knotted limbs and aging trunks speak to one of the key differences between apples and vegetables—this permanence of place, this need for literal rootedness that means far fewer people grow their own apples than grow their own vegetables. Trees (apple and otherwise) have a permanence quite distinct from, say, a carrot patch. They are not easy to take with you, and a given apple's seeds carry a genetic gamble of little or no use to the fans of that particular apple. Apples don't grow true to seed, so if you want another tree bearing the same delicious apple you just picked, you'll have to graft a piece of that tree onto rootstock and wait a few years. Apples also produce, and are produced by, particular landscapes. The regimented rows of large-scale commercial orchards—the earth beneath them stripped of growth, the trees of uniform shape and size to ease harvesting and increase efficiency and consistency—produce the shiny, unblemished apples that we can find year-round at the grocery store. The Westons' orchard, on the other hand, yields a patchwork of sizes, shapes, and varieties as well as resistance or susceptibility to pests, climate, and disease, but not suited for wide-scale commercial sale, distribution, and transport.

Like most cultivars, apples are full of human intentionality: centuries, even millennia, of efforts to get it right.[11] There is a preciousness about orchards like the Westons', full of flavors, textures, and histories that few of us regularly encounter. The Westons' orchard, as much as it is a working farm, also felt like a leafy archive, with a few specimens of each kind of tree, in a range of ages, shapes, and sizes, populating a sloping hillside, with different sections of the orchard hidden behind stands of other trees and shrubs. We would walk through a thicket and suddenly find ourselves in another beautiful "room," the hazy October sunshine making its way through the laden branches. Any orchard offers a set of botanical, historical, and sociological puzzles.

Making Apples

These trees—not only the French Fameuse and Calville—have their genetic and cultural roots on distant shores. How do these foods come to be where they are and to be so entrenched, so connected to memory, identity, and daily life? When you bite into an apple of any sort, you are tasting hundreds of years and thousands of miles of history that all started in the forests at the foot of the Tien Shan mountains in Kazakhstan, where stands of wild apples still populate the foothills.[12] There were cultivated apples in ancient Egypt and ancient Rome. The journey from the Tien Shan mountains to New Berlin, Wisconsin, is a long one geographically, temporally, and botanically, with detours in ancient Rome, eighteenth-century France, or New England along the way. And as rich as this orchard is, it merely scratches the surface of apple biodiversity.

As apples moved across the globe, new domesticated varieties developed that were adapted to unique microclimates. This can happen with intentional and careful breeding, but it often occurs by accident (particularly in nineteenth-century North America) when a discarded apple seed might sprout a tree that survived long enough to bear delicious fruit. Many botanists and other scholars credit the Romans with creating a highly developed apple culture by perfecting grafting.[13] Seed saving doesn't work with apples if you want to end up with the same apple you started with—each seed in an apple contains a different genetic code from the parent tree. Grafting a piece of a tree you know to produce the kind of apple you want allows you to know for sure that you'll get the taste, color, texture, and shape of the original. So the logistics of preserving old apple varieties differ from the method of saving tomato or squash seeds.[14] Skillful grafting and well-chosen rootstock are necessary to carry on a favorite apple variety, today just as in ancient Rome. The Romans brought apple trees and the necessary tools and skills of apple husbandry when they conquered much of Europe, and the first mention of apple grafting was in the second century BCE, although apples were eaten by the ancient Etruscans, Egyptians, and Greeks as well as Romans.[15] There is also a suggestion that humans were cultivating apples even before the onset of more sedentary, agricultural societies.

With the fall of the Roman Empire, many cultivated apple varieties disappeared, a long-ago instance of the loss of biodiversity connected to large-scale political and military upheaval. European monasteries did preserve some of the Roman varieties, as well as the knowledge necessary to care for and propagate the trees.[16] The founder of the Benedictine order advocated planting apples in monastery gardens in the sixth century,[17] and the eighth century saw Charlemagne drafting a gardening and agricultural manual to aid in food production across his empire, including specific instructions about apples.[18] Apples are visible in medieval tapestries and depictions of the *hortus conclusus*, the enclosed garden that was both a pleasurable and a productive space for medieval aristocrats.[19] In medieval tapestries and manuscripts alike, apple orchards offered shelter to amorous couples and a final resting place for monks.[20] The Plan of Saint Gall, one of the few documents depicting a medieval garden plan, shows little crosses next to apple trees, representing the bodies of the lost monks turning, over time, into the sweetness of apples as an orchard and a cemetery coexist.

Apples were an important source of sweetness in medieval Europe, on a continent largely devoid of sugar. Medieval apple consumption concentrated on apple wine and cooked apples, including dried apples later turned into compotes or cooked alongside meat and grains. This preference for cooked over fresh apples reflects a widespread medieval aversion to fresh fruit.[21] In the British Isles, a first wave of apples appeared thanks to the Romans, and a second wave was brought by the Normans about the eleventh century.[22] One source lists thirty-two varieties of apples in thirteenth-century France, including the Rouviau, the Blanc-Duriau, the Blandurel, and the Capendu.[23] Thirty-one varieties were listed in the German states of Hessen and Saxony in the middle of the sixteenth century. The Roter Herbstkalvill grew in the pleasure garden of the prince in Stuttgart in 1565;[24] the Edelborsdorfer was mentioned as early as 1175.[25]

The apple became an integral element, not only of the European diet, but also of literary, artistic, mythological, and religious traditions, far more than plums, parsnips, or peas.[26] Somehow apples and grain are especially symbolic and spiritual compared with eggplant and celery or even the seductive peach. People go to the trouble of creating engravings, watercolors, and other images of all kinds of produce, but apples and wheat occupy pride of place in European literary, mythological, and artistic traditions.

Grafting really began to come back in the sixteenth century, especially in France.[27] Medieval monks and aristocrats had actively cultivated apples, but European apple cultivation truly began to flourish in the seventeenth century as fresh fruit became fashionable at courts from Versailles to Potsdam and beyond.[28] Evelyn Thieme and colleagues, authors of a detailed book about the apple meadows of central Europe, write that "fruit first made a big impression on the [European] aristocracy beginning in the Renaissance. In Italy it was seen as impossibly chic to have a great diversity of fresh fruit. . . . Soon this trend took over on aristocratic estates north of the Alps. The courtly orchard and vegetable garden grew to be a status symbol, and a regular competition began for quality, size, varieties and most exotic fruit."[29] Many dukes and counts reportedly even did their own pruning and bud grafting.

In the eighteenth century, royal pleasure gardens in Berlin, Potsdam, and nearby Bornim all included fruit trees, and competitive fruit cultivation grew swiftly as aristocrats and kings bred increasingly exotic fruits. Apples were one component of this conspicuous consumption, though far less exotic than the pineapples, winter citrus, or coffee beans grown in frigid northern winters thanks to technology, copious amounts of coal or wood to heat the greenhouses, and legions of staff.[30] Royal fruit collecting declined (alongside the decline in royalty) after the French Revolution.

In the nineteenth century, across Europe, fruit breeding increasingly moved from the aristocracy to the middle class.[31] Fruit enthusiasts formed clubs of "pomologists," or fruit experts, published handbooks on fruit cultivation, and held fruit fairs and exhibitions. This work involved not only apples but also all manner of produce. In his superb book *Forgotten Fruits*, Christopher Stocks describes major differences in English apple growing between the eighteenth and nineteenth centuries.[32] In the nineteenth century, categorization and classification of fruit and vegetable varieties (as well as animal breeds) increased greatly in England and the European continent, but also in the United States. Over time the goal of much fruit breeding across Europe was less about creating diversity than about growing produce that satisfied particular notions of "excellence," including high yields, firm flesh, and the ability to tolerate long storage. The nineteenth century provides the lion's share of what we today consider heirloom produce, not just apples. In fact, as early as the late nineteenth century, efforts were beginning in Europe to limit the number of apple varieties available.[33]

Pomology burgeoned in that century, as more and more bourgeois nurserymen (almost always men) and hobby botanists began meticulously identifying and propagating apple varieties, nurturing chance seedlings and developing new varieties.[34] These systems of classification also have wide-ranging histories and cultures, emerging over time and building on or refuting past systems of classifying growing things. *The Oxford Companion to Food* tells us that "the history of pomology is therefore fundamentally the history of the fruit-eater," since it focuses only on edible fruits and on the fruit itself rather than its botanical origins.[35] The story of pomology is also the story of the ever-shifting attempts to classify fruit and the connections between different pomologies and large-scale societal changes like the rise of industrial capitalism and the decline of aristocratic regimes. There were courtly pomologies that ended with the French Revolution, and massive new pomologies in the late nineteenth and early twentieth centuries in the United States.[36] Apple orchards also spread across the English colonies, and North American apple varieties were even exported back to England. Bunyard also writes of apples from Australia and Tasmania finding their way to England in the early twentieth century. So the global trade in apples began early.

Bunyard tells us that in his (comparatively affluent) English experience of apples, "the right season to eat an apple is a matter of importance; to catch the volatile ethers at their maximum development, and the acids and sugars at their most grateful balance, requires knowledge and experiment. Many apples will keep far beyond their period of maximum flavour, and in some this moment is so fleeting that they are hardly worth growing; a week-end away from home might prove disastrous."[37] One of his friends recommends eating fruit straight from the tree to avoid any deterioration in flavor—an extreme of local and seasonal eating! Bunyard advises that "the first apples [of the season], such as Gladstone, Irish Peach, Feltham Beauty, should be eaten from the tree, or at any rate not kept over till the next day, when they will be flat and unprofitable."[38] On the opposite end of the spectrum, some apples don't reach their zenith until they've sat in the attic for a while. "At the same time [the end of August] comes Lady Sudeley, an apple which every garden should possess if only for its flaming scarlet fruits. The flesh is tender and melting, and at its hour of prime very highly aromatic and juicy. For the best result it should be gathered before it is willing[!], and stored in the fruit room for a week or two and sampled from day to day till the exact moment arrives."[39] The privilege of a fruit room and the time to carefully check for the ideal moment of ripeness imply a level of wealth and leisure unavailable to most apple eaters. Bunyard suggests 1921 as a year whose apples were so perfect that they "will remain long in memory."[40] In addition, he discusses apples like the Cox's Orange Pippin, too acidic at harvest in October, but "as the acid gradually fails, the aromatic ethers develop, and the end of November and early December see them at their height. It then slowly declines, very slowly if properly stored, and even in May, after a sunny summer, it is still worthy."[41]

If we adhere to Bunyard's standards, the proper appreciation of an apple requires a substantial reservoir of knowledge and expertise as well as an orchard and an attic, not to mention a fruit room. At the time he was writing, the people with access to these levels of apple perfection would have either been well-heeled landowners with large houses, grounds, and staff, or farmers living close to their apple trees. In the captivating book *Good Things*, Jane Grigson offers not only delicious apple recipes, but also precise suggestions about what types of apples to use for different recipes, ranging from Cox's to Midwest Baldwin,[42] and English chef and cookbook writer Nigel Slater finds there is "an apple for every occasion."[43] For these English chefs and writers, the apple is a distinctly English cornerstone of the nation's gardens, landscapes, and cooking.

Making Apples American

But how did apple pie, and its apples, become so American? Apples become literally and figuratively rooted in places, cultures, and identities, including the United States. This simple question has significant implications for how we understand both culture and food, the slow accretion of habit and tradition, the loss of this habit and tradition, then its rekindling or (re)creation. Apples arrived in North America with pilgrims and conquistadores. Across the United States, rich regional apple cultivation started to develop as early as the seventeenth century, but it really expanded in the nineteenth century. The founding fathers and similarly landed men planted substantial orchards. Thomas Jefferson had a six-acre orchard much like his fellow landowners, orchards that typically held somewhere around two hundred apple and peach trees, mostly for (hard) cider and brandy, as well as animal fodder.[44] Indeed eighteenth-century New Englanders reportedly consumed thirty-two gallons of hard cider a year.[45]

New apple varieties then developed in North America. American apples were also exported back to Europe. Year by year, season by season, people created new varieties, suited to particular valleys and hillsides and to particular tastes and appetites.[46] Sometimes this happened by accident, in other cases through intentional breeding.[47] Apples were a widespread component of the Anglo conquest of North America, since planting apple trees went along with homesteading and the accompanying radical transformation of land use (and attendant power relations).[48] Kerrigan (and others) show that apples (and peaches) were also in widespread cultivation by Native American communities. "An awareness of Indian orchards invites us to reexamine the old narratives of European conquest of the New World. The presence of cultivated orchards of Old World fruit on the lands of many of the Indian peoples of the Great Lakes is evidence of one of the many ways in which Native Peoples of the region responded to the biological, military, and political intrusions into their territory. The fact that these orchards have been largely ignored or forgotten tells us much about the powerful myths embedded in the popular story of white conquest and Indian dispossession in the Great Lakes region."[49]

Apples, and the attendant social patterns, move across landscapes. Many of the apple varieties I found at the Westons' may have a long tradition in the United States but came originally from fruit breeders in England, France, Germany, or the Netherlands. Unique varieties developed in the United States, in part because of the habit of planting apples from seeds rather than grafts. Most of the resulting apples would have been good only for cider making (and even then the quality of the end product would have varied), but here and there an excellent dessert apple sprouted from one of the seeds, then lived on through generations of grafts. Pollan and others credit the North American practice of planting cider apples from seed with the origins of many good eating apples (completely by chance).[50] That is, John Chapman ("Johnny Appleseed") and others planting seeds, rather than grafts (in an effort to make hard cider widely available) across North America greatly opened up all kinds of genetic possibility that had not been as prevalent in Europe, where grafting far exceeded planting from seed. There are plentiful stories of trees sprouting from a seed in a compost pile and being left alone long enough (about seven years) to bear great eating apples: apples like the Paula Red and even the Golden Delicious and the Macintosh.

All this apple growing, as seemingly random as it was when it began, quickly became more organized. The American Pomological Society was codifying apples by the mid-nineteenth century, in pursuit of "excellence" as well as qualities useful for the commercial apple market. Distinguishing a new flavorful or useful variety could be profitable through selling not only specific (and particularly appealing) apple varieties, but also grafts and saplings of these trees. Fred Lape recounts that until the 1920s the qualities most prized were that apples be good keepers and that they taste good both raw and cooked.[51]

Apples in the United States became highly regional, connected to local and regional history and identity, something discussed in detail by Rowan Jacobsen in *American Terroir*.[52] There are distinct collections of Maine apples, Ohio apples, New York apples, Southern apples, Northern California apples, or Utah apples.[53] Maine celebrates the Great Maine Apple Day, and the Madison, Wisconsin, farmers' market has had heirloom apples for a long time. Particular apples may grow particularly well in one region or another: "At one time each apple growing region in this country had its local favorites—the Newtown Pippin on northern Long Island, Fameuse along the St. Lawrence River, Willows and Gilpins from West Virginia and York Imperial from Pennsylvania," writes Lee Riech of the New York State Agricultural Experiment Station.[54] Some of these apples are new North American varieties, while others (like the Fameuse) are European varieties that arrived in North America as grafts and found their way into farms and gardens.

Great tomes like *Old Southern Apples* or *The Apples of Maine* meticulously catalog a given region's apples, and each region of the United States has its local favorites, most of which have long disappeared from commercial production.[55] As one reporter recounts, speaking with Ezekiel Goodband from Vermont's Scott Farm, "The Baldwin apple originated . . . in Wilmington, Mass., and there is a monument today where the first tree grew. The hard, deep red apple was famous for its hardy pies. They were baked and served for breakfast, and the pies were very different from 'the sugary things they are now,' Goodband said. But in 1934 there was a great freeze that killed most of the Baldwin trees."[56] Immigrants from Europe to Pennsylvania brought apples from home, establishing orchards adjacent to their new homes. Across the country, apple biodiversity flourished. By the 1930s, writes Tim Henley, there were fourteen hundred apple varieties unique to the South, and ten thousand across the United States.[57] Over time, farmers and gardeners discovered varieties particularly suited to their markets and microclimates.

Maine offers just one example of this regional specificity. European settlers in Maine had scion wood of their favorite varieties sent from England and, we learn from *Apples of Maine*, the area near Hallowell, Maine, "today still supports great numbers of crumbling trees whose fruit, names long forgotten, look suspiciously like many of England's most famous apples."[58] Scions are the slips of apple tree topped by a bud that can then be grafted onto rootstock. The rootstock, today usually dwarf or semi-dwarf, provides the hardy foundation on which the desired fruit will grow. The scion carries a different genetic code than the rootstock it is grafted onto. "Think of it: seemingly, every little hamlet in Maine with its amateur farmer/horticulturalists creating new fruit like angels in the Garden of Eden!" (3). In cases where people were growing so many apples from seeds, they freed up into their landscapes and diets all this genetic material that had been locked down by centuries (bordering on millennia) of European apple grafting, which strongly discouraged the widespread planting of apples from seeds. "There was, at this time, practically no market for apples, for poor indeed was the rough homestead that could not boast several dozen trees," for eating, but above all for cider (4). In the mid-nineteenth century, the grafting of scion wood became more popular, in order to have better eating apples, and people like Captain Salmon Holmes and Moses Sears traveled through the area "topworking countless older trees to more promising fruit." Markets for apples also grew in North America as cities grew (6). "Thus, the past with its glories and its mistakes, its struggles and its victories, is written. We have seen fruit growing in Maine evolved from a mass of seedling trees through a hardly less chaotic period of testing and experiment to a stage where through market demands, its catalog of varieties seems fairly well fixed" (12). This book is four hundred pages about the apples of Maine. That's a lot of detail and specificity, and a lot of apples connected to a single state.

Many of the apples that originated in the United States are chance seedlings that ended up producing fruit people enjoyed, so they grafted scions from these trees to other rootstock. The French Russet "was apparently confined to the seacoast near Waldoboro and Wiscasset. In 1876, it was listed as one of thirteen leading varieties of winter apples grown near Waldoboro and as late as 1910, was still grown to some extent but was of little or no importance" (121). Everything about this passage is fascinating (well, to me): that this poor apple was of "little or no importance" by 1910, and that it was called the "French" Russet but seemed to grow only in this tiny patch of Maine seacoast. The author comfortably includes the Alexander apple in a list of the apples of Maine, although "this variety was introduced into England from Russia in 1817, and imported by Manning to Massachusetts about 1830" (15). Reading his descriptions, the tremendous challenges of apple identification, as well as the blurred edges of these pomological boundaries, become quite clear. Nomenclature has its complexities across the plant and animal kingdoms, and apples are no exception.

My own apple history is closely connected to the central coast of California. Six little apple trees, almost as old as I am, provided the leafy frame of my childhood and often very tart additions to my lunch box. Like so many corners of the United States, this part of the world has a unique apple history. Newtown Pippins grow especially well in this climate. As fruit hunter David Karp recounts, Newtown Pippins first arrived on the central California coast in the 1850s, and by the 1920s they covered twelve thousand acres.[59] We took school field trips to some of these orchards, picking apples and watching the cider presses work, and I remember seeing a little friend get stung by a bee (the hazards of setting foot outside the classroom). But, as with tomatoes, the twentieth century saw the decline of these regional varieties as apple production transitioned to increasingly standardized varieties that could be shipped long distances and stored for long periods in low-oxygen warehouses rather than in attics and cellars, then appear unblemished in the grocery store: the familiar Golden Delicious, Gala, or Granny Smith.

Many apple-growing regions of California have changed over the twentieth century. In 1908, Pajaro Valley, near Santa Cruz, was home to fourteen thousand acres of apples containing a million trees.[60] Today there are two thousand acres, many of the apple trees having given way to strawberries, raspberries, and housing developments.[61] Sonoma, once home to thirteen thousand acres of apple orchards, now has just three thousand, in part because vineyards provide a much greater return per acre than apple orchards, and in part because of competition from imported apples—China, for example, produces more than half of the world's apples, sold at very low prices.[62] Furthermore, the USDA documented nine thousand varieties of apples in 1906, but a mere six hundred by 1980.[63]

Commercial apples grow in orchards wholly different from those common in other centuries, when orchards sustained not only apple biodiversity but also insects, flora, and fauna, including serving as lambing grounds for sheep, and the aforementioned monastic burial grounds. Much apple production today (certainly of supermarket apples) takes place in the context of large-scale agribusiness rather than small family farms. The fruit is generally harvested by migrant laborers, and apple picking is especially hard work. As a field boss at one of the farms studied by Seth Holmes in his *Fresh Fruit, Broken Bodies* explained, "Picking apples is the hardest job on the farm. Apple pickers work five to ten hours a day, seven days a week, carrying a heavy bag of apples over their shoulders. They repeatedly climb up and down ladders to reach the apples."[64] Supermarket apples have qualities desirable to many producers and consumers alike—uniformity, predictability, and a lack of scab and worms. When I buy apples from the Westons, I may get quite a range of shapes, colors, flavors, and textures even among the same variety from the same tree. Some of the apples I buy from them keep for ages, while others must be eaten right away (and sometimes I discover this too late, but an apple strudel or crisp can still be forgiving). Supermarket apples, on the other hand, have to be highly predictable year-round to keep consumers reaching for them, and this is made possible through a combination of breeding, technology, transport, storage in oxygen-less warehouses, and global markets, as well as legions of generally low-paid laborers who are subjected to pesticide exposure and to the physically grueling work of picking apples by hand.

Apple grafting is slow, careful work. It takes a long time to make a new tree, and even longer to make an entirely new apple variety.[65] This is not instant gratification gardening. In general you grow apple trees only if you own land, or if you plan to be somewhere for a while. There are ways that culture, appetite, and desire can run up against biology or botany. In characteristically detailed fashion, *The Oxford Companion to Food* explains that "in the Middle East and most of Asia the climate does not suit apples except in some cooler, hilly areas. Thus they are grown in the upland, but not the lowland, parts of Lebanon. India produces apples in the northern hills and some are grown in Nepal and on the mountain slopes of E. Java. China has grown apples since well before AD 1000, and its crop now accounts for 41% of the world harvest. Japan produces apples extensively."[66] There ultimately are limits to how and where apple trees will grow, even though people certainly succeed at pushing those limits with combinations of breeding, technology, and widespread spraying. Apples also pose specific challenges, such as codling moths (the proverbial worm in the apple) and scab, conditions that can be sprayed for. There are heirloom varieties that are highly resistant to pests and disease and others that are highly susceptible. Orchards require a significant investment of time, money, and real estate, and a single ice storm or early frost can do tremendous damage to the crop and to the farmer's income. Without pruning and other care, neglected apple trees also cease to be reliable producers.

The trees themselves changed as commercial apple production increasingly relied on dwarf rootstock. No longer tall (or standard) or even medium tall, commercial apple trees are short and compact and also generally very dependent on pesticides. Dwarf rootstocks like Malling IX and Malling-Merton have become integral to apple cultivation. They prevent the tree varieties grafted to them from becoming large and unwieldy, like the apple trees of earlier eras. Thus the landscapes have changed with the switch to dwarf trees, as have the apples themselves. People in the United States tend to like sweet and reddish apples with smooth skin, but rough-skinned brown and yellow apples like Roxbury russet, St. Edmund's Pippin, and Seek-No-Further were once very popular.[67] Much as happened with tomatoes and other produce, many people attribute the disappearance of the heirloom apple to the success of the Red Delicious and Golden Delicious and to the changing tastes of consumers. The ability of these commercial apples to grow quickly and uniformly, their capacity to withstand long storage and lengthy journeys in trucks, as well as the growth of supermarkets more broadly, contributed to the demise of heirloom apples. Some people argue, however, that it was precisely these (in some people's minds) insipid apples that laid the groundwork for the return of the heirloom apples. After a generation of predictable apples, more and more people began to search for the apples they remembered from their childhood, or for apples with more tantalizing flavors, aromas, and colors, not to mention names, much like what went on with tomatoes.

The Ben Davis, for example—an apple I had never seen in a market—was once one of the most popular apples in the United States, and particularly widespread in the South. Countless apples like this receded from extensive cultivation, apples like "Grimes Golden, Magnum Bonum, Virginia Beauty, Albemarle Pippin, Summer Rambo, and Blacktwig."[68] Some of them persist in localized ways, like the Albemarle Pippin that still grows widely in Albemarle County, Virginia, but even those are difficult for most consumers in the United States to come by. As Lape wrote more than thirty years ago, "Think of the different tastes one will never know, the fascinating names of apples never to be tasted: The Fallawater whose only claim to distinction seems to have been its size; the Blue Pearmain, one of a whole group of Pearmains; and the Black Gilliflower, a long red apple with a pointed nose . . . [or] . . . the Kittigeskee, which originated with the Cherokee Indians in western North Carolina, was sent to France in 1860, and proved popular there, but is now forgotten here."[69] People cut down trees or allowed them to run wild, and the public's desire for sweetness and predictability prevailed. When Lape was writing in 1979 he found that Northern Spy was "still being sold, usually at top prices, at the older orchards in the Northeast. One can buy it occasionally in the larger cities, at special stores and exorbitant prices."[70] As with tomatoes, changes in the structure of farming and retail sales played a tremendous role in the disappearance (or vastly increased rarity) of certain varieties. Almost all the apples we eat today are far more standardized and predictable. In some respects supermarket apples represent a kind of collective forgetting—of flavors, textures, and aromas, of landscapes and foliage. Forgetting can be far more difficult to study than remembering, because its traces are much harder to discern.[71]

Saving Heirlooms

But while shiny, reliable apples cornered the market, people like the Westons continued to grow these nearly forgotten old-fashioned apples. Like other heirlooms, apples capture individual passions and inspire deep devotions. One thing that becomes very clear in reading so many newspaper and magazine articles and books about apples (often containing copious pages of meticulous cataloging of varieties compiled by apple devotees) is the importance of committed individuals, passionate apple advocates who devote varying combinations of time, money, land, and skill to finding and preserving old apple varieties. Across the country and the world, people from all kinds of backgrounds find a real calling in antique apples.

Creighton Lee Calhoun, "a retired Army officer, gentleman farmer and dedicated apple collector . . . is racing against the clock, rushing to save a heritage most Southerners don't even know they have."[72] Calhoun's *Old Southern Apples*, published in 1995 (revised and expanded in 2011), lists sixteen hundred named varieties as having once been grown in the South, though only two hundred antique Southern apple varieties are known to exist today.[73] Calhoun was a force behind the orchard at Horne Creek Living Historical Farm in Pinnacle, North Carolina.[74] Tom Burford was also promoting heirloom apples in Virginia in the mid-1990s, and Wisconsinite Dan Bussey is working on a comprehensive guide to North American apples while also preserving an extensive archival orchard at the Seed Savers Exchange farm in Decorah, Iowa, and teaching new generations to graft, prune, and make cider. Another key figure is Carlos Manning, who "began his search for old apples by phoning elderly people in the hollows, asking about their orchards. If it sounded promising, he would show up, cut a few twigs and buds, and leave, bearing untold genetic treasures: Maiden Blush, Winesap,[75] Wolf River, Yellow Transparent and Yellow Sheepnose, all lost from common memory. He'll sometimes drive as far as 200 miles in search of grafting wood—a six-hour trip each way, on West Virginia roads."[76] Similarly, "apple sleuth Tom Brown believes the Battlefield apple is still out there somewhere, and he is determined to find it. The retiree from Clemmons drives rural roads, hikes mountain trails and knocks on doors in search of a taste of history: old Southern apples, like Guilford County's own Battlefield."[77] Many of the apple fans described in newspaper articles also wrote books themselves, such as the surprisingly thick volume on the history of Maine apples, the methodical account of Southern apples, and a guide to the best North American apples.[78] Weaver, Creasy, Yepsen, Lape, Janik, and many authors play important roles both as apple preservers themselves and by spreading the word about apple biodiversity, history, and flavor.[79]

Long before generic antique apples began to appear in restaurant reviews and mainstream food writing, nurseries and home gardeners were busily grafting cuttings from old trees onto new rootstock, scouring the countryside for forgotten apple trees, and building their own collections of old apples. One response to a global fruit glut in the early 2000s was to turn to heirloom apples.[80] They are one of many responses by family farmers to changing economic conditions and efforts to hang on to the family farm through diversification—corn mazes and pumpkin patches, apple picking and farmers' markets. As with forgotten tomatoes and turnips, countless individuals across the United States and around the world preserve varieties in their backyards and gardens. In fact nurseries and small-scale orchardists are crucial to understanding the origins of the heirloom apple movement.

Even as so many apple trees and apple varieties began to disappear from landscapes and lunch boxes, committed individuals across the country (and around the world, as this movement has been very strong in Germany, England, and other parts of Europe) began to seek out and preserve these threatened apples. Some of this work began in the 1980s, in a highly informal way. Lone apple aficionados drove through forgotten valleys in search of old trees, using old botanical prints and models to identify the fruits of forgotten trees—ideally with apples from the sunniest side of the tree, as the sun-kissed cheek of those apples best reveals the true color of a particular variety. These apple experts also spread the word to nursery owners and cooks and converted people into die-hard fans of heirloom apples.[81] Today the number of projects dedicated to bringing back old apple varieties is extensive.[82] This solitary work continues, but in the meantime there are so many groups and individuals actively engaged in seed saving, whether conducting official interviews, reading through newspapers, or simply talking with friends, family, or strangers on planes and trains, that seemingly everyone knows someone who loves old apples.[83] Extensive work was going on in the 1970s and 1980s to preserve edible biodiversity in the United States (and certainly elsewhere as well) and this work expanded greatly in the 1990s and 2000s, becoming increasingly visible in mainstream media, even as extensive work continued behind the scenes. People care for apples, preserve them, curate them, seek them out.

There are also larger, more official groups dedicated to preserving old fruit varieties, cultivating less familiar varieties, and creating new ones. The American Pomological Society, for example, is a key organization preserving and disseminating the trees themselves as well as knowledge about them.[84] It was founded in 1848 "to foster the science and practice of fruit growing and variety development" and lists as its core mission "to promote the study and culture of fruit and nuts . . . to disseminate information pertaining to fruit and nut cultivars . . . to register new fruit and cultivars."[85] The Midwest Fruit Explorers and the Backyard Fruit Growers Association (whose website proclaims: "So many apples, so little time . . ." and whose newsletter has a circulation of 350, centered in Pennsylvania) are two smaller-scale regional groups invested in cultivating not only heirloom varieties, but also rare varieties (and fruit other than apples).[86] They offer grafting workshops, newsletters and journals, and opportunities to exchange information. These apple activists are also very much aware of the links between apples and memory, and many hurry to capture not only grafts of the few remaining trees of a particular variety, but also the knowledge and memories of the aging people who grew up with these trees.

Slow Food has also taken up the cause of heirloom apples. Seven apple varieties are in the Slow Food Ark of Taste, the project aimed at identifying and preserving varieties of edible plants and animals that are particularly at risk of disappearing. There are more than 1,600 entries in the Ark of Taste worldwide, and 172 in the United States.[87]

The apples included in the Ark of Taste are Capitol Reef, Granite Beauty, Harrison, Hauer Pippin, Hoover, Newtown Pippin, Sebastopol Gravenstein, and Sierra Beauty. In the early twentieth century, Bunyard wrote of the Gravenstein's already being forgotten, but Slow Food and other groups and individuals have worked to bring it back.[88] Seed Savers Exchange—an early and important actor in heirloom fruit preservation, offering melons, huckleberries, and ground cherries—also has an heirloom apple orchard. I walked through that orchard one July with Dan Bussey, Dave Snyder (one of the cofounders of the Chicago Rarities Orchard Project), and many others, learning how to bud graft—something done in summertime, unlike bench grafting, which is done in winter. We crouched in the dirt, affixing tiny buds to tiny slits in rootstock growing out of the sun-warmed earth, then wandered through the collection of dozens of antique apple trees, well preserved up here on this breezy, sunny hillside. Tree by tree, apple by apple, old genes (and flavors and memories) get carried into the future, preserving biodiversity, variety, and, above all, possibility.

New England, the South, the Upper Midwest, California, and the Pacific Northwest—each region has its heirloom darlings and commercial hits, clearly evident in the apples selected for the Renewing America's Food Traditions project. Five apples made it into the RAFT list—Gloria Mundi: "also called the Mammoth, the Melon, and the Ox, it was first recorded near Red Hook, New York, before it spread to New Jersey and adjacent Pennsylvania by the beginning of the nineteenth century"; the Harrison cider: the earliest record of it is from 1803, and it is now "nearly lost forever from American tables"; the Magnum Bonum: "a fine Southern apple" from 1828; Nickajack: "said to have originated where Cherokees lived along Nickajack Creek in Macon County, North Carolina, this heirloom apple likely dates back to the late 1700s"; and Sierra Beauty: "first discovered around 1890 growing in the Sierra Nevada. It is derived from a seedling apple, one presumably found as a remnant of miners' movements following the California Gold Rush, for it next appeared in mining camps above the town of Chico in Butte County in 1923."[89] Individuals and groups actively narrate heirloom fruit and bring it back into broader use and public awareness. And across the country, groups and individual orchards (including the Westons) hold grafting and pruning workshops.

Writing about Apples

In popular food writing, particularly newspapers, heirloom apples receive far more attention than any other produce besides the tomato. Apples (and other heirloom fruit) run the gamut from a very generic description ("heirloom apple tart" at a restaurant) to extensive historical detail and intense family connections. The increase in popularity of heirloom apples is reflected in, and in part shaped by, an increase in newspaper coverage. With apples in particular, this trend took off in the 1990s, although the earliest newspaper article I found mentioning antique apples was in the *Washington Post* in September 1979. The article pointed out, more than thirty-five years ago, what today is a more familiar concept: that "there are between 14,000 and 16,000 varieties of apples, but less than a dozen show up regularly on our supermarket shelves. Where are the apples of yesteryear—the Snow Apple, the Gravenstein, the Sheepnose, the Cox Orange Pippin?"[90] The answer at the time was here and there, and in an occasional nursery catalog like the one issued by J. E. Miller Nurseries in Canandaigua, New York.

Apples, along with tomatoes, are the heirloom foods most connected to their stories in popular food writing. Compared with other produce, apple variety names show up more often too. This is in part because there are far more varieties of apples than, say, eggplants or peas. One of the more popular motifs is a given apple's connection to Thomas Jefferson or George Washington, and both men were avowed fans of the fruit.[91] Eventually restaurant reviews and apple tastings became an important part of spreading the word about apple biodiversity. The Sonoma Antique Apple Nursery, now the Tree of Life Nursery, held an apple tasting in September 1990, and other tastings followed.[92] In the early 1990s, reporters already were regularly writing about the return of heirloom apples, and antique apple trees were readily available at a handful of nurseries across the country. "Antique apples and recent arrivals with international ties are the current darlings of backyard apple orchardists. It's fun to grow a fruit with a lineage that goes back a century or longer," the *San Jose Mercury News* pronounced in 1994.[93] That same year, the *Washington Post* described the heirloom apple trend as "exploding."[94] An heirloom apple tasting was held at New York's Union Square Greenmarket in November 2000, for instance, and in

2003 there was one at the Adams Morgan farmers' market in Washington, DC. Apples in the Park, with food prepared from heirloom apples by New York chefs, took place in Union Square Park in November 2000. A dinner at the White House in 2000 featured "smoked loin of lamb with a sauce that included 'heirloom apples' planted in York, Pa., in the 19th century."[95]

"People into the nostalgia of history buy these apples," explained one farmer who grows old varieties.[96] The stories may be personal or regional or may focus on particular historical figures. "When [apple expert] John Bunker comes across a ragged old apple tree by the Maine roadside, he sees more than a tree," an amateur historian's scenario goes: "Bunker, 46, sees—in his mind's eye—a Civil War–era farmer biting into a new and tasty apple. Or he imagines an early settler discovering a wild apple tree in the woods, or an 18th century housewife drying apples for winter storage."[97] Bunker adds, "These apples are a link with the past. . . . [E]ach has a history. They are a living incarnation of amazing things that happened 100 or more years ago. . . . Looking at an apple is almost like looking into a crystal ball and seeing who's there."

One reporter found as early as 1996 that "nostalgia for old plants is in vogue. Growing old plants from heirloom seeds or eating antique apples links us with plants our grandparents and great-grandparents enjoyed."[98] In restaurant reviews there is almost never a mention of the variety—it's just "heirloom apple tart," with no particular apple specified. In fact, when you find yourself being served heirloom anything, I would (for many reasons) strongly advocate asking the name of the variety. At the same time, there is often more historical detail to the apple narrative than to that of, say, carrots. There is a lament in much of the writing about apples, a sense that things used to be better, although Henry David Thoreau was already taking this tone in the era people look back on so fondly today.[99] In the 1980s the themes are not that different from the themes in the 2010s. An in-depth article appeared in the *New York Times* in October 1989 singing the praises of antique apples and explaining many different varieties. Red and Golden Delicious apples, originally developed in the 1800s, had come to dominate the US market, the writer declared, "but there is muttering in the ranks and a growing demand for apples with personality. Nurseries are beginning to feature antique-apple trees, and the apple industry is developing stock that yields more flavorful fruit."[100] This tone of discovery and of educating readers about lost and recently found varieties appears repeatedly from the 1980s through today.

As early as 1986, food journalists were associating antique apples with culinary trendiness, although this association never reaches the heights with apples that it does with tomatoes. "Is your produce market up-to-date? If it is first with the fashions you'll be finding Italian-style chicory, cinnamon basil, red and yellow currant tomatoes, antique apple varieties and up to 40 varieties of figs," the *Washington Post* gushed in 1986.[101] In another account, we hear that "heirloom apples will begin to be trendy and more readily available. New York is an apple-producing state and we're all just a little bit fatigued with Red Delicious—it's about time."[102] In 1998 one reporter wrote that "so-called heirloom apples gained a kind of cachet a few years ago in foodie circles."[103] A few years later another wrote, "Vegetables in vogue are pea tendrils, Jerusalem artichokes, tomatillos, parsnips, squashes, celery root, greens, fennel, heirloom tomatoes and heirloom potatoes . . . and the trendiest fruits include blood oranges, Meyer lemons, heirloom apples, grapefruit, figs and dates."[104] The availability of antique apples in markets is even used as an indicator of gentrification.[105] And people express fears that the widespread popularity of heirloom apples, and the cresting of the trend, may lead to inferior ones appearing on the market (as arguably has happened with mass-produced heirloom tomatoes).[106] Newspaper after newspaper offer a list of heirloom varieties with their tempting names and qualities, educating readers about their options. There is also a lot of taste-making going on in the apple coverage, encouraging people to develop a taste for these foods, with lush descriptions of their flavor and color as well as careful instruction on whether they are cooking apples, eating apples, or both. Many of the apple articles also educate people about the "best" apples to eat.[107]

People seek out these apples for many reasons, much like the reasons for pursuing heirloom tomatoes: novelty, flavor, and connection to the past. Flavor appears consistently in popular writing as a reason to grow these apples, both the quality of the flavor and the variety of flavors available. Some apple fans advise peeling and slicing the apple rather than biting into it so as to more directly taste the apple flesh on the tongue, unobstructed by the comparatively low-flavor skin. Flavor can vary based not only on the variety, but also on where on the tree a particular apple grew—on a sunny branch or in shadow. Looks, on the other hand, are not as significant a category for home gardeners, although they are very important for commercial apple producers. Many apple varieties are mottled or russet, with a rough, dull skin hiding crisp, flavorful flesh. The Calville Blanc d'Hiver may connect me in some way to sixteenth-century France, as I eat an apple that is a direct descendant of a very similar apple eaten by a French person centuries ago. But I wouldn't love it if it didn't taste good and, above all, if it weren't crisp. For me (though certainly not for everyone), texture is the most important feature when I eat an apple. My aversion to soft, grainy, or mealy apples can certainly make a bowl of heirloom apples somewhat hit-and-miss. People may be attracted to particular apples because of childhood memories or because of taste (and knowledge) acquired later in life. And as with other fruits and vegetables, the expansion of the taste for heirloom apples has helped to strengthen apple biodiversity.

National Apples

Fruits and vegetables (and other foods as well) can also become important parts of identity, meaningful for people's sense of who they are. The heirloom apple revival has hit the United States as well as many European countries. Even in our globalized era, apples continue to be associated with particular countries and regions. Varieties become American (or French or English) over time, shifting their connection to identity, memory, and place. People invest apples, even more than most vegetables, with national and regional identity. Lape describes the Northern Spy as "purely an American apple."[108] What, exactly, does it mean for an apple to be American—or French or English? The ways apples (and other fruits and vegetables as well) take on national identities reveals the ways culture can be both changeable and deeply felt. National tastes affect what apple varieties are chosen and also how people categorize them.[109] Catalogs of apple varieties regularly list the country where an apple variety was first developed, as well as the year it was identified and propagated in France or the Netherlands, England or Canada.

In *The Anatomy of Dessert*, Edward Bunyard proclaims, "No fruit is more to our English taste than the Apple. Let the Frenchman have his Pear, the Italian his Fig, the Jamaican may retain his farinaceous Banana, and the Malay his Durian [a very powerful-smelling fruit that I address in more detail in a later chapter], but for us the Apple."[110] Given the apple's Kazakh and later Roman origins, its transformation into something that Bunyard (who admittedly was inclined toward hyperbole) saw as so distinctly English is something that could take place only over time, and with a fair amount of effort. Not only do particular apples develop in particular countries, but different nations apparently have varying collective tastes, even to the point of preferring the same apple at different stages of ripeness. Bunyard claims that "Reinette de Canada, that spoilt darling of the Parisian restaurateur, is [still] very good in March and April. We [the English] prefer it still crisp and juicy, whereas French taste waits for the *fondant* [melting] stage, which arrives later."[111] This is definitely a case of differing national tastes, and the idea that you would keep (and know how to keep) apples until they reach the flavor and texture that you—as an individual or a nation—prefer was new to me when I read Bunyard for the first time. Personally, I find the thought of an apple at the *fondant* stage extremely unappealing.

Some of these attitudes about apples illustrate Bourdieu's concept of the habitus—that set of unspoken tastes, predilections, preferences, and habits that guides our actions in daily life. The habitus sits very deep in our bodies and our psyches, initially acquired in our youth and thus steeped in our family, community, region, and nation of origin.[112] It influences what we reach for in the course of a given day, how we carry ourselves, and what we seek to gaze on, experience, or ingest. These tastes are carried by individuals, but acquired and exercised in the social world. Stocks captures some of this intertwining of taste and culture and national identity, as the fruits and vegetables he is trying to "rescue . . . from undeserved obscurity" are clearly English.[113] "There are onions named after islands, redcurrants named after castles, even a parsnip named after a popular song. . . . [T]he history of their introduction, adoption and improvement has mirrored the transformations in British society from the Roman conquest right through to the present day. Fashions in food have changed just as radically over the centuries as fashions in clothing."[114]

One example of a powerful connection between food and national identity is Bulgarian yogurt—far afield from apples, but illustrative of the deep ties that can emerge between food, identity, and place. Ethnographer Maria Yotova examines the sequence by which Bulgarian (and later Japanese) consumers came to identify a particular microbe, *Lactobacillus bulgaricus*, and its effect on milk, with Bulgarian national identity. Bulgarian yogurt became particularly popular in Japan, where many people (even those who don't like it) eat it in the belief that it is healthful. "The making of Bulgarian yogurt comes to demonstrate once again that common national memories and understandings are sometimes more strongly articulated in shared smells, tastes and visions . . . : in other words, in the non-verbal, even intangible and invisible (like *Lactobacillus bulgaricus*) forms."[115] Not only is food a source of identity, community, and connection, it can also be a source of differentiation, distinction, and exclusion.[116]

There is definitely a proprietary quality to heirloom apples, visible in the copious catalogs of apple varieties, ranging from nineteenth-century pomologists' manuals to detailed inventories of specific hills and valleys. While the origins of some apples remain mysterious, for others there is a very clear record of precisely whose compost pile yielded a particularly precocious seedling (like the Keswick Codlin, whose "original seedling was discovered around 1790 growing on a Cumbrian rubbish tip"), or what breeder perfected a once-popular, now-forgotten variety.[117] Apples are also routinely categorized by nation, and a lot of these varieties emerged as nations were emerging. These are not timeless traditions. Historians, sociologists, and others refer to the invention of traditions and the imagining of communities as important ways beliefs and practices that feel very permanent to us today actually have very particular historical origins.[118] These inventions and imaginings are neither flimsy and superficial nor easy to change, and in fact they constitute crucial elements of how we understand ourselves and our place in the world. The past that people reach for when they reach for an heirloom apple is a specific historical moment and geographic place—eighteenth-century France, nineteenth-century Maine, Revolutionary Virginia—resting atop the long history of apples' migration around the globe.

Over time, botanists, monarchs, farmers, and consumers invented apple traditions and imagined apple communities. Apples are bound up in national identity in the United States, including the connections between apple pie and other patriotic symbols, but extending to things like orchards planted in honor of the Bicentennial.[119] As far as apple pie goes, many sources credit the English with bringing apple pie to North American shores (although the Dutch get the credit for Dutch apple pie).[120] There is a very succinct recipe for what might be an apple pie in a fourteenth-century English cookbook: "FOR TO MAKE TARTYS IN APPLIS. Tak gode Applys and gode Spycis and Figys and reysons and Perys and wan they are wel ybrayed coloured wyth Safroun wel and do yt in a cofyn and do yt forth to bake wel."[121] In addition, "the typical American pie . . . descends from fifteenth-century English apple pies, which, while not quite the same, are similar enough that the relationship is unmistakable. By the end of the sixteenth century in England, apple pies were being made that are virtually identical to those made in America in the early twenty-first century."[122]

This linkage of apples and identity also takes place in many other countries. In Germany, for example, apples are sometimes labeled in national terms (*alte deutsche Apfelsorten*, "old German apple varieties"), but quite often in local and regional terms as well (*Märkische Äpfel*, *Äpfel des Alten Lands*, or an apple wine called the "Swabian national drink").[123] While the language around many of these apples, in Germany as well as the United States, implies a timeless tradition stretching back into a misty past, many of these apples and the landscapes they populate are relatively new. In the United States something one hundred years old can seem ancient, whereas in Europe being a century old barely merits attention. Many of the apple varieties making a comeback across both Europe and America today and cloaked in this aura of the past, however, were first bred in the nineteenth century in the midst of the categorizing and breeding fever that swept both continents then.[124] Furthermore, many of the apples returning to the scene in Germany today, for example, were first bred decades or a century or two ago in France, England, the Netherlands, or even Canada and the United States.[125] Even in a book dedicated to "German apple varieties," the authors include plentiful examples of English, French, Dutch, and North American apples, including the Pineapple Renette from Holland and the Baumanns Renette developed in Alsace in 1800.[126] But the

Golden Renette Freiherr von Berlepsch, a golden, striped apple, was developed in the Rhineland.[127] Within Germany, plenty of people distinguish the apples of one region from those of another, but all these apples are also understood as German, in opposition to Dutch, English, French, or North American apples.[128]

Apple Places

Across Europe and the United States, people preserve old varieties of apples in heirloom orchards, public meadows and parks, and on the grounds of living history museums. Farmers have to make a living, so while aficionados often cultivate heirloom trees mostly as a hobby, others apply a specific strategy to fill a niche market. Many people in the United States encounter heirloom apples only in annual forays to pick-your-own orchards or on occasional trips to living history museums that may have planted a few traditional apple trees. Pick-your-own orchards are less a way to lay in stores for the long winter than an opportunity for a pleasant fall day out, although the orchards with a twenty-pound minimum certainly push you toward picking enough apples to last awhile. Farmers' markets give city dwellers comparatively easy access to heirloom apples.[129] There are also edible apples with expressive names like the Berlin Sheep's Nose (which does look a lot like a sheep's nose), and ambitious projects across the European continent to preserve "native" apple varieties, from Ireland to Hungary.

Orchards become places where people preserve biodiversity, but also cultural memory—flavor, textures, and colors of the past as well as qualities that may be useful in future apples, and the details of past growers and eaters of these apples. One fall I traveled to Old World Wisconsin, an open-air museum, with some loyal friends, and we wandered around the autumn landscape.[130] There was an apple display set up near the restaurant, selling bins of apple varieties I'd never seen in my life. Big mealy apples, tiny tart ones, with unfamiliar names and beautiful blushes. I went home with a paper bag full and cut up a bunch into an apple crumble, eating the smaller, crisper ones on their own. This was possibly my first conscious effort to cook heirloom apples, and I was delighted at the alchemy of mixing the great mealy "pie apples" with tiny sour ones, pushing my apple crumble in a direction it never could have taken with Golden Delicious or Granny Smith. When you add butter and brown sugar and walnuts, not to mention heat, the original structure of the apples breaks down into something sweet and tart and warm, the heirloom or at least unfamiliar qualities melting into a delicious apple crisp.

Across the United States (and much of Europe) in recent decades, people have used apple trees to encapsulate these shared understandings of the past and to preserve and convey elements of past ways of life. Even a single tree can offer a compelling narrative: "The original seedling of Newtown Pippin stood near a swamp on the estate of Gershom Moor in Newtown, Long Island, until 1805, when it died from exhaustion from the cutting of too many scions for grafting, the price of popularity."[131] Poor exhausted tree, too beloved to survive. Lape also recalls his own apple tree memory: "My most vivid memory of the orchard on our farm was the old Spitzenburg tree, hollow in its upper core, with a hole where the flickers nested each spring when the tree was pink in flower, and hanging red with fruit in October, like a jewel among the other trees."[132] This recollection also highlights personal, individual memory. In the case of edible forgetting, the creator of the Cox's Orange Pippin was Richard Cox, whose "villa and gardens [at Colnbrook in Berkshire, England] have long since disappeared, replaced by modern housing and a car park. No one thought to preserve them, and the original Orange Pippin tree is said to have blown down during a gale. Other than its name, The Lawns today bears no sign of its place in culinary history, which is a shame."[133] Some historical trees persist into the present, while others vanish without a trace.

One site of extensive apple biodiversity and attendant edible memory is the USDA's Plant Genetic Resources Unit in Geneva, New York, which has a seed bank, a living orchard, and cryogenically preserved cuttings.[134] There are also fruit repositories in Corvallis, Oregon, and Davis, California.[135] Places like these also offer the opportunity to walk through, and eat, these remnants of the past.[136] There are places that intentionally preserve old apple varieties both to hold on to apple biodiversity and to give visitors a visceral connection to past ways of life. There is a Johnny Appleseed trail in north-central Massachusetts, and Filoli Mansion and Gardens in Northern California, thirty miles south of San Francisco, maintains an heirloom fruit orchard.[137] One reporter asks, "Bored with bland supermarket apples and pears? Yearning for the flavors you remember as a child? Taste what you're missing at the Filoli Friends' Day Fall Festival."[138] At Filoli, the "gentleman's orchard" contains more than 670 trees, featuring traditional varieties of apples, pears, Asian pears, and a host of other pomes (some of which, like azorole and hales, I'd never heard of!), stone fruit, grapes, and other fruit and nuts. The renovation of the orchard began in the late 1990s, when there were only about 150 trees left from the original thousand planted at the estate in 1918. Filoli's website explains that the orchard renovation was done both to preserve a wide range of fruit germplasm and because "historic fruit cultivars are both living legacies and evidence of our past cultural history. The curators of Filoli's fruit collection place emphasis on historical connections."[139] "The orchard's surviving authentic trees have been left standing, and were also propagated onto new rootstock and replanted. The lower orchard has also been planted with 670 new heritage fruit trees. . . . In accordance with Filoli's accessions policy, the orchard is planted only with historically appropriate fruits."[140] Some of these apple varieties exist only here. In 2003 Filoli started occasionally supplying apples and pears to Chez Panisse. Visitors could also participate in fruit tastings, take tours of the orchard, drink cider, eat tarts made from the estate's apples, and even buy fruit trees in the gift shop.[141]

In keeping with the frequent associations between Thomas Jefferson and American heirloom apples, Monticello is another key apple place. The Thomas Jefferson Center for Historic Plants began offering heirloom apple varieties in 2001.[142] The lady apple and the Ralls Genet, French heirlooms that were grown in the United States in the nineteenth century, were both available as bare-root saplings. In 2006 Monticello held its eighteenth heirloom apple tasting.[143] Tom Burford, a devoted apple activist, often leads apple tastings at Monticello. The curators and researchers for historical gardens can use things like Thomas Jefferson's careful garden diaries, noting the days when peas were sown and, a reasonable number of weeks later, served for dinner.[144] This is a place to expose the public to information about "old" seeds, to distribute seeds, cuttings, and seedlings as well as instructions, and to preserve elements of biodiversity such as "some of Jefferson's favorite apple trees, like the Albemarle pippin, a good eating apple that keeps well; Esopus Spitzenburg, a deep-red eating apple that thrives in colder climates, and the Newtown pippin, a crisp, yellowish-green apple that's not too sweet and not too tart."[145]

The Tower Hill Botanic Garden just outside Worcester, Massachusetts, also has a collection of antique apple trees, and each year it sells visitors hundreds of scions.[146] They have over a hundred varieties of relatively rare apples, based on a collection started in a Depression-era government plan to take out abandoned fruit trees in the state. The project was responsible for the destruction of thousands of trees, but the head of the project, S. Lothrop Davenport, also held on to a few dozen varieties, first in his own orchard in Massachusetts, moving them to Old Sturbridge Village in 1973. The orchard was then moved to its current location in the late 1980s. Scion sticks cost a mere $3.50, for those willing to do their own grafting. The catalog also lists the date and place of origin of the particular variety. In 2008-9 it offered 119 varieties, including some dating back to the seventeenth century, with provenances ranging from Russia, England, France, and Canada to many US states. Both dates and origins are sometimes followed by a question mark, reflecting the difficulty of identifying the precise date and place of origin of particular apple varieties. Apple tastings and sales of scions also spread the popularity of these varieties.[147]

Canterbury Shaker Village in New Hampshire also has an heirloom apple orchard: "In the small orchard at the Shaker Village living history museum in Canterbury, heirloom apples just give a nostalgic feel, says David Bryant, the property's land manager. He said about 75 trees were restored from an original Shaker orchard of about 240 trees there and are now bearing fruit. Those varieties include Pippins, Newtons, Dutchess [*sic*] of Oldenbergs, Arkansas Reds, Winesaps and others."[148] John Bunker of FedCo Seeds finds that "you can go to a museum and you can see the beds that (early Mainers) slept in or the dishes they used or whatever, but with an heirloom apple you actually are experiencing the same taste that they found worthy of replicating. . . . To me, some of these varieties are strange-tasting, and I think, well, I'm learning something about these people by eating the food that they ate."[149] That experience—of eating other people's memories and components of other people's daily lives—is repeated again and again in farmers' markets and living history museums, restaurants and backyards. This closely resembles what Alison Landsberg refers to as "prosthetic memory"—the sensation of experiencing a past we ourselves never lived through.[150] The English chef Nigel Slater recalls the first apple tree he planted in his garden, intentionally evoking his childhood: "The young tree, barely three feet high, was planted with white phlox underneath in an attempt to realize a haunting childhood memory of the smell of ripe apples mixed with the powdery scent of fading *Phlox paniculata*.... For years I had walked around with this childhood scent in my head. And now here it was in a garden of my own making."[151]

Forgetting Apples

For every historical orchard or storytelling tree, there are countless forgotten orchards and neglected or vanished trees, traces and remnants of past ways of life—past habits and economies. Throughout Europe and the United States, there are vanished orchards, the orchards of the Roman legions, Charlemagne's subjects, Benedictine monks, struggling farmers, and eighteenth-century gentlemen. All disappear with time—in part because apple trees tend to live only a century or so, with notable exceptions, and in part because the world changes around them. They persist only in scanty records—the occasional engraving, medieval tapestry, or inventory scrawled on parchment. Apples populate both forgotten and remembered landscapes. Apples are very much about land, and as land use changes, so do apples. There are many mentions of orchards' disappearing to make way for subdivisions. Pollan's search for the Chapman (Johnny Appleseed) orchards is an excellent illustration of the ways landscapes disappear, obscuring their history.[152] Pollan finds parking lots and strip malls, weedy rivers and vacant lots, in his search for apples once planted to supply the young nation's thirst for hard cider. In the nineteenth century, Thoreau lamented that "the era of the Wild Apple will soon be past," exhibiting a keen sense of forgetting in the landscape. He saw the apple husbandry of his day as modern and soulless, but the apples that were new then are now viewed with nostalgic affection. Stocks also discusses the underlying landscapes, the ways the development of cities and suburbs, industrial parks and factories, erases the past uses of the land, and thus these layers of culinary memory and practice as well as varieties of apples and other fruits and vegetables. He describes a single tree as "the last survivor of an ancient monastic orchard" and offering hope for new generations from that survivor.[153] We can also think about forgotten gardens and orchards on a global scale.

Supermarket apples also mean the loss of the habits of putting up apples, either drying them or turning them into applesauce, or knowing how to store different kinds of apples. There are apples that can be picked in the fall but won't reach their peak of flavor until Christmas, so people used to store them in the attic in anticipation of a Christmas treat. We lose (as a society) both tastes and habits, the familiar roughness of a russet in your hand or on your tongue, for example, the dull brown skin concealing a crisp, juicy, snow-white interior. Specific names and images in archives, old books, and forgotten orchards offer a way to follow today's apples back in time.

For all these living history museums and botanical gardens, most past apple landscapes have been erased and forgotten. Suburbs take over farmland, grocery shopping becomes something people do once a week by car, and transcontinental refrigerated shipping has moved much commercial apple growing to Washington State (and even more to China). An abandoned orchard on North Manitou Island in Michigan used to produce fruit for the Chicago markets, but now spindly, unproductive, and neglected trees are the only trace of this past.[154] It is striking to see a mention of traces of Seneca orchards in the landscape of New York State: "In the early years of this century two old apple trees remained of the old Indian orchards near the Geneva Experimental Station in New York State."[155] Two trees can tell us of past ways of living on and eating off the land.

Abandoned orchards provide a tangible way to think about the dynamic relationship between remembering and forgetting. Across the country, apple activists scour the countryside for old apple trees, exploring quiet valleys and neglected islands. It can take years, or even decades, to definitively identify a variety or produce a fruiting tree from a graft. Such devoted memory work is often done very individually. In orchards, culture, agriculture, and nature blend together. People lay their hands on the landscape over decades and centuries. Orchards are more persistent than wheat fields or vegetable patches, but they still disappear, through neglect or the ax and chainsaw. Landscapes are littered with forgotten apple trees that, left unpruned, become less and less productive. Others vanish in gale-force winds, the owners waking to find a venerable apple irreparably toppled, to be sawed up for firewood. There are references in censuses and surveys, orchards and nurseries, letters describing dessert apples and strolls through flowering orchards. Specific landscapes reflect these changes in apple culture: forgotten southern valleys, remnants of orchards along English motorways, the recovered (and forgotten) fruit meadows of Austria and Germany. Not only the apples but also the knowledge about growing, processing, cooking, and preserving disappear, as does knowing what to do with a diverse array of apples.

Even more than cooking, making cider requires a set of skills, tools, and tastes that have largely vanished from much of the United States.[156] In many regions of Germany and Austria where apples and pears grew well, villages were once ringed by tall, handsome apple and pear trees, many growing fruit for hard cider rather than for cooking or eating raw. But as the villages expanded in the later twentieth century, the trees vanished one by one, felled by developers and road builders and city foresters. Changes in apples are also linked to changes in technology and markets. Many cider apple trees were eliminated from European landscapes, often intentionally. In West Germany, Schermaul tells us, "from 1957 to 1974, 14,000 hectares of orchards [specifically *Streuobstwiesen*, "scattered fruit meadows"] fell victim to the ax. In addition, road construction, the clearing of property lines, and large-scale housing developments destroyed countless additional fruit meadows."[157] Such meadows, however, have experienced a resurgence across Germany and Austria in recent years, as existing meadows are preserved and new meadows are planted with old apple varieties traditional to particular regions.

Cider is especially emblematic of heirloom food (and drink). The resurgence of heirloom apples brings a resurgence of hard cider and the landscapes that produce it. All is not lost. Many heirloom apples are more suited to making hard cider than sweet cider, since hard cider calls for a balance of sweet and tart or even bitter fruits. Cider making requires another layer of skill and investment of both time and money, and it needs a specific kind of tree and creates particular landscapes in apple-growing areas. In the 2000s hard ciders are becoming more widely available in Europe and in the United States. One of the cider makers is AeppelTreow Winery, where they grow "200 varieties of antique fruit on 15 acres in southeastern Wisconsin in [an] attempt to replicate old English, French and U.S. colonial ciders from historic recipes."[158] In the 2000s fermented cider began making a serious comeback, including brewers like Virtue Cider in Michigan and Farnum Hill from Poverty Lane Orchards in New Hampshire, among many, many others.[159] People sometimes misunderstand the meaning of cider and cider apples, mistakenly assuming that nineteenth-century cider was the sweet stuff drunk on crisp autumn weekends today, rather than the varyingly alcoholic drink that it actually was. Cider gets a surprisingly short entry, only a brief paragraph, in *The Oxford Companion to Food*.[160] The *OCF* claims that American cider has traditionally not been made from cider apples, unlike European cider, which is made from apples bred specifically for the purpose.

Apples created (and create) far stronger stuff as well: "Farmers made applejack by placing fermented cider outside during the winter and removing the ice that formed, leaving a potent alcoholic liquid."[161] Prohibition played a big role in bringing cider traditions to an end and felling the orchards that produced the lightly alcoholic hard cider and the far more potent applejack. One summer, at the Annual Seed Savers Exchange Conference and Campout in Decorah, Iowa, I attended a cider workshop in the basement of a barn, packed with people learning about one particular way to make cider—quite different from the way I'd seen cider made in Austria, above all lacking the great living layer of microorganisms that seals in the cider and keeps out the oxygen. The room was full of fresh-faced young back-to-the-landers and urban home brewers as well as venerable farmers in overalls. People murmured and discussed among themselves, posing good-natured questions to the leader of the workshop, Dan Bussey—one of the most knowledgeable people around on the subject of heirloom apples.

I have also spent many hours in an Austrian meadow scattered with venerable old pear and apple trees, some far taller than most fruit trees planted today—the original full height apple and pears, not grafted onto dwarf or semi-dwarf rootstock. The cider trees become distinctly visible in spring, their unmistakable crowns of white blossoms settled into hillsides and front yards. The trees mark the change of seasons, and as winter comes these towering trees full of often misshapen pears and apples cast off their fruit.

In Austria cider is called *Most* and is made from a sometimes motley assortment of windfall fruit collected from stands of *Most* trees planted in rural barnyards and along country lanes. In the cider making I experienced there, apples and pears behind the rural Austrian house that I often visited when I was living in Vienna were picked up one by one and dropped into metal mesh baskets and old paint buckets. The trees' owners filled the back of an old yellow Volkswagen truck with the windfalls and the fruit they could reach by ladder from these *hochstamm* ("high-trunk" or "standard," i.e., in apple terms, very tall) trees, then drove the harvest to the village cider press. The old VW would return to the house with plastic casks full of the cloudy fresh-pressed cider, and the casks would be hauled down slippery stone steps into a centuries-old cellar at the top of the meadow. Some people add a bit of sugar or some medlar (an apple-like fruit that helps preserve the *Most*), but most people, like the cider maker who lived in this old Austrian house, just let the yeasts in the air aid fermentation.

This family's *Most* fermented in the cool cellar as energetic molds reached out of the brickwork and embraced the outside of the barrels. A sealing layer of scum would build on the top of the liquid inside the barrels, so the barrels mustn't be moved. When the *Most* was finally drinkable, someone had to take an old pitcher and walk the length of the big meadow behind the house to get to the *Mostkeller*, then carefully carry the full pitcher back to the house. This cider making is handed down through generations. I could read a book or attend a seminar, of course, but there is something to be said for learning in the shadow of an old hand. For me, drinking this tannic cider, often mixed half and half with sparkling spring water in a half-liter glass, was as refreshing as it was novel. The cider maker himself shook his head one day when he saw me photographing the tableau of the *Most* pitcher and our dinner all laid out on the picnic table at the edge of the meadow. But part of my appreciation of the *Most* was also the preciousness of sitting together in the shade of the old walnut tree (which appears again in the epilogue), talking about Lou Reed or politics or village gossip, watching the sunlight slowly fade in the leaves of the trees from which the *Most* had come.

Apples and other heirloom foods resonate strongly with diverse members of the public—the eager brewers in that barn basement in Iowa, but also the readers of food blogs and the chefs and reviewers of fancy restaurants, as well as home cooks and gardeners. The attachment to the past that sends people to living history museums in the countryside or modern speakeasies in Brooklyn also sends them off in search of traditional, old-fashioned, historical food, or edible memory—in ways that can help to preserve apple biodiversity as well as the landscapes and habits that accompany it. The complex cultural, botanical, and geographical history of apples—perhaps even more than of tomatoes or turnips—reveals the highly changeable qualities of culture itself. In the late twentieth and early twenty-first centuries, many people in the United States (and elsewhere) either discovered or, less frequently, personally recalled an appetite for the flavors, colors, aromas, textures, and shapes of thousands of apple varieties unavailable in supermarkets. And for all the troubles and challenges of the contemporary food supply in the United States, these farmers, gardeners, pomologists, and other savers of seeds and trees create fecund pockets of biodiversity across the country, often well out of view—decentralized ways of holding on to the past but also looking toward the future. Apples come to be about places too, hooked into regional or national economies and identities. There are hidden apple trees across the country, apples rooted to places and to families, seed saver orchards in Iowa, and a rainbow of apple varieties at urban farmers' markets. Changes in the landscape correspond to changes in what and how we eat.[162] A single apple can yield a lot of sociological lessons, from France to New Berlin, from the eighteenth century to the twenty-first. As with vegetables, the heirloom phase is just the most recent moment in the history of apples, in their shifting meanings and uses.

Collective forgetting can reduce biodiversity, and the converse is also true. A collective attachment to the past—translated into appetites, desires, and actions—happens on the literal outskirts and the margins, in well-tended or abandoned gardens, backyards, orchards, nurseries, and estates, but also increasingly in the limelight. These apples come back in part because of the meanings people attach to them. Bringing them back involves networks and activism. And they persist in the daily practices of people tending trees, farms, and gardens, pruning or making cider as the season dictates. They also come back because of the hard work of committed activists, work that helps to create and in turn benefits from the broader popularity and resurgence of heirlooms, as people turn their attention to both the past and the future. As Bunyard writes, "There is in the Apple a vast range of flavours and textures, and for those who adventure in the realm of taste, a field for much hopeful voyaging."[163]

· 4 ·

*Forgotten Turnips
and Other Vegetables*

IN SOCIOLOGICAL PURSUIT of memorable vegetables, I headed
out beyond the tomato patch, into the world of multicolored potatoes,
crooked eggplants, and bright red carrots. I wondered, for starters, if
anything was as popular as the tomato. The short answer turned out to
be no. But some heirloom vegetables do ride the coattails of heirloom
tomatoes, and even less popular ones—the forgotten turnips, celery,
or leeks—are preserved by home gardeners, seed saver groups, and
small-scale farmers, grown for a targeted clientele or for their own dinner tables. Furthermore, these varieties' fates may change again just as
they have changed in the past. Looking through old seed catalogs, botanical prints, cookbooks, and still life paintings, I encountered shapes,
colors, and sizes of fruits and vegetables largely absent from grocery
shelves today, but once highly popular and widely consumed. I also
headed to farms and gardens to see vegetables in action.

One day I drove out to the Hollister, California, location of Mariquita Farm, one of the two farms that supplied my parents' CSA box.
Heading to Mariquita from the coast that summer morning, the fog
was so thick I had the windshield wipers on as I drove along Highway
101, dotted here and there with signs indicating I was on El Camino
Real, the route linking the California missions.[1] This string of largely
eighteenth-century settlements left significant political and cultural

imprints on the state, as well as botanical, agricultural, and culinary marks, but this terrain has changed noticeably in the past few centuries.[2] The fields and pastures as I saw them that day reflected just the most recent moment in the political, economic, and agricultural history of this particular valley.

The layers of space and memory in California have always intrigued me. Hiking in the foothills of the Sierra Nevada, we would come across grinding stones worn by centuries or millennia of grinding acorns. Closer to home on the coast, we regularly found black, ashy middens along the shore, flecked with iridescent fragments of the abalone eaten by generations of Native American residents. These objects and spaces make it clear that people had been living in this supposedly New World for a long time, in ways that Spanish, Russian, and Anglo settlers generally did their best to eradicate. Indeed the Native American population of California went from approximately three hundred thousand in the late eighteenth century to about twenty thousand in 1900, owing to a combination of disease, warfare, and outright murder.[3]

The Spanish missionaries left traces in the physical landscape of the state along the El Camino Real, including the wild mustard that blossoms in spring in traffic medians, scrubby fields, and orchards. My mother would tell us that every patch of bright yellow wild mustard was the site of a Spanish missionary picnic, the seeds scattered by their apparently careless use of mustard. As a little girl I'd look out the window of the station wagon, imagining a cluster of hair shirt–clad friars somewhat incongruously reclining in the golden grasses (perhaps with a nod to Friar Tuck), enjoying a picnic and unable to keep their mustard contained. I've since heard similar stories from California friends, albeit with important variations, such as the scattering of mustard seed to mark the road between the missions, while other sources credit everyone from the conquistadores to nineteenth-century ranchers with the introduction of the now-invasive plant.[4]

On the way to Mariquita I also drove past hundred-year-old orchards reflecting different waves of desire for fruit, the erasure and displacement of Native American communities, and the imprint of the Spanish land grants still visible to the trained eye beneath the layers of freeways and subdivisions that sometimes still bear the names bestowed upon the land by a long-ago Iberian monarch or Mexican governor.

In the early twentieth century, when the lack of refrigeration and extensive transnational shipping networks still made it difficult to get out-of-season or far-off produce, dried apricots and prunes grown in this fertile soil were very popular. As this changed and fresh fruit became easier to get, the dried-fruit industry receded, and many of these orchards yielded to the march of nearby Silicon Valley.

I drove past cow-calf operations, small orchards, and vast fields being harvested by dozens of farmworkers bundled up in layers of sweatshirts and bandanas, first against the morning chill and later against the mid-day sun.[5] As I neared the farm, I drove past a Victorian farmhouse as instructed, letting myself in at a red metal gate. It's not often in my urban life that I swing open a farm gate. The farmer, Andy Griffin, took me for a closer look at the origin of my mother's vegetables.[6] The farm buzzed with bees and ladybugs. Nestled in this fertile valley, a riot of chili peppers, Italian greens, and purple Sicilian artichokes were thriving in the coastal push and pull of fog and heat. These vegetables, with their genetic origins in faraway places, were now destined for the kitchens of local restaurants and residents. But how did these particular vegetables arrive in this particular valley? What constellation of tastes has developed to shape this landscape? These questions began on this farm, but in subsequent months and years they took me deep into books, archives, and libraries.

There were rows and rows of green tomatoes, waiting for a few more weeks of central coast sunshine. There seemed to be a fair number of weeds—or what at first glance appeared to be weeds. In fact, many of these plants served dual purposes: some in high demand as greens at local restaurants (there's sometimes a fine line between a weed and a coveted side dish); some helping to manage the pests on this pesticide-free farm. At the time, Griffin didn't grow many heirloom varieties, tomatoes or otherwise. Because his farm is organic, it is necessary to plant varieties that are very well suited to the microclimate, whether they are heirlooms or not. When we spoke a couple of years ago, he was growing very few heirloom tomatoes, for which this climate is challenging. He grows pesticide- and herbicide-free artichokes, surrounded but not harmed by weeds, including purple Sicilian artichokes that he sells only to restaurants, because they're too unusual for the CSA box. As he puts it, he grows what wants to grow in a given place, which may or may not be an heirloom. This book's focus on heirlooms does not imply that they are the only way to go, and understandably many farmers mix heirlooms and hybrids, depending on what their customers want and on the demands of their particular climate.

The sun came out as we walked through the fields. A faithful old dog accompanied us, as often happens when I visit farms, orchards, and gardens, just as my shoes always get muddy and my nose gets sunburned. In the thick early morning fog, I never imagined it could heat up as it did, until the dog finally capitulated and lay panting in the shade of the tractor while Griffin's employees, mostly men who had emigrated from Mexico, continued harvesting, packing, and tending crops in the growing heat. Weeding, tilling, planting, and harvesting are hard physical work, and on a farm this small most of that work is done by hand rather than by machine. But it is also done in air and soil free of the toxic pesticides and herbicides that are essential to much non-organic farming.

Through the capable hands of Griffin and his employees, the appetites of restaurant patrons and CSA subscribers translate directly into strips of crops, particular landscapes that stand out in contrast to the monocultures of nearby Salinas Valley—making it apparent that this is a different kind of space and a different kind of agriculture. These landscapes harbor both edible biodiversity and highly diverse flora and fauna and microbial life deep in the soil, a marked contrast to the silent dearth of insects, microbes, and weeds in neighboring fields more heavily reliant on herbicides, insecticides, and nitrogen-rich fertilizers. In this part of the world there is extensive monoculture. There are patches of land that have been covered in conventional artichokes and strawberries year after year for as long as I can remember, and ever-increasing expanses of lettuce, broccoli, and the more recent vineyards stretch deep into the Salinas Valley. Mariquita is comparatively very diverse and very small. The farm is planted in strips of different crops, often with weeds growing robustly between the plants (where they aren't a nuisance). Visually this differs starkly from most of the farmland in the region, where acre upon acre is covered in the same crop. Here there are rows of chili peppers, tomatoes, Italian greens, beets, kale, all kinds of squashes, and a stand of elderberry trees that shades a parking lot for the farmworkers and the occasional visiting sociologist. There was row after row of all kinds of peppers: Hungarian, Romanian, round and curvy like tomatoes, little yellow pods, or long, curling dark red ones. As we were looking at the peppers, suddenly half a dozen men showed up with stacks of plastic packing totes on their shoulders—it was time to pick the Romanian peppers, but Griffin told them to leave the hotter peppers in the field.

As I noted above, scholars like Guthman and others emphasize that tastes in food have tangible, and at times dramatic, consequences for particular landscapes and particular economies, as well as for the lives and bodies of workers and consumers.[7] The popularity of McDonald's means a landscape scattered not only with golden arches, but also with vast fields of genetically modified corn and soy. On the other hand, the tastes of a handful of restaurant owners (and their patrons) in California directly leads to fields of organic Italian greens alive with bees and other fauna and flora, taking up acreage in the otherwise fairly monocultural agricultural valleys of California's central coast. The growing popularity of heirlooms and other unusual or traditional foods creates further demand, and landscapes change to meet that demand. This popularity creates alternative spaces of both production and consumption.[8]

The development of industrial agriculture requires, in part, that people have appetites for (or no alternative to) its products, and marketing departments and ad agencies put a lot of effort into cultivating these appetites in ways that are profitable for the companies selling this food. A collective forgetting of the flavor of a good August tomato can come in handy when you're trying to sell tomatoes with less flavor but more resilience. What we reach for every day has a history, a politics, and a geography: Granny Smiths or baby carrots, backyard lettuce or a neighbor's excess tomatoes. There is a push and pull of taste as well, with the rhythm of the seasons and as farmers respond to but also guide their customers' tastes. Griffin has been around since the early days of Alice Waters. Like many longtime farmers, he has watched vegetable trends come and go, and he knows that chefs in particular want things that will set them apart: rare vegetables no one else will have—things like amaranth and agretti, greens that some see as weeds and others see as heirlooms or even sacred seeds (amaranth).[9] Rarity, exclusivity, and scarcity are key to understanding the popularizing of heirlooms.[10] His business is also helped by Greek and Italian restaurateurs whose customers have a taste for agretti and other greens. Griffin includes few edible weeds and mysterious roots in his CSA boxes, but when my mother started subscribing, especially early in the season before the strawberries and Swiss chard started appearing, she had to do some serious research to identify some of the vegetables and learn how to cook them. She was definitely aided by Griffin's weekly newsletter, essays, and recipes, but she commented offhand that it was a good thing she'd retired and had time to manage her vegetable box each week.[11]

When we think about heirloom vegetables, as William Woys Weaver notes, we also have to think about both cooking and gardening, which are very interdependent.[12] Cooking is the alchemy—or the straightforward chemistry—by which these raw materials are transformed.[13] Over time many people have lost the knowledge of how to grow, preserve, and prepare them—as well as a taste for them in the first place. There are old cookbooks with recipes that call for vegetables we home cooks may never have heard of, and at the other extreme, recipes that call for all kinds of prewashed, prechopped, premade foods.[14]

Vegetable Mobility

Not only is Andy Griffin's farm an example of tastes shaping landscapes, it also reveals the phenomenal mobility of both tastes and vegetables themselves. After Columbus's voyages, the tomato eventually became essential to much Italian food, chili peppers infuse much of the world's cuisines, and Europe adopts the potato.[15] None of the plants cultivated on Griffin's land have their evolutionary origins here. Tastes and habits alter with the movement of empires, conquest, and trade, political alliances and new technologies of production and distribution.[16]

One year Griffin grew zucchetta rampicante and other relatives of the butternut squash, thinking that the butternut's suitability for a CSA box might mean that its relatives would be a good fit as well. But the squashes turned out to be much too big to fit in the boxes, and many were not particularly flavorful. The newsletter for the week they were harvested showed a mountain of enormous dusty-colored squashes—destined in part for the goats' and donkeys' winter dinners. Squash is a New World food, but this squash has an elaborate Italian name. Its name and its appearance reflect the dramatic aftereffects of the Columbian Exchange, the tectonic movement of food around the globe in the wake of Columbus's voyages, discussed in greater detail in the next chapter. This imposing squash's ancestors originated in the Americas, but centuries of European gardeners and farmers led to new varieties developed on European soil that became deeply ingrained in the food culture of a particular region of Italy.

How do vegetables come to be where they are and to be crucial elements of gardens, kitchens, and daily life? When I asked this question it quickly became clear that heirloom varieties are just the most recent trend in the uses and meanings of vegetables. Vegetables are wrapped up not only in the histories and memories of individuals, families, and communities, but also in global social change—colonialism and imperialism, centuries of slavery and waves of immigration, changing empires and revolutions, not to mention new technology and changing tastes. Traditions that may feel quite stable within a given generation often have dynamic and by no means predictable histories, leading to the traditional qualities we may observe today.

Vegetables (and other foods) may be incorporated into culinary traditions very quickly or very slowly. The concept of an heirloom variety rarely involves an unbroken tie to a place-bound vegetable past. Instead, vegetables carry the traces of past movements of people and seeds. It takes a lot of work to turn them into heirlooms—to attach them to particular habits and places, to root them in a group of people and a particular patch of soil or set of geographic coordinates. Even the European food cultures prized by so many American food writers rest on a foundation of mobility and often dramatic change. Minor ice ages or cataclysmic wars, botanical innovations and global exploration can alter entire systems of food production and distribution, in the blink of an eye or over centuries. So can the intentional creation of everything from French haute cuisine (carefully constructed and codified), to the efforts to get post–World War II Italians to like shopping at supermarkets.[17] Not only Mariquita, but most farms and gardens in the United States are growing things that have their genetic origins far away. There are important exceptions, like the fields and gardens of Native Seeds/SEARCH in Arizona, which focus on growing traditional and botanically indigenous foods of the Southwest, but even maize—so essential to culinary and cultural traditions across North America—has its evolutionary roots firmly planted farther south.[18] As I visited farms and gardens, I also delved into historical accounts of vegetables, and it became clear that vegetables have long been subject to fickle appetites as well as to much deeper geopolitical and economic change.

Forgetting Turnips

What kinds of changes have vegetables undergone over time? And what are the fates of particular vegetables in this era of heirloom food? When I began my search in mainstream food writing for coverage of forgotten turnips, celery, and other less glamorous vegetables, I found very little. Particular blogs, authors, and chefs zeroed in on particular heirloom vegetables at various moments, but there was no comparison with the coverage of heirloom tomatoes or apples. My initial inclination was to think that this silence reflected forgetting. But in fact these supposedly forgotten vegetables inspire extremes of devotion in some seed savers, gardeners, and farmers, and it is to these people (more than to urban diners and famous chefs) that they owe their survival.

My research into popular food writing yielded almost nothing about leeks, cauliflower, turnips, and a host of other heirloom vegetables. Overall, I found far fewer mentions of all these vegetables combined than of heirloom tomatoes. Some fruits and vegetables are more evocative than others, but I was truly surprised at the dearth of writing about heirloom vegetables overall compared with heirloom tomatoes and apples.[19] At the same time, every one of these vegetables provokes passionate commitment in at least a handful of gardeners, eaters, or chefs.

The history of a given heirloom variety rarely reaches back beyond the eighteenth century (and more frequently the nineteenth), although there are some fundamental exceptions, such as pre-Columbian potatoes, beans, and corn. A very wide range of historical moments and geographic locations can provide the narrative necessary for a given vegetable to qualify as an heirloom. As with tomatoes, the heirloom phase in these vegetables' careers is just the most recent moment in centuries—even millennia—of changing uses and meanings. For starters, some vegetables that languish in obscurity today were once highly fashionable or essential to the daily nourishment of vast numbers of people. Much vegetable life has moved in and out of fashion. As Guthman and others assert, these fashions—these changing tastes—have direct consequences for fields and bodies, for physical and social landscapes.[20]

I expected the specific memories and stories attached to these vegetables to play a crucial role in public discussions of heirloom vegetables, but they were almost entirely absent from most newspaper food writing. Even those heirloom vegetables that do appear with some frequency often lack deep stories. At least in popular discussions of food, and in venues where much ink is spilled over heirloom tomatoes (and to a lesser extent antique apples), turnips, leeks, beets, and other vegetables are not as charged with connections to the past as tomatoes, apples, or even grain. Even the origins of vegetables that receive relatively extensive coverage—like heirloom beets, beans, squashes, lettuce, pumpkins, and carrots—are rarely part of the tale. Most articles don't even mention the name of the variety but leave it at "heirloom celery" (on the rare occasion that heirloom celery makes an appearance).

Why, then, are some fruits and vegetables remembered while others are forgotten? And what are the consequences of this forgetting? For starters, something like leek biodiversity is not integrated into the culinary lives of large numbers of people, outside of a few leek-loving regions of the world. There may also be botanical reasons for this—simply the lack of the same biodiversity available with tomatoes, potatoes, and apples. How much has to do with cooking? You don't have to cook heirloom tomatoes, but turnips and leeks often need some cooking, which may dilute their flavors and texture and color considerably compared with raw tomatoes or raw apples. I doubt that any other vegetable, fruit, or grain will experience the same change in fortunes as the tomato. Heirloom tomatoes dominate in part because of their great variety in color, flavor, and texture. Heirloom leeks (forgive me, lovers of leeks attuned to subtleties I have not yet learned to perceive) do not present this same aesthetic variety, nor do a host of other vegetables. That said, taro root, for example, is eaten in vast quantities around the globe cooked rather than raw (raw taro root is toxic), yet consumers can readily distinguish different varieties of taro, even when it is cooked and pulverized.

One farmer offered a useful theory about why lettuce, for example, might spark less interest than tomatoes: "People don't reminisce about the great red Batavian lettuce they ate when they were kids the way they recall tantalizing tomatoes and mouth-watering melons."[21] And lettuce clearly does not pack the same nutritional punch as beans, which play a huge role in global eating habits. This comparative lack of media references may also occur because most fruits and vegetables have far fewer heirloom varieties: there simply aren't as many kinds of leeks or turnips as tomatoes, and the differences are more subtle than the vivid variations in tomato varieties. In addition, non-heirloom tomatoes and apples are also particularly popular, so it makes sense that the heirloom varieties would also be particularly popular. In *Forgotten Fruits*, Christopher Stocks writes that "of all the vegetables . . . cabbages are perhaps the least glamorous, with the possible exception of turnips. Maybe this explains why the history of individual varieties is so sparse: while the introduction of a delicious new apple might be cause for general rejoicing, the launch of a new type of cabbage is unlikely to generate such widespread celebration. . . . What it isn't—and what it has probably never been—is fashionable."[22]

Food writer Jane Black concurs: "What I thought was interesting about heirloom tomatoes is the way most people are only like that about tomatoes. You rarely hear people demanding heirloom radishes or cucumbers, though they certainly exist. (I have seen heirloom beans and beets on menus though. Next big thing?)"[23] Based on my research, yes, they are in line to become fashionable for a tiny segment of the population, but not on anything close to the scale of apples or tomatoes.[24] Not surprisingly (to me, at least), *Portlandia* captures this phenomenon in a dramatic sketch about the attempts to make heirloom celery the next big thing. As one review of the sketch sets the scene, "Kale is cool, Brussels sprouts are back, heirloom tomatoes are hot, and the head of the [fictitious] Produce Sales Headquarters is very happy. But there's one outlier to the up-and-to-the-right sales charts that the organization is seeing with other vegetables: celery."[25] Despite the comedic and imaginary challenges of marketing heirloom celery in the universe of *Portlandia*, there is certainly a coattail effect; the popularity of heirloom tomatoes paved the way for "heirloom" to become a meaningful way of describing a host of vegetables.

One article asserts that heirloom iceberg lettuce really is no different in taste and texture from regular iceberg lettuce.[26] This critical

approach to heirlooms is not uncommon, and some of the appreciation of heirlooms happens because people learn the story behind these
foods. One of the few mentions of the history of lettuce refers to George
Washington's predilection for fresh greens, and Colonial Williamsburg plants colonial lettuces in their demonstration nursery.[27] "Meals
back in the days of Gen. George Washington consisted of more than
just meat, bread and potatoes. There was a fondness for greens during the 18th century. Each morning, Washington ordered his regimen-
tal officer to gather leafy plants growing near the camp and distribute
them among the men. Wesley Greene, a garden historian with Colonial
Williamsburg in Virginia, likes to share that bit of information when he
tells visitors about the heirloom lettuces growing in the demonstration
Colonial Nursery on Duke of Gloucester Street."[28] Washington's insis-
tence on daily foraging was owing not only to his fondness for greens,
but also to the necessity of supplementing the meager provisions available for his soldiers, as well as concerns about scurvy, which had devas-
tated the redcoats in the first winter of the war.[29]

The story of heirloom lettuce is not as crucial to the survival of lettuce, because of the coattails effect and the importance of private preservation. Much of the lettuce coverage has to do with mesclun replacing iceberg, with a strong emphasis on aesthetics and variety over story
and origins. Overall, popular writing about lettuce is short on emotional
content or cultural narrative, other than an occasional mention of the
eighteenth-century taste for salads. But lettuce has had great commercial success. Heirloom lettuce became part of an economic niche,
profitable to grow and sell to restaurants or for a premium at farmers'
markets.[30] It is certainly not the only produce lacking emotional narrative in public discourse. Pumpkins, for example, receive frequent mentions but are almost never called by their variety name, and almost no
storytelling accompanies their coverage.

I was surprised by the references to heirloom beets, even though
they still pale compared with the coverage of tomatoes (a mere ninety-
seven mentions of heirloom beets in the same time period, for example). In 2000, Marian Burros wrote in the *New York Times*, "Beets are
following the fashionable pattern of purple potatoes, heirloom tomatoes and golden raspberries. These heirloom varieties, long lost in the
quest for standardized fruits and vegetables, until small farmers began

growing them again, have helped make the beets more appealing, and not one of them has ever seen the inside of a can."[31] Almost all references to beets occur on restaurant menus, and very little in the way of stories is attached to them. Occasionally the names or colors get mentioned: "Italian heirloom beets"; Bull's Blood; MacGregor's Favorite (in a gardening context); "some golden, some candy-striped"; "Chioggia beet: An heirloom beet with red and white rings in its interior" (this description appears in an article titled "Food Mysteries Solved," one of many, many references to heirlooms as something new and exotic rather than traditional and familiar);[32] "Chioggia is an Italian heirloom beet."[33] Mostly they are simply "heirloom beets," with all this term seems to promise: flavor, color, rarity, authenticity, exoticism, good taste on the part of the chef and the restaurant patron? A specific name is mentioned only a few times, and there is not a single origin story. In the context of newspapers, the story of beets turns out to be irrelevant, other than the general story contained in the word "heirloom," which somehow elevates these beets above their (industrial, mass-produced?) brethren. Here "heirloom" both confers cultural cachet and is a tool of advertising, a necessary element for the menu of an upscale restaurant. Discussion of biodiversity was a consistent omission in newspaper writing on heirloom food.[34] The word "heirloom" becomes a resonant stand-in for all kinds of specific history.[35]

Turnips are in many ways emblematic of "forgotten" heirlooms. Only a handful of newspaper articles refer to them, including a couple of restaurant reviews, one describing a soup, "served in white espresso cups . . . a puree of hoekurai, an heirloom turnip,"[36] and another mentioning a roasted heirloom turnip and pear gratin.[37] That said, there are people who fervently appreciate turnips. A small town in Vermont organizes an entire festival around a specific turnip variety. Antoine Jacobsohn, an heirloom vegetable expert living in France, recounts how he "really discovered turnips. Turnips are highly variable and very tasty if one doesn't turn them to mush." He even has a favorite turnip from a particular farmer in a particular French suburb.[38] We get glimpses into the importance of turnips in the lives and diets of particular chefs, communities, or the characters created by famous authors. Christopher Stocks quotes Mark Twain: "On rainy days he sat and talked hours together with his mother about turnips. When company came, he made it his loving duty to put aside everything else and converse with them all day long of his great joy in the turnip."[39]

Stocks writes that "without the Spanish Inquisition our carrots might never have been orange, while the French Revolution was at least partly responsible for the triumph of British strawberries in the nineteenth century. Even the humblest root crops have their claims to fame: beetroot, for example, is in part responsible for the abolition of slavery, while swedes [a type of turnip] helped lay the foundations for the Industrial Revolution."[40] The familiar, homey, even pedestrian carrot has a dramatic history. Carrots appear in considerable numbers in newspaper writing, but with almost no indication of their long journey from their origin in Afghanistan (where they were purple and yellow), and the fact that today's orange carrots descend from carrots grown by refugee Mennonites goes unmentioned.[41] At a farmers' market in Vienna I bought *ur-Karrotten*, supposedly the original carrots, whose blood-red centers turned my soup a disconcerting pink. Much of the carrot story vanishes as heirloom carrots hitch a ride with heirloom tomatoes. The first mention I found of heirloom carrots was in the *Boston Globe* in 1997, offering suggestions about what to plant in a home garden.[42] Although more popular than the turnip, the carrot, too, has so far failed to really take off as an heirloom in popular culture, nor do its origin stories figure significantly in this popular coverage.

Eggplants are one of the few Asian vegetables that feature as heirlooms, although still almost always without a backstory. Coverage of them in the media, while surprisingly frequent, seemed to be about shape and color rather than either origin or, say, unique heirloom flavor. *GQ* instructs its gentlemen readers: "That little weedy patch behind your apartment doesn't have to look like a jungle or junkyard. With as little as 500 square feet, you can grow all sorts of coveted produce-aisle specialties—exotic hot peppers, striped heirloom eggplants, even asparagus."[43] But despite the occasional article with a title like "Learn More about Fascinating Eggplant!,"[44] there doesn't seem to be much passion for the heirloom eggplant. Heirloom radishes are mentioned more than other vegetables, but almost always in restaurant reviews, and in one case used as an example of frivolousness: "According to [Alice] Waters and her sprouting acolytes, growing heirloom radishes on the White House lawn will help address issues as diverse as obesity, teen diabetes, and global warming."[45] Lizzie Collingham's history of curry recounts how many of the British in the early days of colonialism disliked a lot of Indian vegetables, like eggplant. "The British in India never really took to Indian fruit and vegetables. 'I have often wished for a few good apples and pears in preference to all the different kinds of fruits that Bengal produces,' wrote a homesick accountant from Calcutta in 1783. The Anglo-Indians thought that aubergines and okra tasted slimy and unpleasant. Jean-Baptiste Tavernier described how the East India merchants at all the seventeenth-century European factories planted extensive kitchen gardens with vegetables familiar to them from home, such as 'salads of several kinds, cabbages, asparagus, peas and principally beans, the seed of which comes from Japan.'"[46]

The cucumber's origins are called out here and there, but it too falls into this B-list of vegetables. There is a very early mention of heirloom cucumbers, in 1988, in an article discussing heirlooms more broadly. Another article describes "some grand heirloom cucumbers with romantic names—Boothby's Blond from Maine, West India Burr Gherkin, Armenian Yard Long and Crystal Apple White Spine Cucumber." This article also cites Weaver and the cucumber's origins in Asia, as well as its popularity among ancient Greeks and Romans.[47] But that's about it for discussions of the cultural backstory of cucumbers, whose ancestors appear to have been wild cucumbers in the Himalayan foothills.[48]

Beets and other heirloom vegetables are also used, here and there, to pillory overly precious trends. By 1998 *GQ* (which seems to be oddly concerned with heirloom produce) had already listed heirloom vegetables as one of the most overrated concepts of the year.[49] By 2010 another reporter could write that "funky health-food stores evolved into the designer supermarket Whole Foods. Ciabatta trickled down from Chez Panisse to Jack in the Box. And now, everywhere you look, stylish, discerning rebels . . . drink small-batch vodka infused with heirloom beets at underground farmers markets. They wear limited edition blue jeans made in historic North Carolina denim mills using vintage shuttle looms."[50] These heirlooms become emblematic of tastes that are fancy, and even excessive: "And in an upscale take on the salad bar, diners can build their own. You grab one of the little pencils on the table and mark up to 10 items on a sheet listing 35 ingredients, among them Dungeness crab, toasted pine nuts, Point Reyes blue cheese, heirloom endive, wild arugula and so on."[51] For vegetable after vegetable, in certain contexts "heirloom" becomes a truncated reference to something desirable or even over the top, only rarely filling in even a particular variety, not to mention a place or a story. There are a host of vegetables that receive almost no mention in the popular press. Garlic's origins and background, for example, receive little attention despite its immense popularity. As one journalist writes, "Everybody knows about heirloom tomatoes and apples, the historic varieties that have endured for decades or even centuries in garden plots and back yards. But heirloom garlic?"[52]

There is very little on heirloom broccoli, despite the widespread popularity of broccoli in its non-heirloom form. Broccoli's "origins are lost to history," according to one article, a statement that applies to much of the vegetable world; but it was grown by the Romans and grown in North America in the eighteenth century.[53] Even vegetables that are comparatively popular in their non-heirloom form garner relatively little media coverage—broccoli, peas, or cauliflower come up short when measured against tomatoes or apples.

Thus most of the world's vegetables do not appear in popular writing about heirloom vegetables in the United States. There is hardly any discussion of heirloom peas, either dried or fresh—just a handful of articles, mostly about gardening, with very little social or cultural significance attached. Here and there they find their way into the media and into farmers' markets. The *New York Times* reported in 2000: "Heirloom tomatoes, apples, beans and potatoes have become almost commonplace in farmers' markets, but this is the first year in which peas have become consistently available in varieties that were grown decades ago, before crossbreeding for long shelf life and truck travel led to vegetables that were more sturdy than sweet and flavorful."[54]

Despite the widespread popularity of non-heirloom spinach, there is also basically nothing in the media on heirloom spinach, other than a couple of mentions of restaurants. Heirloom collards and okra were each mentioned only a few times, despite the centrality of these foods to soul food, Cajun, Gullah, and other cuisines.

Indeed, what popular food writing, both books and articles, tends to classify as "heirloom" is generally a much narrower range of food than would fit the standard definition (varieties that are open-pollinated, developed before World War II, and possess some kind of meaning and story). Much of this writing targets audiences that are predominantly (though certainly not exclusively) white and relatively affluent. The list in newspaper food writing of vegetables with few or no mentions in their heirloom state is long (and incomplete): Brussels sprouts, cassava, celeriac, celery, chard, chickpeas (one of the first cultivated crops), chicory, Chinese cabbage, cowpeas, endive, fennel, Jerusalem artichokes, kohlrabi, leeks, mâche (as "heirloom mâche"), mustard greens, parsley, parsnips, rutabagas, salsify, scorzonera, tomatillos, and yams received little or no mention as heirlooms. I developed the list of searchable vegetables by looking at heirloom vegetable books and seed catalogs, food encyclopedias, and stacks of garden books and cookbooks about heirloom food. But these sources omit much of the world's vegetable riches.

Many tropical and Asian vegetables seem to fall outside the language of heirlooms, yet what constitutes heirloom produce for Hmong farmers in Minnesota, for example? The concept of heirloom produce has very specific geographical and historical boundaries, which I think can and should be expanded. Just because a vegetable dates back to the era before industrial agriculture does not mean it will inevitably be labeled an heirloom.[55] The term "heirloom" seems, at least in popular media in the United States, to get attached most frequently to fruits and vegetables associated with European and, to a lesser degree, African American and Native American communities and traditions. Asian and Mexican vegetables rarely receive the label, nor does anything from tropical latitudes, and the limits of the terms help us think about culture, including boundaries and identities.[56] I call this chapter "Forgotten Turnips" not so much because heirloom turnips are at such great risk of disappearing forever, but because the patterns with which they appear in media coverage, restaurants, and markets tell us that the heirloom label alone is not enough to catapult them to popularity.

Off the Beaten Path

Judging by newspapers in the United States, one might think that heirloom turnips have begun to vanish from the earth. Nevertheless, although they may be "forgotten" by most of us and largely absent from supermarket produce sections and restaurant menus (with notable exceptions), they live on in the gardens of turnip fanciers and in seed banks. At a time when so much is at risk of disappearing, a wide array of individuals has stepped forward to help preserve old varieties.[57]

Some of these engaged individuals are gourmets seeking the flavors and textures of long-forgotten vegetables and old-fashioned fruit. Others are intrepid gardeners or living history volunteers seeking the plants and animals of a particular time period. Their hard work has led to much success in preserving vegetable and fruit biodiversity. In a country as shaped by immigration as the United States, the biodiversity found in home gardens and urban allotments is very extensive. A lot of edible biodiversity ends up in culinary subcultures, local communities, market gardens, or particular chefs' kitchens. And as with tomatoes, elite tastes for certain vegetables do not keep others from eating these same things. The consumers of heirloom varieties occupy both ends of the socioeconomic scale, both within the United States and beyond its borders. Community and home gardeners, or the seed savers contributing their carefully saved seeds to local seed exchanges, are rarely wealthy.[58] Such places include the Global Garden Refugee Training Farm in Chicago, where a group of families from Bhutan and Burma is using a vacant lot in Chicago's Albany Park neighborhood to grow a mixture of vegetables and herbs familiar from home and those that are popular among visitors to the farm stand and other buyers.[59]

For most people in the global West and North today, in the United States and Europe and other industrialized countries, the kitchen garden is a relic of the past. Even those of us who have enough land for a garden may emphasize flowers, grass, or ornamental plants over a truly sustaining kitchen garden. It takes work to make a garden, especially a productive one. Barbara Kingsolver's year of living off her garden (and other nearby sources of food) makes this clear.[60] In many Russian cities, however, such gardens have played a huge role in helping average people weather economic uncertainty and hard times, both before and after the collapse of the USSR. And Becky Nicolaides, for example, writes about the blue-collar suburbs of Los Angeles, where the lots were big enough for families to have economically viable chicken coops, vegetable gardens, and fruit trees, supplementing their diets and their incomes with the eggs, chickens, and produce generated on these large lots.[61] The kitchen garden ebbs and flows in importance, but it persists both nationally and globally.

In Milwaukee, the Victory Garden Initiative (recalling the victory gardens all across the United States during World War II) has started planting productive edible gardens across the city, including groves of hazelnuts and other nut and fruit trees. Places like Growing Power, Walnut Way, Alice's Garden, Milwaukee Urban Gardens, and the many other community gardens in the city are spaces where people grow both hybrids and heirlooms, seeking out familiar and unfamiliar vegetable flavors, colors, shapes, and textures.[62] In Chicago, endeavors like Growing Home, Growing Power, and the Peterson Garden Project fill vacant lots with lush gardens and edible biodiversity and connect a range of residents of the city to the land where they can garden, to each other, and to a wide array of produce (as well as eggs and honey in some cases).[63] Some of those gardens are, in fact, on land once used by World War II–era victory gardens. Here the popularity is really more among gardeners than restaurant patrons, and the important biodiversity work is done by a combination of committed activists and home gardeners and cooks.[64]

Susan Price, a gardener and author of an in-depth portrait of Minnesota vegetable gardeners, describes the layers of vegetable loss and forgetting as well as memory and creation:

> In the late 1600s, the Ojibwe, pushed west to Minnesota by white settlement, brought seeds of corn, pumpkins, beans, squash, and potatoes. Two hundred years later, Norwegians came with beet and cabbage seeds, apple tree scions, and rhubarb roots. As the Hmong arrived in the 1970s and 1980s, they brought seeds of various mustards, melons, squash, and cuttings of their medicinal plants. "We were afraid we couldn't find these plants here," one of the Hmong gardeners told me, echoing what many have felt leaving their homelands.

This description of the many layers of gardening, culture, habit, and memory in Minnesota is echoed across the country and around the globe.

Price portrays thirty-one Minnesota gardens planted and tended by an assortment of Minnesota residents, with a particular focus on immigrants from far-off places.[65] So, for example, she describes how thirty-three elderly Korean residents tend a garden at a Minneapolis apartment complex, full of wild sesame and taro, balloon flowers and *toduk* (both with edible roots), which grow alongside onions, chard, and spinach, planting foods familiar from their earlier lives in Korea and difficult, expensive, or impossible to find in stores.[66] Beatrice Garubanda, who emigrated from Uganda to Minnesota, grows a mix of vegetable varieties—some familiar from her Ugandan garden, others newer additions well suited to the Minnesota climate.[67] Astra Landa, a Latvian immigrant, creates a similar mix of familiar flavors from home and newer varieties in her Minnesota garden.[68] Likewise, Simeon Okwulehie grows a wide range of peppers he grew up with in Nigeria, to ensure spiciness in his cooking. And he believes his cooking is a way for his children to be connected to his country of origin, so that they will find Nigerian food familiar and appealing when they visit family there. Both his garden and his kitchen contain these flavors and vegetables "familiar to Nigerians but exotic to most Minnesotans," like the Igbo vegetable *Telfairia occidentalis*, a leafy green rooted in Igbo culinary and horticultural traditions.[69] Not all plants transported from warmer climates do well in Minnesota (some gardeners report trouble growing yucca, chipilín, or chayote). And the gardens are a way for some people to feel more at home in a new place.[70] Minnesota weather means no guava or citrus for Laotian refugees, but "the essential Laotian vegetables are thriving."[71] In Hmong gardens, gardeners intentionally create flavors, nutrients, and a social space where memories of life in Laos are kept alive.[72] Seitu Jones, another gardener profiled by Price, "sees himself in a long line of black gardeners reaching back to his great-grandfather, a slave who fought in the Civil War and then came upriver to farm." He not only has his own gardens but has helped establish small parks and gardens around the city, as well as Frogtown Farm, serving residents of one of the most diverse neighborhoods in Minneapolis.[73] Other people, needless to say, are happy to leave the hard work of farming and gardening behind on moving to a city or a new country.[74]

Chapter Four

Vegetable Landscapes

Many of us in the United States (at least those with relatively easy access to food shopping) don't have to give much thought to where our vegetables come from—and indeed, without more accurate labeling, it's pretty difficult to determine the origin of a particular bunch of broccoli, or whether a given food contains genetically modified organisms. Where did your grandparents' vegetables come from? Certainly cans, in part. My great-aunt Kay, who grew up in Los Angeles, recalled lots of pot roast and canned vegetables, with some vague memories of getting fresher produce from Japanese truck farmers, but few of those vegetables made it onto the table in any recognizably fresh way. Markets, old restaurants, old gardens, and city farms and dairies fade as time passes but can leave traces in the urban landscape. These trends, this disappearance from view, can be read in the landscape.

Whether carefully preserved, nearly vanished, or clearly fake, elements of the culinary past are etched into cityscapes. Although little remains of them today, London had more than four thousand hectares (about ten thousand acres) of market gardens in the early nineteenth century.[75] Street names, old signs chiseled into stone or done in now-peeling paint, arrangements of streets, converted market halls (sometimes turned into discos or shopping malls), and surviving traditions all bear witness to past forms of producing, distributing, and eating food. Heirloom varieties also appear in a wide range of public gardens, at living history museums or historical houses, in the plaza in front of San Francisco's city hall and on the Mall in Washington, DC.[76] When Slow Food planted a garden in the plaza of the San Francisco Civic Center, heirlooms suddenly found their way into the middle of the city. At Old World Wisconsin, farmhouses conveying the daily lives of the state's immigrant farmers in the nineteenth century are surrounded by vegetable gardens that complement the architecture—the particular layout and plantings of the garden reflecting what and how the inhabitants of those buildings might once have planted their vegetables. As a relatively new transplant to Wisconsin myself, my California self is fascinated by the heavy hand of the seasons on this garden, the unmistakable ways in which the plants register the glorious rain and sunshine of the summer, or the swift onset of late fall when the tomatoes die back and bright squash peek out of withering vines.[77]

Memory transforms landscapes. Gardens and fields, as well as barns and houses, can be reservoirs of memory—can remind people of past ways of living or teach about them in the first place. These ways include the techniques of farming and animal husbandry, but also the crops and animals themselves. There is a sense of authentic recipes and authentic kitchen tools and preparation techniques to accompany the historical things coming out of the vegetable garden.[78] The gardeners at Colonial Williamsburg plant flowers and vegetables and fruit that resemble what archaeologists and garden historians think the eighteenth-century gardens of this town would have contained.[79] Thomas Jefferson's Monticello and George Washington's Mount Vernon contain gardens full of plants that researchers have uncovered in these founding fathers' archives, turning the dusty pages of historical documents into living and edible archives of fruits and vegetables.[80] West of Chicago, at Garfield Farm Museum, old vegetable varieties and old animals also come together. They regularly hold a kind of heirloom vegetable fair, with heirloom seed aficionados displaying and selling their wares— tomatoes, potatoes, garlic, eggplants, and chilies—while old breeds of turkeys, sheep, pigs, and cattle were displayed nearby. These are intentionally communicative spaces. The National Colonial Farm at Accokeek, Maryland, grows colonial farm crops of the Chesapeake region, and Old Sturbridge Village in Sturbridge, Massachusetts, has a collection of heirloom vegetables from New England.[81] Such gardens can be found in Europe as well, in old monasteries, manors, and farmhouses open to the public.

I once visited the autumnal seed-saving garden at Arche Noah, for example, a living archive in the grounds of an eighteenth-century monastery garden in Austria.[82] A late September mist hung over the vineyards on the surrounding hillsides, and the aging apple trees and crumbling stone walls gave off a pleasant aura of mild decay. The garden was full of the last tomatoes and tomatillos and of plants grown from seeds ordered from Seed Savers Exchange, saved by local farmers, or brought to Austria by refugees. These are three-dimensional, multisensory spaces that also preserve, display, and advocate for biodiversity. In living history museums, culture and agriculture come together, with heirloom fruits and vegetables exhibited (either in gardens or on tables) not far from craft demonstrations, historic farmhouses, and heirloom livestock.

But heirloom vegetables and biodiversity also appear in far less public or official places. Bitter melons grow on Chicago street corners, community gardeners from Afghanistan or Belize grow chilacayote and Malabar spinach in Hayward, California, and Hmong farmers in Wisconsin plant a mixture of Laotian and typical Wisconsin vegetables.[83] Nazarea finds that modernity intensifies impulses to save old breeds and varieties: "In many instances, heirloom plants play a central role in the restoration of landscapes of remembrance."[84] Seeds can certainly be connected to identity. The Bicentennial in 1976, for example, "caused many American gardeners to reassess their historic roots, encouraging a renewed interest not only in early American life but also in the various ethnic communities that cultivated distinctive kitchen gardens in the nineteenth century."[85] One of my students recently waited after class to tell me about the heirloom carrots he had seen at the local Pik'n Save and to ask just what an heirloom carrot might be.

It is unlikely that turnips will ever achieve the popularity reached by tomatoes, but networks exist, groundwork has been laid, and the tools and techniques and habits of preservation extend to other vegetables as well.[86] When we speak of "saving" seeds, this does not mean freezing them in time. Saving them from one season and planting them the next keeps the genome changing, adapting bit by bit to new conditions, pests, and appetites. Farmers and gardeners who save seeds both help to preserve elements of the past and lay the groundwork of edible possibility for the future.

· 5 ·

Mobile Vegetables

IN SOME RESPECTS, an average supermarket in the United States today carries an amount and variety of produce unprecedented in human history. As recently as the 1960s, Judith Jones, the editor who brought Julia Child to so many kitchens and bookshelves in the United States, complained about the lack of parsley in supermarkets.[1] Parsley! Today parsley is easy to find in an average grocery store, and even tomatillos and jicama are fairly commonplace. British seed saver and author Simon Hickmott recounts that red peppers and eggplants—two staples of contemporary supermarket produce sections—were unusual in English supermarkets as recently as the 1960s.[2] Eggplant, squash, or beans move back and forth between being exotic and being familiar.[3]

Both the more standardized fruits and vegetables in the produce section and the diverse edibles we call heirlooms occupy just the most recent moment in long careers, one end of a continuum of connections between food, memory, meaning, and place,[4] a snapshot in the history of vegetable life and love. Long before anyone considered these foods heirlooms, other trends influenced vegetable consumption. As Rachel Laudan writes in *Cuisine and Empire*, "Migrants and travelers, including colonists, diplomats, soldiers, missionaries, and merchants, took their cuisine with them. . . . Along the roads and across the oceans, they took their know-how, their cooking equipment, and the plants and animals necessary to replicate their cuisines elsewhere. Cuisines have tended to expand and contract with empires."[5] Heirlooms are created over time, and there have been dramatic changes in vegetable fortunes in the past. So the wave we are seeing today is part of the ebb and flow of food and politics, economics, tastes, and habits. All of the biodiversity discussed in the previous chapter, along with sustenance and cultural memory, rests on a much deeper botanical and historical foundation. In this chapter I look more closely at how the meanings of vegetables change over time and also as foods move across space and between groups of people. By first examining the Columbian Exchange, then looking more closely at what might constitute definitions of "American" food, and finally examining the vegetable heritage of Europe, we can see how malleable our tastes in food can be, how quickly they can change, while also being felt so deeply.

Most of what are now considered heirloom varieties originated in Europe and, to a lesser extent, Africa. Plants from distant places come to be integral elements of daily life in their "new" homes, year by year, century by century. This investigation of changing tastes across time and space helps place the current heirloom trend in a much broader historical and geographical context. It also reveals that what many of us today perceive, and experience, as stable food cultures have undergone great upheavals in past decades and centuries. Eating habits that may seem stable to the contemporary outside observer or practitioner of those habits can have contentious, even violent origins. Politics, technology, taste, class, even the weather affect tastes and trends. Ships and the maritime world play vital roles in the history of food and its transformation across time and place, as do overland trade routes.

Many of the fruits and vegetables eaten today originated in Mexico and Central America, Africa, and Central Asia. Although great global migrations of foods have also occurred in other times and places, one of the most momentous of these transfers was the massive and rapid movement of plants, animals, people, and microbes around the globe that took place in the wake of Columbus's voyages to the so-called New World, which the historian Alfred Crosby dubbed the Columbian Exchange.[6] "In one direction went rice, wheat, sugar cane and the coffee bush; in the other maize, potatoes, haricot beans, tomatoes, manioc and tobacco."[7] New World foods like tomatoes, potatoes, and peppers become vital to the cooking pots and dinner tables of places far afield from Central or South America. Many of today's heirlooms were Columbus's novelties, or regarded as dangerous nightshades. The new became familiar, even beloved and fundamental to people's sense of well-being (and constitutive of identity). This exchange involved violence and tectonic shifts in power, practices, and meaning, and it took place at both micro and macro levels, in the context of geopolitics and kitchen gardens alike. Columbus first ate corn on Cuba in 1492, bringing it eastward even as explorers and conquerors brought sugar and other crops west.[8] Sugarcane was already being grown in Madeira in the fifteenth century using the labor of enslaved African men and women, laying the groundwork for a post-Columbian slave trade closely connected to sugar, with cataclysmic consequences. Chili peppers, beans, potatoes, and cassava each illustrate the profound mobility and cultural malleability of cultivated plants, another connection to conquest and global movement.

In *Neglected Crops: 1492 from a Different Perspective*, J. E. Hernández Bermejo and J. León suggest that certain cultural factors led to the easy adoption of Old World cultivars in the New World: "Certain non-American plants contained colours with a symbolic importance and, moreover, coincided with the food habits of the indigenous peoples."[9] In this great "exchange" of germplasm, farming techniques, traditions, people, and microbes, many foods, habits, and traditions also vanished or were systematically wiped out, along with the people who died in its wake. Hernández Bermejo and León continue, "In the tropics, deserts, or temperate zones, not even the peasant farmers have any recollection of certain plants that were once cultivated."[10] Thus both the seeds (and their DNA) and even the memory of those seeds and their fruits are long gone, revealing the importance of memory and biodiversity and practice. The chayote, for example, apparently leaves little or no trace in the archaeological record. ("Its fleshy fruit . . . does not allow it to be preserved and, as far as is known, no pollen grains or other structure of this species have been identified on archaeological sites.")[11] We still eat the chayote today, but its origins are difficult to trace.[12]

Not only do we remember and forget specific foods, but we remember and forget stories attached to them—often stories of violence, loss, and death, which disappear over decades and centuries as these foods become fond memories of childhood and anticipation of pleasure for many people. Planting, preserving, and cultivating plants and preparing the food they supply can be a tool of resistance and survival. Soul food and the African American culinary traditions from which it emerged, discussed below, exemplify these multiple meanings. The combination of African and North American foods (e.g., black-eyed peas, collards, grits, and okra) that arose out of the cultural clash surrounding slavery became a source both of strength and of pleasure. Popularized and celebrated by chefs like Edna Lewis and, more recently, Bryant Terry, it remains very much a part of American diets.[13]

Four plants are particularly illustrative of these intersections of massive global change and edible memory: cassava, peppers, beans, and potatoes. Cassava is a crop that captures much of this dynamic: it is intimately connected to slavery and an integral element of regional food cultures in South America, Africa, and Asia. Nowhere in my research did I come across the notion of "heirloom" cassava.[14] Yet 230 million metric tons of cassava are grown worldwide each year.[15] Cassava "was berated as being as tasteless as sawdust by the Europeans, but it played a major role in the conquest of the New World by the military and the religious."[16] The authors of *Neglected Crops* write of the "numerous cultivars of cassava . . . and cultivars of numerous fruit species, [that] remained in the region as disquieting reminders of what the diet had been like before contact had been made with the Amazonian peoples."[17] Cassava, in other words, when read properly, can tell a story of cataclysmic changes in populations. Its origins lie in the Amazon, but once loaded into the holds of European ships, it quickly spread, becoming a staple of many global cuisines as well as a more processed additive to all kinds of foods. Estimates of cassava domestication range from two thousand to seven thousand years ago—it is an ancient food, and largely impervious to bad weather and pests.[18] Cassava has a long history in the United States in some respects, but it gained popularity here much later with migrants from Puerto Rico, Cuba, Brazil, Nigeria, and other places. It is an essential element of many of the world's cuisines (especially Brazilian and West African), as well as being eaten in many immigrant communities in the United States, yet it is not part of any mainstream heirloom movement. For some it is exotic fare, for others it is pleasant but familiar. Context matters immensely, and the widely differing interpretations of this simple root remind us that one person's heirloom may be another's daily bread, or else an unfamiliar (and perhaps unappealing) exotic.

One example of the code switching that can happen with food is the set of meanings attached to cassava (also known as manioc and *farinha*) in Bahia, Brazil. Geographer Susan Paulson found that Brazilians often see cassava as an African crop, even though the plant is actually indigenous to Brazil. As early as the sixteenth century, Portuguese traders brought cassava to Africa, where it quickly (and literally) took root. Cassava came "back" to Brazil as provisions in the holds of ships carrying enslaved men and women, and it was grown on the *rocados*, the plots where enslaved people in Brazil grew their own food.[19] Furthermore, Paulson finds that as valued and meaningful as cassava is among some members of Brazil's population (in the form of *farinha*, or cassava meal), particularly Bahians who are descendants of those enslaved African populations, "Brazilian magazines sometimes deplore *farinha* as empty calories that produce slothful unshapely bodies, variously associating eating 'excessive' *farinha* with disease, poverty, ruralness, darkness." So manioc has multiple meanings—sloth or strength, degenerative or sustaining, and becomes a way to embrace or disparage a particular group identity.[20] Eaten on both sides of the Atlantic, cassava was a staple of the slave trade and plantation systems.[21]

Less calorically significant than cassava—but still a vital source of nutrients, flavor, and symbolism—is the pepper. *The Oxford Companion to American Food and Drink* describes the early and swift geographic spread of peppers: "The chiles for Spanish and Hungarian paprikas arrived in their respective countries, well before 1600, by very different routes. Spain's were brought, by Columbus and later navigators, from the Caribbean, Mexico, and Peru. Hungary's arrived overland via Ottoman Turks, who got them from Arab and Indian traders, who got them from Portuguese navigators, who in turn got them from what is now Bahia, Brazil," and all in the space of a few decades.[22] Peppers are essential to many food cultures, a part of identity, a part of what it means to feel nourished, full, alive, or loved. They inspire passionate devotion in the most disparate corners of the globe.[23] Festivals and fans honor them, a significance that bears little relation to the lack of newspaper coverage of "heirloom" peppers in food writing in the United States. They are worthy of many books on their own, and other writers have discussed them in depth.

Sustaining Beans

Beans are just beans, all with similar molecular structure, but they take on widely varying symbolic and cultural, culinary, and botanical forms—snap, shell, dry, or field, fava or broad (*Vicia faba*), lima or butter, runner, soy, or tepary (*Phaseolus acutifolius*), for example. Beans are fundamental to global culinary traditions, reaching back not only centuries (as many of the more common heirloom fruits and vegetables do) but millennia. And there are both New World beans (like the varieties of *Phaseolus vulgaris*, tepary, kidney, and lima beans) and Old World beans (or pulses) like fava beans, chickpeas, and lentils, all firmly entrenched in regional economies, habits, identities, and religious beliefs long before the Columbian Exchange. Within the Aztec and Inca empires, kidney beans served as a form of tribute, for example.[24] The variety and significance of beans as staples around the world mean that their story is intricate and almost limitless.[25] Their nutritional significance may partially explain the attention they receive.[26]

Beans are vital and diverse components of seed banks across the country (and the world), packing a lot of nutritional bang for the buck.[27] Dry beans receive by far the most attention in coverage of heirloom vegetables in popular food writing. The origin stories of beans also receive more attention than those of any other heirloom vegetables. In popular food writing, they were mentioned in the context of restaurants and home cooking as well as shopping, seeds, and gardening. People describe their beauty and the often subtle variations in flavor. These beans get described in vivid language, with emphasis on color and shape: "Many customers are seduced by the heirloom beans' extraordinary beauty. Displayed in big woven baskets . . . they are as alluring as glittering jewels."[28] Heirloom beans then began appearing in restaurants as well. "Chez Panisse Café in Berkeley, Calif., has doubled its use of beans in the last five years," a writer in the *New York Times* noted in 1989.[29]

Cultivation of beans in the New World began sometime between 7000 and 3000 BCE, and according to *The Oxford Companion to American Food and Drink*, dishes developed millennia ago "are recognizable as part of U.S. culinary heritage."[30] That in itself is a more complicated concept than it may seem at first glance. Indeed, the question of what constitutes American culinary heritage runs throughout this book. This is also one of the relatively few instances where the timing of an heirloom can go back much further than the nineteenth century. Beans can evoke Aztec, Anasazi, and other native North American culinary cultures. Four species of *Phaseolus* had been domesticated in the New World, including the tepary bean, which dates back to at least 3000 BCE.[31] Today the website of Native Seeds/SEARCH lists common, fava, lima, runner, and tepary beans, a mix of indigenous varieties and more recent arrivals—a total of 115 varieties.[32] Seed Savers Exchange offers dozens of beans, and Slow Food lists twenty-two varieties in its Ark of Taste.[33] In most of these cases the beans have been collected with stories attached, as in the case of the O'odham Pink: "The O'odham Pink Bean is a bush bean native to the desert borderlands of Sonora and Arizona. This bean has been an important resource for the O'odham people since the early eighteenth century. Reports from the early 1900s indicate that, as a staple crop of the Tohono O'odham, nearly two million pounds were produced annually. Unfortunately, this highly cherished crop—that was once widely cultivated across the southwest—has few remaining producers."[34] A different model for seed preservation (and consumption) is Rancho Gordo, which offers cooking beans for sale: "The origin of individual beans can be tricky but most Rancho Gordo beans are new world crops, meaning they are indigenous to the Americas. Many of them are close to extinction. All of them are delicious and easy to prepare."[35]

One story in particular is frequently invoked with respect to beans, in newspapers, magazines, and books: the bean called Cherokee Trail of Tears. As one reporter recounts, "Like so many heirloom vegetables, it has a story. In 1838, Cherokee Indians were rounded up by the federal government and relocated from Alabama, Georgia, North Carolina and Tennessee to Oklahoma. More than 4,000 Cherokee died from disease, hunger and exhaustion during the trek. The Indians took the bean with them and planted it the next spring. From then on, it's shared the name of the journey."[36] The bean has been included in Slow Food's Ark of Taste: "The Cherokee Trail of Tears bean memorializes the forced relocation of the Cherokee Indians in the mid-nineteenth century. They carried this bean throughout this infamous walk, which became the death march for thousands of Cherokees; hence the 'Trail of Tears.' In the face of its poignantly dismal history, the shiny, jet-black seeds are used with pride in many traditional American Indian dishes."[37] In 2000, Martha Stewart even called on her readers to "re-plant history with heirloom seeds," asking, "Would you like to grow the same corn that was carried by the Cherokees over the Trail of Tears? How about tomatoes cultivated by Shakers in Pittsfield, Mass., or thousand-year-old beans that were found in a cave in Utah?"[38] Stewart explicitly offers her readers a connection to the past through cultivating and eating seeds with histories. This is precisely what I mean when I talk about eating other people's memories. The recurrent invocation of the Trail of Tears, as well as the popularity of something like Carolina Gold rice (a variety of rice that was cultivated in South Carolina with enslaved labor and is now being planted and sold online and in restaurants), also underscores that the stories attached to heirloom foods are not always stories of triumph or happiness, but can also recall suffering and struggle.[39]

In an article about heirloom New World beans in 1984, the "guerrilla gardener" being interviewed talks of growing "pre-Columbian beans . . . you can taste exactly what your ancestors did when they came to America."[40] But whose ancestors? This is a common approach in much of the coverage of heirlooms—writers sometimes presume (often correctly) that much of their audience has little experience with the vegetable being described. This case implies an audience of immigrants, or rather descendants of immigrants. In fact, these beans are also the flavors experienced by the ancestors of many people whose roots on this continent go back millennia rather than centuries.

This assumption gets to the heart of the complexity of the word "heirloom" as used to describe vegetables. Whose heirlooms are these? If beans come to be carriers of collective memory, whose collective memories are they? On one hand, some writing on the subject presents heirloom food as exotic, even if it is quite familiar to people in a particular community or tradition. The urban garden plots and kitchen tables, backyards and cooking pots of this country are full of all kinds of fruits and vegetables that might be considered heirlooms based on the definition of them as deriving from non-hybrid seeds predating the mid-twentieth century. Yet they rarely receive the heirloom label. On the other hand, mainstream descriptions of heirloom vegetables largely or entirely ignore a huge amount of vegetable life.

Sacred and Frightening Potatoes

Pink tomatoes and blue potatoes may be heirloom varieties, but for me they were once completely unfamiliar. The first time I roasted a pan of blue potatoes from the farmers' market, I was delighted not only by the visual departure from a lifetime of russets, Yukon Golds, and reds, but also by the unfamiliar tastes and textures shining through the olive oil and herbs covering the chunks of potatoes. Today blue potatoes are relatively easy to find in supermarkets and farmers' markets, but shoppers in the United States still have available only a small fraction of the world's potato biodiversity. (There are approximately four thousand edible potato varieties, many of them preserved at the International Potato Centre in Peru.)[41]

The potatoes to be found at the supermarket and the farmers' market are simply the latest stage in millennia of potato transformations.[42] Anthropologist Sophie Coe reports that "travelers visiting Peruvian markets today see a range of potato varieties undreamed of in their homelands. The tastes and textures vary as much as the looks, and Peruvians consider our commercial potatoes watery, insipid, and boring."[43] Potatoes were so important to the spiritual and physical sustenance of the Inca (and continue to be so in contemporary Peru and neighboring countries) that they appear in sacred ceramics, and were grown up and down the Andes, as early as 8000 BCE.[44]

Potatoes were changed by arriving in Europe and being carried from there to North America, where they changed again. The year 1573 brings the first documented reference to potatoes in Europe, in Seville.[45] Carolus Clusius, a European humanist who was the overseer of several botanical gardens, brought potatoes (and tulips!) to the Netherlands in 1590,[46] and potatoes were planted at the Seitenstetten Abbey in Austria as early as 1620 and in Alsace by 1660.[47] The potato did not really take hold in Europe as a whole until the eighteenth or even the nineteenth century. But like maize, it was locally successful at earlier dates. In 1720 Friedrich Wilhelm I of Prussia ordered farmers to plant potatoes, but they resisted.[48] "Sometimes potato advocacy was backed by force: Austrian peasants were threatened with forty lashes if they refused to embrace it."[49] By one account, when potatoes were introduced in the Austro-Hungarian Empire, they had to be guarded by soldiers so that the farmers would not rip them out of the ground at night. Another version of the soldiers guarding potatoes story reports that Prussian Emperor Frederick the Great tried to get local farmers interested in planting potatoes by posting guards around fields planted with potatoes.[50] What European peasant in the eighteenth century wanted to plant potatoes? This was for many of them an untested crop imported from far away, with a reputation for being poisonous (thanks to its resemblance to the deadly nightshade, as well as the actual ill effects of eating potatoes that had turned green in the sunlight), but it took hold in some places much earlier than others, and made slow progress across the continent, particularly in places where the soil did not support abundant grain harvests. At one point potatoes were even planted for their foliage rather than their tubers. Antoine-Augustin Parmentier, a French chemist and pharmacist, is credited with bringing potatoes to France in 1760, having been exposed to them as food for humans (rather than food for livestock) while held captive by the Prussians. He later convinced Marie Antoinette of their value to the point where she wore potato flowers in her hair, and in 1787 a feast at Versailles was dedicated to the potato.[51] Potatoes gained popularity in France so quickly that they were planted in the Tuileries gardens during the Revolution, outliving Marie Antoinette and their other royal champions.[52]

The potato, then, found some of its first European fans in the monasteries of Europe and later made its way onto the tables of the nobility. It was centuries after it first arrived on European shores that it then became such an essential component of the broader European diet. Karl Marx himself wrote about the scabby potatoes that served as the primary nourishment for the urban proletariat in mid-nineteenth-century Europe. There are many stories about potatoes' being planted in prominent urban spaces in times of trouble and hunger—in the Tuileries during the French Revolution but also, more recently, in Vienna's Heroes' Square or on the Mall in Washington, DC, during World War II. Potatoes grew in importance during the Napoleonic Wars in the early nineteenth century, according to journalist Tom Standage, as they began to shed their reputation as either poison or animal fodder: "The potato made slow progress in the following years, being consumed only by the very rich (it was prized by some aristocratic gardeners and was served as a novelty) and the very poor (it became a staple food among the poor, first in Ireland, and then in parts of England, France, the Low Countries, the Rhineland and Prussia)."[53]

The way New World crops get adopted in Europe has a lot to tell us about edible memory, how people over centuries, decades, or even just a few years incorporate a new food into their most precious traditions. The example of the potato's first being grown in Europe as a "botanical curiosity" is a prime instance of a whole continent of people learning to like something, a change that occurs with many foods beyond fruits and vegetables.[54] Colonialism and empire contribute to these changing tastes. In England, for example, "the ships that sailed for Canada, Jamaica and Australia were laden with Sheffield knives and Lancashire cloth, and returned with holds full of wheat, sugar and wool."[55] That imported sugar and wheat became integral to the English diet and also to conceptions of what it meant to be English. Potatoes, once so feared, were later popularized in India by the colonizing British, according to Lizzie Collingham's research on curry: "How the potato came to India is unclear. The Portuguese or Dutch may have brought the first specimens to the subcontinent, but they were unusual enough in 1780 for the governor-general Warren Hastings to invite his fellow council members to join him for dinner when he was given a basket of potatoes by the Dutch."[56] As Collingham notes, potatoes, tomatoes, and other New World foods are now essential ingredients in Indian cooking.

People learn to like and then love something they (or their ancestors) once feared and hated. Something that was sacred and fundamental in Peru turns into something fancy (Marie Antoinette with potato flowers in her hair), then essential. Other people's memories become memories for a new group of people. For centuries the "progress" of potatoes across Europe—and out of the category of botanical curiosity and into daily life—was plodding and slow. After much resistance, the potato became a fundamental element of European eating habits. Potatoes play a deeply mixed role in Irish national identity, in particular, but they are also central components of cuisine from England to Croatia and beyond.

The production and consumption of potatoes have changed significantly over the twentieth century and into the twenty-first. The area of agricultural land planted in potatoes in Austria, for example, dropped in the twentieth century, from 215,562 hectares in 1937 to 31,000 hectares in 1993 (partly as people began feeding pigs grain rather than potatoes).[57] Similar changes have occurred in the United States. According to James Lang's very informative *Notes of a Potato Watcher*, the USDA found "several thousand varieties" of potatoes in the United States in 1909, but by 2001 half of the potatoes grown in the United States were Russet Burbanks.[58]

More recently, however, interest in preserving old varieties of potatoes has grown in Europe, the United States, and South America.[59] Potatoes have even become the subject of books, films, and museums: in Lower Austria, there is a Potato Museum devoted in part to Pfarrer Johann Jungblut, an early potato advocate. In northern Germany, farmer Karsten Ellenberg specializes in growing old-fashioned potatoes. He began the project in 1997 and today offers his customers 20 types of potatoes and grows 150 varieties. He has developed his own varieties, and he also grows the controversial "Linda" potato. The potato's original breeder wanted to pull it from the market after thirty years, to make way for newer and more profitable varieties, but Ellenberg and other farmers insisted on continuing to grow it. The case is still unresolved.[60] Other people continue to grow the Lumper, which failed with such tragic results in nineteenth-century Ireland, leading to famine. As Stocks explains, "The idea of growing something that was responsible—albeit indirectly—for the deaths of a million people may seem faintly distasteful, but the Lumper potato has such an extraordinary history it surely deserves to be preserved."[61]

American Food

"What is American food?" asks Andrew Smith in *The Oxford Companion to American Food and Drink*. "Is it traditional foodstuffs, such as maize, beans, squash, domesticated in the Americas? Is it warmed-over British fare, such as meat, potatoes, puddings, and sandwiches? Or perhaps special holiday treats—turkey, cranberries, corn on the cob, candied sweet potatoes, or Christmas cookies? Is it ethnic foods brought by continuous waves of immigrants—tacos, pizza, spaghetti, and fortune cookies—bastardized in America?" Smith goes on to ask if it is represented by fast food, processed food, California cuisine, cookbooks, or the Food Network.[62] Asking, "What is American food?" also means asking what it is to be American. Food is at the heart of personal and national identity, and it is deeply connected to memory.[63] Inevitably, it is thus a rich source for the study of collective memory and identity, whether of farms and fields, school lunches, or historical kitchen gardens. This kind of memory is simultaneously very personal and intricately connected to political and economic structures. These memories of food, whether we are eating other people's memories or our own, have tangible consequences.

Vegetables move, but people move too, and immigration can provide stark changes in habits, as well as a longing for the familiar.[64] Seeds themselves are inherently mobile, easily transported by birds, humans, and the wind. So food, and especially old-fashioned plant varieties and animal breeds, may be intertwined with the history of a specific place or region but may also tell us stories of migration and global journeys. Many of the "heirloom" varieties now making a comeback in the United States have long histories of mobility; some were sewn into immigrants' hatbands and skirt hems. But in the language of popular books and newspapers, there are basically no tropical heirloom foods. Only rarely do broad categories of South Asian, Southeast Asian, Chinese, or Japanese vegetables get called heirlooms in Western media. The more closely I looked at newspaper articles, books, and seed catalogs, the more I noticed these contours and silences in the kinds of foods, places, and histories accorded the heirloom label. Yet there is another way to think about this: when you look a little deeper, heirloom varieties are everywhere.[65]

Chinese cooking, for example, has been present in the United States since at least the mid-nineteenth century, but very few Chinese vegetables appear in the heirloom categories in popular food writing. From the 1850s until the passage of the Exclusion Act in 1882, there was substantial immigration to the United States by Chinese men.[66] Given the immigration of so many Chinese men, as well as the direct role many of them played in food production, it seems there should be much more of a Chinese legacy in the ranks of heirloom vegetables as they started farms and gardens in California, planted in part with fruits and vegetables from home.[67] As work on the railroads in the Los Angeles area dried up, for example, many former track workers began farming on the outskirts of the city and sold produce first by horse-drawn carts, and then at the market established in the old Los Angeles city plaza. Indeed, "in the days before refrigerated railroad cars, Chinese vegetable peddlers were the principal source of fresh produce in the city of Los Angeles."[68] Chinese food was Americanized by the late nineteenth and early twentieth centuries, which presumably had an effect on vegetable production as well.[69] Immigration laws have direct consequences for food patterns.[70] The 1982 book by George and Nancy Marcus, *Forbidden Fruits and Forgotten Vegetables*, intentionally omits "the entire range of peculiarly Oriental foods—winter melon, lotus root, burdock, and the like—as these are dealt with at greater length in other cookbooks."[71] These categories presume habits and tastes based on country of origin, even in an immigrant nation and long after key moments of immigration. That particular book is really a collection of recipes, where "we have also included a number of fruits and vegetables that are actually abundant here; neglected by most Americans these are generally used within certain groups or locales—collards by Southerners, dandelions by Italians, celery root by those of northern European stock."[72]

In *Forbidden Fruits*, the Marcuses set out to learn how to enjoy and prepare these forbidden and forgotten foods, literally eating other people's memories. The authors bring together an eclectic mix of what they see as "ethnic, exotic, and neglected produce."[73] Many things are surprising about this passage, in light of what many of us can find in our local supermarket today. They write as white Euro-Americans, setting out to explore the foods of nonwhite and somehow non-American people and places, but foods that in fact were already very American in the sense that the foods of new arrivals to this country have always constituted American eating.[74] In the early 1980s the Marcuses found that "it is not uncommon now to see kale and mangoes vying with corn and tomatoes in produce bins, not just in specialty shops and ethnic groceries but in chain stores as well."[75] The novelty of mangoes and kale for these authors, and the widespread familiarity of these two foods for so many people in the United States today, illustrates the significant changes in the fates of particular foods in a relatively short time. In the changing popularity of particular vegetables, we observe the move from being exotic to being familiar, the imprint of ethnicity and immigration, and the experience of eating other people's memories.[76]

Similarly, in 1986 Elizabeth Schneider released a 546-page book, *Uncommon Fruits and Vegetables: A Commonsense Guide*, meant to "guide you through the burgeoning produce section." She explicitly sees these "uncommon" foods as connected to the immigrants who brought them to the United States. "Taxonomic classification changes as the science does: the appearance of a chromosome or two, the discovery of a hidden ovule will move a plant from one grouping to another." Common names are often confusing (and change considerably from one region to the next), but even the more reliable binomial classifications are not written in stone.[77] Arugula is the first full entry, a strong indicator of the changes that have occurred in the nearly thirty years since the publication of that thorough guide to "uncommon" foods, many of which have since become common—and, for many Americans, were already quite common in the 1980s.

Corn and tomatoes themselves were once terribly exotic to people in Europe, Asia, and Africa. Likewise the very fruits and vegetables the Marcuses or Schneider single out as exotic are someone else's childhood memories. This is not a criticism of these authors, but note how the description is written from a particular perspective: they refer to "our mothers," the mothers of the authors, as being unfamiliar with this produce: "It would never have occurred to our mothers to serve dandelions or bake with persimmons, to buy papayas or fry plantains, although the former could have been seen downtown in Italian markets and the latter bought uptown in Spanish bodegas."[78] But plenty of mothers (and fathers!) in the United States were cooking plantains and serving dandelions at the time, just within smaller communities and often with relatively recent immigration in their background. Most of what journalists, activists, gardeners, and others call heirlooms arrived in the United States precisely through immigration.

People immigrating bring with them not only seeds but also gardening techniques, appetites, and traditions. The German "farmer's garden" typically planted by the so-called Pennsylvania Dutch, a "rural kitchen garden, enclosed, divided into quadrants, and usually featuring raised beds," came with a specific approach to cooking the things it produced.[79] These can be small worlds of longing and hope, and attempts to mitigate displacement.[80] The seeds, seedlings, and saplings immigrants carried to the United States are now fundamental elements of American cooking, with a widespread (if also often highly regional) presence in farmers' markets and grocery stores targeted to particular immigrant groups.

In the United States these connections between food and memory are necessarily multicultural, in part because the layers of Native American agriculture and culinary traditions were also so varied, and in part because of the almost frenetic movement of species and varieties up and down the Americas and back and forth across the Atlantic and the Pacific in the seventeenth, eighteenth, and nineteenth centuries. Particular peppers, tomatoes, or apples leapfrog over large expanses of land and sea, following the routes of individual conquistadores or entrepreneurs. In the Chesapeake region, "Native Americans grew corn, sweet potatoes, melons, and a variety of squash and beans. They harvested strawberries, blackberries, persimmons, acorns, hickory nuts, and black walnuts, and hunted deer, turkeys, and small game. They also ate oysters, crabs, and fish."[81]

Gardening was very popular in nineteenth-century America, and there are distinct regional garden styles from this era.[82] Southern gardens, for example, "have many cultural influences as part of their gardening history. Native Americans, Spanish explorers, French missionary priests, African-Americans, and British settlers" contributed to this variety, and "black-eyed peas, millet, okra, peanuts, rice, and yams are all African foods that became part of Southern cooking."[83] Kitchen gardens used to be essential, close to a matter of life and death, and they also shaped people's lives with seasonal agricultural work.[84] Gentlemen gardeners, however, also created new varieties, and some are today considered heirloom plants. William Woys Weaver finds a great array of European, American (in the sense of the continents of North and South America), and African plants in nineteenth-century US kitchen gardens.[85] One of the great joys of heirloom vegetables in the United States is the sheer diversity of the seeds themselves, and of the culinary and regional traditions with which they are interwoven.

Ramps and pawpaws, two staples of contemporary trendsetting restaurants, were key elements of this regional cooking. Having grown up myself with no knowledge of ramps or most other foraged foods, I even took a cooking class about wild foods—the same ramps, morels, nettles, and lambs' quarters eaten with seasonal regularity and no hint of trendiness by so many of my fellow Americans, albeit well out of the mainstream until relatively recently.

Some of the food cultures of North America are older than some current European food cultures. Moreover, there is a deep regionalism to American food, as well as an inherently multicultural quality. This is partly why the idea of stable food culture can seem incomplete. Reverence for stable food culture can also imply a reverence for a perceived homogeneity in a given population (also overlooking the heterogeneity of many European countries). Food in the United States is an inherently hybrid affair. But so too is much European food—the highly international foods that formed the cooking of the Austro-Hungarian Empire, for example. In fact this complexity is the essence of food cultures— varying degrees of change over time, relationships between memory, identity, territory, and botany that, in any given generation or era, can mask their distant origins and come to seem timeless and essential. The meanings of these foods are deep, but also changeable.

Mobility and meaning, memory and disappearance are all exemplified in the story of diverse African American culinary (and particularly vegetable) traditions. Much of this food constitutes some of the oldest agricultural imports to North America. African and African American foods are utterly fundamental to American food. *The Oxford Companion to American Food and Drink* separates the history of African American food into two distinct eras—the African origins in the seventeenth to nineteenth century, then subsequent changes in the United States. The book says of this earlier era and its origins:

> Yams were the staple of the Ashanti, the Yoruba, and the Ibo; plantain (and later cassava) was favored by the tribes of the Congo and Angola; rice, millet, and eventually maize pleased the tribes of present-day Senegambia, Sierra Leone, Ivory Coast, and Liberia . . . sorghum, black-eyed peas, sesame seeds, Bambara groundnuts, eggplant, okra, spinach, cabbage, kidney beans, mushrooms, onions, maize, tomatoes, mustard greens, collard greens, lima beans, cucumbers, sugar cane, sweet potatoes, bananas, lemons, mangoes, limes, peaches, coconuts, watermelons, wild game, wild ducks, goats, pigs, chicken, guinea hens, cattle, shrimp, cod, flounder, catfish, crab, salt, Melegueta pepper, coriander,

ginger, saffron, thyme, sage, sweet basil, mint, parsley, curry, hazelnuts, and kola nuts.[86]

This list of well-established foods in the African (particularly West African) diet reflects significant movements of edible plants across great stretches of the globe.[87] Maize, tomatoes, peppers, and lima beans all found their way from the Americas to West Africa and had become entrenched in African gardens, farms, and cooking by the time the horrors of the slave trade began in earnest. Conversely, African vegetables have been in North America for almost four centuries. Furthermore,

> the South's penchant for deep frying and for boiling, its way with confections (sugar was a status symbol), its emphasis on leafy greens, its use of sweet potatoes, peanuts, peppery sauces and spices and even the introduction of ingredients such as okra and sesame seeds were African driven. Many Southern foods and recipes also can be traced straight to the earliest British colonists in Virginia, where the region's native population introduced settlers to corn (the source of grits and hominy), berries, beans, peas, squash and wild greens, as well as the abundance of native animals and seafood, from wild turkeys to oysters. But no group has had a greater hand in Southern cuisine than Africans, who brought with them foods, techniques and spices, and used them liberally.[88]

Edna Lewis (and, later, with Scott Peacock) played an important role in bringing southern cooking to other parts of the United States.[89] In their obituary of Lewis, who died in 2006 at the age of eighty-nine, Eric Asimov and Kim Severson describe her as "the granddaughter of a former slave whose cookbooks revived the nearly forgotten genre of refined Southern cooking while offering a glimpse into African-American farm life in the early 20th century."[90] The Southern Foodways Alliance and the Southern Seed Legacy work, in quite different ways, to both preserve and publicize Southern cooking and gardening. And products like Anson Mills grits appear in expensive restaurants, but also connected to projects of culinary and botanical preservation. Clearly much is going on away from the mainstream, in backyards and roadside restaurants, even after Southern food is receiving a growing amount of scholarly and popular attention.

Various African food cultures took root and formed foundations for highly regional cuisines like the Gullah-Geechee rice table of the Carolina lowlands and Sea Islands, and the Creole dishes of Louisiana. Gumbo, for example, has deep African roots, but possibly also Choctaw influence.[91] And it is important to remember the influence of the Caribbean on North American food, in part as a crossroads between Europe, Africa, and South America. Cooking in the United States owes much to the Caribbean and to the movement of European, South American, and African food cultures through the Caribbean and into North America.[92] Much later, "with the civil rights movement of the 1950s and 1960s, 'soul food' became an interest for white liberal cooks, although segregationists in the South had enjoyed a modified version for more than a century."[93] Some argue that the concept of soul food is in many ways a northern invention.[94]

Other legumes, like cowpeas, are essential to African diasporic cuisine—the foods eaten in Africa and in places around the world where many people of African descent live today, including (but not limited to) the Garifuna in Central America, much of the population of Brazil, and the United States. This bean takes the westward route of the Columbian Exchange, moving from Old World to New World in the holds of ships, often as they carried African men and women into the New World and generations of slavery. The cowpea (*Vigna unguiculata* L. Walp.) is "an annual legume . . . also commonly referred to as southern pea, blackeye [*sic*] pea, crowder pea, lubia, niebe, coupe or frijole. Cowpea originated in Africa and is widely grown in Africa, Latin America, Southeast Asia and in the southern United States."[95] A dish like hoppin' John, based on cowpeas, contains layers of history and memory. These layers include the genotype of the black-eyed peas themselves, originating in Africa and changing slowly after arrival in the Americas. The dish eaten today—at home and in restaurants across the country, including places like Marcus Samuelson's Red Rooster—involved centuries of acquiring the taste for it, of linking hoppin' John to memories of home, both physical and emotional sustenance, and enjoyment.[96] The bean was carried in the holds of slave ships as a provision along with yams, maize, and other relatively long-lived staples. The cowpea was planted in Jamaica and other earlier plantation settings, then grown widely in the American South, moving from the cooking pots of enslaved men and women to the tables of white southerners as well. As Judith Carney recounts,

Among the celebrated foodways of the Americas are many which evolved in former plantation societies. *Hoppin' John*, *jambalaya*, and *gumbo* are as emblematic of the US South as the pepper pot stews and bitter greens are of the Caribbean, salt fish and ackee of Jamaica, and the palm-oil flavored dishes and bean fritters of Bahia . . . but there is relatively little attention to the fact that African ingredients give these foodways their distinctive culinary signatures. The accent on rice and bean dishes, okra, collards, sorrel, palm oil, black-eyed and pigeon peas, ackee and other African foods compels serious consideration of the ways these food staples arrived and gained legitimacy in plantation societies.[97]

Hoppin' John also comes about from the knowledge of preparation techniques—rubbing off the skins, balancing seasonings, cooking times, and so on. These layers, for this or any other traditional dish, also include the knowledge of growing and preparation techniques and contain the traces of African culinary practices and their refraction through slavery and the New World. Originally cooked over the hearths of enslaved men and women, the dish also found its way far beyond these spaces, even into fancy restaurants and glossy cookbooks.[98] Indeed, hoppin' John encapsulates much of the shifting (and persistence) of meanings and uses that can happen as food moves through both time and space.[99]

Judith Carney found that, contrary to more recent scholarship, many European writers of the time credited enslaved men and women with importing African foods to the New World.[100] More than thirty-five thousand voyages took place carrying enslaved people across the Atlantic.[101] Each of these voyages necessarily involved carrying large quantities of provisions in the holds of the ships. Carney discusses the importance of enslaved people growing their own food, although with little time and space (67). African foods were also quickly adopted by Native Americans living close to plantations, and vice versa, knitting together cooking traditions in ways that shape how many Americans eat today (68). African women in particular began cultivating and cooking African foods on this new continent, bringing African techniques of cultivation and preparation, and incorporating available North American foods as well. These foods may also have been sold at markets or integrated into plantation kitchens (73). "In such ways, and with little historical commentary, African crops and food products stealthily made their way into the kitchens and onto the plates served to planters and their families. Enslaved Africans and their descendants left culinary fingerprints throughout the Americas that are often forgotten" (74). Indeed, "the basic need for sustenance, and access to land on which to produce it, gave Africans and their New World descendants the opportunity to reconstitute in part familiar foodways and with it, memory dishes that would serve to remind them of the societies they had been forced to leave. Today these foodways are experienced by white and black alike as regional cuisines, creolized signatures of the historical confluence of foods and peoples from three continents."[102]

The story of the calas, a kind of fritter, also exemplifies these changes in meaning across time and space. "The name . . . is almost certainly African, deriving from a series of cowpea-based fritters generally called 'akara' or 'akra' (sometimes 'akla') in West Africa, and 'acras' in much of the Afro-Caribbean diasporas, but 'callas' in Curaçao. The beans are soaked and the skins are painstakingly rubbed off to give the fritters a pure white color. In Trinidad and Haiti, salt-cod fritters—also snow white—also are called acras. The lengthy description in the *Picayune's Creole Cook Book* noted that in former (perhaps slavery) times, the calas women pounded the rice in mortars, an African technique."[103] So this is a mixture of seeds (genotype), processing and cooking techniques, and a change of language, technique, and ingredients across time and space. Bryant Terry, author of several vegan cookbooks devoted to soul food and other African diasporic culinary practices, says that "many African-Americans in generations past would enjoy [diets] replete with these nutrient-dense leafy greens—collards, mustards, turnips, dandelion greens, legumes such as butter beans and black-eyed peas."[104] These eating habits were certainly born in part of poverty and hard times, but also became anchors of meaningful and pleasurable cuisines.

The trajectory of soul food and its predecessors is in part a case of eating other people's memories, from the Old World to the New World, through the slave trade, to cooking traditions in the US South, moving northward to current popularity.[105] Not only cooking techniques but also specific vegetables become associated with particular culinary and horticultural traditions in the United States.[106] For example, "closely identified in America with the South, okra is a vegetable with a long history and strong culinary traditions on five continents," including being cultivated by the ancient Egyptians.[107] Okra and gumbo, linguistically, have their origins in West Africa, reflecting the connection of this vegetable to the slave trade. My white mother, raised in a modest house in affluent Pacific Palisades, has distinct memories of eating canned okra as an accompaniment to her own mother's very mainstream 1950s cooking.

For all the often justifiable hand-wringing that goes on about the contemporary American diet, the foods, and seeds, available in the United States are incredibly diverse. This diversity is certainly not equally accessible to all, and overall it is not taken advantage of as widely as it might be, but nonetheless there is a culinary richness and diversity in the United States, due in part to immigrant gardening and cooking habits and in part to the native cultivars like corn, squash, and New World beans and the cooking and cultivation practices associated with them. Stable food cultures are not as stable as they might appear. Many of us end up eating other people's memories, and over time those memories become our own. The unfamiliar becomes not only familiar, but beloved. In turn, the familiar may become unfamiliar, even inaccessible. The twin properties of novelty and nostalgia, familiarity and the exotic are at work.

Vegetal Europe

In addition to the global scope of the Columbian Exchange, and the anchoring of African foods in American cooking, we can see less cataclysmic but still striking changes in the fates of particular vegetables within Europe from the Roman era to today. Those peas, for example, that many of us now unthinkingly pull out of the freezer, either to thaw for dinner or to ice a sore joint, were once the talk of Paris, all the rage among eighteenth-century French aristocrats.[108] Kale—widely popular and high status in both the United States and Europe today—was long the food of the poor in Scotland.

Tastes change with migration patterns and the rise and fall of empires, as well as with the development of new technologies and agricultural practices, marketing schemes, and economic eras.[109] Immigrant communities may, in turn, change the tastes of the receiving country or region—Italian food, Chinese food, and sushi are now integral parts of

Americans' eating habits.[110] Curry in England or kebabs in Germany become part of people's daily lives and arguably part of the national cuisine. Change can also be instigated by large corporations that spend considerable money, time, and energy to give us an appetite for what they produce or sell.

Or change can come from French queens and Prussian emperors pushing the European populace to eat something unsettlingly unfamiliar, even frightening—the potato. Or consider the French colonial power in Vietnam attempting to persuade people to trade rice for baguettes that could be baked in central ovens rather than using the individual fires built for each family's pot of rice (as Calvin Trillin wryly expressed it, the *banh mi*, the now-classic Vietnamese sandwich on a baguette, is "the only good argument for colonialism").[111] Other tastemaking campaigns include Heritage Food USA's work to popularize the heritage turkeys so carefully preserved by a handful of small-scale poultry farmers, or attempts by Jamie Oliver, Alice Waters, Michelle Obama, and many others to cultivate a taste for fresh fruit and vegetables among schoolchildren (and their parents).

This vegetal shape-shifting is by no means exclusive to the fast-paced twentieth and twenty-first centuries. In fact it goes back much further. English food writer Jane Grigson finds that "salsify, scorzonera, fennel, celeriac and globe artichokes appeared in all the best vegetable gardens [in the seventeenth] and through the eighteenth century. . . . [T]hey are now ranged at the posh or exotic end of the supermarket counter, and appear only in the most upmarket greengrocers and market stalls."[112] Of course she was writing a few decades ago, and in the meantime fennel and artichokes, at least, have found their way into more and more produce sections and away from the posh end. However, at least in the United States, salsify is still a bit hard to come by, and vegetables continue to be subject to changing appetites, marketing campaigns, and habits.

Simply looking back at *Forbidden Fruits* by George and Nancy Marcus, we can see recipes and explanations of celeriac, chayote, dandelion, fennel, greens (collard, mustard, rape, and turnip), Jerusalem artichoke, kale, mango, okra, papaya, persimmon, plantain, pomegranate, quince, salsify, and Swiss chard.[113] Today it would be hard to call mangoes, Swiss chard, or most of the other fruits and vegetables listed here either forbidden or forgotten. In each section of the book, the authors instruct readers in the history of the fruit or vegetable, but also in the art of choosing the right ones, something that must be taught only if these are fruits and vegetables readers did not grow up with. Many of the "forgotten" foods they list have become much more widely popular in recent years, and all of them were very familiar (and neither forgotten nor exotic) for particular families and communities at the time the book was written (1982). The authors point out that dandelions or papayas would have been familiar to them if they had grown up in Little Italy or Spanish Harlem.

Such changeability is not new. Although European vegetable trends may have been more prevalent among aristocrats and adventurers, the consumption patterns of peasants and factory workers changed over the centuries as well. Many of the culinary traditions that present themselves to us as long-standing (and particularly healthy or illustrious) are often of relatively recent invention—even potatoes and tomatoes go back only a few centuries in European cooking, and two world wars (not to mention countless other uprisings and revolutions) created great ruptures in food cultures and transformations in agricultural practices. Much of the European continent lived off pulses and gruels, diets that bear little resemblance to French haute cuisine or the vibrant flavors of contemporary Italian cooking. For example, "the standard meal of an eighteenth-century German rural labourer," Lizzie Collingham tells us, "was 'gruel and mush,' a soupy combination of grains and lentils. This was typical fare for the rural population throughout Europe. . . . In the eighteenth century three-quarters of all European foods were derived from plants, and even the fat in the diet was drawn predominantly from plant oils." Over the nineteenth century, meat consumption increased, and few Europeans today are eating large quantities of gruel and mush.[114]

Individuals, families, classes, and whole societies acquire—and lose—particular tastes over time. These changes in tastes may come about through intentional marketing schemes and heavy-duty political lobbying, like the dramatic increase in the amount of corn (in processed form) in our diets since the 1970s.[115] They may result from a new technique for processing "baby" carrots, or government campaigns to get us to eat certain foods (often heavily lobbied for) every day. Changes in tastes may also be altered through small alterations in soil and climate, or when an impassioned advocate of turnips or microgreens comes to town.[116] Such tastes can and often do have consequences for biodiversity. Furthermore, observing these changes over time reveals substantial transformations, even in places that appear to many of us to have stable food culture. Something as personal as our taste for a particular vegetable is still nested in the interactions of politics and economics, as well as culture and class.[117] They can also be shaped, in recent years, by the profusion of media about food—television shows (and entire networks), books, blogs, and the like.

Much sociological work has found important connections between taste and class, and the ways tastes for certain objects or experiences are shaped in part by our class backgrounds and play a role not only in reproducing social status, but also in very salient forms of identity.[118] Changing tastes in vegetables are connected to larger societal transformations, whether technological development of processing nitrogen for fertilizer (with unprecedented changes in agriculture) or fluctuations in eighteenth-century French courtly life. The foods we grow up with constitute a set of memories, familiar tastes that we may later reject or embrace.

As cities grew rapidly in nineteenth-century Europe and the United States, the division of labor meant more and more people had to buy most or all of their food, rather than growing it themselves. Jane Grigson cites the laments of various food historians about the disappearance of all kinds of vegetables from dinner tables and markets even earlier, *in the sixteenth century*, as English cities grew larger and more people had to rely on others to grow their food.[119] These worries echo today's concerns that no one is eating enough vegetables. But urbanites in England and elsewhere, from the sixteenth century up to the early twentieth, still drew largely on the ring of farms circling their particular city until the industrialization of agriculture really took off after World War II. While there was well-developed global trade for certain products— spices, sugar, and rum (inextricably wrapped up with slavery), fresh fruit, and vegetables for the hungry masses generally came from the farms close to the cities.[120] But the contents of these fields certainly changed in the wake of the Columbian Exchange.

In *Forbidden Fruits and Forgotten Vegetables*, the Marcuses refer to "the distinctive vegetables of French *haute cuisine*—leeks, artichokes, asparagus."[121] Asparagus has experienced a radical change in fortunes over time. Thomas Moffett found that in the course of the sixteenth century, asparagus went from "a meat for such Emperours as *Julius Caesar*: now every boord [or table] is served with them."[122] In other words, they had become so popular as to lose their appeal among elites and trendsetters in the 1500s, not unlike complaints today that heirloom tomatoes have become too popular. People were eating both wild and cultivated asparagus. Asparagus is another Mediterranean vegetable that made its way across Europe to England and then to North America. Jane Grigson asks, "How would you describe the best asparagus? . . . The answer will tell me more about you than about absolute standards of asparagus perfection. Italians like white asparagus with a yellowish head. . . . The French like their violet and green and white spears. And the English and Americans like unblanched, tender greenness."[123] Grigson's example of a fancy vegetable and national tastes for particular forms also reveals the ways a single vegetable can range from being very high status to very pedestrian, and also how its consumption can follow the lines not only of class but also of nation.

T. Sarah Peterson has a research question that speaks to this vegetal morphing: "Why did food change so drastically in seventeenth-century Europe?" She sees the Renaissance (and its attendant changes in the political and religious orders) turning its back on the sweet and heavily spiced food of the medieval era, so connected to astrology and alchemy, and replacing them with a cuisine rooted (or at least reputed to be rooted) in a classical emphasis on salty and acidic flavors.[124] She sees, among other changes, the vegetables of the ancients becoming very popular among Renaissance elites: artichokes, cardoons, asparagus, cabbage, onions, and parsley. Wanting to be like the ancient Romans culturally and intellectually, Renaissance elites set out to eat like them as well. Riding the tide of this trend, the artichoke, for example, became widely available by the sixteenth century, whereas a century earlier it had been very hard to find.[125]

There was clearly a seventeenth-century European enthusiasm for the vegetables (and other foods and flavors) of the ancients: "As the kitchen garden burst its medieval boundaries, a striking number of the new vegetables were linked to the texts of the ancients. In the south of

France an explosion of horticultural interest, Le Roy Laduire observes, transformed those 'bleak collections of leeks, cabbages, and turnips' of the fifteenth century garden into profuse collections of vegetables. By 1604 a garden at Nimes had blanched lettuce, head or Milanese cabbage, headed endive, cauliflower, artichokes, turnips, parsley, fennel, and melons."[126] Parsley, too, experienced a sixteenth-century resurgence precisely because of its presence in ancient texts, lending it an aura of authenticity, health, and illustrious lineage. "Parsley now 'swam' with new authority in sauces, and many varieties of onions and cabbages were developed and became widely available."[127] This change was naturally also shaped by class, trends of the elites not necessarily being shared by the rest of the population. Grigson also writes about parsley, something I don't address at length, since I've left it by the wayside along with other plants we might consider herbs (fodder for future writing projects). She captures the decline of parsley from a staple of Roman cooking to a footnote in the English kitchen: parsley "reminded Pliny of holidays away from Rome—'You see sprigs of parsley swimming on milk everywhere in the country.' And in England it reminds us—of what? Boiled cod, on Good Friday, the relationship of centuries and civilizations reduced to green flecks in a white sauce."[128] Ouch! Parsley's journey hasn't improved much; this once-illustrious herb is often casually tossed on restaurant dishes as they head out to diners, a garnish as compulsory as it is uneaten.

Kale offers another fine example of the changing fates of green foods, albeit in the opposite direction. Kale has triumphed over lesser vegetables, beloved by many new converts, yet also spurned as a sign of a trend past its peak and of excessive dietary virtue. Whole Foods announced in early 2014 that collards were the new kale;[129] and it now routinely appears on lists of overhyped and fatally hipster vegetables. But kale was once almost exclusively the food of the poor. It was particularly important in Scotland, the Marcuses tell us, where "every family had its own patch of kale, and the rude enclosures attached to every country cottage became known as kailyards. This term was later associated with a school of Scottish poets and writers who at the end of the last century took up themes of rural life, writing sentimentally of a vanishing era. Perhaps more bitter associations with the realities of poverty . . . prompted many immigrants to America to relegate kale . . .

to a list of our most neglected vegetables."[130] It couldn't be much different today, where kale is ubiquitous, a marker of culinary virtue, consumed in great quantities in green smoothies and crunchy raw salads.

Artichokes, too, experienced changes in both meanings and fortunes. "Heirloom artichokes," for example, appears in only two newspaper articles, and only as very brief mentions. Artichokes originated in the Mediterranean and grow in only a narrow range of places in the United States, one being close to where I grew up on the central California coast. My school friends reportedly got shot at with rock salt when trying to pluck (or rather, steal) artichokes from the unfenced fields. Artichokes are a deep part of my own edible memory, dating at the very least to a photograph of me at two in a smiley face sweatshirt, proudly holding a big stainless steel bowl of homegrown artichokes for the camera. For me, the artichoke elicits far more personal memory than the tomato. I wasn't attuned to different varieties of artichokes, since almost all that were grown nearby were globe artichokes. Unaware of the artichoke's illustrious and geographically dynamic past, I simply appreciated the meaty leaves and above all the tender heart, learning at an early age how to scoop the choke out with a spoon. We would have little Pyrex dishes holding a dollop of mayonnaise from a jar or, for my mother, melted butter, for dipping the leaves and the quartered hearts. In fact there is a subtle family tradition of feeling obligated to share the heart with others at the table, with parents making sure children get enough heart and children checking that everybody else has a fair share. It's in eating an artichoke—far more than a tomato—that I most feel the presence of my coastal California family, and to this day artichokes almost invariably grace the table on the first night of a visit home.

Artichokes followed a circuitous path from the ancient Romans to North Africa, where new varieties were developed and re-imported to Europe. This suggests, first, that other vegetables with similarly European pedigrees do not really make it to heirloom status of any significance. Artichokes were eaten by European kings and queens, Arab gardeners, and Martha Washington, not to mention Italian immigrants. They were grown in colonial Virginia in the 1720s and even in Revolutionary New England.[131] Yet I had to teach many midwestern friends how to eat them. As widespread as artichokes were, they have not made it into the lexicon of heirlooms or into a broader collective memory. Their past popularity compared with the lack of interest today also highlights the extensive changes vegetables can experience over time, in conjunction with changes in tastes and appetites.

Leeks similarly offer a range of high status and low status, as well as national identity. Stocks asserts that "for some reason—perhaps because they are less inherently variable than some other crops—leeks never captured the imagination of Britain's nurserymen. Only two kinds of leek were available to the eighteenth-century gardener: the narrow-leaved French or Flanders leek and the newer, broad-leaved London or London Flag."[132] Grigson tells us that "leeks must be one of the oldest vegetables. They grew leeks (and still do) in Egypt. Leeks spread north, green and fresh in beastly winters."[133] She writes of leeks as being poor people's food in Europe for thousands of years. "Not so in America. Here leeks are rare . . . and so expensive that they are ironically called 'rich man's asparagus.'"[134] These arrangements of roots, leaves, flavors, colors, and DNA can take on whole new meanings in different cultural and economic contexts.

All kinds of edible plants fade in and out of daily use, fashion, and memory. Alexanders, for example, are a Mediterranean plant whose stalks taste, according to *The Oxford Companion to Food*, like something "between celery and parsley. . . . Alexanders was supplanted in the 18th century by the improved kinds of celery which were then developed. It is now almost forgotten as a foodstuff, although it still grows wild in much of Europe, including Britain. It is common around the sites of medieval monastery gardens, where it had been cultivated as *petroselinum Alexandrium*."[135] Such physical traces of past uses can yield clues to the previous existence of particular gardens and dietary habits.

The Jerusalem artichoke, too, experiences both a great global shift and rapid changes in fortune: "Of all the vegetables American Indians gave to Europe (potatoes, corn, squash, and tomatoes among them), none was so rapidly adopted by Continental cooks as the Jerusalem artichoke—nor did any fall so quickly out of favor."[136] By the early seventeenth century, Jerusalem artichokes had made their way from Cape Cod and other realms of the East Coast of North America to the courts of Europe. "By 1629, however, the apothecary to King James I, John Parkinson, complained in his *Paradisus in Sole* that they 'are by reason of their great increasing, grown to be so common here with us at London, that even the most vulgar begin to despise them, whereas when they were first received among us, they were dainties for a Queene.' Ultimately, overabundance turned this at-first-fashionable food into fodder for livestock, which remained its primary use in Europe until it was reintroduced into *haute cuisine* in the nineteenth century."[137] This is just one more example of the ebb and flow of vegetable trends. Today they grow on the roof of that meat-packing plant back in chapter 1, serving both as a vegetable and as a windbreak.

Salsify was once very familiar and now is almost entirely absent from cooking in the United States, although it was often eaten by the founding fathers.[138] Although it is originally from Europe, it was very common in nineteenth-century American cookbooks, and it even grows as a weed along the East Coast. I first encountered salsify (or more likely *scorzonera*) in a little wine tavern on the outskirts of Vienna, in a bowl in the refrigerated case along with potato salad, pig knuckles, and thinly sliced cucumbers bathed in heavily sweetened vinegar. The salsify looked like little white cylinders, swimming in a milky white dressing. They were nutty, sweet, and delicious. In German they're called *Schwarzwurzel*, "black root." They grow with a tough dark skin that can be challenging and messy to peel. Salsify is popular in Austria, available in glass jars in any supermarket, but difficult to find in the United States, even though varieties of it also grow wild by roadsides.

Wild greens like ramps (a wild onion, *Allium tricoccum*) and sorrel fell utterly out of fashion in much of Europe in the wake of World War II, provoking unpleasant memories of hard times, only to be rediscovered in the early twenty-first century and to appear on the menus of the most fashionable restaurants.[139] "From time immemorial," the Marcuses write, "as winter passed and the first shoots pushed up from the earth, country folk took to the woods and fields to gather the delicate spring greens."[140] Today there is quite a trend toward wild and foraged foods, perhaps most intensively embodied in the Danish chef René Redzepi, the so-called chefs' top chef whose restaurant Noma has repeatedly been named the best restaurant in the world.[141] Wild greens can be the food of war—what people eat when agriculture starts to fall apart—or they can be served in some of the world's most expensive and highly regarded restaurants. Familiarity depends on where you stand, where and how you grew up, who has shown you around the vegetable world, and what culinary trails you follow in adulthood.

Lost Plums
& Found Mangoes

AS WITH VEGETABLES, rare and nearly forgotten fruits speak to global histories and memory (and forgetting) both private and collective, and flourish under the care of individual farmers and small groups of enthusiasts. One of the many people preserving fruit biodiversity is Andy Mariani. His orchards on the edge of Silicon Valley, tucked between subdivisions and dry golden hills, contain a rich reserve of stone fruit germplasm, and acres of vibrant, thriving trees.[1] This orchard is in many ways emblematic of the concept of heirloom food—a pocket of biodiversity including fruit with long histories connected to global movements and individual appetites. When I visited the orchard one summer, I arrived a little early on a Saturday morning, taking an exit I'd never used before off a freeway I've known my entire life, Highway 101, heading into the Santa Clara Valley. As I approached the turnoff, the sun broke through the fog, revealing housing developments creeping up into the yellow hills. As the road wound down the off ramp and toward the orchard, a new shopping complex of big box stores announced its grand opening, and row upon row of townhouses and McMansions filled this part of the valley. I drove by an abandoned orchard, a few unruly fruit trees in dry scrubby ground. It's easiest to see the orchard remnants in the springtime, when telltale white and pink blossoms peek out above backyard fences, the wild edges of office parks, and highway rights-of-way. There are also many California microclimates—stone fruit thrives on the outskirts of Silicon Valley, somewhat protected from the maritime fog and enjoying copious summertime heat and sunshine. An hour away, where I grew up, only apple trees could tolerate the pea soup fog of our summers.

Growing up, I'd always heard that the Santa Clara Valley was once filled with fruit trees, and each time we drove through on a family trip my father lamented their displacement by tract homes. So it surprised me to hear from Mariani that much of the area had actually been home to vineyards long before the valley was filled with fruit trees. Fruit trees began to displace the vineyards in part because of Prohibition, although wine-making continued in the area, both officially for religious purposes, and unofficially for other purposes. But the orchards also grew more widespread because of improvements in irrigation (the vineyards were dryland farmed, while the stone trees required irrigation), and the potential, at the time, for fruit trees to offer greater profits—a reversal of today, where vineyards are highly profitable and spreading across the state.[2]

Of course, for some people stone fruit is even easier to turn into alcohol than grapes are—a couple of fruit trees, a home-built still, and you're just a bit shy of a bottle of plum brandy or apricot schnapps, things many central European farmers made on the side (and often out of view of the tax authorities) and handed out to landless friends in unlabeled bottles. When I lived in Austria, we often had a clear glass bottle of "X-Schnapps" on the kitchen shelf, named after the farmer who made it and "labeled" with just a piece of yarn tied around the neck. We would bring it out for guests as a (not particularly smooth) taste of the countryside or, after a hearty meal, a highly flammable digestif.

Plums grow well in various regions across the United States, but they took to California particularly well. Plums, including those specifically meant to become prunes, have a century or more of history in the area. French monks in an abbey near Agen and Bordeaux reportedly had a well-established prune-growing operation in the sixteenth century, and as Jane Grigson tells us, "cuttings of the famous French prune [the *prune d'Agen*][3] were stuck into raw potatoes, then in sawdust, and packed in two leather trunks to make the long trip around Cape Horn to [Louis] Pellier's orchard at San Jose [Pellier was the French nurseryman who first introduced plum trees to California]; he grafted them to stocks of native wild plum."[4] These French prune plums thus found their way to the dry but fertile valleys of coastal California.

I arrived shortly before Mariani's farm stand opened and watched the parking lot fill with eager fruit buyers. The store itself filled up as Mariani showed me what they had in stock at the time. There were no fresh apricots at all, mostly plums, nectarines, and peaches, as well as dried fruit, jams made of Blenheim apricots, and also some vegetables—heirloom cucumbers, tiny pale green zucchini, great squash blossoms, and diminutive eggplants. Two twenty-something men anxiously asked where the Baby Crawford peaches were. Mariani told them they were out of luck; the Baby Crawfords were done for the year. The young men were crestfallen: Hadn't they just bought Baby Crawfords not long ago? How could they be done already, meaning nearly a year would have to pass before they could taste this fruit again? Mariani suggested the Angelus or the O'Henry as an acceptable replacement, though he specifically steered them away from the Fay Elberta. There's no question that flavor is driving much of the demand for the fruits of this orchard, and these two young men had to content themselves with, in their minds, the runners-up (although in my mind even the runners-up are spectacular peaches whose likes I've rarely tasted elsewhere).

Most of Mariani's business relies on the annual cherry harvest, and many of the heirloom and new fruit varieties he grows are more to satisfy his own taste buds and curiosity than to make a living. The fruit at the farm stand itself is a pretty good deal, and some people there clearly were regular shoppers—a retired farmer from the neighborhood, an older couple who seemed to have a well-orchestrated routine for securing the best of the day's fruit offerings, and those two young men with a hunger for Baby Crawfords. Mariani also offers more expensive specialties, including fifty-dollar boxes of greengage plums shipped to wherever you want. These plums are very difficult to buy commercially in the United States, although they are grown fairly widely in France and other parts of Europe. In the back room of the farm stand, Mariani showed me how the greengages are packed to be shipped overnight, in a cardboard box with two layers of foam, with tiny hollows for the plums. The greengages were amazing, about the best fruit I'd ever tasted—rich and creamy, jammy and complex. Out in the orchard he picked them off the branches and handed them to me, just one of dozens of fruits I tasted as we walked through the trees.

The name greengage alone lets us in on some secrets of the fruit world. A wild plum from Asia Minor, transformed somewhere in France to the Reine Claude, Queen Claude, then hopping across the English Channel to become the greengage.[5] Like much produce, these plums are both humble and mighty, grown and eaten in private for free, or celebrated at an exclusive dinner party thousands of miles from the trees they were grown on. Indeed, shipping thirty-six greengage plums by overnight delivery (they're picked ripe, so the clock is ticking before the perky plums melt into overripe puddles) reminds me of the practice at baroque dinner tables. European aristocrats would try to outdo each other in providing ever more impossible dessert fruits, sparing no expense either for transport from distant places or for the latest in greenhouse technology, and of course the labor of untold numbers of people working to put dessert on the table but not getting to enjoy it.[6] The ability to grow pineapples and oranges off-season in the European North was directly connected to a supply of cheap labor to stoke the fires heating the orangeries and pineries, and to the increased availability of cheap coal.

Fruit hunter and writer David Karp is a great fan of Andy Mariani's, ordering a box of greengages from time to time.[7] Another literary member of Mariani's network is David Mas Masumoto, a farmer and author who writes lovely books about farming in California's San Joaquin Valley.[8] As like-minded appreciators of rare fruit talk to one another, read each other's books, exchange recipes and anecdotes, seeds and stories, they build networks, some quite informal, simply of friends and correspondents, as well as more formal clubs and online communities. This kind of grassroots sharing of affection for rare and old-fashioned fruits and vegetables has been essential to the survival, persistence, and revival of a lot of edible biodiversity.

The layers of memory and history intrigued me—vineyards I'd never known about, then stone fruit, then tract homes, bits of the past peeking out of the landscape of the present. Mariani showed me a hundred-year-old grapevine wrapped around the side of a shed that used to be the base of a water tower. I'm always interested in these agricultural remnants, bits of edible history easy to overlook, that begin to reveal themselves only when you start asking around and digging through archives or abandoned gardens. Mariani picked a bunch of tiny sweet, dusty grapes that we ate, spitting the seeds onto the dry earth. As we walked through the orchards and talked in the busy back room of the farm stand, Mariani also emphasized something I've heard from many seed savers. For him and so many others, the point of preserving the old varieties is not to make time stand still. Many of the people involved in seed saving and biodiversity preservation find it is possible to care meticulously for traditional varieties while at the same time actively creating new ones. And they emphasize the importance of subjecting the old varieties to the evolutionary pressures that simply happen when plants are grown out and exposed to pests, diseases, or changes in climate. Mariani's orchards are not a museum, not an attempt to stop time, but rather a lively mix of old and new, of preservation and invention. His varieties are old and new, and even the old are unfamiliar to most of us, combined with the Kazakh varieties that have been added for breeding new varieties.

We drove out to an orchard planted on land he rents from the neighbors, whose dogs barked at the truck as we drove down the rutted driveway. At first glance the orchards look pretty uniform. It's not as if you can read flavors, cultural history, or breeding techniques from a bunch of trees, and Mariani wondered out loud how many trees I needed to look at to get the picture. It turned out I needed to look at a lot. I needed to see the scars of grafts and the meticulous labeling and to realize that (to my layperson's eyes) the heirloom trees were indistinguishable from the newly bred varieties. It was highly educational to learn a little more about how to read an orchard, to hear Mariani tell the story of a given tree, and to taste the latest stage in the forward motion of stone fruit over thousands of years. Walking through so many rows of trees also led to something I hadn't expected: tasting dozens of plums, above all; a few other fruits here and there, but by and large plums in every possible shape and color and flavor.[9]

As we walked through the orchards, Mariani would pull fruit off the tree and hand it to me. "Taste this," he said, "and this." Wiping the dust off on my jeans, I bit into plum after plum warm from the sun, encountering flavors you simply can't get anywhere else. I ended up eating pounds of fruit straight from the tree, spitting pits into the weeds.

So many flavors. I discovered—and ingested—far more plum diversity than I had ever imagined before beginning this project. I got a crazy sugar high from all that very ripe fruit. Every peach and nectarine and plum I tasted was completely distinguishable from the last, each a unique balance of sour and sweet, soft flesh and smooth skin. Muddy and squinting in the sun, I would wait as Mariani rustled through the branches to find a perfect plum or white nectarine on the sunny side of the tree, twisting it open and offering me half. Although I don't know much about wine, I have on occasion tasted very non-winey things in a glass, and in these plums and peaches and nectarines there were all kinds of other flavors (and textures) going on. The predominant flavor was sweetness, but sometimes paired with skin so tart it made my mouth pucker, with juices that were creamy or acidic, with the taste of lemons or pineapples layered beneath the plum flavor. Some already tasted as concentrated as jam. These peach trees and plum trees require a certain amount of sun, casting their genetic lot for a short couple of weeks, then calming down for the rest of the year.

If you look more closely at an orchard, and if you have an expert guide as I did, it is not impossible to see the trees for the forest. Little metal tags or long plastic ribbons hanging from the trunks hint at the careful record keeping in some computer or filing cabinet. While some of the orchards contain large numbers of the same kinds of trees, on closer inspection others are highly diverse. Looking even more closely, I could see, over and over again, the scars of the grafts, the careful work of attaching the scion that will bear the fruit you want to the tree trunk that will support it. In one of the orchards the grafts are bright yellow, and many were done by a graduate student wanting to polish her grafting skills. In a few years her work will literally bear fruit. Another surprise waited in what, from afar, looked like uniform stands of trees. In a living fruit archive near the farm stand, Mariani showed me that some trees had completely different colors and varieties of plums growing on different branches. To keep track of his collection of old varieties, he had grafted many varieties to a much smaller number of trunks, so that we could circle each tree and pluck six or seven different varieties of plums—quite a surprise to see so many colors of fruit ripening on the same tree. I use a photograph of that tree when I give lectures about gardens, plants, and memory, because that tree is a paradox, preserving old-fashioned flavors and varieties in an unconventional form.

A recurring theme in my research is that once somebody tells me how to see (or taste) something, I often see it and taste it in an entirely new way. This is a strange thing about taste—while it is so personal and so seemingly absolute, many of us find our tastes changing profoundly over a lifetime. Researching this book has brought many new foods into the realm of things I like, just as my parents' weekly vegetable box has greatly expanded their vegetable horizons. Simple exposure can sometimes be enough,[10] but it may also require a little instruction— whether it's the stories and recipes included in the weekly vegetable box or the expert knowledge of someone like Andy Mariani,[11] guiding me through his orchard, which felt like walking through the delicious pages of some three-dimensional encyclopedia. There are limits, however, certain things that simply won't taste good to me no matter how much I learn about them or how expert the person who introduces me to them—mealy apples, for example, or more than one or two heirloom beets at a sitting.

And honestly I wasn't much of a plum fan before my visit to Mariani's orchards. When I was growing up we had two very unproductive plum trees (no comparison to our busy little apple trees that produced great piles of fruit every year), and even as an adult it rarely occurred to me to buy a plum, since I so often found the supermarket plums a disappointment.[12] But these hours spent in the midday sun, among the rustling leaves and the uneven mud of the irrigated fields, made me a convert. I won't go out and spend fifty dollars on a box of greengages anytime soon, but I promise to give plums a fair shake in the future. And in the meantime, my family and I are now incapable of driving past Mariani's orchard without taking the turnoff and stocking up on whatever is in season, buying up dried apricots if the fresh fruit is done for the season.

I once pointed out some Satsuma plums to a friend at a farmers' market, and she found them not especially attractive—an odd dusty brown-green. But once she tasted the deep red flesh with its layer of tart skin, she saw something new in those unfamiliar colors. If you don't spend much time around plums, you might not know that one of their special qualities is skin that is either translucent or opaque, so that a plum may combine the skin color and the color of the flesh beneath. In addition, most plums, when left alone, develop a powdery bloom that, depending on your point of view, may add to their beauty or look dangerously like mold.

There is so much activity around heirloom plums in orchards like Mariani's, but so very little notice of them in the popular press. When I sought out heirloom plums in popular food writing, the few newspaper articles that mention heirloom plums allude to specific histories or use the idea of an heirloom plum to indicate trendiness, for example. In reference to artisanal chefs and farmers in Montreal, the *New York Times* writes that "they are . . . growing heirloom plums introduced to New France by priests in the 17th century; and making cheeses that rival those of the home country."[13] Compared with apples or tomatoes, heirloom stone fruit is definitely being preserved under the radar of mainstream food writing.[14] The engagement of growers and consumers with these fragile fruits rarely appears in popular media, resulting in a comparative silence about heirloom plums and peaches in the same pages where tomatoes and apples get top billing. I think this lack is due in part to their profound perishability. For many fruits, not just plums, it is very difficult to get them to markets at peak ripeness.

Mariani showed me funny plums with big beaks, which would be difficult to sell because the beaks get bruised on the way to the market. Much of what he grows is meant to be tree ripened, which can be said of very little fruit found at the grocery store. I could see clearly how challenging it must be to transport some of these varieties. Stone fruit is far more perishable and ephemeral than apples, with implications for how it gets to market and how much stone fruit biodiversity most of us encounter in grocery stores and farmers' markets. By the end of our walk through the orchards, my bag was laden with fruit. What I couldn't eat on the spot as we walked up and down the rows of trees, I stuffed into the shoulder bag I always used in my fieldwork—expandable to hold even a change of clothes, but compact enough to carry a notebook and, in the olden days, a camera. That trusty bag had been filled with produce before (not to mention books, wet bathing suits, seedpods, or my lecture notes), but this visit to the orchard was the beginning of the end for it. By the time I got home, it was already starting to ooze syrup onto the car seat, from plums begging to be put into a tart (which I did as soon as possible before they disintegrated). That bag was never the same, forever smelling like mildly fermented plums. But that's the price of perfectly ripened stone fruit: much of it is not well suited to being carted miles to market. Gorgeous plums and peaches and nectarines do make their delicious way to farmers' markets and grocery stores, but much of that array of flavor and color remains close to the orchard it came from. Small wonder there are so many ways to turn ripe fruit into something else (jam and marmalade, dried fruit, powerful clear spirits).

These plums perishing in my bag felt like a small-scale version of the dilemma that faces much of the world: How can we enjoy ripeness and sweetness at any distance from the fruit's origins? This conundrum is solved on a massive scale by the development of hardy, transportable varieties of everything from bananas to strawberries to papayas. But there is often a stark difference in flavor, aroma, texture, and even color between the transported fruit and the fruit eaten near the tree or bush or plant of origin. I am not trying to be precious about fruit flavor here or advocating that we eat only homegrown fruit. I am observing this quandary that also reveals webs of longing, appetite, and desire stretching across time and space—the hunger for ripe stone fruit that is completely impossible to satisfy in January in Wisconsin, or someone else's memory of a multitude of banana varieties from a childhood in the tropics, impossible to satisfy with the meager variety of bananas available in even the most import-packed produce store in the United States. The practice of canning fruit in temperate climes has faded—the only way to "transport" flavor, sweetness, ripeness, color, and particular vitamins from the peak weeks of the summertime harvest into the depths of winter. Distance, sweetness, ripeness, perishability, transport, flavor, geography, place, and sun all combine to create these complicated webs of fruit consumption. They can be motivated by a longing for childhood, for summer, for the tropics, for micronutrients, for sweetness. And fruit seems to kindle desire in a way that vegetables often do not.

Mariani also told me, in a later conversation, that he has spent much of his fruit-growing career chasing the flavor of a peach he ate as a child. Similarly, English chef and writer Nigel Slater, ever effusive about fruit and childhood, says of damson plums, "The trees you come across in old gardens and hedgerows are laden with nostalgia for me, their crop—

in pies, jam, and tender-crusted tarts—being the single best thing about my country adolescence."[15] The damson orchards in England largely disappeared during and after World War II owing to sugar rationing, since damsons are best eaten cooked with sugar. As Slater recounts, with the decline in the availability of sugar, "many ancient orchards were torn up."[16] But some still grow in Cumbria and Shropshire, where the fruit was apparently once used to color yarn and thread for the area's cotton and wool mills.[17]

Fruit trees are very place-bound, literally much more rooted to the landscape than annual vegetables. Heirloom fruit works differently than heirloom vegetables in several respects. First, much fruit grows on trees or bushes that may live for decades or even centuries. This is quite a contrast to peas, squash, and other vegetables that don't last even a year, the tangled dying vines and leggy plants easily pulled out of the ground at the end of the growing season. Their seeds can be saved, of course, but the plants themselves die off, and the whole system is far more transportable than a peach tree or an apple tree. For home gardeners, heirloom fruit requires a more substantial investment of time and real estate than a vegetable patch. People plant fruit trees for the long haul, whereas peas can be harvested within a couple of months of planting and carried somewhere else as a pocketful of dried seeds. Fruit trees and berry bushes also require regular care to continue producing; proper pruning in particular is essential for fruit production and the health of the organism, another gardening task not necessary for vegetables.

Local Fruits and Local Flavor

Plums and other stone fruit are obviously extremely fragile when perfectly ripe. Even at the farmers' markets where a kaleidoscope of heirloom tomatoes and antique apple varieties might be available, I never find even close to that range in heirloom plums, peaches, or cherries. Not far from Mariani's plums, all kinds of other fruits are growing in people's gardens and allotments, full of plants and trees tended by recent immigrants and long-term residents alike: "If you're looking for proof of 'ethnic diversity' in Silicon Valley, just check out the backyard fruit orchards. There you will find fabulous newcomers from such places as New Zealand, Australia, Japan and China plus a renewed interest in heirloom fruit from Germany, France and England. Together, these new immigrants and old-timers add a wonderful new look and taste to trees that can be grown here. The University of California Cooperative Extension includes these oldies and goodies in its list of recommended varieties."[18] It almost seems as if this reporter is talking about people rather than fruit, reflecting the diversity of the area's population and its gardens. There is a certain conflation of people and plants, and a deep connection between plants and places. There is no one-to-one mapping of territory, culture, and memory. Fruits (and other foods) lose or gain popularity among different groups, depending on changing tastes, immigration patterns, new techniques of preservation or transportation of perishable varieties, and even changing geopolitical conditions.

Eating locally is a very different experience for people who stay in their childhood homes than for people who live far from the fields, orchards, forests, markets, and gardens of their earliest memories. Even my own move of two thousand miles meant a change in the fruits I eat. I think in particular of the rhubarb eaten so heartily in Milwaukee, cared for and transplanted over generations, which I never encountered in California. And moving to Milwaukee greatly changed my access to citrus, avocados, and artichokes that, granted, would not grow well in our foggy yard but at least were grown nearby. No neighbor in Milwaukee appears at my front door with a paper bag full of homegrown avocados, Meyer lemons, or persimmons, as routinely happens to my parents. But many fruits have to be either picked before ripening, then ripened in warehouses or in transit, or else picked too close to ripeness, making them liable to be damaged in transport or to rot quickly if not bought and eaten immediately. We should also not assume that nostalgia inevitably accompanies immigration—some people may think "good riddance" and be happy to leave particular foods behind.

Many heirloom foods are just as exotic to those eating them as what many in the United States have more conventionally thought of as exotic food—the spiky fruits or copious greens that have been available in any big city's Chinatown for decades, as people far from the places of their own or their parents' childhood seek out those familiar flavors and textures. The colors and shapes may evoke memory, but the foods are also delicious and anything but exotic—instead, they are familiar, common, everyday. The same piece of fruit can mean very different things to different people. Durians and mangoes, cherries and McIntosh apples, all constitute the deep memories of someone's childhood. Almost none of these foods are mentioned in newspaper food writing about heirlooms, yet these are global heirlooms—foods often made even more poignant because of their perishability, the near impossibility of tasting fruit as it was meant to be tasted, or as it remains in memory.

Almost no tropicals are called heirlooms in popular food writing. Some of this may have to do with latitude—most of the foods that receive the heirloom label in popular food writing can be grown in North America (although much that can be grown here and technically fits the heirloom definition also fails to be called that). Botany and chemistry definitely limit what people in North America do and do not eat, although this has changed with advances in both breeding and transportation. The development of bananas that can be picked green, for example, has made it possible to have cheap bananas in the United States. This access, however, came with a corresponding set of political and economic exploitation, and with a striking lack of diversity in genetics, flavor, and texture.[19]

The term "heirloom" does generally seem to be reserved for fruits and vegetables that have been grown successfully in the United States since the first half of the twentieth century. But if an heirloom is simply an open-pollinated or otherwise non-hybrid plant variety dating back at least to the first half of the twentieth century, then the cultivated foods of the native inhabitants of North America should all have that label too, as well as the countless tropical fruits and vegetables brought to North America by immigrant communities and their descendants. Some of these fruits make it into the pantheon of Slow Food's Ark of Taste.[20] The traditions being restored are diverse and often relatively new. The fruit species themselves originate not only in North America but on other continents, although the varieties are often developed in the United States. There are concrete ways of bringing these fruits back, and tensions exist between remembering and forgetting, between stable traditions and dynamic communities. These foods are not and should not be frozen in time.

The draw of exotic fruit is nothing new. Today seasonal heirloom tomatoes and locally raised heritage turkeys might serve as a kind of status symbol, a sign of both good taste and environmental awareness. They might also be part of a larger movement to reduce carbon footprints and sustain local economies. But in other times and places, culinary status symbols have been anything but local or seasonal. The opulent dessert courses of baroque-era Europe, for example, demanded serving trays piled high with off-season fruit imported from far-off lands or grown in costly orangeries and pineries.[21] These orangeries were often large structures, usually with a south-facing wall of leaded glass, to capture the winter sunshine. They generally had an elaborate heating system under the floor to provide additional warmth to the citrus, figs, and pomegranates, as well as decorative palms and other plants with no business in northern latitudes.

Such produce was a way for the gentry to demonstrate their wealth and taste—and also their class and power. They proved it by the legions of gardeners (and, in the case of status-seeking gardeners like Thomas Jefferson and George Washington, enslaved men) who kept the fires burning to heat the glasshouses and by the far-reaching and violent extraction of fruit and other resources from colonized lands. As they were creating microclimates in Europe with glasshouses, colonialism moved things from one climate to the next. With technology, cheap labor, and large quantities of coal, they could conjure these fruits in European latitudes or ship them from the lands where they originated, something that continues today. Today's exotics are tomorrow's memories, and far more children in the United States today are growing up with avocados and mangoes, for example, once unheard of at this scale.

Familiar and Far Away

As in other chapters, I set out to see what presence various heirloom foods had in popular food writing. About tropical and subtropical fruit I found almost nothing. There are no references at all to heirloom avocados, for example. Yet avocados have been eaten in the United States since the nineteenth century, when they were introduced from three directions (California, Florida, and Hawaii).[22] They originated in a region of Mexico and Central America but had spread to Peru and elsewhere before the Spanish conquest, and the Spanish soon brought them to the Caribbean as well.[23] At least five hundred varieties of avocado exist today, and the archaeological record indicates that they have been cultivated for seven thousand years.[24] And what is more an heirloom than something that's been eaten for seven thousand years? Sophie Coe describes guacamole as a recipe transferred almost directly from the Aztecs to the present day.[25] Avocados are also a foundation of my own edible memory, alongside artichokes and backyard apples. One of my favorite sandwiches was a ripe Haas avocado mashed and spread on whole wheat or, even better, tangy sourdough bread and sprinkled with salt. (Let's not forget I was growing up in California in the seventies.) When I was living in Vienna, researching elements of this book and much of my half-written next book, the only avocados in the markets were usually rock hard, shipped from South Africa, of a variety I found oily rather than creamy like the Haas of my childhood. Mexico can ship avocados year-round, leaving them on the tree until needed. Half of the world supply of avocadoes today comes from Michoacán.[26]

Like avocados, bananas rarely receive the heirloom label, despite having been fundamental elements of various food cultures around the world for centuries, even millennia. There is incredible banana biodiversity, but the bananas we see in most supermarkets in the continental United States have little to do with the banana biodiversity in other parts of the world (sixty-seven species and over two hundred varieties).[27] Imagine choosing from two hundred *different* bananas! The banana seems to have originated in Malaysia or Indonesia, but even a few thousand years ago bananas were already being grown in India, and they were in China by 200 CE. Arab traders brought bananas from Southeast Asia to the Near East and Africa in the seventh century. Starting in Madagascar, bananas were cultivated across the African continent by the fourteenth century.[28] In the New World, bananas were first planted on the island of Hispaniola in the early sixteenth century (intended in part as a food source for enslaved people). As happened with many other foods, including rice,[29] bananas spread so widely and at such an early date that many people thought they were New World natives. Indeed, *The Oxford Companion to Food* found that "the spread of the banana in S[outh] America was so rapid, often anticipating the progress of the colonists, that some early writers were convinced that it had existed in S[outh] America, among the Inca, before the Spanish conquest."[30]

Despite sophisticated technology, many foods simply will not grow if the conditions are not right. Thus there is no commercial banana cultivation in the continental United States. Bananas were at first sustenance for slaves in the Americas, then luxury goods for global elites, and finally an "inexpensive food for the poor as well as a food of the health-conscious middle and upper classes."[31] Even the bananas so familiar today are relatively new: "Handsome, big, yellow, Caribbean bananas began to appear in Europe as well, ousting the small brown Canary ones."[32]

Bananas became more accessible in North America in the 1870s. According to sociologist Mimi Sheller, "It was only with the late-nineteenth-century reduction of transatlantic journey-times by the use of steam-powered ships, the invention of refrigeration and the development of new techniques for canning and boxing fruit, that the relationship between mover and moved would be reversed"—in other words, that the fruit traveled to North Americans and Europeans rather than the Europeans and North Americans traveling to the tropics.[33] There is evidence of an incredible appetite for tropical fruits in late nineteenth-century England, for example. According to Mimi Sheller, "*The Fruit Trade News* reported in December 1901, that . . . 'the buyers seem on the wait for the fruit, and many of the loads are sold without being unloaded,'" fifty thousand bunches of bananas a week.[34] Indeed, the number of bananas imported to England nearly doubled just from 1904 to 1905, from 1,416,873 bunches to 2,395,351 (295). This skyrocketing demand, and the colonial relations of production, quickly led to monoculture by the early twentieth century (a problem that continues to plague the banana industry) (296). "Wardlaw described how thousands of acres of virgin forests, populated by monkeys and birds and full of valuable and useful trees and plants, were indiscriminately felled by North American fruit companies, who left the wood to rot. They were then planted over in bananas, only to be abandoned a few years later due to Panama Disease [*Fusarium oxysprocum*, a fungal disease]" (296).

In other words, Western and Northern appetites—as Sidney Mintz and other scholars make clear—have dramatic consequences for the people and landscapes of the tropics. Consumer demand for a particular kind of banana, and for predictability and uniformity, led directly to monocultures, which quickly became susceptible to fungal infec-

tion, leading to rapid deforestation and continued monoculture crop-
ping as the fruit companies transitioned from the Gros Michel banana
to a (temporarily) more fungus-resistant variety, the Giant Cavendish
(298). The fungus led to the creation of acres and acres of new banana
plantations, which in turn led to the uprooting of the workers, who had
to break camp and follow the ever-changing locations of banana plantations.[35] In the late 1950s and early 1960s, boxing bananas rather than
shipping them on the stalk allowed companies to develop a brand identity and customer loyalty, and stickers started appearing on individual
bananas in 1964. The use of advertising, in part through the enter-
tainer Carmen Miranda (a Portuguese immigrant to Brazil, "imper-
sonating the exuberant and independent Afro-Brazilian street vendors
of Bahia"), was meant to create a bridge between European and North
American consumers and this once-exotic but now deeply familiar fruit
(298). Bananas are a huge global industry, shaping landscapes and lives
around the globe, a concept hard to comprehend when we're packing a
single banana in a lunch box or baking banana bread from fruit left too
long on the kitchen counter.[36]

Another form of banana is the plantain, eaten as a staple by an estimated four hundred million people, with thirty-seven million metric
tons grown in 2010.[37] Plantains originated in India and Malaysia but
quickly moved around the world in the wake of missionaries, merce-
naries, and the slave trade, and by the seventeenth century plantains
could be found worldwide.[38] Thus for many people to whom plantains
today are a fundamental element not only of daily meals but also of
identity and memory, the plantain was a relatively recent addition.
People were eating other people's memories four hundred years ago.
Plantains are staple foods in eastern and central Africa, and somewhat
less so in the West Indies, southern India, and Southeast Asia.[39] Today
plantains are available around the world, responding in part to the appetites of people who have emigrated from the tropics to more temperate regions.[40] And though Whole Foods in Milwaukee may occasionally have a small box of plantains, I can find a plentiful supply across
town at El Rey, the flagship location of a local chain that describes itself
as "Milwaukee's Authentic Hispanic Grocery Store." They carry abundant stacks of unripe, partially ripe, and fully ripe plantains (carefully
separated), since different recipes call for different stages of ripeness.

I discovered this the hard way on my first attempt to make plantain empanadas, prompting an eleventh-hour race across town to buy riper plantains.[41]

The question "Whose heirloom?" fits very well with tropical fruit. Many foods are hugely important in other parts of the world but largely peripheral in the United States. Breadfruit, for example, is native to the Pacific Islands, and there are more than two hundred cultivated varieties.[42] In fact, Captain Bligh's ill-fated journey was intended to bring breadfruit from Tahiti to the West Indies as a potential staple food for enslaved populations.[43] The jackfruit (which can reach ninety pounds) and the jambolan are two other examples—nutritionally and symbolically important on other shores but rarely eaten in the United States. *The Oxford Companion to Food* notes that "the [jambolan] tree and its fruits have religious significance for both Buddhists and Hindus. The latter believe that the god Krishna holds the fruit in special regard."[44] Many fruits play central roles in people's diets elsewhere in the world but are of comparatively minor importance in the United States, in part because many of them don't grow well in the forty-eight contiguous states. The custard apple also falls into this category, as do the duku, the langsat, the rambutan, the soursop, and the sugar apple.[45] The coconut, however, has made its way robustly into American eating habits, including the current craze for coconut water, or my mother's Easter brownies—frosted with buttercream frosting, then covered in shredded coconut dyed green to look like grass, with a jelly bean resting like an Easter egg in the coconut on each brownie. There is a fruit called a bullock's heart, now grown in tropical areas throughout the world and incorrectly called custard apple, cherimoya, and sugar apple.[46] Cactus fruits like prickly pear are another whole group rarely, if ever, referred to as heirlooms, yet they fulfill the definitions of this term for many people in the United States, Mexico, and elsewhere.

Much transported fruit still is far inferior in texture and flavor to fruit eaten closer to the tree: for example, the lilikoi that falls from a friend's mother's tree in Honolulu is left to ripen on the concrete patio, then eagerly scooped out for breakfast or cocktails. Or the papayas that are exquisite within a few miles of the tree they grew on, but far less appetizing once transported to the mainland. Still, many tropical fruits have become more common in grocery stores—the guava, the papaya, or the mango, for example—but often are not nearly as enjoyable as they would have been closer to home. The mango has experienced a great increase in popularity in the United States, although we still see just a handful of the five hundred to a thousand varieties estimated to be cultivated today, and I know people who complain bitterly about the contrast between the mangoes they can get here and the mangoes they remember from their childhoods on other shores.[47] The mango "has been cultivated in India since 2000 BC or earlier. . . . [It] is much loved wherever it is found, and appears in many myths and legends. In Indian Vedic literature it is spoken of as a transformation of the Lord of Creatures, Prajapati, who later became the Lord of Procreation."[48] The mango spread eastward to China and was also cultivated in Persia by the 900s. "By this time the mango had become a status symbol in India. The Moghul ruler Akbar (1556–1605) planted an orchard of mango trees at Darbhanga in Bihar, called Lakh Bagh because the number of the trees was supposedly one lakh (100,000). For a long time the cultivation of mango orchards in India remained the prerogative of rajas and nawabs," a high-status pursuit. In the sixteenth century the mango moved to Africa, and in the eighteenth century it went on to Brazil and then to Hawaii, Florida, and Mexico a century later.[49] Part of the mango's success in coming to market is because the fruits can ripen off the tree; in fact harvesting them before they are ripe can stave off a worm infestation.[50] But again, note that as recently as the early 1980s the mango seemed highly exotic to many people in the United States. Not very long ago, mangoes were being written about as a fruit whose flavor and use must be explained to readers,[51] but today at least a few varieties are readily accessible in grocery stores. There is a tension between the strange and the familiar. What is lost in a lot of food writing is that even the most supposedly exotic or unfamiliar fruit is likely someone's heirloom, someone's childhood memory or family staple.

The cargo holds of great container ships and airplanes are full of quickly ripening fruit, sent through a litany of fumigations and customs officials, and coming from the great fruit plantations marching across the terrain of tropical republics, worked by legions of fruit growers. Pineapples, too, were once unusual in both the United States and Europe, and highly desired. The pineapple has long been a staple in the United States despite its unwillingness to grow in North America.

Pineapples are originally from Brazil, though their precise botanical origins are a bit unclear. *The Oxford Companion to Food* reports that "no primitive form of the modern pineapple, which is almost invariably seedless, has been found, and the evolution of the fruit we know remains a mystery; but cultivation had certainly spread from Brazil to the W. Indies before the Europeans arrived."[52] Pineapples began to be grown in Europe once the Dutch developed advanced hothouse technology, but these fruits were still only for elites.[53] "Fashionable enthusiasm for pineapples can be seen in the frequency with which they appear as a decorative motif in the buildings and furniture of the next hundred years. Hothouse cultivation of pineapples as an expensive luxury continued in several European countries into the 19th century, and was developed into a fine art by the great Victorian gardeners of the 19th century in England."[54] And from the start of its time in Europe, the pineapple was an upper-class indulgence.[55]

The extreme popularity of pineapples in Europe, combined with the challenges of transport, led to all kinds of expensive innovations. As Sophie Coe writes:

> It is hard to think of a less plausible plant to cajole into fruiting under English conditions, but that is what the competitive gardeners of the British nobility succeeded in doing in the late seventeenth and early eighteenth centuries. It was an abstruse and expensive business, calling for specialized buildings named pineries. . . . Heat was provided by beds of manure and specialized furnaces. . . . The result of all this was that the pineapple became not just a fruit but the embodiment of everything the nobility liked to think that it stood for—wealth, hospitality, and friendship.[56]

But the pineapple bubble burst once they became less of a challenge to acquire. "By the 1820s pineapples could be imported from the West Indies on their plants, so that they became common, and therefore uninteresting to fashion pacesetters."[57] But have I ever come across anyone talking about an heirloom pineapple?[58] No. The fate of a fruit changes radically with a shift in modes of transport and production. Both bananas and pineapples become commonplace, and hearty appetites for these sweet tropical fruits among westerners and northerners turn into stark political, economic, and physical landscapes as great plantations run by multinational corporations occupy land once covered in forests, villages, and farms. What we eat today is just the most recent moment in the trajectory of foods with long histories. A fruit as unfamiliar in US markets as the durian is someone's heirloom, as are vanished banana varieties, but few media accounts of durian or bananas refer to them as heirlooms. In a land of immigrants, gardens can offer a connection to home. But there are limits to this—the climatological impossibility of growing bananas or mangoes in Milwaukee, for example.

I found hardly any mention of heirloom citrus in popular media coverage, despite citrus fruit's popularity, as well as its ancient and venerable history: "All citrus fruits are native to a region stretching from E. Asia southwards to Australia. Collectively they now constitute the third most important group of fruits; only the apples and pears, and the banana and plantain, surpass them in quantity produced and consumed. Botanists have calculated that the history of the citrus trees goes back 20 million years, to a time when Australia was joined to Asia."[59] That's a lot of history. Yet heirloom citrus makes only rare appearances. The lemon is perhaps the iconic citrus fruit, yet as important as the lemon is to European cooking, it's a latecomer.[60] As *The Oxford Companion to Food* notes, "Lemon cultivation in the Mediterranean was certainly the consequence of Arab initiative. Soon after their conquest a fully indigenous orchard production had been established in S. Europe. . . . Arab traders also spread the lemon eastward to China." Although it's not clear if there were lemons in ancient Rome, "in the Near East, the lemon's wide range of culinary uses was explored. *The Treatise of the Lemon*, which was written by Saladin's physician Ibn Jamiya, gives recipes for lemon syrup and preserves."[61] By the sixteenth century, lemons were becoming more important in Italy. Limes grow better in tropical locations than lemons.

There is a host of citrus less common in North American kitchens but essential to cuisines on other shores—the pomelo, the ugli fruit, or the yuzu, for example. The pomelo is an ancestor of the grapefruit and originally from Malaysia and Indonesia.[62] The pomelo has probably been both gathered and cultivated in China for millennia.[63] The calamansi, a cross between the kumquat and the mandarin orange, enjoys particular popularity in the Philippines.[64] The citron is originally from India (as are the lemon and the lime).[65] Somewhat surprisingly, the citron had a lot of religious significance and healing properties. In China it became a symbol of happiness, in India it symbolized wealth, and in Jewish traditions it is eaten for the Feast of Tabernacles.[66] The orange's origins lie in southwestern China and northwestern India.[67] Bitter oranges spread west first, followed five centuries later by sweet oranges. As I was in the final throes of writing this book, heirloom oranges suddenly began appearing at Trader Joe's and Whole Foods, but with no mention of history or even the variety name.

Preservation and Seasons in Europe and North America

In addition to fruits that come from far away, we can look closer to home. Humans have been eating in North America for many thousands of years. That's a lot of edible memory, and a lot of forgetting. The continent was traced with the patterns of people's efforts to find and grow food long before Europeans came anywhere close.[68] There have been at times cataclysmic changes in patterns of eating, growing, cultivating, hunting, and gathering on this continent: "Only a few fruits now of commercial importance, including blueberries, cranberries, strawberries, and cactus pears, are indigenous to the United States. Before the arrival of European settlers, Native Americans commonly gathered raspberries, blackberries, and strawberries that grew wild in openings in the forest . . . wild grapes, blueberries, cranberries, native persimmons, and mulberries . . . native species of plums, typically smaller and more astringent than cultivated imported species, as well as crab apples and chokecherries, grew from coast to coast."[69] The pawpaw, too, was an important indigenous fruit and has experienced a resurgence of late, maintaining a growing number of loyal followers and acquiring new fans.[70] The prickly pear is another vital fruit, although with a smaller growing region than the pawpaw[71]: "Also called Barbary pear, cactus pear, Indian pear, Indian fig, or tuna fig, [the prickly pear] is not a kind of pear or fig, but comes from any of numerous cacti of the genus *Opuntia*."[72] These fruits are essential to Tohono O'odham cooking, for example, described in great detail by Gary Nabhan in *The Desert Smells like Rain*. There are also more wild varieties of grapes in North America than in the Old World.[73] I don't talk about grapes in great detail because they really fall into the category of wine—far too wide-ranging for this particular book. Mulberries, elderflower, and many berries were native to both sides of the Atlantic. These are in some respects the true North American heirlooms.

Whether on the twelfth-century Atlantic coast of North America or in the courtly kitchen gardens of baroque Europe, techniques of fruit preservation were vital in the days before refrigeration. Unlike potatoes, turnips, or even apples, much fruit is highly perishable and difficult to eat at peak ripeness unless you grow it yourself. That doesn't stop people the world over from eating out-of-season or imported fruit with great enthusiasm. A platter of apples or medlars or bael fruit means very different things to different people: comfort and home, or a tantalizing exoticism. Over time, cultures and societies collectively forget how to grow, prepare, preserve, and enjoy various fruits (and vegetables). Many of us (myself included) sometimes see fruit as medicine—a bland banana or a mealy apple eaten to meet the varying guidelines of daily produce consumption. But in much of human history (and certainly still for much of the world's population), fruit has been a pleasure and a privilege, a jolt of sweetness, juiciness, and color in an otherwise monotone culinary life. In temperate climates, seasons mean that the brief moment of ripeness of some fruit is inaccessible the rest of the year. And that moment is worlds away from a dish of cling peaches canned in heavy syrup, available year-round and offering a very uniform flavor, texture, and color.

Specific fruits are harbingers of seasons: the bright persimmons hanging like Christmas tree ornaments in the bare winter branches of a California tree, or the furry quince lurking in the fading foliage of an autumnal Austrian garden, or the rhubarb frenzy that sweeps the Midwest in early spring, eyes and palates hungry for color and flavor after the long, colorless winter. In temperate climates people find ways to hold on to these flavors ahead of the coming winter, despite brief seasons of peak color, sweetness, and flavor. It was while living in Budapest, and later Berlin and Vienna, that I began to understand the seasonality of produce. The collective mania for asparagus, apricots, gooseberries, or tomatoes—and the sudden ubiquity of these foods in market halls and corner stores, on restaurant menus, and even in university cafeterias was a far cry from the forces that long inhibited my own understanding of seasonality as I was growing up on California's central coast, with seasons far more subtle than elsewhere, living largely off oddly seasonless grocery store produce.

We cannot underestimate the importance of preservation in temperate climates, in the form of jams, preserves, drying, and even schnapps. Because so much fruit is so perishable, techniques of preservation have a long tradition around the world. Both blackberries and blueberries were important in Native American diets, often made into pemmican so they would last beyond the brief growing season.[74] Zola writes eloquently of turning fruit into other things in nineteenth-century France: "Jars of preserved fruit, cherries, plums, and peaches . . . flasks of bright green, red, and yellow, suggesting mysterious liqueurs, or exquisitely limpid flower essences," bottling, canning, and distilling the countryside for the city dwellers.[75] Stocks tells us that "the importance of jam in late Victorian Britain is hard to imagine now, but in the days before deep freezers it was impossible to keep soft fruit for any length of time, so bottling, canning, preserving and above all jam-making helped to extend the shelf-life of soft fruit right through the year, and provided a cheap, energy-rich food for the poor."[76] Preserving and drying are ways of holding on to the sweetness, flavors, and calories of the summer.

An example of this practice is a "marmalade kitchen" in the eastern plains of Austria, the culinary heart of Schloss Hof, a massive baroque palace within sight of the former Iron Curtain, a palace whose interiors and gardens have recently undergone a splendid renovation. The kitchen is full of gleaming copper and cool marble, dominated by an enormous farmhouse sink, a massive range, and scrubbed floors, modeled after the kitchens once used to transform the berries and stone fruit of the nearby gardens and orchards into preserves for the estate. It is a beautiful place, but in its forebears legions of servants labored on behalf of the lords of the manor, sweating over kettles and creating opulent meals without the luxury of running water or refrigeration or even good dish soap. Thus the marmalade kitchen and similar sites that "museumize" culinary memory are also ways of thinking about our relationship to the fruits of the garden, and about the labor that goes into transforming raw materials into food on kitchen tables, hospital trays, or the plates of a hundred guests at a prince's banquet. My visit to this kitchen with its surrounding gardens and barnyards, and to dozens of similar places, captured much of what is intriguing about heirloom food—the layers of history and memory, the interplay of hard work and pleasure, biodiversity and necessity, capturing a fleeting moment of summer ripeness for sustenance in the dark and cold months of the year.

Holding on to Stone Fruit

An even more extreme form of preservation than jam or marmalade, in which the original fruit is less recognizable, is through distillation and making schnapps, turning highly perishable fruit into alcoholic drinks as a way to capture sweetness and the energy of the summer sun. Candied fruit is another approach to preservation, though it requires a fair amount of sugar and is labor intensive. Stone fruit has a long history of being dried, turned into preserves, and distilled into alcohol.

Like plums, apricots have been cultivated for millennia and can form the aromatic basis of the sharp schnapps I was often served at farmhouse tables in central Europe. Cultivating apricots began in China four thousand years ago, and eventually they made their way to the Mediterranean by the Silk Road.[77] Nigel Slater credits Henry VIII with bringing the apricot to England in 1542, or at least with having a gardener who imported it from Italy. In each case of fruit mobility, someone has to make the move—carry a sapling or scions or seeds across a border or an ocean, in hopes of impressing a royal employer, attaining commercial success, or adding to a collection of botanical oddities. Much of the apricot stock that appears in supermarkets today I find cottony and unenjoyable. But just up the Danube from Vienna, in the spring the whole Wachau Valley fills to overflowing with apricot blossoms. As Nigel Slater says, "Blossom is all about hope."[78] This is the same valley where the voluptuous Venus of Willendorf figurine was found, a valley that has offered a rich and mild home to humans for thousands of years. The Danube runs down the middle of the valley, and vineyards rise on the hills above, nestled into stone terraces made with a secret knowledge that has nearly died out. As the seasons start to change, the daily news in Vienna brings eager updates on the apricot harvest—the estimated date when the harvest will begin, guesses about how long it will go on and how it will compare with previous years. Has there been too much rain? Too little? Did the summer come on too strong, too soon, or has this pretty Danube valley been steeped in chilly mists deep into late spring?

As the ever-effusive Bunyard writes, "It is in this quiet carnal antici-pation that much of the charm of fruit-growing rests—as we watch the slow processes of development, the fugitive flower, its hopes and fears, the slow swelling of fruit and the dangers it runs, until we have for the survivors an almost maternal love."[79] This intense seasonality brings about both pleasure and appetite, and an acute awareness of the pas-sage of time and the fleeting seasons.

In anticipation of the Wachau apricots, other apricots start showing up in supermarkets as well. Apricots ripen sooner in Spain and Italy, so with Viennese mouths watering for apricots (or *Marillen*), the grow-ing consumer appetite is somewhat appeased with enormous plastic buckets of the small, pale fruits from elsewhere. One of the most popu-lar ways to eat the apricots is in apricot dumplings. You pop out the pit with your finger or the handle of a wooden spoon (the fruit should be ripe enough that the pit easily pushes out the other side) and fill the hol-low with a sugar cube or a lump of marzipan. Then you wrap the apricot in a layer of potato dough, made either from especially floury potatoes or from one of the powdered mixes from the store. The dumplings boil in hot water until they're done and are served rolled in browned bread crumbs and butter, with a sprinkling of sugar. On warm summer days they sometimes make a midday meal in themselves. This is also a for-giving technique for apricots that aren't quite as good as the best fruit of the Wachau Valley. The love for these apricots creates layers of appetite and authenticity. In jars of Wachauer Marille jam, there are tensions between image and marketing, the worry that what's in the jar may not actually be from that particular valley (despite the prices charged). The Marille farmers' organization urges buyers to look for the seal of ap-proval or certificate of authenticity, and the apricots have even received one of the European denominations of origin.[80]

As with apricots, rarely do I see more than three or four varieties of cherries at the farmers' market—but an estimated nine hundred sweet cherry varieties are cultivated around the world (descendants of *Prunus avium*), as are about three hundred sour cherry varieties (from *Prunus cerasus*).[81] As they did with many other things, the Romans carried cherries across Europe, so that they were found in Britain by the first century CE.[82] Wild cherries also covered much of Europe, and the cultivated variety captured the imagination of writers and artists. Medieval artists used cherries to represent "a sweet, pleasing character, and the delights of the blessed."[83]

Indeed, cherries seem to enjoy particular favor among writers, artists, and eaters alike. Bunyard describes a variety of cherries I had never seen anywhere, despite years of paying unusual attention to fruit, until I bought a small cardboard box of them on a return visit to Andy Mariani's orchard. Bunyard describes these elusive cherries with admirable enthusiasm: "Black Tartarian is a large corpulent fruit, bossed and uneven, and history associates it with Prince Potemkin and Catherine the Great, and for such lusty company it is in no way unfitted. The black, finger-staining, napkin-ruining juice makes it perhaps a fruit for garden strolls rather than for the decorous dessert."[84]

As with other fruits, Henry VIII's fruiterer Richard Harris was responsible for establishing more widespread cherry cultivation in England's Kentish orchards. In *Forgotten Fruits*, Stocks points out that "not many would claim that swedes [a type of turnip], say, are as beautiful as they are delicious, but there are few more uplifting sights than a cherry tree in flower."[85] The Waterloo cherry is one of the only foods in Stocks's book created by a woman rather than a man—this nursery and produce-breeding culture in much of Europe and the United States in the eighteenth and nineteenth centuries was an almost exclusively male affair.[86] Cherry production has declined precipitously in England in recent decades: "At its height in the 1950s, there were 17,300 acres . . . of cherry orchards in the United Kingdom. Thirty years later, there were under 1,000."[87] Unlike apples, cherries really do disappear from supermarkets at a certain point: during the last week or so of the season, the cherries grow blowsy and mottled as the growers shake out one more harvest in the heat of summer. But year-round, at least in Wisconsin, I can still buy Mason jars of sour cherries for pies and compotes, catching a taste of summer on my tongue.

Peaches, too, rarely make it to market in the full glory of available biodiversity and at the peak of tree-ripened flavor. Peaches are originally from China, and they ended up growing very well in Persia. The Romans seem to have brought them to parts of Europe, and France then sent its well-developed peaches across the Channel toward England. Peaches can be delicate, and English peaches had to be grown in sheltered places, like the walls of kitchen gardens, often given additional warmth with built-in hot water pipes heated with wood or coal fires. The development of sophisticated techniques of espalier (training fruit along a wall or wire) also helped to produce exquisite fruit. "Perhaps the most famous peaches of France have been those of Montreuil near Paris; but this was not an instance of a special variety, it was rather a special method of cultivation, using espaliers of a different design, to produce fruits of exceptional quality, packed by hand and internationally famed." But these peaches disappear from memory and daily use, as well as from the landscape; by 1993 "there was only one lady orchardist selling genuine Montreuil peaches in the town."[88]

Fruit history offers a constant refrain of decline and rebirth, fruit falling out of favor, landscapes shifting as tastes change (and tastes changing as politics and economics alter landscapes). Now peach production is widespread in the United States.[89] Peach trees are much shorter-lived than apple or pear, lasting only ten to twenty years, so many old varieties have disappeared as old peach trees die off and new peach fashions (for less fuzz, say, or paler flesh) lead to new varieties' relatively quickly eclipsing the old.[90] I had no idea, and this pattern is quite different from that of so many other heirloom varieties. I'd always thought nectarines were new, a response to these kinds of peach fashions, but in Europe they've been around at least since the sixteenth century. Bunyard also names varieties I'd never heard of. The nectarine's origin is a mystery. It is a true peach, not a cross between a peach and a plum, and "fuzzless" peaches appear in late medieval French records as *brugnon*.[91]

The fashion for heirloom peaches receives some disparaging comments, like the imaginary "kiwi-heirloom peach margaritas" offered as a satire of Martha Stewart (in 2002) or mentioned snidely in a restaurant review.[92] Peaches are originally Chinese, but they have become sufficiently American to be listed in Slow Food's Ark of Taste. The listed peach varieties include Baby Crawford, Fay Elberta, Oldmixon Free, Rio Oso Gem, Silver Logan, and Sun Crest.[93] In fact, something like the Oldmixon Free peach is only two hundred or so years old and was widely grown and sold in the nineteenth-century United States. "Currently, it is one of the few peach varieties from this era that is still available. . . . It bursts with a vanilla flavor and a hint of sugary mint."[94] For much of my youth, I mostly ate peaches out of cans, despite living in driving distance from some spectacular peach orchards, like Andy Mariani's and Mas Masumoto's.

Berries too lend themselves to various forms of preservation. More than two thousand varieties of blackberry grow wild in North America, Europe, and Asia.[95] Blueberries also exist in enormous diversity, both wild and cultivated. There is a fair amount of confusion among the names blueberry, bilberry, whortleberry, and huckleberry. The raspberry grows wild across the Northern Hemisphere.[96] According to Stocks, the raspberry "has suffered so many losses that there is not one 'heritage' variety currently available."[97] The raspberry's genus, *Rubus* (belonging to the rose family), also includes the salmonberry, blackberry, dewberry, and cloudberry. "The fruit, though called berry, is technically an etaerio of druplets (a cluster of small fruits with stones)."[98] Berries even become the subject of international conflicts and diplomatic efforts: "In N. Scandinavia where Finland, Sweden, and Norway meet, and the cloudberry thrives, the inhabitants of these peace-loving countries have been known to engage in 'cloudberry wars'; and the Swedish Ministry for Foreign Affairs maintains, or used to have, a special section for cloudberry diplomacy." Further complicating matters, bears have a special fondness for cloudberries.[99] They grow only in far northern latitudes, so they're hard to get elsewhere except as jam.

Wild strawberries are native to the New World and the Old World. American strawberries were brought to Europe as early as the seventeenth century,[100] and the encounter of North American *Fragaria virginiana*, as well as *F. chiloensis*, with much smaller European varieties led to the cultivated strawberries we know today. The English developed new varieties in the nineteenth century: "On the crest of this wave, a market gardener called Michael Keens produced the 'Keens' Seedling,' remarkable for size and flavour. It caused a sensation when it came into cultivation in 1821 and quickly spread to the Continent and to America. Virtually all modern varieties derive from it."[101] As Jane Grigson writes, "Strawberries are one of the fruits of modernity which are better as well as bigger. The fruit our ancestors knew was one species or other of small European strawberry—fruit sacred to the Northern fertility goddess, Frigg, and then to the Virgin. Bulgy modern straw-berries would hardly be recognized by a medieval miniature painter, who ran hautboys—or wood strawberries—round the margins of his Book of Hours."[102] Strawberries were important during the early colo-nization of North America as well: "They had to make do without sugar and cream, but the Pilgrims were mightily solaced by the strawberries they found at Plymouth soon after the landing."[103] In his chapter on strawberries, Stocks writes, "This chapter is haunted by ghosts: the ghosts of strawberries past," since most older varieties of strawberries have disappeared. Stocks attributes this loss not so much to careless-ness with old varieties as to the susceptibility of soft fruit to viruses. Heirloom strawberries are definitely popular in Germany, where straw-berries like the Mieze Schindler survived decades in obscurity deep in-side East Germany, to experience a renaissance of sorts after the fall of the Berlin Wall. This German strawberry was developed in 1932 by a botanist who named it after his wife (Mieze), and while it has an intense flavor, it ships very poorly, partly accounting for its obscurity.[104] Ber-ries are particularly fragile, but they lend themselves particularly well to jam, collecting the sweetness that comes from summer sunshine into something beautiful to eat in the winter, in a time before freezers and off-season shipping.

Persimmons are also good candidates for preservation. There are native North American persimmons as well as Asian persimmons. After Europeans began to settle in North America, "ripe persimmons were eaten by the settlers, or used in puddings, breads, preserves, etc. But the production of persimmon (or 'simmon') beer and wine and other alcoholic drinks was an equally important use."[105] Kaki is a kind of persimmon popular in Japan, with lots of preservation tech-niques surrounding it. It is generally eaten raw in the United States but often dried in East Asia. The fruit can be dried on rooftops, threaded on strings in the wind and sun. As they dry, sugar forms on the surface, and that sugar is sometimes collected and made into cakes—a very spe-cialized kind of sugar! These dried persimmons are also eaten as a New Year's treat in China.[106] The Marcuses explain that "the round, maroon persimmon that our forebears enjoyed (*Diospyros virginiana*) is now en-countered mainly in the wild or on old farms. The round or plum-shape bright orange varieties sold commercially are not native to America.

Originally from China and then Japan, they were introduced here soon after Commodore Perry's intrusion into Japan in 1852."[107] It is not entirely clear to me who the authors see as "our" forebears. That is quite a geographical journey—from Commodore Perry to the corners of old farms in the United States. This is also another example of forgotten fruit landscapes, the persimmon trees neglected in corners of old farms and forests.

Another fruit native to both Europe and North America is the elderflower/elderberry tree. It is a vibrant part of beverage culture in England and Austria (among other places), with juice, cordial, and even fritters made from the blossoms. Elderflower and elderberry are largely unimportant in the United States today but are beloved across Europe and important in regional Native American culinary traditions. There are many rituals, habits, and techniques surrounding the lowly (and in much of the United States, largely forgotten) elderflower. Many of these are curative and even magical—the scent of elderflower supposedly is mildly sedative, and in Europe sleeping under an elderflower tree could conjure elves and fairies.[108] Both berries and flowers have to be cooked—unripe berries are toxic, and even ripe berries make some people distinctly unwell. Recipes order the cook to shake the large clusters of blossoms to remove excess pollen and insects when making fritters, before dipping the whole thing into a runny batter. *The Oxford Companion to Food* also locates elderflower fritters in North America: "They provide, in a more substantial role, the basis of elderflower fritters, sometimes claimed to be an invention of N. American Indians but having a lineage in Europe which goes back to mediaeval times."[109] Elderflower cordial is widely drunk, and made, in many parts of Europe, a pleasant syrup that can be added to still or sparkling water, and even white wine, lemon juice, or champagne. Elderflowers also form the basis of the pale golden St. Germain liqueur.[110]

The elderflower also carries important cultural symbolism. Schermaul writes that "going all the way back to the Neolithic, this nutrient loving shrub has been a loyal companion to humans near settlements, barns, barnyard entrances and trash heaps. . . . Thus our forebears [in Germany] saw the elderflower as the green protector of house and farm, and honored as the home of a kindly spirit—it was the home and life tree par excellence."[111] Chopping down an elderflower tree could even lead to death. They bloom around the summer solstice, and legend has it that eating elderflowers dipped in batter and fried in lard will protect you from illness in the coming year. One Austrian cookbook author recalls that her grandmother always fried the blossoms in pork fat.[112] She also recalls these fritters as being served at the summer solstice. Nigel Slater finds that "most streets, commons, and wasteland support a *Sambucus nigra* [elderflower] or two. Untended gardens are often good hunting grounds [in the United Kingdom]. At last, something for the urban forager."[113] There are countless underutilized elder trees across the United States, blooming unnoticed, the blooms turning into mildly toxic berries that become enjoyable when properly ripened and cooked.

Gooseberries possess much less mystical power and symbolism than elderflower but have still inspired extremes of devotion, particularly in nineteenth-century England. References to cultivated gooseberries first appear in the fourteenth century.[114] While gooseberries are also found in continental Europe (and are indigenous to North America as well), England is where people most worked at their cultivation. In the nineteenth century, for example, gooseberry societies became extremely popular there, moving across class lines as gardeners competed to produce the largest gooseberries each year. Champion gooseberries approached two ounces—close to eight times what wild ones weigh, a point that fascinated Charles Darwin:[115]

> From the late 18th century and throughout the 19th amateur "gooseberry clubs" were set up in the Midlands and the north of England. These held competitions for the best-flavored and, more particularly, for the largest fruit. Johnson (1847) points out that extraordinary results were achieved, especially in the vicinity of Manchester, by "the lowest and most illiterate members of society, [who] by continual experience and perseverance in growing and raising new sorts, have brought the fruit to weigh three times as much as before and that, too, under the greatest disadvantages, not having the privilege of soil, manure, situation, &c. like the gardeners of their more wealthy neighbours."[116]

By the 1980s there were fewer than ten gooseberry clubs left in England.

Grigson recommends early gooseberries ("small, green, primitive and hairy") as "the best sauce for mackerel. That's a habit we seem to have lost, gooseberries with mackerel, let alone with pork, veal, lamb, goose or duck. We've forgotten how well the sweet-sour astringency of young gooseberry puree goes with such rich flavours."[117] Gooseberry sauce just scratches the surface of what we've forgotten. Indeed, she writes, "by tradition, gooseberry sauce is the Maytime companion of boiled or grilled mackerel. The French honour this antique alliance by naming the gooseberry *groseille à maquereau*: in practice they usually serve a puree of sorrel instead." Grigson then provides four recipes "for a sauce which has been eaten for centuries in Germany, France, Holland and Great Britain."[118] She subsequently poses a question I certainly couldn't answer in the affirmative: "Do you follow the country tradition of eating the first gooseberry pie of the season at Whitsunday lunch?" I don't, but maybe I should. If only I could get my hands on some gooseberries.

The gooseberry's fate, and size, changed significantly in the nineteenth century. Bunyard says it "owes its development to the Midland workers who raised new seedlings for competition, whose sole test of merit was weight, and so was the Big Gooseberry born in the smoke and moisture of Macclesfield and other industrial towns."[119] Bunyard also realizes his readers may not all like hairy fruit, so he proclaims that he "will name [the hairy gooseberries] apart from the smooth or merely downy."[120] He then provides a marvelous (and impossible) specificity as to the proper moment to eat them. Once again, as so often with Bunyard, a fruit room is crucial to ideal flavor:

> As to the time and temperature for gooseberry-eating opinions differ. A friend tells me that the moment of moments and the day of days is on the return from church at 12:30 on a warm July day when the fruit is distinctly warm. For my part I prefer gathering while they are still cool and keeping in the fruit room till wanted. But the Gooseberry is of course the fruit *par excellence* for ambulant consumption. The bush should be given to all visitors, as it is thus that we pass back to those days of the prime when fruit was gathered without the dark terror of the annual show hanging over us, and the exercise of gathering, too, is beneficial to the middle-aged, and also stimulates their absorptive capacity.[121]

Where to begin? The idea that the annual (and highly competitive) gooseberry shows would spark a "dark terror," or the benefits of gooseberry gathering to the middle-aged? Perhaps I should add gathering gooseberries to my workout routine. As for the dark terror, Stocks reports, "Lancashire's pre-industrial weavers were a competitive bunch, and in their spare time they bred all manner of things, from whippets and leeks to pigeons and gooseberries. Their preoccupations were surprisingly familiar: speed (dogs and pigeons) and size (fruit and veg)."[122] Gooseberry competitions peaked in 1815, when there were more than 120 shows. My friend Dave Snyder, the former rooftop farmer at Uncommon Ground in Chicago, grew gooseberry plants in the parking lot planters at the restaurant, a hint of English countryside in the heart of this midwestern city.

Many of these fruits become the province of the privileged and the foragers. When I worked on a schooner in Alaska (at the tender age of sixteen), the ship's cook explained to me that the people who ate best in Alaska were the poorest and the richest—the richest could buy whatever they needed, and the poorest would rely on what they could glean from nature. This dynamic played out in our own shipboard eating, as we ventured onto the islands in our rubber boots to gather buckets of wild salmonberries, raspberries, and blueberries—always on the lookout for grizzly bears interested in the same thing, and carrying a sawed-off shotgun (surely as futile as it was illegal) to keep them at bay. We would pull halibut as big as I am from the boatswain's secret fishing grounds. The ship's cook immediately served small slabs of the creamy white flesh raw on sticky, vinegary handfuls of sushi rice. We butchered the rest of the halibut and filled the ship's freezer with Ziploc bags of halibut chunks, some of which I later traded to passing salmon fisherman for glistening, freshly caught salmon—the fishermen desperate for the taste of something other than the gorgeous fish filling their ship's hold. Our lone crab pot was always full enough when we passed it so we could simply set a huge kettle to boil on the deck, toss in the crabs, and eat them then and there, flinging the shells back into the sea they came from. The blueberries, tiny and delicious, each contained its own worm, so we soaked the berries in a bucket of seawater. The worms would flee their cozy homes and swim to the surface, leaving the berries worm-free and ready for our morning pancakes.

Wild fruits abound for those who know where to look, and they leave traces so they can be gathered and appreciated by those paying attention. The Fallen Fruit project in Los Angeles, for example, creates detailed fruit maps and sponsors (as many groups do) the creation of edible urban orchards, identifying or producing fresh fruit available free in the urban landscape.[123] The Beacon Food Forest in Seattle is another example of planting publicly accessible fruit, including quince, in the cityscape.[124]

Old World Fruit

In fact, European and tropical fruits alike exhibit heirloom qualities but fall out of much popular discourse. The pantheon of heirloom food in the United States includes a host of fruits that really came into their own in Europe. These range from currants, which were *illegal* in New York State until 2003, to quince.[125] Quince is another fruit that is beloved by those who know it well but has fallen out of mainstream culinary culture in the United States (or never was part of it). For starters, many people don't need it as they once did. The first time I remember seeing quince growing was at Arche Noah, the seed saver garden in Austria. In a time before refrigeration (and before the year-round availability of relatively affordable fresh fruit), quince lasted deep into winter. It is not eaten fresh but is usually cooked. Like apples and pears, it comes from the Caucasus, "where small, twisted quince trees still grow wild."[126] Quinces arrived in Europe before apples and were important in Greek mythology. Some people speculate that the golden apple that started the Trojan War was actually a quince.[127] The quince never really took off in North America, but it is quite popular in Uruguay, among other places.[128] Jane Grigson writes lovingly of the quince: "The scent and the look of a bowl of ripe quinces in the house in the autumn are enough to make you believe that the golden fruit Earth gave to Hera and Zeus when they were married was quince and not apple."[129] Grigson offers a recipe I certainly have never tasted—quince pie with mulberry syrup, two fruits that are rarely in my shopping basket (and, at least for now, are rarely found at either grocery stores or farmers' markets). She also offers a recipe for Sir Isaac Newton's baked quinces and an "eighteenth century quince pudding."[130]

Quince is very popular in some parts of the world and in particular forms (like quince paste or quince cheese). Top producers in 2011 were

Turkey, China, Uzbekistan, Morocco, and Iran. But quince is largely forgotten or under-utilized in much of Europe (although Spain and Serbia are in the top ten world producers) and North America, where there is no longer the same appetite for it.[131] The Marcuses report that "until recently in America, quinces could only be obtained from trees on old farms or in neglected orchards, whose stock probably dated back to the plants brought here during colonial times, when quinces were a quite popular fruit."[132] The quince also shares some properties with the service tree (*Sorbus domestica*). Schermaul reports that the service tree, both rare and beautiful, was once found in many villages and farms across Germany.[133] Ancient Greeks and medieval monks planted the service tree, and it has begun to return to the landscapes of cider- and apple-loving regions of Germany, for example, where 100,000 have been planted in the past ten years.[134] The fruit of the service tree becomes edible only after a frost softens it, and it is largely used in making hard cider. The medlar is similarly obscure, edible only after it has been bletted (left to begin decaying, ideally after a frost); Charlemagne was responsible for spreading it through Europe.[135] I encountered venerable quince trees within the generous walls of an old monastery garden in Austria (and slipped one quince into my trusty research bag), the first time I'd seen them growing in the wild. I'd also run across baskets of quinces in the autumn farmers' markets in Vienna. Indeed, much of this chapter is about longing, memory, and appetite across time and space.

Pears, not yet mentioned in this book, deserve to be treated at greater length given their cultural and culinary importance. Today there are about a thousand varieties of pears.[136] Pear trees originated, like so much else, in the Caucasus.[137] There were wild pear trees in ancient Greece, and pictures of pear trees grace the walls of Pompeii.[138] The Romans brought cultivated pears to Europe.[139] The pear appears in the *Domesday Book*,[140] and Henry VIII's fruiterer, Richard Harris, brought a number of pears to England, growing them alongside apples, plums, and other fruits in model orchards at Teynham in Kent.[141] As with apples, many of the early pears were cooking pears rather than dessert pears (and cider pears as well), and Europeans didn't eat them raw in any great numbers until the past few hundred years.[142] Pear trees generally grow larger than apple trees, and they need a warmer climate.

They live so long that in Germany some are designated natural monuments.[143] Pear expert James Arbury notes that because pears grown on pear rootstock can live for more than three centuries, those we see today have witnessed, and survived, plenty of political and social upheaval.[144]

At one point pears were more popular than apples, and the two fruits followed a similar course in the sixteenth and seventeenth centuries, becoming the objects of increasingly skilled cultivation and breeding techniques, many developed in France. James Arbury tells us that "it was . . . in the 18th and 19th centuries that the bulk of the fine pears were raised and it is from these pear growers and nurserymen that we have such a wide range today, although this has declined from its heyday."[145] Pears grow particularly well in France (as opposed to England or points farther north or south), and planting pears along warm walls seems to have started in France in the sixteenth century.[146] Pears were brought from France to Germany,[147] and pear espalier techniques developed at Versailles spread far beyond.[148] The seventeenth century is when people started eating pears raw in Germany (which may have less to do with fashion than with botany and the development of more pleasant-tasting pears).[149] There is a pear (described by Theodor Fontane) known as the *franzoser Birne*, the "French pear," and the German language is full of things described as *franzose*: for example, the splendid French bed, essentially a full- or queen-size mattress rather than the two twin mattresses pushed together that the Germans tend to use.

Pears, like other fruits and vegetables, often have murky origins: "Black Worcester, origin uncertain, but one of the oldest pears in cultivation. It appears on the coat of arms of Worcester and was grown there before 1575 when Queen Elizabeth I saw it at Whystone Farm. . . . [It] may even date from Roman times";[150] or the Jargonelle, "origin uncertain, one of the most ancient pears in cultivation, first mentioned by Parkinson in 1629 but possibly much older."[151] Some pears became widely popular and commercially successful, while others languished in obscurity. The Williams' Bon Chrétien, better known in the United States as the Bartlett, originated in 1770.[152] In a bit of English pride, Bunyard asserts, "We may be proud of [the Williams pear] as one of the few universal pears which are of British origin, and behind the old Church at Aldermaston, near Reading, may be seen a simple stone marking the resting place of John Stair, 'Schoolmaster of this Parish— erected by his grateful Pupils.' His other memorial is the pear now known as Williams, but which in his own country is still called Stair's Pear, and since that year of its birth, 1770, it has travelled far."[153] It became the Bartlett pear in North America, then moved on to South Africa, and it was frequently canned.[154]

Warden pears, on the other hand, have not been so popular in recent decades: "The name *Warden* was probably first given to a pear grown at Warden Abbey in Bedfordshire, but the term 'warden' came to signify a type of culinary pear which was much grown in the past. These pears are very hard and often gritty; they ripen slowly and are never soft enough to be eaten as dessert. They are very long keeping, storing under ordinary storage conditions (in a shed or barn) until April or May."[155] So this is clearly a pear from another era, "particularly valuable in the days before cold storage, canning, freezing and imports from the Southern hemisphere."[156] They took hours to cook and were eaten spiced or sweetened.

The nineteenth-century German author Theodor Fontane describes a man who put pear seeds in his pockets when he felt death approaching so that pears would grow out of his grave.[157] There are Asian pears, derived from a different *Pyrus* species than European pears,[158] and cider is frequently made from pears: "Perry pears are fairly small and usually quite astringent (although some are suitable to eat or cook). They are crushed and pressed to produce juice used to make perry, in much the same way as cider and wine are produced. The best perry is a fine drink of a quality equal to good wine."[159] Cider pears were more widespread than dessert pears, since they didn't require as much pleasant weather.[160] Today pears are often grafted onto quince rootstock to keep the trees short (pears grafted onto pear stock tend to grow very large). Arbury writes that "not all pears are compatible with Quince rootstocks, and incompatible cultivars have to be 'double worked,' that is a compatible cultivar has to be grafted on first as an interstock."[161] There was an exceptionally heavy freeze in Europe in 1928–29, so every tree older than that survived that frost, leaving some very cold-hardy pears.[162]

Many other fruits' histories reveal these changes in economies and tastes, landscapes and habits. Bunyard writes, in his inimitable way, "The family of melons is large, and we may divide it, as Melville did the whale, into folios, octavos, and duodecimos."[163] The kiwi didn't become popular until the twentieth century ("a mystery to which Jane Grigson [1982] has drawn attention is why the Chinese did not perceive the possibilities of this fruit. There is little evidence of their having shown any interest in it, except as a tonic for children or women after childbirth").[164] The loquat has been cultivated in China for at least a millennium.[165] The lychee is originally Chinese and has been cultivated for a long time: "During the 1st century AD a special courier service with swift horses was set up to bring fresh lychees from Canton north to the imperial court";[166] and "the 12th-century treatises on the lichi, for example, are essentially lichi club handbooks, rich in metaphor and indulging in the typical . . . conceit of enumerating pleasures."[167] The date is minor in much cooking in the United States but essential in North Africa and the Middle East, and "indeed, in such regions the tree is often the essential plant on which life depends, a universal provider which is said to have 800 distinct uses."[168] The pomegranate is originally from Iran but was widely known in ancient Egypt, Greece, and Rome.[169] There is a curious amount of inaccuracy about fruit in literature and history. For example, there is an ongoing debate about what Eve ate in the garden of Eden (we think of it as an apple, but there is talk of pomegranates, figs, and citrons). Scholars also wonder what Homer's lotus-eaters were actually eating: jujubes? dates?[170] And few have ever heard of azaroles outside the eastern Mediterranean and Iran. Or bael, "a tree which grows wild in much of N. India and SE Asia, belongs to the same family, Rutaceae, as the citrus fruits. . . . Hindus hold the tree sacred to Shiva and use its leaves in his worship. It is sacrilegious to cut down a bael tree, but to die under one assures immediate salvation."[171] So again, one person's heirloom is clearly another person's exotic. Trees that are sacred, physically and spiritually nourishing, in one part of the world may be virtually unknown or considered extraordinary elsewhere. Fruits unknown to most American newspaper readers are in fact integral components of other people's daily lives or culinary memories.

Another "fruit" (although technically a vegetable) that creates landscapes of memory is rhubarb. I once gave a talk at my home campus in Wisconsin about historical kitchen gardens (subject of a future book), including some discussion of heirloom fruits and vegetables. In the question-and-answer session, people's hands flew up to talk about something I hadn't even mentioned: rhubarb. The idea of an heirloom food, and of memory rooted in a garden, not only piqued their curiosity but immediately made many members of the audience think of their own experience with rhubarb. No heirloom rhubarb appears in the media coverage I analyzed. Yet in Wisconsin rhubarb has many of the qualities of a literal heirloom. In Milwaukee people dig up their rhubarb patches if they move to a new home, or bring clumps of their parents' rhubarb plants to new homes (even rentals). Rhubarb is a great relief after the lean season of spring. Here in the Upper Midwest, April and May are still quiet months in the garden, with little or no nourishment yet coming out of the ground. Botanically speaking, rhubarb belongs to the world of vegetables, but in 1947 the Customs Court in Buffalo, New York, declared that legally speaking they belong to the world of fruit, since they are normally eaten more as a fruit (sweet) than a vegetable (savory). Wild rhubarb originates in Asia, and it took a long and meandering path westward. Much of the plant's early use was medicinal, as when it was introduced to England in the sixteenth century[172] and when it was traded on the Silk Road.[173] As Slater tells us, "It was the darling of the Victorian kitchen, finding its way into pies, fools, crumbles, and tarts quite by chance. Tired of the escalating price being asked by Chinese exporters, British apothecaries decided they could grow their own, and imported plants from Central Asia, unintentionally importing the more edible and less medicinal variety."[174]

Rhubarb didn't take off as a non-medicinal food in England until the nineteenth century, in part because most people prefer it cooked with a fair amount of sugar, which was prohibitively expensive in England until about this time.[175] The development of red rhubarb is relatively recent (nineteenth century). Gardeners often force rhubarb, in England but also in Afghanistan. Stocks writes, "Forcing really took off in the 1880s, when a group of enterprising families in the so-called 'Rhubarb Triangle' between Wakefield, Leeds and Bradford took advantage of the fact that local coal was cheap as chips and started raising rhubarb in specially heated sheds."[176] By the end of World War II people left rhubarb behind, owing, in his view, to overexposure plus the new availability of imported fruit.[177] But "the last few years have seen a rhubarb renaissance, as people have rediscovered its subtle flavour and palate-cleansing mix of sweetness and acidity."[178] And many Wisconsinites never lost their taste for the first fruity flavor of the long-awaited spring, or neglected their rhubarb patches. There is even a book titled *A History of Rhubarb Grown in Yorkshire*, one of the most specific fruit histories I've come across in my research: "In Britain the combination of rhubarb and custard is as irresistible to some as it is off-putting to others; and rhubarb crumble, also with custard, is deservedly popular."[179] Rhubarb leaves, however, contain high levels of oxalic acid, making them toxic. Indeed, rhubarb has it all—a fruit *and* a vegetable, eaten with gusto in Afghanistan, Leeds, and Milwaukee, and on the same roller-coaster of fame and infamy, remembering and forgetting experienced by so much of the produce in this book.

In many cases, the foods referred to in popular culture as heirlooms are relatively recent and came from somewhere else. In popular media the term "heirloom" tends to have particular boundaries and connotations. But if our understanding of heirloom varieties has to do with food that predates more industrialized and mechanized agriculture, and that bears a story of its past, then the concept of heirloom food in the United States must be more diverse. In a country so inherently heterogeneous, and born of mobility and immigration, heirloom fruits and vegetables must include not only the favorites that show up repeatedly in newspapers. Some criticize the term "heirloom" for sounding exclusionary, but most people I ran across used the term in a more down-to-earth way. And I suggest that we can expand the understanding of an heirloom. We may crave the first fruit placed on our tongues when we were babies, or a longed-for fruit served at a homecoming, or unattainable tastes lost forever. Heirlooms can reach far beyond tomatoes or apples.

Home gardeners are keepers of biodiversity in vegetables and some fruits, less so in tree fruits, and much less so in grain. Ultimately the heirloom concept allows us to look at something much bigger—this powerful intersection of food and memory, biodiversity and landscape, culture and history. Yes it's about heirlooms, but it's also about how memory is manufactured and uneven, and how it interacts with the material world, refracted through politics and economics, habit and history. What is remembered exists in a kind of silent contrast with the universe of what has been forgotten, what has gone extinct. It's always easier to study what is remembered than what is forgotten. There are iconic, paradigmatic, talismanic trees, orchards, gardens, and specific pieces of fruit; and there is a difference between eating certain foods as a child and coming to them late in life. Today numerous children in the United States grow up eating avocados and mangoes, even in an era when many people are not eating as much fruit and vegetables as we're told we should. Any well-stocked bodega and any produce market in an urban Chinatown will have lots of fruits unfamiliar to many Americans, but quite familiar to people who grow up with them. These markets, fruits, and trees teach us about mobility and perishability, and about appetites and longings across great geographic and temporal distance. The strange becomes familiar, the body and palate grow accustomed. These transformations do have to do with home and place and love and the dinner table, but also with loss.

Epilogue

WITH ALL THE mobility of fruits and vegetables, the changes not only in tastes but also in the technologies of agricultural production, there are forgotten landscapes, remnants that can tell us about the past. Forgotten fruits and vegetables, trees, and bushes appear here and there in history, literature, and landscape. Fruits are more permanent than vegetables, leaving trees or stumps in the ground while ancient vegetable gardens leave little archaeological or vegetal record. My interest is always piqued when I run across information about an abandoned orchard or forgotten fruit trees. These forgotten trees tell us about lost habits and about changes in the production, distribution, and consumption of food. Long-lived pear trees, for example, may be silent witnesses to Spanish colonization in the American West: "The pear and the orange were the fruits, and it was their seeds that the Spanish padres carried with them when they founded missions up the western coast of North American into what is now California. Their old pear trees are still sometimes found growing in the old mission gardens."[1] Apple trees repeatedly surface out of neglected landscapes. In the nineteenth century, Nathaniel Hawthorne wondered, "And what is more melancholy than the old apple-trees that linger about the spot where once stood a homestead, but where there is now only a ruined chimney rising out of a grassy and weed-grown cellar? They offer their fruit to every wayfarer,— apples that are bitter sweet with the moral of Time's vicissitude."[2]

Jane Grigson offers a particular walnut tree as a vivid example of the powerful connection between memory, food, and place.[3] In the prune-growing Agenais district of France, where farmers grew plums well suited for drying in ovens built into the hills, she finds that "one may walk along a sunken lane . . . and come to a hamlet of old cave houses warrening an exposed rock face. There will be a walnut tree or two as a token of past living, a bay tree, some apples, a quince, and a medlar, but the plum trees will have disappeared. Chimneys poke through the slopes of the cliff top above, but there's no smoke. The only other sign of past existence, of life before the First World War, is a blackened flare of rock above a gaping hole at waist height," where "the wives of the hamlet" used to bake their bread and then dry their plums in these cave ovens.[4]

A tree full of forgotten walnuts, melancholy apples, or Spanish pears can be a remnant of a past way of living.[5] Many people in the walnut-growing latitudes of the world today, using them as an occasional addition to a salad or baking, not as a vital source of nutrients, find walnuts relatively cheap and accessible without tending a large tree. The sheer quantity of sustenance available from one walnut tree justifies its existence in a garden or barnyard. Today in much of the global North and West, we can toss a sealed plastic bag of walnut meat into our shopping cart without a second thought about the trees those walnuts grew on or who planted and harvested them, and without the time-consuming work of gathering the big round fruits off the ground, peeling off the skin, cracking the hard shells, and picking out their rich, nutritious meat. Walnuts can be stately, solitary occupants of barnyards, a commanding presence in yards and gardens. In the Austrian meadow where I have spent so many evenings, a single walnut tree grows above the old manure pile, close up against the side of the outbuilding that used to house the laundry and the dairy cows, and later the printing studio of the artist who cared for this tree, which sadly has outlived him.

The outdoor space where the manure had once been collected had a paved floor and a low wall on three sides. The walnut tree once protected the valuable manure from too much rain or sun. When I knew it, manure was no longer stored here, and the area was used as a patio, a place to sit outside on long summer evenings in the cool, fresh breeze from the meadow. We would barbecue, drink white wine spritzers or mugs of hard cider, and talk into the night. This spot was so well shaded by the tree's lush leaves that we could sit outside in the rain for a long time before a single raindrop found its way through the great umbrella of this aging tree, whose days ultimately were numbered. It was a heartbreak when any of the trees in this meadow had to come down, a loss on so many levels: the loss or radical change of the view out onto the meadow; the loss of a certain apple or nut variety from the yearly harvest; and the poignant memory of the person who planted and tended the tree, a reminder of lost loved ones who had once inhabited this space. Like us, fruit and nut trees (indeed, any trees) do not live forever, and one by one they vanish from the landscape, taking with them their fruits and their memories. A tree comes down in a windstorm or gets split by a bolt of lightning, taken unexpectedly and shockingly, or it falls to the ax or the chainsaw, the expansion of a house or a village or a city, the building of a road or a freeway or a shopping center.

There are marked tensions here between remembering and forgetting. For Nigel Slater, "currants bring back memories like those of no other fruit. They provide, by their flavor and the scent of their pruned wood, a clearer memory of my childhood than any photograph album ever could."[6] Slater is not alone in feeling this edible memory so deep in his physical senses. People work hard to bring back some of these forgotten fruits, in what I have elsewhere called landscapes of memory. But here and there, people work to preserve fruit memory not only in the form of trees and bushes, but also as recipes. If this one orchard disappears, making way for a handful of new houses or a parking lot, a single family's memory vanishes, as do a few aging fruit trees. When this happens on a larger scale, we lose something much bigger. One family's loss in the aggregate is a massive scale of forgetting, of habit and appetite but also of biodiversity, the potential reserve of genes to carry us into an always uncertain future. It requires countless huntresses of lost fruit to bring back the forgotten (or nearly forgotten) "genes, aromas, and histories."[7]

The borders of my own childhood were also formed by fruit trees, but my family is especially attached to the apple trees. We felled a diseased bay tree once, without much fuss except that several family members got hurt trying to remove the stump. We recently chopped down a gangly, unproductive, largely ornamental plum tree. No one shed a tear, and three generations of the family worked together to turn the misshapen boughs and unpruned shoots into a magical backyard tent, using a stack of bedsheets and a cushiony unstrung hammock, a perfect refuge for reading stories and building LEGO cities. A few days later the shelter was dismantled, the sheets washed and put away, and the branches unceremoniously chopped up for our winter fires. The tree's absence was barely noted, except that we had more light in the yard and it was easier to get to the compost pile.[8]

But if we'd had to chop down one of the six apple trees in the yard, the mood would have been far less festive. The open space would have been felt as an ache in the heart, and we might have caught the ghost of the tree out of the corners of our eyes. These apple trees have witnessed some of the happiest and some of the most heartbreaking moments in my own life. They occupy the background in countless birthday party photographs, and their tart fruits went in our lunch boxes and filled untold numbers of apple crisps. Loosely following Halbwachs, these apple trees anchor our family memory, serving as a backdrop but also as a reminder of the passage of time.[9] The little trees show their age just as we do, but they still appear anew in the photos (and in the dreams and memories) of the newest generation.[10] We can think of edible memory and edible forgetting within families and communities, but also on a global and historical scale—they are intricately connected.

Kurlansky's *Food of a Younger Land*, a collection of WPA (Works Progress Administration) writings from the 1930s, is certainly a case of edible memory, and of edible forgetting.[11] The writers in the collection recount now lost or vanishing habits and traditions—not just ingredients, not just recipes, but whole sets of social habits and obligations surrounding everything from annual festivals to the appropriate time of day for lunch in a given community. These ingredients and techniques of preparation and preservation were part of the structure of gender roles and labor relations, land use and trade patterns, as well as regulations (or the lack of them). The rough edges get smoothed over time like beach glass, by violence and love, loss and identity. Andrew Beahrs's fascinating account of the American foods included in a feast imagined by a homesick Mark Twain also points to layers of edible forgetting and, importantly, the vanished landscapes that produced these foods: a crystal-clear Lake Tahoe and its brown trout; a nontoxic San Francisco Bay free of the layer of mercury laid down by the later years of the Gold Rush; turtle breeding grounds on the East Coast.[12]

A single walnut or pear tree is not going to solve world hunger, nor is a particular heirloom tomato. In the United States and much of the world, government policies and decisions by large corporations affect patterns of food production and consumption. As we grow up, we also attach meanings and memories to these foods, even if they aren't the tomatoes our grandmothers grew. Many people who today might not patronize McDonald's or buy a cereal that turns the milk chocolate still have powerful childhood memories of these foods, in part because of smell. Olfaction is a powerful memory sense, linked directly to food and to taste. I came across the concept of "emotional calories" in a French book about vegetables, pointing out that foods in general (and vegetables in particular) are sources of nutrition *and* symbolism, objects of commerce *and* meaning.[13] I found echoes of this sentiment in conversations and public lectures, gardens and farms, popular and scholarly literature. Sociologist Michael Carolan's own memory of kolache, for example, transported him back to childhood: "To taste this pastry filled with fruit—which in our family tends to be either prune or apricot—is to be momentarily transported to another place and time. An event made real through a dance between my tongue, taste buds, saliva, and the shedding of molecules from a familiar food."[14] And not only do many people truly enjoy much of today's industrialized food, they may attach just as deep a set of meanings to it as someone who grew up eating heirloom tomatoes. A frozen pizza, for me and my brother, was an exciting sign of a night with a babysitter. I knew it didn't taste half as good as my mother's yeasty homemade pizza (which we got to shape and top to our own specifications), but it was still a culinary thrill.

Even if we're eating the recommended amount of fruit and vegetables every day, we're still consuming only a fraction of the edible biodiversity that's out there. Any fruit, vegetable, or grain has a genetic history—years, decades, centuries, even millennia of breeding, as well as cell-level intervention by scientists in the genetically modified food regularly eaten in the United States (predominantly corn, soy, and papayas). Edible forgetting threatens biodiversity and other kinds of similarly valuable diversity, troves of possibility for the future. If there is only one kind of tomato, not only does the genetic pool become depleted but so does the social memory bank, the ability to compare my grandfather's slow-ripening tomatoes with your grandfather's first of the season, or my mother's seafoam salad with your mother's.[15] Some heirloom varieties become status symbols, but that doesn't restrict access, which rests on a much deeper and broader foundation of solitary seed savers as well as larger groups who have preserved the foods that then become fashionable.

There is rarely much inspiration to think about the genetic or cultural origins of what we're eating, in part because there's so little genetic variation, and we generally don't even know who grew the food, under what conditions, or where. I'm not suggesting that people should feel guilty about not getting enough heirloom eggplant in their diets, but the produce department of your supermarket tells a particular genetic (and cultural, economic, and political) story. I *am* advocating for curiosity. We can, and should, ask a simple question: Where does the food on our plates come from? That question alone contains multitudes— the conditions under which that food was most recently produced and its ancient origins alike—the farmworkers who harvested it, the spouse or chef or grandparent who prepared it, the workers who sold it to you, the chemists who created many of the ingredients, or the genetic origins in far-off fields and forests. The apple in your lunch box may be from the Pacific Northwest or your local orchard, and at the same time it is from the foot of the Tien Shan mountains and the orchards of ancient Romans and medieval monks. A vast current of germplasm, habit, memory, and intention is moving inexorably into the future. In the final weeks of revising this book, when I had called on friends to cook for me, since I was too immersed in writing about food to actually prepare any, I was standing in a friend's kitchen as he made one of my favorite meals (his red beans and rice). This smart, savvy friend said something I have heard from other friends and strangers alike—that I have changed how he thinks about food, that now anytime people start talking about memory and meaning and food, he thinks of me and follows the path of inquiry much further than he once would have. That was, to say the least, very gratifying, and I hope that it is also how some people experience this book. Tastes in food—whether for rare turnips or for sugary breakfast cereal—shape space, since the turnips or grains need to grow somewhere, produced by (and producing) agricultural landscapes.

Gardens and barnyards, farmers' markets and gene banks, as well as delicious produce and sturdy barnyard animals, hold powerful keys to a global and personal past and to the future as well. The food in short supply in much of the world is fundamental to physical survival, but it also plays an essential role in culture and meaning, in our connections to other people and to the past, and in our hopes for the future.[16]

Alongside my interest in food history and culinary memory, a lot of my research has focused on cities, and on how cities change over time. I am especially interested in how memories, stories, and symbols get attached to neighborhoods and landmarks, memorials and parks.[17] These may be stories that are personally meaningful, family memories, or tales connected to the history of a nation. What became very clear in my research is that the stories we tell each other—both within the private realm of friends and family and in the public realm of cities and societies—shape the spaces we inhabit. In addition, however, these spaces also shape the stories we tell, and thus our understanding of ourselves, of the past, and in some cases of the future. I began to pay attention to the link between stories and places, the meanings people read into landscapes, and the ways stones and mountains sometimes speak—or rather, the ways we speak for them. The ways we think about things, talk about things, remember them, and imagine them have consequences for the material world.

Part of the success of the heirloom food movement may have to do with the range of spaces it occupies. For decades heirloom vegetables were largely a private matter, grown in backyard vegetable patches. This very decentralized seed saving helped to preserve biodiversity, albeit in what anthropologist Virginia Nazarea calls a "beautifully haphazard" way.[18] As these heirlooms grew in popularity, they found their way into more and more gardens, and eventually on to farms and into restaurants and farmers' markets.

Gardens, fields, and orchards are also linked to politics and culture, to our conceptions of who we are and who we want to be. As a group of professors at Cardiff University wrote in their compelling *Worlds of Food*, "Buying food may be a private matter, but the type of food we buy, the shops or stalls from where we buy it, and the significance we attach to its provenance have enormous social consequences."[19] These are landscapes crafted by people acting individually and collectively, as gardeners or farmers or corporations or legislative bodies. The Farm Bill in the United States, the extensive agricultural subsidies and protective tariffs around the globe, the fiscal policies of the World Bank and the International Monetary Fund—all shape the landscapes around us and the food that ends up on our plates.

The landscapes we inhabit are mixtures of accident and intention. The recent trend toward heirloom produce and heritage livestock creates objects and spaces that bear powerful messages about collective understandings of the past and the future—about pleasure, nutrition, hunger, and biodiversity. Apples, tomatoes, and their compatriots in agricultural biodiversity become media themselves, unsuspecting carriers of shared understandings of a simpler past or a threatened future. Furthermore, the efforts to preserve these genes *and* to attach resonant meanings to their phenotypes translate into concrete spaces that have complex relations to the symbolic and material qualities of contemporary life.

As individuals and as a society, we learn how to love certain foods, and forget how to love others. Taste is a complicated thing, a mixture of the biology and chemistry of our taste buds and particular foods, but shaped by habit, memory, and culture. Taste in food feels very personal, even visceral. It is a great part of how we experience the world, and of how we understand our places in that world. But our tastes in food (and art and music and clothes and many other things) are also rooted in the social worlds we inhabit.[20] New tastes and appetites become memories over time, both personal and shared, with layers of familiarity and unfamiliarity, movement and tradition.

Making Memory

As many historians, sociologists, and others emphasize, the "past" is not simply delivered to us unchanged by our ancestors.[21] Instead, scholars, hobby researchers, journalists, archivists, and a multitude of others sift through archives and records and photographs and seed banks to piece together accounts of the past. Some elements of the past (edible and otherwise) are carried on into the future, while others vanish irretrievably.

As many of us know from our own often fallible memories, memory even of something as simple as one's own childhood is full of contradictions and inexplicable gaps, ghostly images like dreams and powerful recollections that may wash over us at the chance encounter with a particular smell or taste. Powerful memories are built within a generation (in fact, many people may reject tradition outright in the context of immigration or upward mobility). The food we eat, or that we remember eating in decades past, can tie us to distant people or places or to our grandparents' kitchens and backyards, down the street or an ocean away. In the prosperous parts of the global North, these issues are important but are not always urgently connected to survival. In other parts of the world, where agriculture has not yet been exhaustively industrialized, bitter battles are now being fought, with more looming on the horizon, over who has the rights to the fundamental DNA floating in seeds and animals, who has the right to save seeds and plant them the following year, and whether imported hybrid plants and animals will eliminate local indigenous varieties.[22] While the growth of interest in heirloom plants and animals in the North and West seems to be pulling some varieties and breeds back from the brink of extinction, questions remain about the persistence of global agricultural biodiversity in the face of current, and pending, transformations in agriculture around the world.

We can, and should, take edible memory seriously in settings where communities are at risk of famine, and where local agriculture for domestic consumption is severely challenged. And without essentializing tradition, we can pay attention to local habits, appetites, memories, and livelihoods. These are memories in the making, both personal and collective. Leaves, roots, fruits, and trees (like stones) do not speak for themselves. But (just like stones) when we speak for them, we see them in a new light and treat them differently. Appetites for meaningful things are not the province of elites, and we do a disservice to much of the country (and the world) if we think this. Not everyone has easy access to these memories. My own experience is at one privileged extreme of the edible genome, but people create edible memories across the socioeconomic scale. They come out of lived experience.

When I teach classes about industrialization and urbanization, and how both really took off in Europe and the United States in the nineteenth century, I ask my students how many of them keep pigs in their apartments, or live off the produce of their gardens, or even have eaten something homegrown or homemade that day. Naturally none of them keep pigs, but few have even cooked anything recently. Most of them "nourish" themselves at fast-food counters (including those in the Student Union) or, proving my point even more, eat out of the dreary vending machines just outside the windowless lecture hall. We then have a long discussion about what the division of labor implies, and how city dwellers and suburbanites pay others to sustain them physically while they engage in other work that people need done (insurance claims adjusting, teaching, heart surgery, etc.). Even with the growth in urban farms and gardens (and the fashionable resurgence of canning and pickling), if all city dwellers had to grow their own tomatoes, not to mention milk their own cows, we'd quickly run into serious problems.

Total self-reliance is the only option for some people and a conscious choice for others, but most of us, especially the world's urbanites and suburbanites with little or no access to agriculturally productive land, need the division of labor to survive and rely on the labor of others to make it through the day. We cannot forget about the labor that goes into food—field workers, truck drivers, butchers, cooks, parents, and salespeople—all this labor done by others to feed people. The uniform, industrial tomato is one answer to feeding urban and suburban populations—large scale, predictable, reliable, and comparatively cheap. In the United States a growing number of farms, farmers' markets, food pantries with connections to urban farms and gardens, and CSA programs solve this problem differently, providing more direct links between consumers and producers. The division of labor as it relates to city dwellers and tomatoes can take the form of tomatoes harvested practically green in Mexican hothouses, ripened (or reddened) by ethylene gas, then transported across North America to reach supermarkets in Maine or Wisconsin or anywhere else. Or it can be a farmer in New Jersey packing up tomatoes for the two-hour journey into Manhattan to set up shop at the Greenmarket.[23]

As with archaeological remnants, these genotypes, and the social memory associated with them, are irreplaceable once they disappear. I am not saying we all need to remember all things, or that all things past should be preserved into the future. But if these genotypes vanish, and if we as a society, or as a world, lose them irreparably, we also lose particular tastes and skills, diversity and heterogeneity in the present, and a wealth of possibility for the future. That may be fine in some cases—

we simply replace old ways with new, and even with better ways. But we may also lose options, variety, and contrast.

These genes are also often bound closely to places. Certain sheep may thrive in alpine valleys but not on the rocky plains of Wyoming. Tomatoes may taste very different depending on the soil, and even on the balance of rain, sun, and wind in a given summer. Many of these crops may be well suited to a particular location and a set of skills, like potatoes well adapted to Andean microclimates. Fruits and vegetables are compartmentalized into specific places, geographic patches, terroir, soil, and sun, yet they are also transnational. We can also see this linking into a global edible memory. In effect, we all eat other people's memories. Food and people move across the surface of the Earth, and while some people, and groups of people, are much more rooted to places than others, these connections operate on a continuum.

Memory settles in all kinds of foods, not just in what many of us know as heirlooms. While this book is primarily about heirloom fruits and vegetables, I have found edible memory—taking in stories and memories alongside physical sustenance—in a far wider range of settings. Edible memory is not only a personal recollection of a childhood tomato or apple, but also collective memory in the sense of tapping into collective narratives, other people's childhood memories, in the form of fruits and vegetables that may seem exotic when first encountered in adulthood. This is part of why thinking about collective memory requires thinking about culture. While most of this book deals with plants whose genetic pedigree and rarity qualify them as edible heirlooms, I also want to leave room for a bigger definition of edible memory and for a broader understanding of culinary heirlooms.

This attention to the concept of heirloom food should not lead us to romanticize or idealize traditional foods. Culinary traditions are highly changeable, in ways often overlooked by people advocating a "return" to traditional diets, and "tradition" itself is rarely as straightforward as it seems.[24] There is nothing intrinsically healthier about a diet simply because it is traditional—at the very least because what we may define as traditional actually is a moving target, identifiable but also changeable. Taken to its logical conclusion, the close scrutiny of the fates of heirloom vegetables also illuminates vital issues around the workings of culture and memory, a model of thinking about how culture works and where it is located. These fruits and vegetables reveal a model of culture as both stable and dynamic. Looking at edible memory means investigating how people have saved these plants and animals from extinction, creating possibilities for the future and connections to the past.

Edible memory goes well beyond heirloom varieties. I use heirlooms as a particularly emblematic form of edible memory, but as I conducted my research, I could see that similar patterns clearly were going on with foods that were not technically heirlooms or antiques. The vast attention paid to foodways, but also to the daily practices of people around the world, contributes to a global form of edible memory. In some places today's culinary habits closely resemble those of hundreds or even thousands of years ago. In other places they are quite different. The examples I offer concern one small corner of the much bigger universe of edible memory, deeply local, profoundly global. I hope to set in motion further questions and conversations, and hope that this book is by no means the last word on edible memory.

In dissertation defenses I always ask my students what surprised them in the research process. If I ask the question of myself, here at the end of this book, undoubtedly one of the great surprises is the sheer scope of the subject. The feeling, after seven years of research and writing, that there is so much more to know and learn is oddly exhilarating. The stacks of books littering my dining table (and my desk and my office) as I finished writing, the knowledge that there were countless other people to talk with and places to visit and foods to taste, left me feeling that there was so much more to read and know. There exists a bounty of beautiful, fascinating, and life-changing investigations of everything from chard to chives, wild foods to the botanicals that make up a liquor cabinet. So much more to learn and know, taste and experience. Sets of meanings, memories, and habits can have profound consequences for fields and farmers, landscapes and lunch. The loss of biodiversity threatens our collective edible memory and the landscapes and practices that create it. But the growing taste for heirloom food has contributed to the preservation of edible biodiversity.

If we lose these old varieties—and our curiosity about food's origins—we lose something vital. Life is inherently about loss—nobody gets out of here alive—but there are essential things that carry on past our own short time on the planet. As French sociologist Émile Durkheim wrote, "We speak a language that we did not make; we use instruments that we did not invent. . . . [A] fund of knowledge is passed on to each generation which it did not accumulate for itself."[25] In other words, we are born into a society already humming along, already steeped in habits and proclivities, which may alter within our lifetime but will also continue past our life span. There is a filtering: of the universe of possible foods humans can eat, what actually lands on one's plate each day is shaped by the same web of symbols and economies that shapes other aspects of our lives. Poverty and hard times can restrict what appears on that plate, and globalization in its multiple forms can radically change the contents, as can trends and wealth and taste. This selection and sorting—at a restaurant, a fast-food counter, an outdoor market, a food pantry—are nested in our appetites and memories, in our economic and cultural past and present, in our geographic location.

Food is clearly fraught. It is packed with symbolism, emotions, taboos, anxiety, fear, and pleasure as well as life-and-death questions of politics and economics. Heirloom fruits and vegetables may be a little distraction from the landscape of iceberg lettuce and Styrofoam strawberries, but they are also part of a means of survival, inseparable from both pleasure and necessity, the past and the future, physical and social sustenance. Sometimes the attachment to these fruits and vegetables is nostalgic, sometimes very forward-looking, seeking to preserve endangered genetic material and to ensure future biodiversity by creating and fostering a demand for this produce. The work of actors and activists translates into concrete spaces and discernible messages. These gardens, barnyards, museums, farmers' markets, and gene banks hold powerful keys to the past and, in the view of many of those involved, to the future as well.

We should think not only about edible memory, but also about edible forgetting, for the two are intertwined. There are many questions we can, and should, ask about food. Many have been elaborated very well elsewhere, but new questions emerge from this investigation of edible memory. We can ask, "Whose memories am I eating? How did this pear, muffin, or frozen pizza come to be? What are its botanical and cultural origins?" Even something as personal as taste in food is rooted in layers of society, politics, and economics. What stories are told by your kitchen? Your garden? Your grocery cart? The concept can take us far beyond heirloom varieties, revealing the roots of habits and attachments and the daily patterns of consumption that most of us take for granted.

Eating is something we do every day, something essentially biological—keeping the organism going, delivering protein and carbohydrates and fats to the complicated systems we carry around with us (or that carry us around). Everything we are comes from food, making up our bodies and making the rest of us possible. In watching children shoot up, even watching a newborn turn into a toddler—it is miraculous to think that a daily delivery of nutrients somehow turns into ever more of this tiny cherished person. But food also delivers meanings and memories—what's more iconic than mother's milk, for example?

Food trends don't just come out of nowhere; they sit atop deep reserves of habit, knowledge, and genetic material. Nostalgia and also non-nostalgic attachments to the past can have material and social consequences. Likewise, a tomato is always more than a tomato. While this book is largely about heirlooms, it has implications for the broader connections between food, memory, and the material world. Sometimes there are good reasons to forget, and I am not advocating encyclopedic preservation. Instead, I observe people enacting, practicing, and embodying edible memory. Yes, this book is largely an exploration of how tomatoes and other food come to be seen as heirlooms. But it is also a call to pay attention to a more expansive sense of edible memory—that this concept also explains people's attachments to a much wider range of foods than old-fashioned tomatoes. Edible memory is the boxed spice cake mix and the heirloom apple and its fellow heirlooms. Attending to edible memory reveals deep connections between food and memory, social and physical landscapes—and pleasures and possibilities.

Notes

1. Gary Paul Nabhan's *The Desert Smells like Rain* (Tucson: University of Arizona Press, 2002) discusses the kind of horticulture and food processing and gathering common among the Tohono O'Odham in the area.

2. Many nurseries, gardeners, chefs, and others use "antique" and "heirloom" interchangeably, particularly when it comes to apples. For example, the phrase "antique apple" appears twenty-five times over twenty-five years in the *New York Times*, while the phrase "antique tomato" does not appear once.

3. Michael S. Carolan, *Embodied Food Politics* (Burlington, VT: Ashgate, 2011), 41.

4. I am very grateful to one of the anonymous reviewers of this manuscript for putting this approach in these terms and capturing a process I had not yet found a way to describe succinctly.

CHAPTER ONE

1. This farm is part of the much larger project in that building, known as the Plant, where this former meatpacking plant now houses aquaponic farms, a bakery, and plans for a brewery and an anaerobic digester, among other projects. http://www.plantchicago.com; www.theurbancanopy.com.

2. The United Nations Food and Agriculture Organization (FAO) refers to this kind of biodiversity as agrobiodiversity, which it defines as "the variety and variability of animals, plants and micro-organisms that are used directly or indirectly for food and agriculture, including crops, livestock, forestry and fisheries. It comprises the diversity of genetic resources (varieties, breeds) and species used for food, fodder, fibre, fuel and pharmaceuticals. It also includes the diversity of non-harvested species that support production (soil micro-organisms, predators, pollinators), and those in the wider environment that support agro-ecosystems (agricultural, pastoral, forest and aquatic) as well as the diversity of the agro-ecosystems," and the local knowledge and culture of managing these systems (http://www.fao.org/docrep/007/y5609e/y5609e01.htm). That said, the concept of biodiversity, edible and otherwise, rests on the shifting foundation of systems of biological and botanical classification—the boundaries of families,

genuses, and species are not as fixed as they may feel at a given moment. They come out of particular historical traditions and can be altered with the discovery of, say, new fossils or butterfly populations.

3. The role of various corporations and changes in government subsidies and policies is also fundamental and is discussed in greater depth by many authors, including (but not at all limited to) Michael Pollan, *The Omnivore's Dilemma: A Natural History of Four Meals* (New York: Penguin, 2006); Julie Guthman, *Agrarian Dreams?: The Paradox of Organic Farming in California* (Berkeley: University of California Press, 2004).

4. According to the FAO, 75 percent of agricultural plant genetic diversity was lost over the twentieth century (http://www.fao.org/docrep/007/y5609e /y5609e02.htm), but the origins of that figure are difficult to track down. Techniques for measuring crop genetic diversity continue to be the subject of both debate and new research, and the precise figures (and techniques of calculating these figures) vary somewhat. See Franziska Wolff, "Industrial Transformation and Agriculture: Agrobiodiversity Loss as Sustainability Problem," in *Governance for Industrial Transformation*, ed. Klaus Jacob, Manfred Binder, and Anna Wieczorek (*Proceedings of the 2003 Berlin Conference on the Human Dimensions of Global Environmental Policy Research Centre*, Berlin), 338–55. In terms of apples, apple expert Dan Bussey, for example, has tracked down references to "some 16,000 apple varieties [which] have been named and nurtured over the last four centuries. By 1904, however, the identities and sources of only 7,098 of those varieties could be discerned by a USDA scientist named W. H. Ragan. . . . Since then, some 6,121 apple varieties—86.2 percent of Ragan's 1904 inventory—have been lost from nursery catalogs, farmers' markets, and from the American table. In the southern U.S. alone, it is estimated that only 300 of some 1,600 varieties that once flourished in the region remain." Gary Paul Nabhan, "The Fatherland of Apples," *Orion Magazine*, http://www.orionmaga zine.org/index.php/articles/article/2961.

5. This book focuses on edible plants, but the heirloom movement also includes animals. Heritage turkeys and antique pigs, old-fashioned chickens and rare cattle have all made a comeback in recent years as well. They are beyond the scope of this book, but some sources include Donald E. Bixby, Carolyn J. Christman, Cynthia J. Ehrman, and D. Phillip Sponenberg, *Taking Stock: The North American Livestock Census* (Blacksburg, VA: McDonald and Woodward, 1994); Carolyn J. Christman and Robert O. Hawes, *Birds of a Feather: Saving Rare Turkeys from Extinction* (Pittsboro, NC: American Livestock Breeds Conservancy, 1999); Carolyn J. Christman, D. Phillip Sponen-

berg, and Donald E. Bixby, *A Rare Breeds Album of American Livestock* (Pittsboro, NC: American Livestock Breeds Conservancy, 1997); Janet Vorwald Dohner, *The Encyclopedia of Historic and Endangered Livestock and Poultry Breeds* (New Haven, CT: Yale University Press, 2001); Peter Kaminsky, *Pig Perfect: Encounters with Remarkable Swine and Some Great Ways to Cook Them* (New York: Hyperion, 2005); Andrew F. Smith, *The Turkey: An American Story* (Urbana: University of Illinois Press, 2006).

6.   The heirloom plant movement is not limited to edible plants, and indeed the Center for Historic Plants at Thomas Jefferson's Monticello focuses primarily on ornamental plants, although it also includes edible plants. Roses are perhaps the heirloom tomato of the ornamental plant world, inspiring wholehearted devotion as well as feuds and rifts, as Michael Pollan describes in *Second Nature: A Gardener's Education* (New York: Atlantic Monthly Press, 1991). See also Priscilla Ferguson's discussion of roses in "Trifles," *Contexts* 8, no. 4 (2009): 66–68.

7.   For obvious reasons, these practices are deeply rooted in the body. As Michael Carolan writes, "We think with and through our bodies." Michael S. Carolan, *Embodied Food Politics* (Burlington, VT: Ashgate, 2011), 1. Likewise, Rachel Slocum and other scholars attending to "the 'new materialism' or corporeal feminism [are] interested in what bodies do." Rachel Slocum, "Race in the Study of Food," in *Geographies of Race and Food: Fields, Bodies, Markets*, ed. Rachel Slocum and Arun Saldanha (Burlington, VT: Ashgate, 2013), 27. Many scholars investigating food find that the embodiedness of food memories is underanalyzed. Emma-Jayne Abbots and Anna Lavis suggest that "individual acts of eating are always inherently social and relational, and that the socialities they enact or disrupt are as viscerally corporeal as they are political." See "Introduction, Contours of Eating: Mapping the Terrain of Body/Food Encounters," in *Why We Eat, How We Eat: Contemporary Encounters between Foods and Bodies*, ed. Emma-Jayne Abbotts and Anna Lavis (Burlington, VT: Ashgate, 2013), 3. The scholarly discussions of embodiment remind us that food happens through and in (literally) the body, made and consumed by bodies. Slocum, "Race in the Study of Food," 40.

8.   *Seed Savers Exchange 2013 Yearbook* (Decorah, IA, 2013), 129. See http://www.seedsavers.org/Membership.

9.   The farming population has undergone serious demographic change over the past century or so. There is considerable diversity among farmers across the United States, including racial and ethnic diversity. The number of African American farmers declined from over 900,000 in the early twentieth

century, farming 15.6 million acres, to only 18,000 farmers on 2 million acres just under a century later. US Department of Agriculture, National Agricultural Statistics Service, 1999; cited in Alison Hope Alkon, *Black, White, and Green: Farmers Markets, Race, and the Green Economy* (Athens: University of Georgia Press, 2012), 79. The USDA also has a history of discriminating against African American famers, and in 1997, 15,000 African American farmers filed a class-action lawsuit. Alkon, *Black, White, and Green*, 79. The results of the suit are ongoing (https://www.blackfarmercase .com//Background.aspx). See also Laura Barraclough's work on the racial politics of farming and rural life in Southern California, *Making the San Fernando Valley: Rural Landscapes, Urban Development, and White Privilege* (Athens: University of Georgia Press, 2011).

10. Susanne Freidberg, *French Beans and Food Scares: Culture and Commerce in an Anxious Age* (New York: Oxford University Press, 2004); Barry Glassner, *The Gospel of Food: Why We Should Stop Worrying and Enjoy What We Eat* (New York: Harper Perennial, 2008); Raj Patel, *Stuffed and Starved: The Hidden Battle for the World Food System* (New York: Melville House, 2007); Harvey Levenstein, *Fear of Food: A History of Why We Worry about What We Eat* (Chicago: University of Chicago Press, 2012); John Coveney, *Food, Morals and Meaning* (New York: Routledge, 2000).

11. http://blogs.worldwatch.org/five-global-seed-banks-that-are-protecting -biodiversity.

12. See, for example, John Vidal, "India's Rice Warrior Battles to Build Living Seed Bank as Climate Chaos Looms," *Guardian*, March 17, 2014; the Ethiopian Institute of Biodiversity (http://www.ibc.gov.et), or the 115 community seed banks across Nepal (http://www.bioversityinternational.org/news /detail/community-seed-banks-in-nepal-past-present-future).

13. The topic of heirloom grain is vast and worthy of more extended inquiry, and was originally a part of the research for this book. What I had thought would be a relatively small-scale movement yielding a few sociological lessons turned into a juggernaut of cryogenic seed banks, bootleggers' cornfields, historically accurate wheat fields, and a global network of grain historians and farmers, food activists and geneticists—and so will be treated in greater depth elsewhere.

14. http://www.slowfoodusa.org/index.php/programs/ark_product_detail /turkey_hard_red_winter_wheat. For more on bread and wheat see, for example, Carole M. Counihan, *The Anthropology of Food and Body: Gender, Meaning, and Power* (New York: Routledge, 1999), 25–42; and Steven Laurence Kaplan, *Good Bread Is Back* (Durham, NC: Duke University Press,

2006). There is a copious and fascinating literature on wheat and bread, too vast to list here, but worth exploring.

15. Rachel Laudan, *Cuisine and Empire: Cooking in World History* (Berkeley: University of California Press, 2013). Also see her book on food in Hawaii, *The Food of Paradise: Exploring Hawaii's Culinary Heritage* (Honolulu: University of Hawai'i Press, 1996).

16. Edward A. Bunyard, *The Anatomy of Dessert: With a Few Notes on Wine* (New York: Modern Library, 2006), xxvii–xxviii.

17. Many activists and farmers frame this issue in terms of "seed sovereignty"— the access to open-pollinated varieties—often, but not always, traditional and region-specific. The work of Navdanya, for example, has conserved "more than 3000 rice varieties from all over the country including indigenous rice varieties that have been adapted over centuries to meet different ecological demands. We have also conserved 75 varieties of wheat and hundreds of millets, pseudo-cereals, pulses, oilseeds, vegetables and multipurpose plant species including medicinal plants." http://www.navdanya.org /earth-democracy/seed-sovereignty. Also see the African Biodiversity Network, among other similar projects.

18. Pablo B. Eyzaguirre and Olga F. Linares, *Home Gardens and Agrobiodiversity* (Washington, DC: Smithsonian Books, 2004); Andrea Heistinger, *Handbuch Samengärtnerei: Sorten erhalten, Vielfalt vermehren, Gemüse geniessen* (Innsbruck-Bozen, Austria: Loewenzahn, 2004); Virginia D. Nazarea, *Cultural Memory and Biodiversity* (Tucson: University of Arizona Press, 1998); Nazarea, *Heirloom Seeds and Their Keepers: Marginality and Memory in the Conservation of Biological Diversity* (Tucson: University of Arizona Press, 2005); Nazarea, "Memory in Biodiversity Conservation," *Annual Review of Anthropology* 35 (2006): 317–35; Vandana Shiva, *Stolen Harvest: The Hijacking of the Global Food Supply* (Cambridge, MA: South End Press, 2000); James Robert Veteto, "The History and Survival of Traditional Heirloom Vegetable Varieties in the Southern Appalachian Mountains of Western North Carolina," *Agriculture and Human Values* 25, no. 1 (2008): 121; Veteto, "The History and Survival of Traditional Heirloom Vegetable Varieties and Strategies for the Conservation of Crop Biodiversity in the Southern Appalachian Mountains of Western North Carolina: A Thesis" (PhD diss., Appalachian State University, 2005); Jonathan Winskie and Jessica Murray, "Heirloom Seed and Story Keepers: Growing Community and Sustainability through Arts-Based Research," *Papers and Publications: Interdisciplinary Journal of Undergraduate Research* 2, no. 1 (2013), art. 10.

19. There have also been earlier trends toward various conceptions of health

food and self-provisioning, and many of today's food trends build on this foundation of back-to-the-landers in the 1960s, and even earlier interest in natural foods, biodynamic farming, and the like. The Rodale Institute, still one of the leading organizations with regard to organic farming, was founded in 1947. See Warren Belasco, *Appetite for Change: How the Counterculture Took on the Food Industry* (Ithaca, NY: Cornell University Press, 2006).

20. John Prescott, *Taste Matters: Why We Like the Foods We Do* (London: Reaktion Books, 2012); Gordon M. Shepherd, *Neurogastronomy: How the Brain Creates Flavor and Why It Matters* (New York: Columbia University Press, 2012); Barb Stuckey, *Taste What You're Missing: The Passionate Eater's Guide to Why Good Food Tastes Good* (New York: Free Press, 2012).

21. Carol Nuckols, "Seeds of Change Offers the Uncommon, the Unusual," *Post and Courier* (Charleston, SC), June 25, 1995.

22. See, for example, Counihan, *Anthropology of Food and Body*; Arlene Voski Avakian and Barbara Haber, *From Betty Crocker to Feminist Food Studies: Critical Perspectives on Women and Food* (Amherst: University of Massachusetts Press, 2005); Allison Hayes-Conroy and Jessica Hayes-Conroy, "Taking Back Taste: Feminism, Food and Visceral Politics," *Gender, Place and Culture* 15, no. 5 (2008): 471–73; Laura Shapiro, *Perfection Salad: Women and Cooking at the Turn of the Century* (Berkeley: University of California Press, 2008). In addition, much of the burden of cooking at home still falls to women rather than to men. Counihan writes, "Because women are sometimes obligated to cook for and serve others, food can be a channel of oppression. Yet because cooking, feeding, eating, and fasting can be significant means of communication, food can be a channel of creativity and power." Avakian and Haber, *From Betty Crocker to Feminist Food Studies*, 201.

23. This includes, but is not in any way limited to, Michael Pollan's *Cooked: A Natural History of Transformation* (New York: Penguin, 2013), as well as efforts by people like Mark Bittman, Jamie Oliver, and Michelle Obama.

24. Draft added to the *Oxford English Dictionary* in 2006: "Chiefly N. Amer. Of or designating a variety of plant or breed of animal which is distinct from the more common varieties associated with commercial agriculture, and has been cultivated or reared using the same traditional methods for a long time, typically on a small scale and often within a particular region or family." *OED Online*, s.v. "heirloom, n.," June 2013. http://www.oed.com/view/Entry/85516?redirectedFrom=heirloom.

25. The question of authenticity—how we distinguish between things that are

authentic and inauthentic—has received extensive attention from sociologists and others, including in the realm of food, but also in many other contexts. Cf. Josée Johnston and Shyon Baumann, *Foodies: Democracy and Distinction in the Gourmet Foodscape* (New York: Routledge, 2010); Johnston and Baumann, "Democracy versus Distinction: A Study of Omnivorousness in Gourmet Food Writing," *American Journal of Sociology* 113, no. 1 (2007): 165–204; Tom Mueller, *Extra Virginity: The Sublime and Scandalous World of Olive Oil* (New York: W. W. Norton, 2011); David Grazian, *Blue Chicago: The Search for Authenticity in Urban Blues Clubs* (Chicago: University of Chicago Press, 2003); Gary Alan Fine, *Everyday Genius: Self-Taught Art and the Culture of Authenticity* (Chicago: University of Chicago Press, 2004). With regard to food and authenticity, Pratt asserts that "authenticity is a quality attributed to a range of foods and cuisines. . . . First, there is food specific to a location; second, these food products are the result of a craft process. These two themes are normally found together and both rest on an appeal to tradition: this food is the product of a continuous and collective endeavour, it pre-dates industrialized food systems and its value derives from that opposition." Jeff Pratt, "Food Values: The Local and the Authentic," *Critique of Anthropology* 27, no. 3 (2007): 294.

26. Benjamin A. Watson, *Taylor's Guide to Heirloom Vegetables* (Boston: Houghton Mifflin, 1996), 2–3; see also Suzanne P. DeMuth, ed., *Vegetables and Fruits: A Guide to Heirloom Varieties and Community-Based Stewardship*, vol. 1, *Annotated Bibliography*, Special Reference Brief Series 98–05 (Beltsville, MA: US Department of Agriculture, 1998).

27. Dick Bushnell, "A Pair of Big, Tasty Slicers," *Sunset Magazine* 204, no. 2 (2000): 74.

28. DeMuth, *Vegetables and Fruits*, 5–6.

29. Michel Viard, *Légumes d'autrefois: Histoire, variétés insolites, recettes gourmandes* (Paris: Maison Rustique, 2005); Élizabeth Lemoine, *Les légumes d'hier et d'aujourd'hui* (Paris: Molière, 2002).

30. Nina Planck, "How New York's Greenmarket Went Stale," *New York Times*, April 24, 2004, 17. Also see E. Melanie DuPuis and David Goodman, "Should We Go 'Home' to Eat?: Toward a Reflexive Politics of Localism," *Journal of Rural Studies* 21 (2005): 359–71; Richard Tellström, Inga-Britt Gustafsson, and Lena Mossberg, "Local Food Cultures in the Swedish Rural Economy," *Sociologia Ruralis* 45, no. 4 (2005): 346–59.

31. Barbara Kingsolver, *Animal, Vegetable, Miracle: Our Year of Seasonal Eating* (New York: Faber and Faber, 2010).

32. Growing Power was established in 1993 in Milwaukee, Wisconsin. Their

mission is to transform "communities by supporting people from diverse backgrounds and the environments in which they live through the development of Community Food Systems. These systems provide high-quality, safe, healthy, affordable food for all residents in the community. Growing Power develops Community Food Centers, as a key component of Community Food Systems, through training, active demonstration, outreach, and technical assistance. Will Allen, our Chief Executive Officer believes, 'If people can grow safe, healthy, affordable food, if they have access to land and clean water, this is transformative on every level in a community. I believe we cannot have healthy communities without a healthy food system.'" http://www.growingpower.org/about_us.htm. See Will Allen, with Charles Wilson, *The Good Food Revolution: Growing Healthy Food, People, and Communities* (New York: Penguin, 2012).

33. Judith A. Carney, *Black Rice: The African Origins of Rice Cultivation in the Americas* (Cambridge, MA: Harvard University Press, 2002); Susan Davis Price, *Growing Home: Stories of Ethnic Gardening* (Minneapolis: University of Minnesota Press, 2000); Miranda J. Martinez, *Power at the Roots: Gentrification, Community Gardens, and the Puerto Ricans of the Lower East Side* (New York: Lexington Books, 2010); Sharon Zukin, *Naked City: The Death and Life of Authentic Urban Places* (New York: Oxford University Press, 2011), 193–220.

34. Writings on the wide array of edible memories are cited throughout this book, and indeed are too numerous to include even in a bibliography as lengthy as mine. A few of the relevant works include the following: Enrique Salmón, *Eating the Landscape: American Indian Stories of Food, Identity, and Resilience* (Tucson: University of Arizona Press, 2012); Gary Paul Nabhan, *Coming Home to Eat: The Pleasures and Politics of Local Foods* (New York: Norton, 2002); Heid E. Erdrich, *Original Local: Indigenous Foods, Stories, and Recipes from the Upper Midwest* (St. Paul, Minnesota: Minnesota Historical Society Press, 2013); Anne L. Bower, ed., *African American Foodways: Explorations of History and Culture* (Urbana: University of Illinois Press, 2007); Adrian Miller, *Soul Food: The Surprising Story of an American Cuisine One Plate at a Time* (Chapel Hill: University of North Carolina Press, 2013); Herbert Covey and Dwight Eisnach, *What the Slaves Ate: Recollections of African American Foods and Foodways from the Slave Narratives* (Santa Barbara, CA: Greenwood Press, 2009).

35. Alongside these vibrant projects, there are places where food access is made difficult by issues of racial, ethnic, or economic inequality, as well as transportation, affordability, location of markets, and so on. These issues are often contained under the umbrella concept of a "food desert." For

many scholars food deserts are not a straightforward situation—there is much debate about exactly what constitutes a food desert, such as the miscategorizing of bodegas that actually have large quantities of fresh produce. At the same time it can be a useful concept for capturing the many challenges that can get in the way of food access for both urban and rural residents. For more on food deserts and related issues, see Alison Hope Alkon and Julian Agyeman, eds., *Cultivating Food Justice: Race, Class, and Sustainability* (Cambridge, MA: MIT Press, 2011); Nik Heynen, Hilda E. Kurtz, and Amy K. Trauger, "Food, Hunger and the City," *Geography Compass* 6 (2012): 304–11; Jesse McEntee and Julian Agyeman, "Towards the Development of a GIS Method for Identifying Rural Food Deserts: Geographic Access in Vermont, USA," *Applied Geography* 30, no. 1 (2010): 165–76; Alison Alkon, Daniel Block, Kelly Moore, Catherine Gillis, and Nicole DiNuccio, "Foodways of the Urban Poor," *Geoforum* 48 (2013): 126–35; Hilda E. Kurtz, "Linking Food Deserts and Racial Segregation: Challenges and Limitations," in *Geographies of Race and Food: Fields, Bodies, Markets*, ed. Rachel Slocum and Arun Saldanha (Burlington, VT: Ashgate, 2013), 247–64.

36. Alkon, *Black, White, and Green*; Alison Alkon and Christie McCullen, "Whiteness and Farmers Markets: Performances, Perpetuations, Contestations?" *Antipode* 43, no. 4 (2010): 937–59; Julie Guthman, "'If They Only Knew': Color Blindness and Universalism in California Alternative Food Institutions," *Professional Geographer* 60, no. 3 (2008): 387–97; Emma J. Roe, "Things Becoming Food and the Embodied, Material Practices of an Organic Food Consumer," *Sociologia Ruralis* 46, no. 2 (2006): 104–21; Rachel Slocum, "Thinking Race through Corporeal Feminist Theory: Divisions and Intimacies at the Minneapolis Farmers' Market," *Social and Cultural Geography* 9, no. 8 (2008): 849–69; Slocum and Guthman also find that "alternative food advocates have usually been blind to their own whiteness and to the impossibility of non-white populations to follow their 'example'"; cited in Slocum and Saldanha, *Geographies of Race and Food*, 6. Both food and race are embodied, and "alternative food networks articulate white ideals of health and nutrition, offer whitened dreams of farming and gardening that erase the past and present of race in agriculture"; cited in Slocum, "Race in the Study of Food," 38.

37. See, for example, the school garden program begun by Alice Waters and the faculty and students of Martin Luther King Jr. Middle School in Berkeley, California. https://edibleschoolyard.org.

38. http://seedingchicago.com/2012/11/14/urban-farm-to-provide-job-training-and-fresh-vegetables.

39. "With farms in the Englewood and Back of the Yards neighborhoods, as

well as the 10-acre Les Brown Memorial Farm in Marseilles, Illinois, Growing Home seeks *to operate, promote, and demonstrate the use of organic agriculture as a vehicle for job training, employment, and community development.*" http://growinghomeinc.org/learn-more/transitional-employment.

40. http://www.growingpower.org/chicago_projects.htm.

41. http://browngirlfarming.com.

42. Johnston and Baumann, *Foodies.*

43. Carolan, *Embodied Food Politics*, 4, 34–35.

44. Lizzie Collingham, *The Taste of War: World War II and the Battle for Food* (New York: Penguin, 2012), 450.

45. Shepherd, *Neurogastronomy*, 4.

46. http://www.bbc.com/future/story/20120312-why-can-smells-unlock-memories.

47. See, for example, Scott Chaskey, *Seedtime: On the History, Husbandry, Politics, and Promise of Seeds* (New York: Rodale, 2014).

48. http://www.parquedelapapa.org/eng/02somos_01.html. See also http://ourworld.unu.edu/en/the-thriving-biodiversity-of-peru-potato-park.

49. As one example, see the ongoing struggle around genetically engineered maize in Mexico. New permits for genetically modified (GM) maize planting in Mexico were suspended, and the question is working its way through legal and political channels. http://www.reuters.com/article/2013/11/12/us-mexico-corn-idUSBRE9AB11Q20131112. Mexico is the center of maize biodiversity, and GM pollen has already contaminated existing strains of non-GM maize. Cf. http://www.abc.net.au/science/articles/2009/02/24/2499950.htm.

50. Alison Landsberg, *Prosthetic Memory: The Transformation of American Remembrance in the Age of Mass Culture* (New York: Columbia University Press, 2004). Also see David Sutton's intriguing *Remembrance of Repasts: An Anthropology of Food and Memory* (New York: Berg, 2001).

51. Carolan talks specifically about the relation between food and memory, and references Connerton and "habit memory." *Embodied Food Politics*, 39.

52. As the extensive analyses of memory in sociology have made clear, either the past has to be experienced firsthand, or it has to be narrated in images, texts, museums, oral stories, stone markers, or other communicative forms that link those who were not there to the original events. Cf. Maurice Halbwachs, *On Collective Memory* (Chicago: University of Chicago Press, 1992); Pierre Nora, Lawrence D. Kritzman, and Arthur Goldhammer, *Realms of Memory: Rethinking the French Past*, 3 vols., European Perspectives (New York: Columbia University Press, 1996); Erika Doss, *Memorial Mania: Public Feeling in America* (Chicago: University of Chicago Press, 2012); Marita

Sturken, *Tourists of History: Memory, Kitsch, and Consumerism from Oklahoma City to Ground Zero* (Durham, NC: Duke University Press, 2007); and my own *Structures of Memory: Understanding Urban Change in Berlin and Beyond* (Stanford, CA: Stanford University Press, 2006).

53. In 2012, 14.5 percent of households in the United States experienced food insecurity at least at some point in the year, with 5.7 percent who had "very low food security—meaning that the food intake of one or more household members was reduced and their eating patterns were disrupted at times . . . because the household lacked money and other resources for food." Alisha Coleman-Jensen, Mark Nord, and Anita Singh, *Household Food Security in the United States in 2012* (United States Department of Agriculture, Economic Research Service, Economic Research Report Number 155, September 2013), i. In Milwaukee, food insecurity was at 23 percent for the residents of the fourth congressional district in 2008–9. http://www.apl.wisc .edu/poverty_food_security.php. Worldwide, approximately one in eight people in 2011–13 were suffering from chronic hunger, "regularly not getting enough food to conduct an active life." http://www.fao.org/publica tions/sofi/en.

54. Elizabeth Cullen Dunn, "A Gift from the American People," *Iowa Review,* 2012, http://iowareview.uiowa.edu/?q=issue/elizabeth_cullen_dunn.

55. Elizabeth Cullen Dunn, "The Food of Sorrow: Humanitarian Aid to Displaced People," in *Food: Ethnographic Encounters,* ed. Leo Coleman (New York: Bloomsbury, 2012), 141.

56. Elizabeth Saleh, "Eating and Drinking Kefraya: The Karam in the Vineyards," in *Why We Eat, How We Eat: Contemporary Encounters between Foods and Bodies,* ed. Emma-Jayne Abbots and Anna Lavis (Burlington, VT: Ashgate, 2013), 117.

57. Janisse Ray, *The Seed Underground: A Growing Revolution to Save Food* (White River Junction, VT: Chelsea Green, 2012), 75.

58. On foraging, see, for example, my unpublished manuscript (with Ashkan Rezvani Naraghi), "The Culture of Wild Things: Eating Weeds in Hard Times and Haute Cuisine."

59. Peter Dreyer, one of the first readers of the full manuscript, questioned the term but then, in my opinion, captured it perfectly in his description of his own experience of edible memory: "But what exactly is 'our own personal edible past'? I can only presume you mean the foods our personal genetic ancestors ate. However, these are not necessarily our own food memories. For instance, I grew up in South Africa, and Cape Malay food is very much part of my food memories. For me these dishes are thus heirlooms, things I inherited. But I have no genetic Malay ancestors. By comparison,

even though some of my German ancestors were actually Lübeck Schonen-fahrer, Hanseatic merchants just like the Buddenbrooks family, the kinds of meals served up to the characters in Thomas Mann's novel *Buddenbrooks* are fairly foreign to me. As Lizzie Collingham shows, foods have traveled all over the globe and been naturalized with amazing speed; hard to think that before the sixteenth century, India (and Thailand, Indonesia, China et al. too) had never known the chili pepper! Vindaloo is 'simply a garbled pronunciation of [Portuguese] *vinho e alhos.*' In 1526, the Turks conquer Hungary and introduce paprika, which becomes the hallmark spice of Hungarian cooking. And so on. You really can't tie the edible past to one's *ancestral* genetic past. But if 'our own personal edible past' is simply what one *personally* remembers, then for many Americans it is indeed what was available at the Safeway in 1968 (or whenever)." I couldn't agree more (personal correspondence, November 3, 2011).

60. Krishnendu Ray, *The Migrant's Table: Meals and Memories in Bengali-American Households* (Philadelphia: Temple University Press, 2004).

61. Georg Simmel, "The Meal," in *Simmel on Culture: Selected Writings*, ed. David Frisby and Mike Featherstone (Thousand Oaks, CA: Sage, 1997), 130–35.

62. Amy Adamczyk, "On Thanksgiving and Collective Memory: Constructing the American Tradition," *Journal of Historical Sociology* 15, no. 3 (2002): 343–65.

63. Pierre Bourdieu found deep connections between people's tastes in food (and art, music, and other cultural goods) and their class standing. *Distinction: A Social Critique of the Judgement of Taste* (Cambridge, MA: Harvard University Press, 1984). In a very different kind of work, journalist Michael Moss explores the intentional ways in which food corporations use their scientists and marketing departments to cultivate tastes in people in the interest of increasing a given company's profits. Moss, *Salt, Sugar, Fat: How the Food Giants Hooked Us* (New York: Random House, 2013).

64. Robin Wagner-Pacifici and Barry Schwartz, "The Vietnam Veteran's Memorial: Commemorating a Difficult Past," *American Journal of Sociology* 97, no. 2 (1991): 376–420, for example, shows how a cultural object such as the Vietnam Veterans Memorial can be understood only over time, analyzing its emergence and the changing discourses around the seemingly fixed memorial. Other studies examine the changing meaning of various cultural objects over time, including music and food: Bethany Bryson, "'Anything but Heavy Metal': Symbolic Exclusion and Musical Dislikes," *American Sociological Review* 61 (1996): 884–99; Michaela DeSoucey, "Gastronationalism: Food Traditions and Authenticity Politics in the Euro-

pean Union," *American Sociological Review* 75, no. 3 (2010): 432–55; Priscilla Ferguson, *Accounting for Taste: The Triumph of French Cuisine* (Chicago: University of Chicago Press, 2004); Gary Alan Fine, "The Presentation of Ethnic Authenticity: Chinese Food as a Social Accomplishment," *Sociological Quarterly* 36 (1995): 601–19; Wendy Griswold, *Cultures and Societies in a Changing World* (Thousand Oaks, CA: Pine Forge Press, 2003). In her study of French gastronomy, Ferguson asks how a whole new set of rules and practices develops for chefs and for the people who eat what they create, imposing a set of rigid practices and meanings on top of what was once a more disparate set of fields and experiences (599).

65. For more on place, see Tom Gieryn, "A Space for Place in Sociology," *Annual Review of Sociology* 26 (2000): 463–96.

66. On tuna, see Theodore C. Bestor, *Tsukiji: The Fish Market at the Center of the World* (Berkeley: University of California Press, 2004).

CHAPTER TWO

1. Portions of this chapter were originally published in a different form in "The Heirloom Tomato as Cultural Object," *Sociologia Ruralis* 47, no. 1 (January 2007): 20–41.

2. J. F. Adams, *Guerrilla Gardening* (New York: Coward-McCann, 1983), 9.

3. Carolyn Jabs, *The Heirloom Gardener* (San Francisco, CA: Sierra Club Books, 1984), 13; Smith, *Tomato in America*, 153; Adams, *Guerrilla Gardening*, 9; http://news.ucdavis.edu/search/news_detail.lasso?id=7521.

4. Cf. Arthur Allen, *Ripe: The Search for the Perfect Tomato* (Berkeley, CA: Counterpoint, 2010); Barry Estabrook, *Tomatoland: How Modern Industrial Agriculture Destroyed Our Most Alluring Fruit* (Kansas City, MO: Andrews McMeel, 2011); Amy Goldman and Victor Schrager, *The Heirloom Tomato: From Garden to Table; Recipes, Portraits, and History of the World's Most Beautiful Fruit* (New York: Bloomsbury, 2008); Jordan, "Heirloom Tomato as Cultural Object"; Andrew F. Smith, *The Tomato in America: Early History, Culture, and Cookery* (Columbia: University of South Carolina Press, 1994); Tim Stark, *Heirloom: Notes from an Accidental Tomato Farmer* (New York: Broadway Books, 2008).

5. Stewart has also worked closely with Amy Goldman, author of several lush books about heirlooms and a dedicated seed saver herself. Goldman also now serves on the board of the Seed Savers Exchange. Goldman and others like her have made fundamental contributions not only to seed saving, but also by spreading the word about the importance (and pleasures) of heirloom varieties.

6. Stark, *Heirloom*.

7. Ibid. I am grateful to the ever-astute Peter Dreyer for this intimidating list of threats to a garden's bounty (personal correspondence, November 3, 2011).

8. Cf. Lauren Baker, "Tending Cultural Landscapes and Food Citizenship in Toronto's Community Gardens," *Geographical Review*, 94, no. 3 (2004): 305–25; Laura-Anne Minkoff-Zern, "Pushing the Boundaries of Indigeneity and Agricultural Knowledge: Oaxacan Immigrant Gardening in California," *Agriculture and Human Values* 29 (2012): 381–92.

9. Émile Zola, *The Belly of Paris*, trans. Brian Nelson (New York: Oxford University Press, 2007).

10. Urban farming has clearly taken off in recent years, in both well-off and poorer neighborhoods, ranging from tiny gardens to full-fledged farms. See, for example, Will Allen, *The Good Food Revolution: Growing Healthy Food, People, and Communities* (New York: Penguin, 2012); Jane Battersby, "Urban Agriculture and Race in South Africa," in *Geographies of Race and Food: Fields, Bodies, Markets*, ed. Rachel Slocum and Arun Saldanha (Burlington, VT: Ashgate, 2013), 117–35; Price, *Growing Home*.

11. Elaine Johnson and Laura Bonar Swezey, "Heirloom Tomatoes," *Sunset Magazine* 195 (1995): 80–84.

12. Jabs, *Heirloom Gardener*; Virginia Nazarea, *Heirloom Seeds and Their Keepers: Marginality and Memory in the Conservation of Biological Diversity* (Tucson: University of Arizona Press, 2005).

13. Cf. Margaret Gray, *Labor and the Locavore: The Making of a Comprehensive Food Ethic* (Berkeley: University of California Press, 2013), with a particular emphasis on the invisibility of agricultural labor in the Hudson River Valley and in the market for local, seasonal food, performed primarily by first African American and then Latino workers; Alison Pearlman, *Smart Casual: The Transformation of Gourmet Restaurant Style in America* (Chicago: University of Chicago Press, 2013); Sarah Elton, *Locavore: From Farmers' Fields to Rooftop Gardens—How Canadians Are Changing the Way We Eat* (New York: HarperCollins, 2010).

14. Anderson, *Plants, Man, Life*, 177.

15. J. Esteban Hernández Bermejo and J. León, *Neglected Crops: 1492 from a Different Perspective* (Rome: Food and Agriculture Organization of the United Nations, 1994), 117.

16. Cf. Lizzie Collingham, *Curry: A Tale of Cooks and Conquerors* (New York: Oxford University Press, 2006); Smith, *Tomato in America*; and Edgar Anderson, *Landscape Papers* (Berkeley, CA: Turtle Island Foundation, 1976); and Anderson, *Plants, Man and Life* (Boston: Little, Brown, 1952).

17. Alan Davidson, *The Oxford Companion to Food*, 2nd ed., ed. Tom Jaine (Oxford: Oxford University Press, 2006), 802–3.

18. Kenneth F. Kiple and Kriemhild Coneè Ornelas, *The Cambridge World History of Food*, vols. 1 and 2 (Cambridge: Cambridge University Press, 2000), 1870.

19. Ibid., 355.

20. Davidson, *Oxford Companion to Food*, 802–3. Also see Kiple and Ornelas, *Cambridge World History of Food*, 355.

21. Douglas Harper and Patrizia Faccioli, *The Italian Way: Food and Social Life* (Chicago: University of Chicago Press, 2009), 158–59; Anderson, *Plants, Man, Life*, 108–10.

22. Kiple and Ornelas, *Cambridge World History of Food*, 357.

23. Collingham, *Curry*, 149.

24. Ibid., 166.

25. Kiple and Ornelas, *Cambridge World History of Food*, 357.

26. Davidson, *Oxford Companion to Food*, 803.

27. Smith, *Oxford Companion to American Food and Drink*, 590.

28. Smith, *Tomato in America*, 54; Anderson, *Landscape Papers*, 53–54.

29. Kiple and Ornelas, *Cambridge World History of Food*, 1313; Harper and Faccioli, *The Italian Way*, 159.

30. Jo Robinson, *Eating on the Wild Side: The Missing Link to Optimum Health* (New York: Little, Brown, 2013), 142.

31. Christopher Stocks, *Forgotten Fruits: The Stories behind Britain's Traditional Fruits and Vegetables* (London: Windmill Books, 2009).

32. Peter Dreyer, *A Gardener Touched with Genius: The Life of Luther Burbank* (Berkeley: University of California Press, 1985); Jane S. Smith, *The Garden of Invention: Luther Burbank and the Business of Breeding Plants* (New York: Penguin, 2009).

33. Janisse Ray offers an in-depth portrait of many different farmers, gardeners, and seed savers. She writes about the dangers of the loss of crop biodiversity and shows that the ways people categorize these things are also crucial to the heirloom movement, to particular ways of understanding species and varieties, and to nomenclature. Ray, *Seed Underground*, 6–7.

34. Pollan, *Omnivore's Dilemma*.

35. Janisse Ray, *The Seed Underground*, 12.

36. Ibid., 61–62.

37. "Hybridization is a controlled method of pollination in which the pollen of two different species or varieties is crossed by human intervention. Hybridization can occur naturally through random crosses, but commercially available hybridized seed, often labeled as F1, is deliberately created to

breed a desired trait. The first generation of a hybridized plant cross also tends to grow better and produce higher yields than the parent varieties due to a phenomenon called 'hybrid vigor.' However, any seed produced by F1 plants is genetically unstable and cannot be saved for use in following years. Not only will the plants not be true-to-type, but they will be considerably less vigorous. Gardeners who use hybrid plant varieties must purchase new seed every year. Hybrid seeds can be stabilized, becoming open-pollinated varieties, by growing, selecting, and saving the seed over many years." http://blog.seedsavers.org/open-pollinated-heirloom-and -hybrid-seeds.

38. There is now a movement in favor of open-source needs—not only open-pollinated landraces and traditional varieties, but also new strains bred for particular improvements, but available in an open-source format (just like open-source software). Cf. Jack Kloppenburg, "Impeding Dispossession, Enabling Repossession: Biological Open Source and the Recovery of Seed Sovereignty," *Journal of Agrarian Change* 10, no. 3 (2010): 367–88.

39. http://ers.usda.gov/data-products/adoption-of-genetically-engineered -crops-in-the-us.aspx#.U2zLoxAXJ8E. There are many public debates regarding GMOs, including the prohibition of many GMO crops in various countries around the world, as well as the debate about labeling foods containing GMOs in the United States. Cf. Rachel Schurman and William A. Munro, *Fighting for the Future of Food: Activists versus Agribusiness in the Struggle over Biotechnology* (Minneapolis: University of Minnesota Press, 2010); John T. Lang, "Labeling to Distract," *Contexts* 13, no. 3 (2014): 10.

40. A 2014 USDA report confirms the findings of others that call into question the long-term value of many genetically engineered crops when viewed over time, and taking into account the costs of inputs. "The seeds are patented and cost more than conventional seeds—the price of GMO soybean and corn seeds grew by about 50 percent between 2001 and 2010, according to the report. But the companies that sell them say they make weed and insect management easier for farmers and can help increase production. But in its report, the ERS researchers said over the first 15 years of commercial use, GMO seeds have not been shown to definitively increase yield potentials, and 'in fact, the yields of herbicide-tolerant or insect-resistant seeds may be occasionally lower than the yields of conventional varieties,' the ERS report states. Several researchers have found 'no significant differences' between the net returns to farmers who use GMO herbicide tolerant seeds and those who use non-GMO seeds, the report states." Cary Gillam, "U.S. GMO Crops Show Mix of Benefits, Concerns-USDA Report," http://

www.reuters.com/article/2014/02/24/usda-gmo-report-idUSL1N0LT16 M20140224.

41. Estabrook, *Tomatoland*.

42. http://www.nass.usda.gov/Statistics_by_Subject/result.php?DAA9A43A -364E-3CD1-A333-6217203944F4&sector=CROPS&group=VEGETABLE S&comm=TOMATOES.

43. It comes to 86.3 pounds, 20.4 of fresh tomatoes and 66.0 of processed tomatoes. http://www.ers.usda.gov/data-products/chart-gallery/detail.aspx ?chartId=40064&ref=collection&embed=True#.U2O1-Vd5svM.

44. The precise figure is 9,271 acres. http://www.ers.usda.gov/data-products /organic-production.aspx#25762.

45. Smith, *Tomato in America*, ix.

46. Jabs, *Heirloom Gardener*; Hernández Bermejo and León, *Neglected Crops*; Bushnell, "Pair of Big, Tasty Slicers." Heirloom varieties are sometimes grown under these conditions too, but in general they are not well suited to large-scale industrial agriculture and must be grown at a smaller scale.

47. Smith discusses the failure of the Flavr Savr tomato. Andrew Smith, *Eating History: 30 Turning Points in the Making of American Cuisine* (New York: Columbia University Press, 2009), 275.

48. Watson, *Taylor's Guide to Heirloom Vegetables*, 5.

49. William Woys Weaver, *Heirloom Vegetable Gardening: A Master Gardener's Guide to Planting, Seed Saving, and Cultural History* (New York: Henry Holt, 1997); Roger A. Kline, Robert F. Becker, and Lynn Belluscio, *The Heirloom Vegetable Garden: Gardening in the 19th Century* (Ithaca, NY: Cornell University Press, 1980).

50. Jack Kloppenburg, ed., *Seeds and Sovereignty: The Use and Control of Plant Genetic Resources* (Chapel Hill, NC: Duke University Press, 1988), 2.

51. Nazarea, *Heirloom Seeds*, 3.

52. Estabrook, *Tomatoland*; Seth Holmes, *Fresh Fruit, Broken Bodies: Migrant Farmworkers in the United States* (Berkeley: University of California Press, 2013). See also Don Mitchell, "'The Issue Is Basically One of Race': Braceros, the Labor Process, and the Making of the Agro-Industrial Landscape of Mid-Twentieth-Century California," in *Geographies of Race and Food: Fields, Bodies, Markets*, ed. Rachel Slocum and Arun Saldanha (Burlington, VT: Ashgate, 2013), 79–96; Alkon, *Black, White, and Green*; Christopher R. Henke, *Cultivating Science, Harvesting Power: Science and Industrial Agriculture in California* (Cambridge, MA: MIT Press, 2008); Don Mitchell, *They Saved the Crops: Labor, Landscape, and the Struggle over Industrial Farming in Bracero-Era California* (Athens: University of Georgia Press, 2012).

53. http://ciw-online.org.

54. Holmes, *Fresh Fruit*, 43.

55. Jabs, *Heirloom Gardener*; Nazarea, *Heirloom Seeds*; Weaver, *Heirloom Vegetable Gardening*.

56. Jerry McGinn, "'Heirloom' Seeds Untouched by Science Give Adventurous Gardeners Real Taste," *Eugene (OR) Register-Guard*, March 7, 1984.

57. Nazarea, *Heirloom Seeds*, x.

58. Jabs, *Heirloom Gardener*.

59. Ibid., 43.

60. J. R. Hepler, as quoted in Bill Hepler, "America's Youngest Seed Grower," *Heritage Farm Companion*, Summer 2012, 7.

61. Diane Ott Whealy, *Gathering: Memoir of a Seed Saver* (Oakland, CA: Wilsted and Taylor, 2011).

62. Jabs, *Heirloom Gardener*, 47.

63. www.seedsavers.org.

64. www.seedsavers.org/Aboutus.asp.

65. Carolan, *Embodied Food Politics*, 82.

66. http://www.nativeseeds.org/v2/content/SeedlistingCatalog2008.pdf. "Since its founding, Native Seeds/SEARCH has been dedicated to this calling to conserve the rich agro-biodiversity of the arid Southwest because of its genetic and cultural importance." http://www.nativeseeds.org/about -us/historymission.

67. She talks, for example, with Will Bonsall, a dedicated seed saver who has created the Scatterseed Project and also works with Seed Savers Exchange. Ray, *Seed Underground*, 57.

68. She also has some criticisms of Seed Savers Exchange, feeling that it may have become corporate (although mostly she is repeating other people's criticisms); she sees a decline in the number of seeds swapped as the number of seeds it sells increases. Ray, *Seed Underground*, 108.

69. Ibid., 186.

70. See, just as one example, food in the context of colonialism in Parama Roy, *Alimentary Tracts: Appetites, Aversions and the Postcolonial* (Durham, NC: Duke University Press, 2010).

71. Many analysts have investigated changes in tastes for particular products and their production over time, including Italian pork fat, olive oil, cheese, and coffee. See William Roseberry, "The Rise of Yuppie Coffees and the Reimagination of Class in the United States," *American Anthropologist*, n.s., 98, no. 4 (1996): 762–75; Alison Leitch, "Slow Food and the Politics of Pork Fat: Italian Food and European Identity," *Ethnos* 68, no. 4 (2003): 437–62; Angela Tregear, "From Stilton to Vimto: Using Food History to Re-think

Typical Products in Rural Development," *Sociologia Ruralis* 43, no. 2 (2003): 91–107; Anne Meneley, "Extra Virgin Olive Oil and Slow Food," *Anthropologica* 46, no. 2 (2004): 165–76. Recent studies have also focused on the production and consumption of food more broadly, including issues surrounding organics, farmers' markets, McDonald's, and genetically modified crops, in many cases flashpoints of conflict surrounding questions of consumer desire, environmentalism, and markets. See Rick Fantasia, "Fast Food in France," *Theory and Society* 24, no. 2 (1995): 201–43; Julie Guthman, "Meaningful Commodities: Re-thinking Production-Consumption Links through the Organic System of Provision," *Sociologia Ruralis* 42, no. 2 (2002): 295–311; Stewart Lockie, Kristen Lyons, Geoffrey Lawrence, and Kerry Mummery, "Eating 'Green': Motivations Behind Organic Food Consumption in Australia," *Sociologia Ruralis* 42, no. 1 (2002): 23–40; Melissa Caldwell, "Domesticating the French Fry: McDonald's and Consumerism in Moscow," *Journal of Consumer Culture* 4, no. 1 (2004): 5–26; Clare Hinrichs, Gilbert Gillespie, and Gail Feenstra, "Social Learning and Innovation at Retail Farmers' Markets," *Rural Sociology* 69, no. 1 (2004): 31–58; M. Finucane and J. Holup, "Psychosocial and Cultural Factors Affecting the Perceived Risks of Genetically Modified Food: An Overview of the Literature," *Social Science and Medicine* 60 (2005); 1603–12; Naoimh McMahon, "Transforming Society through Purity, Solitude and Bearing Witness?" *Sociologia Ruralis* 45, nos. 1/2 (2005): 98–114; Ariani Lotti, "The Commoditization of Products and Taste: Slow Food and the Conservation of Agrobiodiversity," *Agriculture and Human Values* 27, no. 1 (2010): 71–83; Kees De Roest and Alberto Menghi, "Reconsidering 'Traditional' Food: The Case of Parmigiano Reggiano Cheese," *Sociologia Ruralis* 40, no. 4 (2000): 439–51; Mara Miele and Jonathan Murdoch, "The Practical Aesthetics of Traditional Cuisines: Slow Food in Tuscany," *Sociologia Ruralis* 42, no. 4 (2002): 312–28; Roberta Sonnino, "For a 'Piece of Bread'?: Interpreting Sustainable Development through Agritourism in Southern Tuscany," *Sociologia Ruralis* 44, no. 3 (2004): 285–300.

72. Mimi Luebbermann, *The Heirloom Tomato Cookbook* (San Francisco, CA: Chronicle Books, 2006).

73. http://www.stekovics.at/homepage/folgeseite_engl.html.

74. Jere Gettle and Emilee Gettle, *The Heirloom Life Gardener: The Baker Creek Way of Growing Your Own Food Easily and Naturally* (New York: Hyperion, 2011), 13.

75. Ibid., 4–5.

76. Anne Raver, "Plants Jefferson Grew and Other Heirlooms," *New York Times*, February 25, 1999, F14.

77. "Building on informal pathways of seed exchange that already exist, the Southern Seed Legacy is a decentralized network wherein different organizations and individuals across the South ideally select a manageable group of crops in each agroecoregion as their focus. Different groups and individuals contribute their varied expertise and resources to enhance the network." http://pacs.unt.edu/southernseedlegacy/aboutus.

78. See Carlo Petrini, *Slow Food: The Case for Taste* (New York: Columbia University Press, 2004).

79. Bourdieu, *Distinction*; Priscilla Ferguson and Sharon Zukin, "What's Cooking?" *Theory and Society* 24, no. 2 (1995): 193–99; Leitch, "Slow Food"; Bruce Pietrykowski, "You Are What You Eat: The Social Economy of the Slow Food Movement," *Review of Social Economy* 62, no. 3 (2004): 307–21; Pearlman, *Smart Casual*.

80. www.slowfoodusa.org/index.php/programs/details/ark_of_taste.

81. Other participants include the American Livestock Breeds Conservancy, Center for Sustainable Environments at Northern Arizona University, Chefs Collaborative, Cultural Conservancy, and Native Seeds/SEARCH.

82. Nabhan, Rood, and Madison, *Renewing America's Food Traditions*.

83. "The RAFT Alliance brings local farmers, chefs, fishers, agricultural historians, ranchers, nurserymen and conservation activists together to exchange information, tell the stories of regional foods and food producers, and create publications. Through RAFT, these communities of food producers publish lists of traditional regional foods, telling readers the stories and threats to these foods, and where seeds, nursery stock, or seafood and livestock hatchlings can be purchased to aid in their recovery. The result is the growth of food-concerned communities that are reestablishing healthy local economies." http://www.albc-usa.org/RAFT/ourwork.html.

84. See, for example, Bridget Love, "Mountain Vegetables and the Politics of Local Flavor in Japan," in *Japanese Foodways, Past and Present*, ed. Eric Rath and Stephanie Assmann (Urbana: University of Illinois Press, 2010), 221–42.

85. Gary Paul Nabhan, *Where Our Food Comes From: Retracing Nikolay Vavilov's Quest to End Famine* (Washington, DC: Island Press/Shearwater Books, 2009).

86. My thanks to Ashkan Rezvani Naraghi for his assistance in compiling these articles. When examining all articles in the entire Lexis-Nexis US newspaper database that mention heirloom tomatoes, I found the real uptick beginning in 2003. It seemed to peak in 2008, although there is another uptick beginning in 2011 and continuing through 2013, the last year I analyzed. I also looked at the articles in the same database that mention heir-

loom tomatoes in the context of restaurants, finding a very similar trajectory, although with the highest number coming in 2011 rather than 2008. Finally, I also reproduced the analysis conducted for my 2007 article, where I initially identified the patterns of the heirloom tomato trend, looking at articles strictly from the *New York Times* and the *San Francisco Chronicle*. The number of references to heirloom tomatoes nearly doubled in these sources in the period after my original 2007 article identifying the heirloom tomato trend, also peaking in 2007–8, and experiencing another uptick in 2011.

87. The results of the analysis of 344 articles published in the *New York Times* and the *San Francisco Chronicle* between 1989 (the first mention of heirloom tomatoes in this era) and 2005 are discussed at greater length in Jordan, "Heirloom Tomato as Cultural Object." Coverage increased significantly beginning in the late 1990s. At that time I also broke down the articles by theme, and the primary categories that appeared were (in order of frequency) restaurant reviews and descriptions, gardening, heirloom tomatoes as indicators of elite status, recipes, farming, good flavor, farmers' markets, aesthetics, seed saving, ordering seeds, nostalgia, and biodiversity. This last theme—so essential to the pre-popularity era—figures far less but does periodically appear in media, such as Martha Stewart's paean to the heirloom tomato that opened my article. Based on my initial analysis of gardening manuals and seed-saver projects, I had expected a more consistent invocation of the values of biodiversity. Instead, on both coasts the popular coverage of heirloom tomatoes focuses almost entirely on a combination of pleasure and conspicuous consumption. There is no question that through the 2000s gardening is far and away the primary theme—there are only occasional restaurant mentions. Mentions of other heirloom vegetables in the context of restaurants start to pick up in 2006 to 2007, but they remain much more gardening-centered than mentions of tomatoes.

88. Joyce Goldstein provides an in-depth portrait of many of these chefs, and the ways they shaped people's habits and appetites, in her recent book, *Inside the California Food Revolution: Thirty Years that Changed our Culinary Consciousness* (Berkeley: University of California Press, 2013). Also see Dan Barber, *Third Plate: Field Notes on the Future of Food* (New York: Penguin, 2014).

89. In his work on bread, Aaron Bobrow-Strain finds that despite the advantages of biopolitics (e.g., lessening food-borne disease), biopolitics also contains much power and a tendency to divide and exclude. In addition, he finds that people studying biopolitics need to pay attention "to the *alimentary* or *dietetic* workings of biopolitics; something that Foucault and

most subsequent Foucault scholars have overlooked." Aaron Bobrow-Strain, "White Bread Politics: Purity, Health, and the Triumph of Industrial Baking," in *Geographies of Race and Food: Fields, Bodies, Markets*, ed. Rachel Slocum and Arun Saldanha (Burlington, VT: Ashgate, 2013), 268–69.

90. Frank Bruni, "Looks like Diversity, but It Tastes like Tuna," *New York Times*, October 20, 2004.

91. Authenticity is a complicated and much discussed concept in sociology. See, for example, Richard A. Peterson, *Creating Country Music: Fabricating Authenticity* (Chicago: University of Chicago Press, 1997); Fine, "Presentation of Ethnic Authenticity"; Gary Alan Fine, *Everyday Genius: Self-Taught Art and the Culture of Authenticity* (Chicago: University of Chicago Press, 2004); Grazian, *Blue Chicago*; Pratt, "Food Values." Also see Michèle de La Pradelle's critique of the experience of authenticity in French open-air produce markets: *Market Day in Provence*, trans. Amy Jacobs (Chicago: University of Chicago Press, 2006).

92. Nazarea, *Heirloom Seeds*, 97.

93. Watson, *Taylor's Guide to Heirloom Vegetables*, 5.

94. See John McPhee's descriptions of farmers' markets, presumably in the 1970s (the essay first appeared in 1978 in the *New Yorker*). John McPhee, *Giving Good Weight* (New York: Farrar, Straus and Giroux, 1994).

95. Following Wendy Griswold, "The Sociology of Culture: Four Good Arguments (and One Bad One)," *Acta Sociologica* 35 (1992): 327, it is possible to ask both what heirloom tomatoes *mean* and what they *do*. Such an analysis yields a grounded sociological explanation of how a cultural object emerges over time and also highlights the potential importance of incorporating spatial parameters into analyses of taste. It is useful to explore the ways sociologists of culture understand the rise and fall of cultural objects, an approach particularly well developed in analyses of visual art and music. See Howard Becker, *Art Worlds* (Berkeley: University of California Press, 1982); Tia DeNora, "Musical Patronage and Social Change in Beethoven's Vienna," *American Journal of Sociology* 97, no. 2 (1991): 310–46; Douglas Holt, "Distinction in America?: Recovering Bourdieu's Theory of Taste from Its Critics," *Poetics* 25 (1997): 931–1020. Questions of taste are also crucial to these investigations. Bourdieu, *Distinction*; Michel Lamont and Annette Lareau, "Cultural Capital: Allusions, Gaps and Glissandos in Recent Theoretical Developments," *Sociological Theory* 6 (1988): 153–68; Guthman, "Commodified Meanings, Meaningful Commodities: Rethinking Production-Consumption Links through the Organic System of Provision," *Sociologia Ruralis* 42, no. 2 (2002): 295–311; Howard Becker, *Art Worlds*, 25th anniversary ed. (Berkeley: University of California Press,

2008); Priscilla Ferguson, "A Cultural Field in the Making: Gastronomy in 19th-Century France," *American Journal of Sociology* 103, no. 3 (1998): 597–641; Wendy Griswold, *Cultures and Societies in a Changing World* (Thousand Oaks, CA: Pine Forge Press, 2003); and others point to committed advocates and key actors as being essential to the transformation of cultural objects and the lives of cultural (or art) worlds.

96. Gary Alan Fine, "You Are What You Eat" (review essay), *Contemporary Sociology* 30, no. 3 (2001): 231; Jordan, "Heirloom Tomato as Cultural Object."

97. Many of my academic colleagues have also seen the heirloom food movement (and other culinary trends) as arising in part from a growing appetite for what are seen as more "authentic" foods. There is an understanding of authenticity implicit in the concept of an heirloom, albeit a complex one. Cf. Tregear, "From Stilton to Vimto." See also Johnston and Baumann, *Foodies.*

98. Alice Waters, *The Art of Simple Food: Notes, Lessons, and Recipes from a Delicious Revolution* (New York: Random House, 2010).

99. Access to these kinds of foods is very uneven and is made particularly difficult by poverty. Cf. Alison Hope Alkon and Julian Agyeman, eds., *Cultivating Food Justice: Race, Class, and Sustainability* (Cambridge, MA: MIT Press, 2011).

100. Hinrichs, Gillespie, and Feenstra, "Social Learning," 34.

101. http://www.agmrc.org/markets_industries/food/farmers-markets.

102. Hinrichs, Gillespie, and Feenstra, "Social Learning," 34.

103. As of August 2013, there were 8,144 farmers' markets registered in the United States. http://www.ams.usda.gov/farmersmarkets/facts.htm. Data from the USDA's agricultural census "show that direct food sales—sold by farmers directly to household consumers—rose 49% to $1.2 billion in 2007 from $812 million in 2002" (adjusted for inflation, it's an increase of 30 percent). In that period, 17 percent more farms were engaged in direct marketing, but they totaled "only 0.4% of the $300 billion of farm sales in 2007." Press release, Crossroads Resource Center, February 4, 2009. Barry Estabrook praises the Greenmarket in New York's Union Square, where the selection is "reassuringly slim" in March because of the rules governing the market: "Cheaters can be kicked out." Estabrook and others urge caution when we hear the word "local" at a restaurant—it is a term that is not certified and that can easily be misused. "Unlike *organic, local* has no legal definition attached to it. And there is a considerable disconnect between what consumers and food purveyors consider local." *Gourmet,* July 2006.

104. There have been discussions, in part around the work of Michael Pollan, alleging that food is too cheap—that we are not paying the true costs of cheap

food. Alkon believes Pollan's critique that food is too cheap "ignores the financial concerns of low-income people." Alkon, *Black, White, and Green*, 114.

105. "The Chicago Lights Urban Farm empowers youth and community residents in the Cabrini-Green neighborhood to have increased economic opportunities through access to organic produce, nutritional education, work force training, and microenterprise development. It also provides a safe sanctuary and programs for children and youth to learn about urban agriculture." http://www.chicagolights.org/cgi-bin/WebObjects/cl.woa/wa /b?t=Urban+Farm.

106. Max Weber, "Class, Status, Party," in *From Max Weber*, trans. H. H. Gerth and C. W. Mills (New York: Oxford University Press, 1946), 180–95; Bourdieu, *Distinction*.

107. Bourdieu, *Distinction*. Also see Johnston and Baumann, *Foodies*.

108. "Investigating the Edible: Points of Inquiry in the Study of Food, Culture, and Identity," in *Cooking, Eating, Identity: Speisen als kulturelle Codes in Zentraleuropam*, ed. Moritz Csáky and Georg-Christian Lack (Vienna: Böhlau Verlag, 2014).

109. "Food tastes always have material consequences, not only in actual sensation and bodily reproduction, but also in the sense of the work it takes to provide food. For food tastes are not only produced by representations and passed-on cultural meanings, but also by labor and ecological processes that transform biological material from one state to another." Guthman, "Commodified Meanings, Meaningful Commodities," 306.

110. As Guthman notes (ibid.), Bourdieu's analysis of taste also lends itself, for obvious reasons, to the sociological study of food. Bourdieu makes it clear that food is not only a means of sustenance and a source of symbolic meaning and emotional and physical comfort, but also a technique of distinction. He discusses everything from breakfast to fish (too delicate for working-class men), to greasy meat (too heavy for upper-class women), to cake served on cardboard squares ripped from the box it came in. In such visceral and personal acts, what we put in our mouths is reinforced by and reinforces our social standing relative to others. Yet the audiences for markers of distinction are not always clear. If, as Bourdieu asserts, breakfast is sociologically meaningful, we must also note what a private meal it is. Furthermore, even when people are eating publicly, they are not necessarily eating their greasy meats or delicate fish in front of members of other classes; usually they eat among their own, in restaurants, supper clubs, or workplace cantinas. Perhaps food's role in class distinction must thus be understood not only as flashing certain signs to members of other classes,

but also in terms of the spatiality of eating—in the home, the factory cafe-teria, or the sushi restaurant across from the bank headquarters. Thus not only does what you put in your mouth matter, so does where you put it in your mouth. See Fantasia, "Fast Food in France," and Caldwell, "Domes-ticating the French Fry," on McDonald's in France and Russia. Further-more, where you buy food for home consumption (the spatiality of shop-ping) plays a role as well: Wal-Mart or Whole Foods, the local bodega or an upscale farmers' market like Manhattan's Greenmarkets or San Fran-cisco's Ferry Building. Holt, "Distinction in America"; Sharon Zukin, *Point of Purchase: How Shopping Changed American Culture* (New York: Routledge, 2005).

111. Bourdieu, *Distinction*.

112. While I am concerned here more with cultural objects than with fields, the call to investigate origins of both objects and fields propels my inquiry as well. Ferguson and DeNora both point to the significance of temporal analysis in investigating changing tastes and emergent fields, but their re-sults also indicate the centrality of taste's functioning *in space*, even if they do not emphasize this intriguing result of their analyses. Whether it is bar-ring non-elites from admission to "complicated," and thus high-status, concerts in Vienna (through overpriced tickets or limited tickets distributed to a limited circle) or producing and serving food at prices and in settings unreachable for many in France, distinction and the ability to enjoy par-ticular aesthetic objects are being enacted in part in spatial ways. Certainly in DeNora's discussion the genius of Beethoven is at the heart—the pure aesthetic object—but she makes it clear that complicated music is enjoyed in what amounts to carefully guarded social and physical spaces. DeNora, "Musical Patronage." For Ferguson, a set of nonspatial practices is key—the discourse developed in cookbooks and food writing ("Cultural Field in the Making," 602)—but it intersects with the intense physicality and spatiality of gastronomy; the kitchens and restaurants where such food is produced and eaten, where chefs and diners can apply and refine the tastes and prac-tices they are acquiring with regard to gastronomy.

113. Julie Guthman, "Can't Stomach It: How Michael Pollan et al. Made Me Want to Eat Cheetos," *Gastronomica* 7, no. 3 (2007): 75–79.

114. For a list of CSA farms, see http://www.localharvest.org/csa.

115. The demand for organic food has increased significantly over the past two decades. Lockie, Lyons, Lawrence, and Mummery, "Eating 'Green,'" 23; Guthman, "Commodified Meanings, Meaningful Commodities," 305.

116. Allen, *Ripe*.

117. At his Craftsman Building in 1913, Gustav Stickley also opened the Crafts-

man Restaurant. William Grimes, *Appetite City: A Culinary History of New York* (New York: North Point Press, 2010), 176–77. "Framed sepia photographs of the Craftsman Farms reminded diners that the food on their plates reflected a socio-artistic vision. . . . Even more revolutionary, at a time when industrialized food production was ascendant, the Craftsman promised to shrink the distance between farm and restaurant. 'My theory about a restaurant is that to be the right sort of an eating place it must be closely related to its source of supplies,' Stickley wrote, more than half a century before Alice Waters made a religion of the idea at Chez Panisse" (177). And the Four Seasons, in the late 1950s in New York, was also championing "uncompromisingly fresh [ingredients], cooked with herbs from the restaurant's own garden," emphasizing food appropriate to the season (276). A bit later, "The new focus on fresh ingredients and their pure expression reflected the spirit of the 1960s, with their questioning of tradition, hostility to the calcified forms of the past, and search for authenticity" (287).

118. The heirloom food movement has definitely taken hold in Great Britain. One of the more famous members of the movement is the Prince of Wales, who raises both heirloom produce and heirloom animals on his Highgrove Estate. His work is very popular among food activists in the United States. Kim Severson, "For U.S. Food Elite, an Unlikely (Crowned) Hero," *New York Times*, April 25, 2007, F5. The rediscovery of British agricultural products is quite visible in the pages of popular magazines like *British Country Living* and in the growing landscape of local foods and products available in both shops and restaurants.

119. Brad Weiss, "Configuring the Authentic Value of Real Food: Farm-to-Fork, Snout-to-Tail, and Local Food Movements," *American Ethnologist* 39, no. 3 (2012): 614–26.

CHAPTER THREE

1. http://www.fedcoseeds.com/trees/search.php?item=1551&.

2. Michael Pollan, in *Botany of Desire*, provides a lively discussion of the importance of hard cider as a healthy drink (and Johnny Appleseed's role in making it widely available by distributing the apple saplings he had grown from seed). Also see Rowan Jacobsen, *Apples of Uncommon Character: Heirlooms, Modern Classics, and Little-Known Wonders* (New York: Bloomsbury, 2014).

3. Frank Browning, *Apples* (New York: North Point Press, 1998); Edward A. Bunyard, *The Anatomy of Dessert: With a Few Notes on Wine* (New York: Mod-

ern Library, 2006); Creighton Lee Calhoun, *Old Southern Apples: A Comprehensive History and Description of Varieties for Collectors, Growers, and Fruit Enthusiasts*, 2nd ed. rev. and exp. (White River Junction, VT: Chelsea Green, 2010); Kate Colquhoun, *Taste: The Story of Britain through Its Cooking* (New York: Bloomsbury, 2007); James Crowden, *Ciderland* (Edinburgh: Birlinn, 2008); Jabs, *Heirloom Gardener*; Jennifer A. Jordan, "Apples, Identity, and Memory in Post-1989 Germany," in *Debating German Cultural Identity since 1989*, ed. Anne Fuchs, Kathleen James-Chakraborty, and Linda Shortt (Rochester, NY: Camden House, 2011), 46–64; Fred Lape, *Apples and Man* (New York: Van Nostrand Reinhold, 1979); Gregory McNamee, *Movable Feasts: The History, Science, and Lore of Food* (Westport, CT: Praeger, 2007); Gary Paul Nabhan, Ashley Rood, and Deborah Madison, *Renewing America's Food Traditions: Saving and Savoring the Continent's Most Endangered Foods* (White River Junction, VT: Chelsea Green, 2008); James Russell, *Man-Made Eden: Historic Orchards in Somerset and Gloucestershire* (Bristol, UK: Redcliffe, 2007); Raymond Sokolov, *Why We Eat What We Eat: How the Encounter between the New World and the Old Changed the Way Everyone on the Planet Eats* (New York: Summit Books, 1991), 157–62; Christopher Stocks, *Forgotten Fruits: The Stories behind Britain's Traditional Fruit and Vegetables* (London: Windmill, 2009); Ben Watson, *Cider, Hard and Sweet: History, Traditions, and Making Your Own* (Woodstock, VT: Countryman Press, 2008); Roger B. Yepsen, *Apples* (New York: W. W. Norton, 1994); Peter Wynne, *Apples* (New York: Hawthorn Books, 1975); Jörg Zirfas, *Apfel: Eine kleine kulinarische Anthologie* (Stuttgart: Reclam, 1998); John P. Bunker, *Not Far from the Tree: A Brief History of the Apples and the Orchards of Palermo, Maine, 1804-2004* (Palermo, ME: John Bunker, 2007); Edward A. Bunyard, *A Handbook of Hardy Fruits More Commonly Grown in Great Britain: Apples and Pears* (London: John Murray, 1920); Joan Morgan, Alison Richards, and Brogdale Horticultural Trust, *The Book of Apples* (London: Ebury Press, 1993).

4. Sources for antique apples include Southmeadow Fruit Gardens in Michigan and the Sonoma Antique Apple Nursery in Sonoma, California, among many others.

5. Harold McGee, "The Curious Cook: Stalking the Placid Apple's Untamed Kin," *New York Times*, November 21, 2007. In *The Botany of Desire*, Michael Pollan also points out that the apple changes as breeders, and consumers, seek more and more sweetness.

6. Estabrook, *Tomatoland*.

7. The Institut National de l'Origine et de la Qualité in France defines terroir as a "delineated geographical space in which, in the course of its history,

a human community accumulates collective production skills, based on a system of 'interactions' between a physical and biological environment and a set of human factors. The socio-technical itineraries that come into play in this setting impart a typicality, and generate a reputation for the goods/produce originating from the geographical space in question." http://hal .archives-ouvertes.fr/hal-00922129. See also the fine discussions in Rowan Jacobsen, *American Terroir: Savoring the Flavors of Our Woods, Waters and Fields* (New York: Bloomsbury, 2010). Also see Amy Trubek (including a profile of Wisconsin's L'Étoile and chef Odessa Piper), *The Taste of Place: A Cultural Journey into Terroir* (Berkeley: University of California Press, 2008).

8.   Bunyard, *Anatomy of Dessert*, 11, 13.

9.   Karen Herzog, "Few Reasons to Holler over This Year's Apple Harvest," *Milwaukee Journal Sentinel*, September 10, 2012.

10. An orchard, wizened or new, should not be romanticized. Apple growing is not a simple endeavor, and orchardists of all stripes face a yearly onslaught of pests and diseases, combating many of them with some very extreme chemical treatments. See Browning, *Apples*; and Holmes, *Fresh Fruit*.

11. This point is made with particular clarity and eloquence by Michael Pollan in *Botany of Desire*.

12. Erika Janik, *Apple: A Global History* (London: Reaktion, 2011); Browning, *Apples*; Lape, *Apples and Man*.

13. Browning, *Apples*; Lape, *Apples and Man*; Janik, *Apple*.

14. *Better Homes and Gardens* explains apple breeding, in response to a reader's question about growing apple trees from the seeds of grocery store apples: "Most apples are grown from grafted trees and will not come true from seed. The seeds might germinate, and they could develop into productive trees, but the fruit might not be similar to the fruit you purchased. Fruit breeders plant thousands of apple seeds every year from controlled crosses they make. Of these seedlings, no more than one or two are expected to make it into commercial production. If you want an apple tree that develops tasty fruit, you should buy a known variety from a nursery or mail-order source. You can find almost any variety of trees available, and trees you purchase will fruit in a much shorter time. A seed-started tree could take 8–10 years to fruit. Also, apple trees started from seed will have no dwarfing characteristics. Unless you have a large yard, they may be too big for your site." http://www.bhg.com/advice/gardening/fruit/how-do-i-plant-apple -seeds-saved-from-grocery-store-apples.

15. Davidson, *Oxford Companion to Food*, 26; Kiple and Ornelas, *Cambridge World History of Food*, 1720.

16. Eckart Brandt, *Mein grosses Apfelbuch: Alte Apfelsorten neu entdeckt; Ge-*

schichte, Anbau, Rezepte (Munich: Bassermann, 2008), 37–38; Pollan, *Botany of Desire*.

17. Brandt, *Apfelbuch*, 38.

18. Karl Josef Strank and Jutta Meurers-Balke, eds., *Obst, Gemüse und Kräuter Karls des Grossen: "... dass man im Garten alle Kräuter habe ..."* (Mainz am Rhein: Philipp von Zabern, 2008).

19. Frank Crisp and Catherine Childs Paterson, eds., *Mediaeval Gardens* (New York: Hacker Art Books, 1979).

20. Dieter Hennebo, *Gärten des Mittelalters* (Munich: Artemis, 1987), 29.

21. Marina Heilmeyer and Clemens Alexander Wimmer, *Äpfel fürs Volk* (Potsdam: Vacat, 2007), 43; Adam Leith Gollner, *The Fruit Hunters: A Story of Nature, Adventure, Commerce and Obsession* (New York: Scribner, 2008), 48.

22. Lape, *Apples and Man*, 13; Kiple and Ornelas, *Cambridge World History of Food*, 1219.

23. Joan Morgan, Alison Richards, and Brogdale Horticultural Trust, *The Book of Apples* (London: Ebury Press, 1993).

24. Erika Schermaul, *Pardiesapfel und Pastorenbirne: Bilder und Geschichten von alten Obstsorten* (Ostfildern, Germany: Thorbecke, 2005), 57.

25. Ibid., 59.

26. Cf. Browning, *Apples*; Brandt, *Apfelbuch*; Janik, *Apple*.

27. Davidson, *Oxford Companion to Food*, 27.

28. Heilmeyer and Wimmer, *Äpfel fürs Volk*, 43. See also Evelyn Thieme, Jutta Schneider, and Michael Will, *Streuobstwiesen: Alte Obstsorten neu entdeckt* (Ostfildern, Germany: Thorbecke, 2008), 14, 38; Schermaul, *Paradiesapfel und Pastorenbirne*, 39; Brandt, *Apfelbuch*, 39.

29. Thieme and Schneider, *Streuobstwiesen*, 38; my translation. Gollner also describes the changing aristocratic attitudes to fresh fruit. Gollner, *Fruit Hunters*, 50.

30. Heilmeyer and Wimmer, *Äpfel fürs Volk*, 32.

31. Cf. Stocks, *Forgotten Fruits*, 4.

32. Ibid.

33. Brandt, *Apfelbuch*, 46.

34. Davidson, *Oxford Companion to Food*, 621.

35. Ibid., 620.

36. Ibid., 620, 621.

37. Bunyard, *Anatomy of Dessert*, 5. I had initially thought that "grateful" was a typo, but in this context it means "pleasing to the mind or the senses, agreeable, welcome," according to the *Oxford English Dictionary*.

38. Ibid., 8.

39. Ibid.

40. Ibid., 4.

41. Ibid.

42. Jane Grigson, *Good Things* (Lincoln: University of Nebraska Press, 1971), 256–57.

43. Nigel Slater, *Ripe: A Cook in the Orchard* (Berkeley, CA: Ten Speed Press, 2012), 22.

44. Tim Hensley, "Apples of Your Eye," *Smithsonian* 33, no. 8 (2002): 111–18.

45. Kiple and Ornelas, *Cambridge World History of Food*, 1308.

46. "By 1850 thousands of named apple varieties for fresh eating, cooking, drying, pickling, and making cider, apple butter, applesauce, vinegar, wine, and even livestock food were listed in nursery catalogs. There was considerable diversity of varieties in New England, the Middle Atlantic, the upper Midwest, and the Northwest." Thomas Burford, "Apples," in *The Oxford Companion to American Food and Drink*, ed. Andrew F. Smith (New York: Oxford University Press, 2007), 21. Burford also states that "in 1905 W. H. Ragan's *Nomenclature of the Apple: Catalog of Known Varieties Referred to in American Publications from 1804–1904* listed seventeen thousand apple varieties grown in America." That is a vast number, and it is certainly possible that some of these seventeen thousand names refer to the same apples.

47. For more on the process of breeding new apple varieties, see, for example, the history of the Honeycrisp apple, developed at the Minnesota Agricultural Experiment Station. As the University of Minnesota website explains, the apple was "named the Minnesota State Fruit in 2006. This honor was bestowed for several reasons. It is a great tasting apple. It is a very popular apple. And, it helped revive a declining apple growing industry and brought much needed revenue to small to medium sized, family-run orchards. Because of the broad appeal of Honeycrisp's flavor and texture, it sells at a premium price." http://www.apples.umn.edu/Honeycrisp.

48. As Pollan writes, "An orchard is also an idealized or domesticated version of a forest, and the transformation of a shadowy tract of wilderness into a tidy geometry of apple trees offered a visible, even stirring, proof that a pioneer had mastered the primordial forest." *Botany of Desire*, 16.

49. William Kerrigan, "Apples on the Border: Orchards and the Contest for the Great Lakes," *Michigan Historical Review*, 34, no. 1 (2008): 27. "A two-way trade in varieties arose. Gravenstein, the best of the N[orthern] German and Danish apples, became popular in the USA. American Mother, a red, juicy, mid-autumn apple, enjoyed a vogue in Britain in the 19th century." Davidson, *Oxford Companion to Food*, 27.

50. "Breaking Ground: The Call of the Wild Apple," *New York Times*, November 5, 1998.

51. Lape, *Apples and Man*, 45.

52. Jacobsen, *American Terroir*, 68, also quotes Pollan and talks about apples' Americanness.

53. http://www.mofga.org/Default.aspx?tabid=294.

54. Lee Riech, "Grow Your Own Apples and Have the Pick of Flavor," *New York Times*, October 27, 1985 (http://www.applejournal.com, http://www.allaboutapples.com/orchard, http://www.nafex.org).

55. See, for example, Calhoun, *Old Southern Apples*; George Albert Stilphen, ed., *The Apples of Maine: A Compilation of the History, Physical and Cultural Characteristics of All the Varieties of Apples Known to Have Been Grown in the State of Maine*, adapted from a thesis submitted by Frederick Charles Bradford to the University of Maine at Orono, 1911 (Otisfield, ME: Stilphens Crooked River Farm, 1993).

56. Cate Lecuyer, "Core Curriculum," *Brattleboro (VT) Reformer*, October 9, 2006. For more on Scott Farm's extensive collection of heirloom apples, see http://scottfarmvermont.com.

57. Hensley, "Apples of Your Eye," 111–18.

58. Stilphen, *Apples of Maine*, 2; subsequent page numbers are given parenthetically in the text.

59. David Karp, "It's Crunch Time for the Venerable Pippin," *New York Times*, November 5, 2003.

60. Ross Eric Gibson, "The Hall That Apples Built," http://www.santacruzpl.org/history/articles/6.

61. Maria Gaura, "Core Business of Apples Losing Ground in Watsonville," *SFGate*, November 15, 2013, http://www.sfgate.com/food/article/Core-business-of-apples-losing-ground-in-4986387.php#page-2.

62. Alastair Bland, "California's Disappearing Apple Orchards," *Smithsonian*, November 2, 2011, http://www.smithsonianmag.com/people-places/californias-disappearing-apple-orchards-125394178/?no-ist.

63. "Heirlooms: Harvest Days," *Intelligencer Journal* (Lancaster, PA), October 5, 2005.

64. Holmes, *Fresh Fruit, Broken Bodies*, 73.

65. Apple botany is fascinatingly complex and to a large extent beyond the scope of this book. There are also people who know infinitely more than I do about apple growing, cider making, and all the other practices described here.

66. Davidson, *Oxford Companion to Food*, 27.

67. Lynne Ames, "The View from Yorktown; Antique Apples Reveal Couple's Earthy Side," *New York Times*, May 30, 1999.

68. Ralph Berrier Jr., "Heirlooms from the Orchard: Virginia's Antique-Apple

Growers Revive an Unmistakable, Southern Flavor," *Roanoke (VA) Times*, September 21, 1997.

69. Lape, *Apples and Man*, 42–43, 45. Lape concludes on a worried note: "The present picture of the eating apple in the United States, and perhaps in the world, cannot be viewed without apprehension."

70. Ibid., 26.

71. Cf. Paul Connerton, *How Modernity Forgets* (Cambridge: Cambridge University Press, 2009); Paul Ricoeur, *History, Memory, Forgetting*, trans. Kathleen Blamey and David Pellauer (Chicago: University of Chicago Press, 2004).

72. Kathleen Purvis, "A Bite out of Time; Antique Apple Varieties Have Old Southern Appeal," *Richmond (VA) Times Dispatch*, October 9, 1996, F1.

73. Berrier, "Heirlooms from the Orchard."

74. See http://www.nchistoricsites.org/horne/horne.htm.

75. But Peter Dreyer, one of the early readers of this manuscript, had easy access to Winesaps in his region, finding that they are "scarcely lost from common memory" (personal correspondence, November 3, 2011).

76. Bill Gifford, "Fruits of His Labor: Carlos Manning's Job Is in a Coal Plant, but His Life's Work Is Hunting Down Obscure Varieties of Apples and Rescuing Them from Extinction," *Washington Post*, October 18, 1998.

77. Jane Welborn, "Apple Sleuths Hungry for Bites of History," *News and Record* (Greensboro, NC), October 6, 1999. "Devoto and the Bateses belong to a small cadre of growers keeping all-but-forgotten apple varieties alive in Northern California. The group includes John Hooper of Oz Farm, who grows 45 apple varieties on four acres in Mendocino County; Dave Hale of Hale's Apple Farm in Sebastopol; Joel and Renee Kiff, who grow 65 varieties in Healdsburg on what started as an experimental plot for the University of California; and Shirley and Lee Walker, who grow White Pearmain, Baldwin, Ben Davis, Wagener and other old apples on the Sebastopol ranch that Lee's grandfather planted in 1914." Jane Fletcher, "Apples of Our Eye," *San Francisco Chronicle*, October 10, 2001.

78. Tom Burford, *Apples of North America: Exceptional Varieties for Gardeners, Growers, and Cooks* (Portland, OR: Timber Press, 2013).

79. Weaver, *Heirloom Vegetable Gardening*; Rosalind Creasy, *The Edible Heirloom Garden* (Boston: Periplus, 1999); Janik, *Apple*; Yepsen, *Apples*; Lape, *Apples and Man*.

80. Gary Dennis, "NH Apple Growers Look for Heirloom Niche Market," *New Hampshire Sunday News*, September 15, 2002.

81. As David Karp explains, "starting in the 1970's and 80's, Watsonville apple

growers suffered from competition with the much larger shippers of Washington State, and found they could make more money with vegetables, berries and flowers. Meanwhile, retail chains consolidated, cut back on apple varieties and bypassed Pippins for more widely available but tasteless grass-green Grannys. Today the chief source of fresh Newtowns is the Hood River Valley in Oregon, where some 500 acres remain. Paradoxically, their main market is California, where the Northwest Pippins prevail over local ones because when grown in the drier climate inland they do not russet near the stem, and the colder early spring gives them a taller, more typical apple shape." Karp, "Crunch Time," 5.

82.   The groups are too numerous to mention here, but examples include the Maine Pomological Society (http://www.maineapples.org/directory), the California Rare Fruit Growers (divided into local chapters), or orchards like the Westons in Wisconsin or Century Farm Orchards (growing many of Creighton Calhoun's apples) in North Carolina (http://www.century farmorchards.com).

83.   The references I make here to individuals and organizations should in no way be seen as an exhaustive list, nor should the exclusion of a particular project be seen as a reflection of its importance.

84.   http://www.americanpomological.org.

85.   Ibid.

86.   http://www.sas.upenn.edu/~dailey/byfg.html, http://www.midfex.org.

87.   http://www.slowfoodusa.org/index.php/programs/details/ark_of_taste.

88.   Bunyard, *Anatomy of Dessert*, 9.

89.   132 (Gloria mundi); 118 (Harrison); 142 (Magnum); 147 (Nickajack); 36 (Sierra). Nabhan, Rood, and Madison, *Renewing America's Food Traditions*. Many of the sources I analyzed strike a note of concern about the disappearance of apples, like this press release from the American Society for Horticultural Science: "The apple trees of yesteryear are slowly disappearing. Many apple varieties common in the United States a century ago can no longer be found in today's orchards and nurseries. But some historic apple trees still survive in abandoned farmsteads and historic orchards throughout the U.S. Now, scientists interested in conserving these horticultural treasures have set out to identify and catalogue them, working to discover if the last remnants of historical trees may still be alive in American landscapes." "Study Confirms Diversity of Apple Trees Endures in American Southwest," October 27, 2009. http://pressrelease.ashs.org/index.php?option=com_content&view=article &id=1052:conserving-historic-apple-trees&catid=1:hortscience&Itemid=3. "Arguably the most ubiquitous fruit, apples exist in over 7,000 varieties and

have a long history in many parts of the world. One of the first fruits to be cultivated, *Malus pumila*'s direct ancestors are thought to have originated in Caucasus, the region bordering Asia minor. . . . Gravenstein, for example, a variety of apple that used to be common in this country's early history, has all but disappeared from production. Even locally, few farmers continue to produce it, though they are available at Berkeley farmers markets." Melissa Swanson, "Fall Is Here, Which Means Diversity of Local Apples," *Oakland (CA) Tribune*, October 4, 2005, 1.

90. Susan Dooley, "Seeds of a Party—Picking the Apples of Your Eye," *Washington Post*, September 24, 1979, B5. Again region matters, as Peter Dreyer (personal correspondence, November 3, 2011) points out that the Cox's Orange Pippin is "available at just about any greengrocer's stand in England."

91. Hensley, "Apples of Your Eye," 111–18.

92. Katherine Bishop, "What's Doing in the Wine Country," *New York Times*, September 2, 1990, 10.

93. Joan Jackson, "The Apple Gang," *San Jose (CA) Mercury News*, January 13, 1994.

94. In 1994, of 95 million 42-pound boxes of apples sold, 62 million were predicted to be Red Delicious, with Golden Delicious coming in second place with 15.8 million boxes and Granny Smith in third place at 8 million boxes. Walter Nicholls, "Apples Beyond Delicious," *Washington Post*, September 14, 1994, E11; Felicia Gressette, "Here's How to Choose and Use Fall Produce," *Pittsburgh Post-Gazette*, October 6, 1993.

95. Lawrence L. Knutson, "Presidents Past and Present Celebrate White House's 200 Years," *Gettysburg Times*, November 9, 2000.

96. Apple grower Peter Ten Eyck, quoted in Andrea Peyser, "New Empire Apple Causing Excitement," *Evening News* (Newburgh, NY), October 18, 1982.

97. Lloyd Ferriss, "Amateur Historian Sees Past through Antique Apple Trees," *Portland (ME) Press Herald*, October 6, 1996, 4G.

98. Marty Hair, "Bulb Biz Blooms at Old House Gardens," *Times Union* (Albany, NY), October 27, 1996.

99. Thoreau, *Wild Apples*, 147.

100. Marcia Adams, "Food: Apple Polishing," *New York Times*, October 8, 1989.

101. Phyllis C. Richman, "Richman's Table: The Greening of the South Bronx," *Washington Post*, April 9, 1986.

102. Janice Okun, "Snooty Foods of the Future," *Buffalo (NY) News*, November 29, 1995.

103. Gifford, "Fruits of His Labor."

104. Cheramie Sonnier, "Fading Fad," *Advocate* (Baton Rouge, LA), July 15, 2004.

105. Steven F. Peterka, "Getting Intuit," *Chicago Sun-Times*, August 6, 1995, 19.

106. David Karp, "Apples with Pedigrees Selling in Urban Edens," *New York Times*, October 20, 2004.

107. Sonnier, "Fading Fad."

108. Lape, *Apples and Man*, 26; Pollan, *Botany of Desire*, 46.

109. Davidson, *Oxford Companion to Food*, 27.

110. Bunyard, *Anatomy of Dessert*, 3.

111. Ibid., 17.

112. Bourdieu, *Distinction*.

113. Stocks, *Forgotten Fruits*, xi.

114. Ibid.

115. Maria Yotova, "'The Bacillus That Makes Our Milk': Ethnocentric Perceptions of Yogurt in Postsocialist Bulgaria," in *Why We Eat, How We Eat: Contemporary Encounters between Foods and Bodies*, ed. Emma-Jayne Abbots and Anna Lavis (Burlington, VT: Ashgate, 2013), 183. She asks, "What are people actually ingesting when they eat yogurt; a specific bacterium, authenticity, a nationalist tradition, or a health-giving substance?" (168). Slocum expands on this idea in terms not only of the nation but also of racial formations and identities. "Producing and maintaining racial identity is dependent, in part, on holding on to food habits and tastes, which are themselves imagined as cuisines belonging to racialized groups or nations. ... Eating and cooking as acts at once intimate and public, empowering and complicit, are constitutive of racial identity and its politics." Slocum, "Race in the Study of Food," 28.

116. Slocum and Saldanha, *Geographies of Race and Food*, 1. Also see Susan Paulson, "Sensations of Food: Growing for the Nation and Eating with the Hand in Bahia, Brazil," in *Geographies of Race and Food: Fields, Bodies, Markets*, ed. Rachel Slocum and Arun Saldanha (Burlington, VT: Ashgate, 2013), 108, where food is a marker and creator of difference. Alkon also describes how markets can, and do, become spaces of community, connection, and identity; but community can also mean exclusion, and it's important to ask who's in and who's out. Alkon, *Black, White, and Green*, 88, 95.

117. Stocks, *Forgotten Fruits*, 19.

118. Cf. Eric J. Hobsbawm and Terence O. Ranger, *The Invention of Tradition* (New York: Cambridge University Press, 1983); Benedict Anderson, *Imagined Communities: Reflections on the Origin and Spread of Nationalism* (New York: Verso, 1983); Amy Adamczyk, "On Thanksgiving and Collective Mem-

ory: Constructing the American Tradition," *Journal of Historical Sociology* 15, no. 3 (2002): 343–65; Kennan Ferguson, "Mastering the Art of the Sensible: Julia Child, Nationalist," *Theory and Event* 12, no. 2 (2009); Jennifer A. Jordan, "Elevating the Humble Dumpling: From Peasant Kitchens to Press Conferences," *Ethnology* 47, no. 2 (Spring 2008): 109–21; Nir Avieli, "Vietnamese New Year Rice Cakes: Iconic Festive Dishes and Contested National Identity," *Ethnology* 44, no. 2 (2005): 167–87; Avieli, "Roasted Pigs and Bao Dumplings: Festive Food and Imagined Transnational Identity in Chinese-Vietnamese Festivals," *Asia Pacific Viewpoint* 46, no. 3 (2005): 281–93; Jeffrey Pilcher, *Que vivan los tamales!: Food and the Making of Mexican Identity* (Albuquerque: University of New Mexico Press, 1998); Carol Palmer, "Milk and Cereals: Identifying Food and Food Identity among Fallahin and Bedouin in Jordan," *Levant* 34 (2002): 173–95; Harper and Faccioli, *Italian Way*.

119. I find it useful to bring together two powerful social scientific ideas: Benedict Anderson's imagined communities and Bourdieu's concept of habitus. The meanings of particular traditions and daily habits may change across both time and space, but they also settle deeply in bodies and hearts. See my essay "Investigating the Edible." Anderson, *Imagined Communities*; Bourdieu, *Distinction*.

120. Reay Tannahill, *Food in History* (New York: Stein and Day, 1973), 299.

121. http://www.gutenberg.org/cache/epub/8102/pg8102.html.

122. Judith H. Gerjoy, "Apple Pie," in Smith, *Oxford Companion to American Food and Drink*, 20.

123. Günther Nething, "Reminiszenzen an ein schwäbisches Nationalgetränk," *Stuttgarter Zeitung*, October 9, 2006; Landschafts-Förderverein Nuthe-Nieplitz website, http://www.foerderverein-nuthe-nieplitz.de/lfv/index -lfv.htm. Also see my discussion in Jordan, "Apples, Identity, and Memory," 46–64.

124. Cf. Heilmeyer and Wimmer, *Äpfel fürs Volk*.

125. Ernst Simader, *Mostland Oberösterreich* (Linz, Austria: Trauner, 2006); Christoph Wagner and Lois Lammerhuber, *Most* (Vienna: Pichler, 1999); Manfred Franz, *Vom Streuobst zum Apfelwein* (Kreuzwertheim, Germany: Wittbach, 2005); Gudrun Mangold, *Most: Das Buch zu Apfel- und Birnenwein* (Tübingen: Silberburg, 2003).

126. Walter Hartmann and Eckhart Fritz, *Farbatlas alte Obstsorten* (Stuttgart: Eugen Ulmar, 2008); Willi Votteler, *Altbewährte Apfel- und Birnensorten* (Munich: Obst- und Gartenbauverlag des Bayerischen Landesverbandes für Gartenbau und Landespflege, 2008).

127. Votteler, *Altbewährte Apfel- und Birnensorten.*

128. Cathleen Paech, "Vom Aussterben bedrohte Apfelsorten gesucht," *Die Welt*, January 13, 2003. Today there are more than seven thousand varieties of apples worldwide. Kiple, *Movable Feast*, 34.

129. "'There are growers out there who have seen customers looking for the unusual apple,' Taylor said. 'They still market to neighbors but you'll also find them going to markets in the metro areas.' Perry said he finds markets in Boston that want the strange varieties like the Blue Pearmain—a mild eating and cooking apple and a favorite of Henry David Thoreau—and Maiden's Blush, good for drying and cooking. 'We go to specialty food places and restaurants,' he said. Some, like Black Gilliflower, are a favorite for cider-making businesses." Gary Dennis, "A Mac, a Cortland, a . . . Burgundy?" *Union Leader* (Manchester, NH), October 1, 2003.

130. http://oldworldwisconsin.wisconsinhistory.org.

131. Lape, *Apples and Man*, 35.

132. Ibid., 27.

133. Stocks, *Forgotten Fruits*, x.

134. Pollan, *Botany of Desire*, 53, 57.

135. Andrea Peyser, "Old-Time Apples Now Just Taste Curiosities," *Intelligencer Journal* (Lancaster, PA), November 25, 1982.

136. Pollan, *Botany of Desire.*

137. www.filoli.org.

138. Christine Feldhorn, "Hot Stuff," *San Francisco Chronicle*, October 5, 1994, 2/Z1.

139. "The Gentleman's Orchard at Filoli," pamphlet, Fioli Mansion and Gardens, Woodside, CA.

140. Megan Richards, "Filoli Gardener's Reference," 2007, Filoli Mansion and Gardens, Woodside, CA.

141. Cynthia Liu Wollman, "Tasting of Heirloom Fruit Rings in Autumn at Filoli," *San Francisco Chronicle*, October 3, 2003.

142. "In the Garden," *Washington Post*, February 8, 2001.

143. Theresa Curry, "Autumn Is for Apples in Virginia," *Virginian-Pilot* (Hampton Roads, VA), October 15, 2006.

144. Anne Raver, "The Seeds of Yore," *New York Times*, January 24, 1993, A13. Also see http://www.monticello.org/site/house-and-gardens/overview-fruits-monticello.

145. Ibid.

146. Tim Knauss, "Apples Aplenty," *Post-Standard* (Syracuse, NY), September 23, 1991.

147. The Garfield Farm and Inn Museum in Kane County, Illinois, offered an antique apple grafting class in 1992. Mary Gillespie, "Field Museum Helps Gardeners Grow," *Chicago Sun-Times*, March 13, 1992.

148. Gary Dennis, "NH Apple Growers Look for Heirloom Niche Market," *New Hampshire Sunday News*, September 15, 2002.

149. Meredith Goad, "An Aficionado, George Stilphen Knows His Heirloom Apples," *Portland (ME) Press Herald*, November 3, 2002.

150. Alison Landsberg, *Prosthetic Memory: The Transformation of American Remembrance in the Age of Mass Culture* (New York: Columbia University Press, 2004). See, for example, the apples planted at Horne Farm in Pinnacle, North Carolina: http://www.nchistoricsites.org/horne/horne.htm gives more detail.

151. Slater, *Ripe*, 6.

152. Pollan, *Botany of Desire*, 16.

153. Thoreau, *Wild Apples*, 164; Stocks, *Forgotten Fruit*, 7.

154. "Forgotten Fruit: Long-Abandoned Manitou Orchard Could Revive Lost Apple Varieties," *Grand Rapids (MI) Press*, September 23, 2001, A27.

155. Lape, *Apples and Man*, 10.

156. Jacobsen, *American Terroir*, 62–83.

157. Schermaul, *Paradiesapfel und Pastorenbirne*, 18; my translation.

158. Michael Muckian, "Wisconsin Shines with Distinctive Wines," *Capital Times*, July 9, 2007, http://urbanext.illinois.edu/apples.

159. Jennifer Snelling, "Cider: The Fermented Apple Drink Makes a Comeback," *Eugene Register-Guard*, November 2, 2005. See also http://virtue cider.com and http://www.povertylaneorchards.com/farnum-hill-ciders.

160. Davidson, *Oxford Companion to Food*, 186.

161. Hensley, "Apples of Your Eye," 115–18. Also see Pollan, *Botany of Desire*, 22.

162. This is a point made by Pollan, *Botany of Desire*, 6, and Guthman, *Agrarian Dreams*, among others.

163. Bunyard, *Anatomy of Dessert*, 4.

CHAPTER FOUR

1. Cf. Tomás Almaguer, *Racial Fault Lines: The Historical Origins of White Supremacy in California* (Berkeley: University of California Press, 2008); Les Field and K. Tsianina Lomawaima, *Abalone Tales: Collaborative Explorations of Sovereignty and Identity in Native California* (Durham, NC: Duke University Press, 2008); Kent G. Lightfoot, *Indians, Missionaries, and Merchants: The Legacy of Colonial Encounters on the California Frontiers* (Berkeley: University of California Press, 2006).

2. Tim Stanley, *The Last of the Prune Pickers: A Pre-Silicon Valley Story* (Irvine, CA: 2 Timothy Publishing, 2009).

3. http://www.calisphere.universityofcalifornia.edu/calcultures/ethnic _groups/ethnic4.html.

4. Cf. the varyingly conflicting accounts at http://kathyatwood.hubpages .com/hub/Visiting-Father-Serras-Missions-in-California; http://mission tour.org/related/stories.htm; and http://lashp.wordpress.com/2009/05 /22/wild-mustard-a-plant-with-a-checkered-past.

5. See, for example, Mitchell, *They Saved the Crops*.

6. For some of Andy's writings, see http://www.mariquita.com.

7. Guthman, "Commodified Meanings, Meaningful Commodities," 306.

8. Julie Guthman, "'If They Only Knew': Color Blindness and Universalism in California Alternative Food Institutions," *Professional Geographer* 60, no. 3 (2008): 387–97. Guthman rightly criticizes the notion of alternative agriculture in the sense that so many people are then left behind in mainstream agriculture.

9. In one newsletter Griffin wrote: "In this week's harvest box I've included an heirloom Italian green called *agretti*, or *Salsola soda*, which is a close cousin to the tumbleweed. *Agretti* is a tender, succulent herb when harvested young, with a pleasing, sour taste." http://www.twosmallfarms.com/two small.articles.html/agretti.html.

10. See Johnston and Bauman, *Foodies*, for a rich discussion of the pursuit of what consumers perceive as culinary exoticism and authenticity.

11. Indeed, even practiced cooks can find cooking time consuming in otherwise busy schedules. Many feminist commentators and others, while recognizing the pleasure and multiple advantages of home cooking for many people, have criticized elements of the recent calls for people in the United States to engage in more home cooking, saying this approach inaccurately portrays home cooking as inherently healthier or more virtuous than other forms of food preparation and places an undue burden on women, who continue to do most home cooking. In much of the world, for example, street food is a quick, nourishing, and affordable source of sustenance for millions, even billions of people. Similarly, there are companies, schools, and other institutions worldwide committed to providing comparatively healthy food on a large scale and at affordable prices.

12. Weaver, *Heirloom Vegetable Gardening*, 2. Also see Deborah Madison, *Vegetable Literacy: Cooking and Gardening with Twelve Families from the Edible Plant Kingdom* (Berkeley, CA: Ten Speed Press, 2013); Lynn Coulter, *Gardening with Heirloom Seeds: Tried-and-True Flowers, Fruits, and Vegetables for a New Generation* (Chapel Hill: University of North Carolina Press, 2006).

13. See Harold McGee, *On Food and Cooking: The Science and Lore of the Kitchen* (New York: Scribner, 2004).

14. For more on cooking and identity, see Kennan Ferguson, "Intensifying Taste, Intensifying Identity: Collectivity through Community Cookbooks," *Signs: Journal of Women in Culture and Society* 37, no. 3 (2012): 695–717.

15. Kurt Michael Friese, Kraig Kraft, and Gary Paul Nabhan, *Chasing Chiles: Hot Spots along the Pepper Trail* (White River Junction, VT: Chelsea Green, 2011), is a very thorough and intriguing look at peppers in a global context.

16. Sidney W. Mintz, *Sweetness and Power: The Place of Sugar in Modern History* (New York: Penguin Books, 1986); James C. McCann, *Maize and Grace: Africa's Encounter with a New World Crop, 1500–2000* (Cambridge, MA: Harvard University Press, 2005); Evan D. G. Fraser and Andrew Rimas, *Empires of Food: Feast, Famine, and the Rise and Fall of Civilizations* (New York: Free Press, 2010).

17. Emanuela Scarpellini, *Material Nation: A Consumer's History of Modern Italy* (New York: Oxford University Press, 2011).

18. Anthony Boutard, *Beautiful Corn: America's Original Grain from Seed to Plate* (Gabriola Island, Canada: New Society, 2012); Betty Harper Fussell, *The Story of Corn* (Albuquerque: University of New Mexico Press, 1992).

19. I began by reproducing the method I used in an early tomato piece, asking, What is the ebb and flow of the public discussion of heirloom fruits and vegetables? Just as I did for tomatoes, I read all the newspaper articles I could find about heirloom vegetables. They made it clear that a taste for heirloom vegetables was actively expanding throughout the 1990s and 2000s, but there was no comparison with the number of articles covering tomatoes. In the 1980s, the few mentions of heirloom vegetables tend to be about gardening and acquiring seeds. The importance of restaurant reviews increases in the 1990s, and even more in the 2000s. There is also a marked increase in the mainstream popularity of heirloom varieties in the 1990s and 2000s. In addition, these articles revealed dramatic disparities in the frequency with which different vegetables are discussed. The vegetable that received the second most mentions was squash, but the squash descriptions included almost no references to their origin stories. Instead, restaurants, farmers' markets, and gardening received the most mentions. The third most frequently referenced vegetable was lettuce, which was mentioned far more often than I expected, but as with squash, the accounts were almost devoid of stories. The earliest mention I found in popular newspapers was of a chef growing mesclun greens in 1991. I also used an extensive collection of books on heirloom vegetables, including these: Doreen G. Howard, *The Return of Flavor: Heirloom Vegetables, Herbs, and Fruits* (Brentwood, TN:

Cool Springs Press, 2013); Bill Laws, *Spade, Skirret and Parsnip: The Curious History of Vegetables* (Stroud, UK: History Press, 2006); Bill Laws, *Fifty Plants That Changed the Course of History* (Buffalo, NY: Firefly Books, 2010); Jack Staub, *Alluring Lettuces* (Layton, UT: Gibbs Smith, 2010); Bill Thorness, *Edible Heirlooms: Heritage Vegetables for the Maritime Garden* (Seattle: Skipstone, 2009); William Woys Weaver, *100 Vegetables and Where They Came From* (Chapel Hill, NC: Algonquin Books of Chapel Hill, 2000).

20. Guthman, "Commodified Meanings, Meaningful Commodities," 306.

21. Sandy Cullen, "Living a Life of Lettuce," *Wisconsin State Journal* (Madison, WI), September 7, 2004.

22. Stocks, *Forgotten Fruits*, 48.

23. Jane Black, "Free Range on Food: Staffers Solve Your Cooking Conundrums," *Washington Post*, August 12, 2009.

24. A search of the Lexis-Nexis database of United States newspapers (which is a selection of newspapers, not a complete collection of all newspapers) between 1985 and 2013 yielded the following numbers of references to heirloom versions of these foods: beans 196, beets 97, pumpkin 80, squash 65, lettuce 62, potato 52, eggplant 43, pepper 42, radish 20, kale 18, sweet potato 18, cabbage 14, turnip 9, olives 6, peas 6, okra 5, Brussels sprouts 3, spinach 3, chickpeas 2, artichoke 2, celery 1, chicory 1, onions 1, parsley 1, rutabaga 1. There were no mentions for heirloom cassava, celeriac, chard, cowpeas, endive, Jerusalem artichokes, kohlrabi, leeks, mâche, mustard greens, parsnips, salsify, scorzonera, tomatillos, or yams.

25. http://blogs.sfweekly.com/foodie/2014/02/portlandia_boldly_makes_celery.php.

26. Tim Rutten, "The Deceit of the Iceberg," *St. Petersburg Times*, November 12, 1994, 3D.

27. Kathy Van Mullekom, "Lettuce Educate You: Looking Back at the History of a Salad Staple," *Macon (GA) Telegraph*, July 13, 2006, D1.

28. Kathy Van Mullekom, "Exchange for Heirloom Lettuce Seeds," *Chattanooga (TN) Times Free Press*, July 15, 2006, F6.

29. David McCullough, *1776* (New York: Simon and Schuster, 2005), 61.

30. Guthman, *Agrarian Dreams*; Thomas McNamee, *Alice Waters and Chez Panisse: The Romantic, Impractical, Often Eccentric, Ultimately Brilliant Making of a Food Revolution* (New York: Penguin, 2007).

31. Marian Burros, "Who Put the Beet in the Mousseline?" *New York Times*, May 31, 2000, F1.

32. Janice Okun, "Food Mysteries Solved; What Are These? The Exotic New Ingredients Tantalizing Our Taste Buds," *Buffalo (NY) News*, July 13, 2005, C1.

33. Jeanne Jones, "Fans of Beets Will Love This Soup," *Intelligencer Journal* (Lancaster, PA), September 20, 2006, A6.

34. A search of the Lexis-Nexis newspapers (limited to US newspapers, using keyword search of "heirloom [vegetable name]" from the earliest mention through 2010) showed beans as the most discussed heirloom, with twice as many mentions as second-place squash. Rounding out the top ten are lettuce, pumpkin, carrot, pepper, potato, eggplant, radish, and cabbage. Arguments about the preservation of biodiversity, however, rarely found their way into the newspaper coverage I analyzed, though they were present in books and on seed-saving websites.

35. Johnston and Baumann, *Foodies.*

36. Catherine Quillman, "Restaurant Is a Blend of Tastes," *Philadelphia Inquirer*, June 12, 2005.

37. Jennifer C. Berkshire, "The Veggie Table; Chef Digs Up a Wealth of Fresh Fall Produce," *Boston Herald*, October 13, 2002.

38. Quoted in Mary Blume, "In Praise of All Local Produce Great and Small," *New York Times*, July 21, 2001.

39. Stocks, *Forgotten Fruits*, 221, quoting Mark Twain, *Roughing It* (1886).

40. Ibid., xii.

41. Smith, *Oxford Companion to American Food and Drink*, 95.

42. Carol Stocker, "Gardener's Week," *Boston Globe*, February 6, 1997.

43. "Grow Your Own," *GQ* 70, no. 5 (May 2009): 112.

44. Larry A. Sagers, "Learn More about Fascinating Eggplant," *Deseret (UT) Morning News*, May 16, 2008.

45. David Martosko, "Obama's Right to Hold Off on Foodies' Organic Agenda," *Chicago Sun-Times*, February 6, 2009, Op-Ed.

46. Collingham, *Curry*, 165.

47. Marty Hair, "Cool Is a Cucumber," *Detroit Free Press*, August 7, 2001.

48. The cucumber "appears to be most closely related to . . . a wild species that is still quite common in the foothills of the Himalayas." Stocks, *Forgotten Fruits*, 87.

49. *GQ*, PR newswire, August 19, 1998.

50. Greg Beato, "Sorry, White Bread. There's a New Loaf in Town," *Washington Post*, August 15, 2010, B03.

51. Kim Severson and Carol Ness, "What's New," *San Francisco Chronicle*, May 14, 2003, E2.

52. Patricia Sharpe, "Primary Flavors," *Texas Monthly*, April 2004, 206.

53. Pamela Goyan Kittler, "Broccoli," in Smith, ed., *Oxford Companion to American Food and Drink*, 70.

54. Melissa Clark, "My Those Are Lovely Peas You Have," *New York Times*, July 12, 2000, F3.

55. See Wendy Griswold, "A Methodological Framework for the Sociology of Culture," *Sociological Methodology* 17 (1987): 1–35.

56. The achocha is just one example—a fruit widespread in South America and Mexico, eaten and cultivated for many generations. Davidson, *Oxford Companion to Food*, 3.

57. Nazarea, *Heirloom Seeds*; Stark, *Heirloom*; David Buchanan, *Taste, Memory: Forgotten Foods, Lost Flavors, and Why They Matter* (White River Junction, VT: Chelsea Green, 2012). Of course far more people are doing this without books being written about them or by them.

58. Price, *Growing Home*; Veteto, "History and Survival" (PhD diss.); Veteto, "History and Survival" (article), 121.

59. http://www.chicagoreader.com/chicago/global-garden-farmers-market -urban-farming-refugees/Content?oid=10815893.

60. Barbara Kingsolver, Steven L. Hopp, and Camille Kingsolver, *Animal, Vegetable, Miracle: A Year of Food Life* (New York: HarperCollins, 2007).

61. Becky M. Nicolaides, *My Blue Heaven: Life and Politics in the Working-Class Suburbs of Los Angeles, 1920–1965* (Chicago: University of Chicago Press, 2002); Melissa Caldwell, *Dacha Idylls: Living Organically in Russia's Countryside* (Berkeley: University of California Press, 2010).

62. http://www.growingpower.org; http://www.walnutway.org; http://milwaukeeurbangardens.org; http://victorygardeninitiative.org. Also see LaManda Joy and Teresa Gale, *Fearless Food Gardening in Chicagoland: A Month-by-Month Growing Guide for Beginners* (Chicago: Peterson Garden Project, 2013).

63. http://growinghomeinc.org/learn-more/chicago-urban-farm; http://www .growingpower.org/chicago_projects.htm; http://www.petersongarden .org.

64. Nabhan, *Coming Home to Eat*; Nazarea, *Heirloom Seeds*.

65. Price, *Growing Home*, viii. Also see Patricia Klindienst, *The Earth Knows My Name: Food, Culture, and Sustainability in the Gardens of Ethnic Americans* (Boston: Beacon Press, 2006), for in-depth accounts of connections between garden, memory, and immigration across the United States.

66. Price, *Growing Home*, 41.

67. Ibid., 66.

68. Ibid., 73.

69. Ibid., 86.

70. Ibid., 94.

71. Ibid., 117.
72. Ibid., 193.
73. Ibid., 123.
74. In South Africa, for example, Battersby found that many people may garden during economic crises but stop when things improve. In addition, "recent migrants viewed growing food in the city as a retrogressive rather than progressive step." Battersby, "Urban Agriculture and Race in South Africa," 127.
75. Stocks, *Forgotten Fruits*, 188.
76. http://www.nybg.org/gardens/test_garden.php?id_gardens_collections =59.
77. See Marcia Carmichael's beautiful discussion of the historical gardens at Old World Wisconsin: *Putting Down Roots: Gardening Insights from Wisconsin's Early Settlers* (Madison: Wisconsin Historical Society Press, 2011).
78. I include an extended discussion of authenticity in the context of gardens and plants in Jennifer A. Jordan, "Landscapes of European Memory: Biodiversity and Collective Remembrance," *History and Memory* 22, no. 2 (Fall/Winter 2010): 5–33.
79. Michael Laris, "Historical Harvests for Cultivated Tastes; Farmers Bring Back 'Heirloom' Produce," *Washington Post*, September 2, 2002.
80. http://www.mountvernon.org/gardens; http://www.monticello.org/site /house-and-gardens/site-vegetable-garden.
81. Weaver, *Heirloom Vegetable Gardening*, 29.
82. Jordan, "Landscapes of European Memory."
83. On ethnobotany, and the established links between plants and culture in Hayward, see Johanna Silver, "The Global Garden," *Sunset*, April 2011, 64. See also Priscilla McCutcheon, "Returning Home to Our Rightful Place: The Nation of Islam and Muhammad Farms," *Geoforum* 49 (October 2013): 61–70.
84. Nazarea, *Heirloom Seeds*, 97.
85. Weaver, *Heirloom Vegetable Gardening*, 29.
86. There is a strong trend toward heirloom vegetables in Japan, particularly in Kyoto prefecture. As historian Eric Rath writes, "The focus on vegetables in Kyoto cuisine has seen even more interest in the last two decades with the revival of 'traditional Kyoto vegetables' (Kyo dento yasai). . . . The term *traditional Kyoto vegetables* is a neologism coined in 1987 to designate local heirloom varieties grown in Kyoto prefecture . . . before 1868. The Kyoto area is home to forty-seven of these traditional vegetables, more than in any other region in Japan. . . . One reason for the appeal of Kyoto vegetables is their perceived intimate connection with the city's landscape and cul-

tural legacy," to the point that the vegetables are even named for the Kyoto neighborhoods where they were once grown. Eric Rath, *Food and Fantasy in Early Modern Japan* (Berkeley: University of California Press, 2010), 23. "I have a passion for certain kyoyasai (vegetables of Kyoto)," Elizabeth Andoh writes, "like Horikawa gobo (burdock so fat that the center can be hollowed out and the root stuffed with a forcemeat of fish or chicken before being braised), kintoki ninjin (blood red carrots that turn sweet when cooked) and Kamo nasu (plump, nearly seedless eggplants that are fabulous when broiled with miso).... These and other traditional vegetables are grown from heirloom seeds on small farms near Kyoto." Andoh, "In Japan, 'Eat Your Vegetables' Is a Pleasure," *New York Times*, June 22, 2003.

CHAPTER FIVE

1. Judith Jones, *The Tenth Muse: My Life in Food* (New York: Anchor Books, 2008).
2. Simon Hickmott, *Growing Unusual Vegetables: Weird and Wonderful Edibles and How to Grow Them* (Bristol, UK: Eco-logic Books, 2003), 8, 10. Also see Roger B. Yepsen, *A Celebration of Heirloom Vegetables: Growing and Cooking Old-Time Varieties* (New York: Artisan, 1998), 6–7.
3. Rachel Laudan, *Cuisine and Empire: Cooking in World History* (Berkeley: University of California Press, 2013); Vanina Leschziner, "Epistemic Foundations of Cuisine: A Socio-Cognitive Study of the Configuration of Cuisine in Historical Perspective," *Theory and Society* 35, no. 4 (2006): 421–43; Harvey A. Levenstein, *Revolution at the Table: The Transformation of the American Diet* (New York: Oxford University Press, 1988); James E. McWilliams, *A Revolution in Eating: How the Quest for Food Shaped America* (New York: Columbia University Press, 2007); Rao Hayagreeva, Philippe Monin, and Rodolphe Durand, "Border Crossing: Bricolage and the Erosion of Categorical Boundaries in French Gastronomy," *American Sociological Review* 70, no. 6 (2005): 968–91; Benjamin N. Lawrance and Carolyn de la Peña, eds., *Local Foods Meet Global Foodways* (New York: Routledge, 2012).
4. There is a wealth of food histories addressing many of these changes, too numerous to list comprehensively, but a few selected volumes include Laudan, *Cuisine and Empire*; Felipe Fernández-Armesto, *Near a Thousand Tables: History of Food* (New York: Free Press, 2002); Raymond Sokolov, *Why We Eat What We Eat*; Paul Freedman, ed., *Food: The History of Taste* (London: Thames and Hudson, 2007); J. L. Flandrin, M. Montanari et al. *Food: A Culinary History from Antiquity to the Present* (New York: Columbia University Press, 1999).

5. Laudan, *Cuisine and Empire*, 5.

6. Alfred W. Crosby Jr., *The Columbian Exchange: Biological and Cultural Consequences of 1492* (Westport, CT: Greenwood Press, 1972).

7. Fernand Braudel, *Civilization and Capitalism, 15th–18th Century*, vol. 1, *The Structures of Everyday Life* (1979; repr., Berkeley: University of California Press, 1992), 163.

8. Tom Standage, An *Edible History of Humanity* (New York: Walker, 2009), 113.

9. Hernández Bermejo and León, *Neglected Crops*, 28; Charles C. Mann, *1493: Uncovering the New World Columbus Created* (New York: Knopf, 2011).

10. Hernández Bermejo and León, *Neglected Crops*, 31.

11. Ibid., 79.

12. Squash has an ancient history in New World and Old World alike (albeit in different forms). See Sophie D. Coe, *America's First Cuisines* (Austin: University of Texas Press, 1994). Coe also offers long excerpts of the detailed accounts of food in the Aztec world. When we talk of heirloom varieties it can be very important to look back this far. Coe wonders, "What led certain plant foods to be accepted by the Europeans and the modern world, while others were rejected?" (27). Also see Amy Goldman, *The Compleat Squash: A Passionate Grower's Guide* (New York: Artisan Books, 2004).

13. See, for example, Miller, *Soul Food*.

14. I write about cassava in greater detail elsewhere. Taro is another food that is a staple in certain regions of the world but limited in its consumption in the United States: "Today at least six hundred varieties of taro are grown in New Guinea. Among the most prized is a red one that tastes sublimely buttery. So valued is it that in the Telefomin area a poor person is referred to as a man without red taro." Tim Flannery, *Here on Earth: A Natural History of the Planet* (New York: HarperCollins, 2010), 138.

15. "Global production of cassava has nearly doubled over the past 30 years to about 230 million metric tons in 2010. Over half is grown in Africa, with a third in Asia and 14% in Latin America. Nigeria is the largest producer, growing 38 million metric tons in 2010. Other major producers are Brazil, Indonesia, Thailand, and the Democratic Republic of Congo." http://www.cgiar.org/our-research/crop-factsheets/cassava.

16. Coe, *America's First Cuisines*, 18. "Although depopulation is the main indicator of the loss of cultural knowledge, a better index is the number of tribes wiped out during this process, since the disappearance of an ethnic group means that all its acquired knowledge and most of its agricultural artifacts (including the varieties of its crops) have also vanished. With a loss

of between 90 and 95 percent of the original population, it is estimated that at least 80 percent of the ethnic groups have disappeared." Hernández Bermejo and León, *Neglected Crops*, 198.

17. Hernández Bermejo and León, *Neglected Crops*, 198–99.
18. Kiple, *Movable Feast*, 131.
19. Paulson, "Sensations of Food," 109. "Manioc is a key constituent of the bodies of poor rural Bahians and of the smallholder landscape, or should we say foodscape, through which they move."
20. Ibid., 110.
21. Ibid.
22. Gary Allen, "Chile," in Smith, ed., *Oxford Companion to American Food and Drink*, 117.
23. Friese, Kraft, and Nabhan, *Chasing Chiles*; Dave DeWitt, *The Chili Pepper Encyclopedia* (New York: William Morrow, 1999).
24. Hernández Bermejo and León, *Neglected Crops*, 47.
25. Ken Albala, *Beans: A History* (New York: Berg, 2007); Steve Sando, *The Rancho Gordo Heirloom Bean Grower's Guide: Steve Sando's 50 Favorite Varieties* (Portland, OR: Timber Press, 2011).
26. The cowpea's precise botanical origins are somewhat unclear—some evidence suggests origins in China or tropical Asia, but there are also wild cowpeas growing in Africa. Kiple and Ornelas, *Cambridge World History of Food*, 1764. As Peter Dreyer writes (personal correspondence, November 3, 2011), "The term 'pulse' as found in the Bible (see, e.g., one of the earliest vegetarian testimonies, Daniel 1:12–15, but in the King James Version, because other versions translate just as 'vegetables') would presumably have covered fava beans, lentils, chickpeas, and various field peas (such as the cowpea, or black-eye pea, *Vigna sinensis*, which is native to India, but had doubtless found its way to the Levant by then), but not the many varieties of *Phaseolus vulgaris* (kidney beans, etc.), which are New World plants and did not appear in Europe until after Columbus." Other sources place the cowpea or black-eyed pea as originating in Africa. http://www.hort.purdue .edu/newcrop/afcm/cowpea.html; Davidson, *Oxford Companion to Food*, 221.
27. "There are many classes of dry beans produced in the United States, but only the top 14 [*sic*] are specifically enumerated by USDA. These are pinto, navy (pea) bean, Great Northern, black, small white, large lima, baby lima, light red kidney, dark red kidney, pink, small red, cranberry, blackeye, garbanzo (large chickpeas), and small chickpeas. Several others such as adzuki, yellow eye, white kidney (cannellini), white marrow, and anasazi are

generally covered in a miscellaneous category." http://www.ers.usda.gov
/briefing/drybeans/faq.htm.

28. Janet Fletcher, "The Bean Bonanza: Out of the Pod and into the Limelight,"
    San Francisco Chronicle, October 5, 1994, 1/ZZ1.

29. Trish Hall, "Beans, Old or New, Win Fans among Chefs and Nutritionists,"
    New York Times, January 25, 1989.

30. Ruth Tobias, "Beans," in Smith, ed., *Oxford Companion to American Food
    and Drink*, 39.

31. Coe, *America's First Cuisines*, 30–31.

32. http://shop.nativeseeds.org/pages/seeds.

33. Arikara Yellow, Bolita, Brown and White Tepary, Cherokee Trail of Tears,
    Christmas Lima, Mississippi Silver Hull-Crowder cowpeas, Four Corners
    Gold, Hidatsa Red, Hidatsa Shield Figure, Hopi Mottled Lima, Jacob's
    Cattle, Lina Cisco's Bird Egg, Marrowfat, Mayflower, Mesquite Pod Flour,
    O'odham Pink, Rio Zape, Santa Maria Pinquitos, Sea Island Red peas, Tur-
    key Craw, and True Red Cranberry. http://www.slowfoodusa.org/index
    .php/programs/details/ark_of_taste.

34. http://www.slowfoodfoundation.com/ark/details/953/oodham-pink
    -bean. Also see Nabhan, *Coming Home to Eat*.

35. http://www.ranchogordo.com/html/rg_varieties.htm.

36. Doug Oster, "Plotting to Grow Vegetables," *Pittsburgh Post-Gazette*, June 5,
    1999.

37. http://www.slowfoodfoundation.com/ark/details/948/cherokee-trail-of
    -tears-bean.

38. Martha Stewart, "Replant History with Heirloom Seeds," *Contra Costa
    Times*, July 14, 2000.

39. http://ansonmills.com/products/23. Carolina Gold is also listed in Slow
    Food's Ark of Taste.

40. "Gardener Extols 'Heirloom' Produce," *Eugene (OR) Register-Guardian*,
    March 17, 1984.

41. Anne Raver offers a discussion of ordering heirloom seed potatoes from
    catalogs and having success. Raver, "Time to Replace the Lawn with a
    Potato Patch," *New York Times*, April 17, 1994, A39. Also see http://www
    .potato2008.org/en/potato/biodiversity.html, and James Lang, *Notes of a
    Potato Watcher* (College Station: Texas A&M University Press, 2001), 61.

42. See Andrew F. Smith, *Potato: A Global History* (London: Reaktion Books,
    2011.

43. Coe, *America's First Cuisines*, 182.

44. Ibid., 21.

45. Lucas Rosenblatt and Edith Beckmann, *Das goldene Buch der Kartoffel* (Weil der Stadt, Germany: Hädecke, 2013), 8.

46. Ibid., 9.

47. Braudel, *Civilization and Capitalism*, 169. In addition, "Maria Theresa and Joseph II encouraged the cultivation of potatoes, for which evidence appears around 1740 in Pyhrabruck in the Waldviertel." http://www.aeiou.at /aeiou.encyclop.e/e712473.htm; my translation.

48. Rosenblatt and Beckmann, *Goldene Buch der Kartoffel*, 16. After 1740, Frederick the Great planted potatoes around Berlin and had soldiers guard them. (Here the story goes that this was to provoke curiosity, and that farmers stole the potatoes.)

49. Standage, *Edible History of Humanity*, 121.

50. http://www.pfaelzer-grumbeere.de/news/pfalzer-bauern-brachten-die -kartoffeln-nach-preusen.

51. Rosenblatt and Beckmann, *Goldene Buch der Kartoffel*.

52. Ibid., 18; Stocks, *Forgotten Fruits*, 172.

53. Standage, *Edible History*, 120.

54. Hickmott, *Growing Unusual Vegetables*, 9.

55. Collingham, *Taste of War*, 21.

56. Collingham, *Curry*, 165.

57. http://aeiou.iicm.tugraz.at/aeiou.encyclop.e/e712473.htm.

58. Lang, *Notes of a Potato Watcher*, 44.

59. Rosenblatt and Beckmann, *Goldene Buch der Kartoffel*, 24–26, 27–29.

60. http://www.hauskirchen-online.com/Museum.htm; http://www.epoch times.de/articles/2008/07/23/315723.html.

61. Stocks, *Forgotten Fruits*, 182.

62. Smith, *Oxford Companion to American Food and Drink*, vii. See Dana Goodyear, *Anything that Moves: Renegade Chefs, Fearless Eaters, and the Making of a New American Food Culture* (New York: Riverhead Books, 2013), for a more recent exploration of the contours of American food.

63. The French historian Pierre Nora developed the idea of a *lieu de mémoire* as a site not only *of* memory, but created *by* memory. Nora, Kritzman, and Goldhammer, *Realms of Memory*; Gunther Hirschfelder, *Europäische Esskultur: Eine Geschichte der Ernährung von der Steinzeit bis heute* (Frankfurt am Main: Campus, 2005).

64. Cf. Hasia Diner, *Hungering for America* (Cambridge, MA: Harvard University Press, 2001).

65. "Nostalgic gastronomy allows migrants the opportunity to live sensuously in a Malaysian identity . . . , to make grocery stores serve these memories . . .

and to engage in practices done in home countries." Slocum, "Race in the Study of Food," 31.

66. "In the 1860s and 1870s, Chinese immigrants became involved in fishing and farming, producing foods for Asian restaurants and markets." Jacqueline M. Newman, "Chinese American Food," in Smith, ed., *Oxford Companion to American Food and Drink*, 119.

67. China is such a vast country, with such diverse climates and culinary traditions, that it's really not accurate to say simply "Chinese" food: "Before the 1940s, most Chinese food [in America] was Cantonese-style, cooked by southern immigrants from Guangzhou." Newman in Smith, *Oxford Companion to American Food and Drink*, 119; Martha Dahlen and Karen Phillipps, *A Popular Guide to Chinese Vegetables* (New York: Crown, 1983).

68. Jan Lin, *The Power of Urban Ethnic Places: Cultural Heritage and Urban Life* (New York: Routledge, 2011).

69. Davidson, *Oxford Companion to Food*, 182–83; Andrew Coe, *Chop Suey: A Cultural History of Chinese Food in the United States* (Oxford: Oxford University Press, 2009).

70. "Racism against migrant food practices has had an active presence in public health and urban planning policy . . . as well as in the multicultural sentiment that once we eat others' food we all get along. . . . Facing isolation, alienation, and longing for home, some migrants use food to bridge a sensual gap. . . . Working against efforts to 'whiten' their diets, migrants created their own food products. . . . Overcoming 'the splitting of memory and lived experience' . . . might be referred to as nostalgic gastronomy . . . because it recreates what one imagines as food from home often using substitute ingredients." Slocum, "Race in the Study of Food," 31.

71. George Marcus and Nancy Marcus, *Forbidden Fruits, Forgotten Vegetables: A Guide to Cooking with Ethnic, Exotic, and Neglected Produce* (New York: St. Martin's, 1982), xi–xii.

72. Ibid.

73. Ibid.

74. Ibid., xii.

75. Ibid., xi.

76. For many scholars, the eating of other people's memories that I talk about is not neutral, and not strictly pleasurable, but can also be "not just the spice, but the staple of the cosmopolitan experience and appetite." Slocum, "Race in the Study of Food," 32. For others, "if we think in terms of foods as 'crossing over' from one dominated to another dominating culture, we will miss the 'messy, mixed-up, interconnected nature of histories, geographies, and identities.'" Likewise, "suggesting that culinary cosmopolitanism can in-

vite engagement with a nation's past and future, Elspeth Probyn . . . argues against reducing this mode of consumption to liberal pretense."

77. Schneider, *Uncommon Fruits and Vegetables*, 11, 13.

78. Marcus and Marcus, *Forbidden Fruits*, xi.

79. Weaver, *Heirloom Vegetable Gardening*, 15.

80. Ibid., 12.

81. Virginia Scott Jenkins, "Food and Drink of the Chesapeake Region," in Smith, *Oxford Companion to American Food and Drink*, 111. See also Barrie Kavasch, *Native Harvests: Recipes and Botanicals of the American Indian* (New York: Vintage, 1979); Gary Paul Nabhan, *Enduring Seeds: Native American Agriculture and Wild Plant Conservation* (Tucson: University of Arizona Press, 2002); Linda Murray Berzok, *American Indian Food* (Westport, CT: Greenwood Press, 2005).

82. Heffner, *Heirloom Country Gardens*, 4.

83. Ibid., 10, 13.

84. Ibid., 168.

85. Weaver, *Heirloom Vegetable Gardening*, 13.

86. Howard Paige, "African American Food: To the Civil War," in Smith, *Oxford Companion to American Food and Drink*, 8. Also see Jessica B. Harris, *Iron Pots and Wooden Spoons: Africa's Gifts to New World Cooking* (New York: Simon and Schuster, 1999); Frederick Douglass Opie, *Hog and Hominy: Soul Food from Africa to America; Arts and Traditions of the Table* (New York: Columbia University Press, 2008); Doris Witt, *Black Hunger: Soul Food and America* (Minneapolis: University of Minnesota Press, 2004).

87. The peanut "was first imported into the United States from West Africa, on the ships that brought the slaves. But the peanut had been brought to West Africa from Brazil by the Portuguese, along with maize and sweet potatoes." Coe, *America's First Cuisines*, 34.

88. Kim Pierce, "Regional Foods Meet Techniques for '90s in New Southern Cuisine," *Milwaukee Journal Sentinel*, August 16, 1998, Food, 5. According to Howard Paige in Smith, *Oxford Companion to American Food and Drink*, field hands' food, of course, was somewhat different: "johnnycake, greens, cornmeal dumplings, hoecakes, cornbread, sweet potatoes, fried fowl, rice, fish, cakes, pies, tarts, cookies, turnip greens, cabbage, nuts, molasses, peach cobblers, apple dumplings, whole hogs, sheep, beef, cheese, candy, coffee, custards, and so forth" (9).

89. Edna Lewis, *The Taste of Country Cooking*, 30th anniversary ed. (New York: Knopf, 2006); Edna Lewis and Scott Peacock, *The Gift of Southern Cooking: Recipes and Revelations from Two Great American Cooks* (New York: Knopf, 2003).

90. Eric Asimov and Kim Severson, "Edna Lewis, 89, Dies; Wrote Cookbooks That Revived Refined Southern Cuisine," *New York Times*, February 14, 2006.

91. Amanda Watson Schnetzer, "Cajun and Creole Food," in Smith, *Oxford Companion to American Food and Drink*, 81.

92. Cf. Jessica Harris, *Sky Juice and Flying Fish: Traditional Caribbean Cooking* (New York: Simon and Schuster, 1991).

93. Mark H. Zanger, "African American Food: Since Emancipation," in Smith, *Oxford Companion to American Food and Drink*, 10.

94. See Harris, *Iron Pots and Wooden Spoons*; Harris, *Beyond Gumbo: Creole Fusion Food from the Atlantic Rim* (New York: Simon and Schuster, 2003); Harris, *High on the Hog: A Culinary Journey from Africa to America* (New York: Bloomsbury USA, 2011); Opie, *Hog and Hominy*.

95. http://www.hort.purdue.edu/newcrop/afcm/cowpea.html.

96. For Samuelson's recipe, see http://www.marcussamuelsson.com/recipe /black-eyed-peas.

97. Judith Carney, "Fields of Survival, Foods of Memory," in *Geographies of Race and Food: Fields, Bodies, Markets*, ed. Rachel Slocum and Arun Saldanha (Burlington, VT: Ashgate, 2013), 61. "The transatlantic slave trade forced settlement of more than 10 million Africans in the Americas. . . . A new focus on subsistence draws attention to the slave ship as the conveyor of African foods to the Americas, the food fields of slaves as the nurseries from which these crops propagated, and the role of enslaved Africans in shaping the distinctive foodways of plantation societies" (61).

98. Kim Pierce, "Hoppin' John," in Smith, *Oxford Companion to American Food and Drink*, 302.

99. Covey and Eisnach, *What the Slaves Ate*; Bower, *African American Foodways*.

100. Carney, "Fields of Survival," 62 (succeeding page numbers are given parenthetically in the text).

101. Ibid., 64.

102. "While racial oppression may have kept the enslaved from sharing meals with their masters, it did not keep whites from consuming and appreciating the same foods. . . . Recognition of this shared food heritage consequently now offers unparalleled opportunities to talk about a painful history." Ibid., 75.

103. Mark H. Zanger, "Calas," in Smith, *Oxford Companion to American Food and Drink*, 85.

104. http://www.npr.org/2012/12/28/167528801/tamari-greens-miso-yams -chef-gives-vegans-multicultural-flavor.

105. Bryant Terry, *Vegan Soul Kitchen: Fresh, Healthy, and Creative African-*

American Cuisine (Boston: Da Capo Press, 2009); Bryant Terry, *Afro-Vegan: Farm-Fresh African, Caribbean, and Southern Flavors* (Berkeley, CA: Ten Speed Press, 2014); Andrew Warnes, *Savage Barbecue: Race, Culture, and the Invention of America's First Food* (Athens: University of Georgia Press, 2010).

106. Much of white Appalachian food culture is very similar to soul food, e.g.: "The corn that yields moonshine is also the source of cornbread, roasted ear corn, fried corn, hominy, and grits." Mark F. Sohn, "Appalachian Food," in Smith, *Oxford Companion to American Food and Drink*, 17.

107. Marcus and Marcus, *Forbidden Fruits*, 65.

108. Dominique Michel, Antoine Jacobsohn, and Fabien Seignobos, *Le petit pois* (Arles: Actes Sud, 2001).

109. Bread offers another example of the swift but deeply held changes in people's tastes. Within forty years, 1890 to 1930, bread baking in the United States completely changed, from something done by women at home (generally brown bread), to industrialized mass production of white bread. Bobrow-Strain, "White Bread Politics," argues that this change was shaped by "a larger politics of purity, health, and hygiene circulating through early twentieth-century America," but that bakers "needed to convince consumers that bread had a place on the modern American table." "New emotional attachments to food" developed, and "bread consumption choices became a way in which people positioned themselves and were positioned within social hierarchies" (267, 284–85). "Drawing on the work of Michel Foucault, this article shows how discourses of food safety constitute a form of biopolitics aimed at safeguarding and improving the conditions of life for a defined population" (268).

110. This is a fascinating literature, too vast to cite here. But one piece of note, which nicely combines attention to food, identity, and landscape, is Arijit Sen, "From Curry Mahals to Chaat Cafes: Spatialities of the South Asian Culinary Landscape," in *Curried Cultures*, ed. Tulasi Srinivasan and Krishnendu Ray (Berkeley: University of California Press, 2012), 196–218. See also (again, just two of a wealth of rich and informative blogs) Susan Pachikara's "Cardamom Kitchen," http://cardamomkitchen.blogspot.com, and Luz Calvo and Catriona R. Esquibel's "Decolonize Your Diet," http://decolonizeyourdiet.org, who explain their mission as follows: "As US-born Latinos/as, we have much to learn from the way our ancestors ate. Eating our ancestral foods can help us prevent and treat the diseases that result from adopting the Standard American Diet. The central tenet of our project is '*La comida es medicina*' [Food is medicine]. As Chicana professors, we have seen firsthand the effects of the Standard American Diet on our bodies and on the health of our family, our students, and our community. . . . We

believe that it is time to reclaim our cultural inheritance and wean our bodies from sugary drinks, fast food, and donuts. Cooking a pot of beans from scratch is a micro-revolutionary act that honors our ancestors and the generations to come."

111. Calvin Trillin, quoted in an advertisement for his audio tour, *New Yorker*, December 19, 2011.

112. Jane Grigson, *English Food* (Harmondsworth, UK: Penguin, 1999), 46.

113. George Marcus and Nancy Marcus, *Forbidden Fruits and Forgotten Vegetables: A Guide to Cooking with Ethnic, Exotic, and Neglected Produce* (New York: St. Martin's Press, 1982).

114. Collingham, *Taste of War*, 18.

115. Cf. Pollan, *Omnivore's Dilemma*.

116. See Julie Guthman's discussion of mesclun (as a form of "yuppie chow"): "Fast Food/Organic Food: Reflexive Tastes and the Making of 'Yuppie Chow,'" *Social and Cultural Geography* 4, no. 1 (2003): 45–58.

117. Cf. Bourdieu's discussion of habits and appetites in *Distinction*.

118. This has happened in large part in discussions of Bourdieu.

119. Grigson, *Good Things*.

120. Cf. Mintz, *Sweetness and Power*.

121. Marcus and Marcus, *Forbidden Fruits*, xi–xii.

122. Thomas Moffett, in T. Sarah Peterson, *Acquired Taste: The French Origins of Modern Cooking* (Ithaca, NY: Cornell University Press, 1994), 113.

123. Grigson, *Good Things*, 135.

124. Peterson, *Acquired Taste*, xiii. Also see Laudan, *Cuisine and Empire*, on the emergence of French cuisine, as well as many other monumental changes in cooking around the world.

125. Peterson, *Acquired Taste*, 110–11.

126. Ibid., 119.

127. "In their zeal to put the correct thistles on the table, humanists *cum* natural philosophers carefully compared field specimens with ancient descriptions. Pliny in hand, they tracked the wild asparagus." Peterson, *Acquired Taste*, 122.

128. Grigson, *Good Things*, 207–8. "Parsley, garlic, and onions, unlike artichokes and asparagus, had never fallen into neglect, but now their prominence in ancients' texts boosted their status." Peterson, *Acquired Taste*, 115. "Those onions that could be directly linked to types noted in antiquity were accorded special status." Peterson, *Acquired Taste*, 117.

129. http://www.wholefoodsmarket.com/blog/collards-are-new-kale.

130. Marcus and Marcus, *Forbidden Fruits*, 49.

131. Smith, "Artichokes," *Oxford Companion to American Food and Drink*, 25.

132. Stocks, *Forgotten Fruits*, 112.
133. Grigson, *Good Things*, 185.
134. Ibid., 186.
135. Davidson, *Oxford Companion to Food*, 11.
136. Marcus and Marcus, *Forbidden Fruits*, 39.
137. Ibid.
138. Ibid., 119.
139. Ute Scheffler, *Alles Soljanka, oder wie? Das ultimative DDR Kochbuch, 1949–1989* (Leipzig: Buchverlag für die Frau, 2008), 14. I address wild things and foraged foods elsewhere, including an unpublished manuscript (with Ashkan Rezvani Naraghi), "Wild Things."
140. Marcus and Marcus, *Forbidden Fruits*, 17.
141. http://www.guardian.co.uk/lifeandstyle/2009/aug/12/rene-redzepi -danish-chef; http://www.nytimes.com/2013/05/26/opinion/sunday/breed ing-the-nutrition-out-of-our-food.html?pagewanted=all&_r=0.

CHAPTER SIX

1. http://www.andysorchard.com.
2. Andy Mariani, personal correspondence, May 5, 2014; Richard A. Walker, in *The Conquest of Bread: 150 Years of Agribusiness in California* (New York: New Press, 2004), 33, 226, notes that Prohibition surprisingly didn't hurt the grape industry—people bought fresh grape juice, and wine was still sold for religious purposes.
3. Grigson, *Good Things*, 289.
4. Ibid., 289n. Both Grigson and Elizabeth David were important parts of my culinary education, teaching me much that I didn't learn at home. See Elizabeth David, *French Provincial Cooking* (London: Grub Street, 2007).
5. David Karp, "A Finicky Fruit Is Sweet When Coddled," *New York Times*, September 1, 2004; Adam Leith Gollner, *The Fruit Hunters: A Story of Nature, Adventure, Commerce and Obsession* (New York: Scribner, 2008); Romney Steele, *Plum Gorgeous: Recipes and Memories from the Orchard* (Kansas City, MO: Andrews McMeel, 2011).
6. Leslie Geddes-Brown, *The Walled Garden* (London: Merrell, 2007); Susan Campbell, *A History of Kitchen Gardening* (London: Frances Lincoln, 2005).
7. Karp, "A Finicky Fruit is Sweet When Coddled"; John Seabrook, "The Fruit Detective," *New Yorker*, 78, no. 24 (2002): 70.
8. See, for example, David Mas Masumoto, *Four Seasons in Five Senses: Things Worth Savoring* (New York: W. W. Norton, 2004).
9. "Apples are always called apples, after all, although they come in many dif-

ferent forms. A plum, by contrast, can certainly be a plum, but it can also be a damson, a bullace, a greengage or a Mirabelle—not to mention a cherry plum or a prune." Stocks, *Forgotten Fruits*, 154.

10. Note the research of scientists like Julie Mennella, who have found that tastes are already experienced (and memories of tastes are already being made) in utero. http://www.npr.org/2011/08/08/139033757/babys-palate -and-food-memories-shaped-before-birth.

11. See David Karp's discussion of Mariani and his orchard, "Orchard of Dreams." *Gourmet Magazine*, July 2005, http://www.gourmet.com/maga zine/2000s/2005/07/mariani.

12. "'All plums,' said Nicholas Culpeper, 'are under Venus, and are like women— some better and some worse.'" Bunyard, *Anatomy of Dessert*, 73. I'm not really sure what he means here, but I'm thinking it can't be good.

13. Marian Burros, "BY THE BOOK; Cross the Border and Enter France," *New York Times*, August 7, 2002, 5.

14. In fact, a mere handful of articles mention heirloom plums, yet plums are clearly the object of much work and attention. As early as 1994, journal-ists pegged heirloom fruit as an emerging culinary trend, and in 1997 the *Chicago Sun-Times* described heirloom varieties as "a hot gardening trend." Karol V. Menzie, "DayBreak-Food [Garden]," *Salt Lake Tribune [Baltimore Sun]*, January 19, 1994, C1; Colleen Taylor Sen, "Heirloom Seeds and Plants for Sale at Spring Festival," *Chicago Sun-Times*, May 28, 1997, 6.

15. Slater, *Ripe*, 205.

16. Ibid., 106.

17. Ibid., 206.

18. Joan Jackson, "The World Is Our Orchard: Fruit from East and West Finds Home in Our Back Yards," *San Jose Mercury News*, January 15, 1999, 5E; Pier-rette Hondagneu-Sotelo, *Paradise Transplanted: Migration and the Making of California Gardens* (Berkeley: University of California Press, 2014).

19. Dan Koeppel, *Banana: The Fate of the Fruit That Changed the World* (New York: Plume, 2008).

20. Slow Food's Ark of Taste includes the following foods categorized as fruit (omitting apples, which are listed elsewhere): Algonquian Squash, Ameri-can Persimmon, Amish Pie Squash, Aunt Molly's Ground Cherry, Baby Crawford Peach, Beaver Dam Pepper, Black Republican Cherry, Black Sphinx Date, Blenheim Apricot, Boston Marrow Squash, Bradford Water-melon, Bronx Grapes, Bull Nose Large Bell Pepper, Burford Pear, Califor-nia Mission Olive, Canada Crookneck Squash, Chiltepin Pepper, Crane Melon, Datil Pepper, Elephant Heart Plum, Fay Elberta Peach, Fish Pepper, Fuerte Avocado, George IV Peach, Green-Striped Cushaw, Hatcher Mango,

Hinkelhatz Hot Pepper, Hog Island Fig, Hua Moa Banana, Hussli Tomato Pepper, Inca Plum, Inland Empire Old-Grove Orange, Japanese Massage Dried Persimmon, Jimmy Nardello's Sweet Italian Frying Pepper, Laroda Plum, Louisiana Heritage Strawberries, Louisiana Satsuma, Mariposa Plum, Mayhaw Jelly and Syrup, Meech's Prolific Quince, Meyer Lemon of California's Central Coast, Moon and Stars Watermelon, New Mexican Native Chile, New Mexico Native Tomatillo, Oldmixon Free Peach, Padre Plum, Pantin Mamey Sapote, Pawpaw, Pixie Tangerine of Ojai Valley, Puebla Avocado, Rio Oso Gem Peach, Seminole Pumpkin, Sheepnose Pimiento, Sibley Squash, Silver Logan Peach, Sun Crest Peach, Wenk's Yellow Hot Pepper, Wilson Popenoe Avocado, Yellow-Meated Watermelon. http://www.slowfoodusa.org/ark-of-taste?cp=15&q=&qa=#results.

21. Campbell, *History of Kitchen Gardening*, 155, 158.
22. Smith, "Avocados," *Oxford Companion to American Food and Drink*, 28.
23. Jeffrey Charles, "Searching for Gold in Guacamole: California Growers Market the Avocado, 1910–1994," in *Food Nations: Selling Taste in Consumer Societies*, ed. Warren Belasco and Philip Scranton (New York: Routledge, 2002), 131–54.
24. Davidson, *Oxford Companion to Food*, 45.
25. For more on ancient guacamole, see Coe, *America's First Cuisines*.
26. Jacobsen, *American Terroir*, 156–65, 163.
27. Smith, *Oxford Companion to American Food and Drink*, 33–34. "The history and botanical classification of bananas are subjects best left to experts, . . . for they are of extreme complexity." Davidson, *Oxford Companion to Food*, 56.
28. Davidson, *Oxford Companion to Food*, 56.
29. Judith A. Carney, "'With Grains in Her Hair': Rice in Colonial Brazil," *Slavery and Abolition* 25, no. 1 (2004): 1–27.
30. Davidson, *Oxford Companion to Food*, 57; Kiple and Ornelas, *The Cambridge World History of Food*, 178–81.
31. Smith, *Oxford Companion to American Food and Drink*, 34.
32. Davidson, *Oxford Companion to Food*, 57. On the labor conditions of banana production in historical perspective, see Steve Striffler and Mark Moberg, eds., *Banana Wars: Power, Production and History in the Americas* (Durham, NC: Duke University Press, 2003), and Mark Moberg, *Myths of Ethnicity and Nation: Immigration, Work, and Identity in the Belize Banana Industry* (Knoxville: University of Tennessee Press, 1997).
33. Mimi Sheller, "Skinning the Banana Trade: Racial Erotics and Ethical Consumption," in *Geographies of Race and Food: Fields, Bodies, Markets*, ed. Rachel Slocum and Arun Saldanha (Burlington, VT: Ashgate, 2013), 293.

34. Sheller, "Skinning the Banana Trade," 294; subsequent page references are given parenthetically in the text.

35. Sheller points out that "the ecological vulnerability of banana plantations, in other words, also produced locational instability for workers, and in many cases 'enforced mobility' as uprooted workers were enticed to new banana zones" (298).

36. Sheller also discusses "ethical bananas," the growing awareness of the labor and environmental conditions surrounding banana production, "calling attention to the ways in which consumption patterns [in the global North] cause distant suffering [generally in the global South]" (304).

37. http://www.cgiar.org/our-research/crop-factsheets/bananas.

38. Marcus and Marcus, *Forbidden Fruits*, 91.

39. Davidson, *Oxford Companion to Food*, 612.

40. Ibid.

41. http://elreyfoods.com/aboutus.html.

42. Davidson, *Oxford Companion to Food*, 102.

43. Ibid.

44. Ibid., 415.

45. *The Oxford Companion to Food* describes the coconut as "the most useful tree in the world." It's a drupe; the part we buy is actually the stone of the soft fruit (198–99). The coconut can be considered a fruit, a nut, or a seed, according to the Library of Congress. In addition, there is a lot of controversy about where the coconut even originated, an important reminder that the origin stories of fruits and vegetables may not be entirely known. http://www.loc.gov/rr/scitech/mysteries/coconut.html.

46. Davidson, *Oxford Companion to Food*, 113.

47. http://www.hort.purdue.edu/newcrop/morton/mango_ars.html. Certainly ripeness is not always essential for either mango or papaya, as there are recipes that call for unripe versions of both fruits, like green papaya salad popular in Southeast Asian cooking.

48. Davidson, *Oxford Companion to Food*, 478.

49. Ibid.

50. Like the apple, the mango "does not grow true from seed." Ibid.

51. Marcus and Marcus, *Forbidden Fruits*; Elizabeth Schneider, *Uncommon Fruits and Vegetables: A Commonsense Guide* (New York: Harper and Row, 1986).

52. Davidson, *Oxford Companion to Food*, 608.

53. Ibid., 609.

54. Ibid.

55. Coe, *America's First Cuisines*, 42.

56. Ibid., 41.

57. Ibid.

58. "The pineapple in the painting was more than simply a status symbol, however; it was also a reminder of England's rise as a maritime trading power, and of its ascendancy in the West Indies in particular." Standage, *Edible History*, 107–8.

59. Davidson, *Oxford Companion to Food*, 188. For an in-depth cultural history of citrus, see Pierre Laszlo, *Citrus: A History* (Chicago: University of Chicago Press, 2007). For more on the labor conditions of citrus production, based on the example of Belize, see Mark Moberg, *Citrus, Strategy, and Class: The Politics of Development in Southern Belize* (Iowa City: University of Iowa Press, 1992).

60. Davidson, *Oxford Companion to Food*, 451. See also Toby Sonneman, *Lemon: A Global History* (London: Reaktion Books, 2012).

61. Ibid.

62. Ibid., 619.

63. Ibid.

64. Ibid., 126.

65. Ibid., 187.

66. Ibid., 188.

67. Ibid., 559. See also Clarissa Hyman, *Oranges: A Global History* (London: Reaktion Books, 2013).

68. Nabhan, *Desert Smells Like Rain*; William Cronon, *Changes in the Land: Indians, Colonists, and the Ecology of New England*, rev. ed. (New York: Hill and Wang, 2003).

69. David Karp, "Fruit," in Smith, *Oxford Companion to American Food and Drink*, 243.

70. Karp, "Fruit," 223; Davidson, *Oxford Companion to Food*, 575.

71. For more on pawpaws, see Kerrigan, "Apples on the Border," and Allison Aubrey, "The Pawpaw: Foraging For America's Forgotten Fruit," http://www.npr.org/blogs/thesalt/2011/09/29/140894570/the-pawpaw-foraging-for-americas-forgotten-fruit.

72. Davidson, *Oxford Companion to Food*, 635.

73. C. T. Kennedy, "Grapes," in Smith, *Oxford Companion to American Food and Drink*, 263.

74. Davidson, *Oxford Companion to Food*, 85.

75. Zola, *Belly of Paris*, 99.

76. Stocks, *Forgotten Fruits*, 210.

77. Andrew Mariani, "Apricots," in Smith, *Oxford Companion to American Food and Drink*, 22.

78. Slater, *Ripe*, 12.
79. Bunyard, *Anatomy of Dessert*, 19–20.
80. http://www.wachauermarille.at/Die_Wachauer_Marille.6.0.html.
81. Davidson, *Oxford Companion to Food*, 164.
82. Stocks, *Forgotten Fruits*, 77.
83. Davidson, *Oxford Companion to Food*, 164.
84. Bunyard, *Anatomy of Dessert*, 27.
85. Stocks, *Forgotten Fruits*, 76. Also see Charles Quest-Riston, *The English Garden: A Social History* (New York: Penguin, 2003), 40.
86. Stocks, *Forgotten Fruits*, 86.
87. Slater, *Ripe*, 171–72.
88. Davidson, *Oxford Companion to Food*.
89. Ibid.
90. Ibid., 590.
91. Davidson, *Oxford Companion to Food*, 532.
92. There is a reference to a Chez Panisse party, a recipe, a mention of "kiwi-heirloom peach margaritas" as a satire of Martha Stewart (in 2002), and several articles about (and in some cases by) David Mas Masumoto.
93. http://www.slowfoodusa.org/index.php/programs/details/ark_of_taste.
94. http://www.slowfoodusa.org/index.php/programs/ark_product_detail /oldmixon_free_peach.
95. Davidson, *Oxford Companion to Food*, 81; http://www.chicagorarities.org /crop_resources.html.
96. Davidson, *Oxford Companion to Food*, 654.
97. Stocks, *Forgotten Fruits*, 204.
98. Davidson, *Oxford Companion to Food*, 654.
99. Ibid., 194.
100. Schermaul, *Pardiesapfel und Pastorenbirne*, 107.
101. Davidson, *Oxford Companion to Food*, 759.
102. Grigson, *Good Things*, 302.
103. Ibid., 303n.
104. Strawberries aren't so different from bananas in the dearth of heirloom coverage in mainstream media. There are just a handful of articles about heirloom strawberries.
105. Davidson, *Oxford Companion to Food*, 597.
106. Ibid., 428.
107. Marcus and Marcus, *Forbidden Fruits*, 83.
108. http://www.wildmanstevebrill.com/Plants.Folder/Elderberry.html.
109. Davidson, *Oxford Companion to Food*, 271.

110. See Amy Stewart, *The Drunken Botanist: The Plants That Create the World's Great Drinks* (Chapel Hill, NC: Algonquin, 2013).

111. Schermaul, *Pardiesapfel und Pastorenbirne*, 133; my translation.

112. Franziska Burger, *Grossmutters Kochbuch: Essen und Leben vorgestern, gestern, und heute* (Linz: Denkmayr, 2004), 75.

113. Slater, *Ripe*, 230.

114. Schermaul, *Pardiesapfel und Pastorenbirne*, 115.

115. Stocks, *Forgotten Fruits*, 101.

116. Davidson, *Oxford Companion to Food*, 346.

117. Grigson, *Good Things*, 268.

118. Ibid.

119. Bunyard, *Anatomy of Dessert*, 32.

120. Ibid., 33.

121. Ibid., 34–35.

122. Stocks, *Forgotten Fruits*, 101.

123. http://fallenfruit.org; cf. http://www.nytimes.com/2013/05/12/us/fruit-ac tivists-take-urban-gardens-in-a-new-direction.html?pagewanted=all& _r=0.

124. http://beaconfoodforest.weebly.com.

125. Stocks, *Forgotten Fruits*, 96. Black currants were banned because they were thought to spread a fungus that threatened the timber industry.

126. Davidson, *Oxford Companion to Food*, 645.

127. Ibid., 646.

128. Ibid.

129. Grigson, *Good Things*, 254.

130. Ibid., 263.

131. http://faostat.fao.org/site/567/DesktopDefault.aspx?PageID=567#ancor.

132. Marcus and Marcus, *Forbidden Fruits*, 109–10.

133. Schermaul, *Pardiesapfel und Pastorenbirne*, 139.

134. Helmut Pirc, *Wildobst im eigenen Garten* (Graz, Austria: Stocker, 2002), 34.

135. Ibid., 69; on medlar and mulberry, see Slater, *Ripe*, 5. Bletting goes beyond ripening, and with medlar it is generally understood that bletting means allowing it to freeze and then thaw on the tree. http://treesandshrubs .about.com/od/glossaryofcommonterms/g/Bletting.htm.

136. Davidson, *Oxford Companion to Food*, 591.

137. Marina Heilmeyer, Lutz Grope, Gerd Schurig, and Clemens Alexander Wimmer, *Beste Birnen bei Hofe*, Potsdamer Pomologische Geschichten (Potsdam: Vacat, 2004), 7.

138. Ibid., 7, 8.

139. Schermaul, *Pardiesapfel und Pastorenbirne*, 67; Heilmeyer et al., *Beste Birne bei Hofe*, 9.

140. Slater, *Ripe*, 360.

141. James Arbury, *Pears* (Maidstone, UK: Wells and Winter, 1997), 8.

142. Heilmeyer et al., *Beste Birne bei Hofe*, 12.

143. Ibid., 6.

144. Arbury, *Pears*, 8.

145. Ibid., 10.

146. Heilmeyer et al., *Beste Birne bei Hofe*, 39, 41.

147. Ibid., 51.

148. Ibid., 61.

149. Ibid., 18.

150. Arbury, *Pears*, 36.

151. Ibid., 55.

152. Stocks, *Forgotten Fruits*, 142.

153. Bunyard, *Anatomy of Dessert*, 64.

154. Ibid.

155. Arbury, *Pears*, 11.

156. Ibid.

157. Heilmeyer et al., *Beste Birne bei Hofe*, 20.

158. Arbury, *Pears*, 12.

159. Ibid., 13.

160. Schermaul, *Pardiesapfel und Pastorenbirne*, 67.

161. Arbury, *Pears*, 14. I found, for example, two book reviews, a review of an exhibition of paintings of fruit, Filoli (also including a recipe and suggestions about where to buy them), six restaurant reviews, a discussion of a cooking contest (involving heirloom pear cheesecake pie), and Wisconsin jam makers serving "preserves made with forgotten heirloom pears, apples and currants grown at small local farms." Chris Martell, "Forgotten Fruits," *Wisconsin State Journal*, October 30, 2009; Heilmeyer et al., *Beste Birne bei Hofe*, 6. The Germans compare not apples and oranges, but apples and pears.

162. Heilmeyer et al., *Beste Birne bei Hofe*, 14. "Die meisten sind verschollen." *Verschollen* is an amazing word evoking shipwrecks and disappearances. Ibid., 17.

163. Bunyard, *Anatomy of Dessert*, 43; on melons, see also Amy Goldman, *Melons for the Passionate Grower* (New York: Artisan Books, 2002).

164. Davidson, *Oxford Companion to Food*, 437.

165. Ibid., 463.

166. Ibid., 467.

167. Ibid., 620.
168. Ibid., 243.
169. Ibid., 618.
170. Ibid., 425.
171. Ibid., 51.
172. Ibid., 662.
173. Standage, *Edible History*, 72.
174. Slater, *Ripe*, 499.
175. Stocks, *Forgotten Fruits*, 194; Davidson, *Oxford Companion to Food*.
176. Stocks, *Forgotten Fruits*, 194.
177. Ibid., 195.
178. Ibid.
179. Davidson, *Oxford Companion to Food*, 662.

EPILOGUE

1. Lape, *Apples and Man*, 15. See also http://azstarnet.com/news/local/arti cle_319e839f-144e-5d23-b5a5-47486e562100.html.

2. Nathaniel Hawthorne, *Mosses from an Old Manse*. Also see the abandoned apple tree in Bernhard von Barsewisch and Torsten Foelsch, *Sieben Parks in der Prignitz: Geschichte und Zustand der Gutsparks der Gans Edlen Herren zu Putlitz* (Berlin: Bässler, 2004).

3. Davidson, *Oxford Companion to Food*, 13. Almonds have been cultivated since prehistoric times.

4. Grigson, *Good Things*, 289.

5. Other under-utilized trees covering much of the Northern Hemisphere include white and black mulberries from western Asia and red mulberries from the eastern seaboard of North America. White mulberries were introduced to the North American colonies very early in hopes of producing silk, since silkworms feed on the leaves. Todd Kennedy, "Mulberries," in Smith, *Oxford Companion to American Food and Drink*, 396. "It is likely that the Romans introduced the mulberry to Britain, as well as to France and Spain. Roach (1985) points out that since a tree can live for over 600 years (e.g., the mulberry planted when the Drapers' Hall in London was built, in 1364, which lived until 1969) and comes true from seed, Roman introductions could have survived into Anglo-Saxon times, when the tree was called 'mon-beam.'" Davidson, *Oxford Companion to Food*, 520. James I planted a mulberry orchard on the current site of Buckingham Palace. These are remarkable instances of the sites of forgotten fruits, the vanished remnants of past appetites and habits. The persistence of a fourteenth-century sapling

into the 1969 "summer of love" is also a striking (and unusual) instance of fruit continuity.

6. Slater, *Ripe*, 135.

7. Isabella Dalla Ragione, for example, maintains what she calls "the Garden of Lost Trees." Ragione is a "fruit archaeologist," "or even better, a botanical Indiana Jones, huntress of lost treasure—of genes, aromas and histories. . . . Along the way she tracked down pears which had last been mentioned three hundred years before, in the archives of an Umbrian aristocratic family. . . . In her 'Garden of Lost Trees,' not far from the town of Citta di Castello, she grows pears, apples, figs, plums, cherries, quince, medlars, peaches, and grapes once thought to be extinct: four hundred varieties of fruit." Petra Reski, "Die Liebe zu den verlorenen Fruechten," *Geo*, August 2007, 116; my translation.

8. See Jennifer A. Jordan, "Investigating the Edible: Points of Inquiry in the Study of Food, Culture, and Identity," in Moritz Csáky and Georg Christian Lack, eds., *Kulinarik und Kultur: Speisen als Kulturelle Codes in Zentraleuropa* (Vienna: Böhlau Verlag, 2014), 37–50.

9. Maurice Halbwachs, *The Collective Memory* (1950; repr., New York: Harper Colophon Books, 1980); Pierre Nora, Lawrence D. Kritzman, and Arthur Goldhammer, *Realms of Memory: Rethinking the French Past* (New York: Columbia University Press, 1996).

10. See Jordan, "Investigating the Edible."

11. Many thanks to one of the anonymous peer reviewers of this manuscript for coining the phrase "edible forgetting"—something right in front of me that I hadn't properly named. See Mark Kurlansky, *The Food of a Younger Land: A Portrait of American Food* (New York: Riverhead Books, 2009). Forgetting is not necessarily an accident. As philosopher Nancy Tuana finds in her research on intentional ignorance and forgetting, "Obstetricians in the United States, for example, no longer know how to turn a breech, not because such knowledge, in this case a knowing-how, is seen as false, but because medical practices, which are in large part fueled by business and malpractice concerns, have shifted knowledge practices in cases of breech births to Caesareans." In Nancy Tuana, "Coming to Understand: Orgasm and the Epistemology of Ignorance," *Hypatia*, 19, no. 1 (2004): 196. Likewise, certain foods have been actively forgotten, pushed out by new and more profitable foods.

12. Andrew Beahrs, *Twain's Feast: Searching for America's Lost Foods in the Footsteps of Samuel Clemens* (New York: Penguin, 2010).

13. Evelyne Bloch-Dano, *La fabuleuse histoire des légumes* (Paris: Bernard Grasset, 2007).

14. Carolan, *Embodied Food Politics*, 90.

15. One of my readers suggested I call this "mnemonic intensity and/or breadth."

16. Across the globe there are many projects—some grassroots and local, others highly centralized and official—aimed at preserving germplasm. For example, in the Chiloé archipelago off southern Chile, "in an attempt to halt this loss of the traditional crops, in 1989, a community-supported 'living gene bank' of native varieties was planted." Sue Stickland and David Cavagnaro, *Heirloom Vegetables: A Home Gardener's Guide to Finding and Growing Vegetables from the Past* (New York: Fireside Books, 1998), 77. In addition, "the Dehradun Basmati Presidium has been developed with the Navdanya Trust, which was created by Vandana Shiva to conserve indigenous seed varieties, protect traditional food cultures, and fight agricultural patents. Navdanya, which means 'nine seeds' in Hindi, works with more than 60,000 farmers to promote seed banks throughout Northern India and to develop organic agriculture in India." Anya Fernald, Serena Milano, and Piero Sarado, *A World of Presidia: Food, Culture and Community* (Bra, Italy: Slow Food Editore, 2004), 99. According to Vandana Shiva, "The seed, for the farmer, is not merely the source of future plants and food; it is the storage place of culture and history. Seed is the first link in the food chain. Seed is the ultimate symbol of food security. . . . Free exchange among farmers goes beyond mere exchange of seeds; it involves exchanges of ideas and knowledge, of culture and heritage. It is an accumulation of tradition, of knowledge of how to work the seed." Shiva, *Stolen Harvest*, 8. Without the seeds, what can you do? Seeds are also big business. See also Cary Fowler, *Shattering: Food, Politics, and the Loss of Genetic Diversity* (Tucson: University of Arizona Press, 1990).

17. Diane Barthel, *Historic Preservation: Collective Memory and Historical Identity* (New Brunswick, NJ: Rutgers University Press, 1996); Diane Barthel-Bouchier, *Cultural Heritage and the Challenge of Sustainability* (Walnut Creek, CA: Left Coast Press, 2013); Richard Handler and Eric Gable, *The New History in an Old Museum: Creating the Past at Colonial Williamsburg* (Durham, NC: Duke University Press, 1997); Melinda Milligan, "Buildings as History: The Place of Collective Memory in the Study of Historic Preservation," *Symbolic Interaction* 30, no. 1 (2007): 105–23.

18. Nazarea, *Heirloom Seeds*.

19. Kevin Morgan, Terry Marsden, and Jonathan Murdoch, *Worlds of Food: Place, Power, and Provenance in the Food Chain* (New York: Oxford University Press, 2006).

20. Bourdieu, *Distinction*.

21. Kenneth E. Foote and Maoz Azaryahu, "Toward a Geography Of Memory: Geographical Dimensions of Public Memory," *Journal of Political and Military Sociology* 35, no. 1 (2007): 125–44; Jordan, *Structures of Memory*; Brian Ladd, *The Ghosts of Berlin: Confronting German History in the Urban Landscape* (Chicago: University of Chicago Press, 1997); Jeffrey Olick and Joyce Robbins, "Social Memory Studies: From 'Collective Memory' to the Historical Sociology of Mnemonic Practices," *Annual Review of Sociology* 24, no. 1 (1998): 105–41; Barry Schwartz, *Abraham Lincoln and the Forge of National Memory* (Chicago: University of Chicago Press, 2000); Lyn Spillman and Brian Conway, "Texts, Bodies, and the Memory of Bloody Sunday," *Symbolic Interaction* 30, no. 1 (2007): 79–103; James Young, *At Memory's Edge: After-Images of the Holocaust in Contemporary Art and Architecture* (New Haven, CT: Yale University Press, 2000); Jay Winter, *Remembering War: The Great War between Memory and History in the Twentieth Century* (New Haven, CT: Yale University Press, 2006).

22. Kloppenburg, *Seeds and Sovereignty*; Jack Kloppenburg Jr., *First the Seed: The Political Economy of Plant Biotechnology* (Madison: University of Wisconsin Press, 2005). See also Brandon Keim, "Voracious Worm Evolves to Eat Biotech Corn Engineered to Kill It," http://www.wired.com/2014/03/rootworm-resistance-bt-corn.

23. Estabrook, *Tomatoland*. The division of labor also shapes home cooking, school lunches, and vegetable gardening, issues receiving particular attention today. See, for example, Mark Bittman, *How to Cook Everything* (New York: Houghton Mifflin Harcourt, 2006); Michelle Obama, *American Grown: The Story of the White House Kitchen Garden and Gardens Across America* (New York: Crown, 2012); and Jamie Oliver, *Jamie's Food Revolution* (New York: Hyperion, 2011).

24. In her discussion of olive oil and Slow Food, for example, Anne Meneley points out that "meanings and symbols attached to food, as Mintz notes, are shaped in particular economic and historical contexts, regardless of claims to 'timelessness,' and we must assume that marketing practices are part of these contexts." Meneley, "Extra Virgin Olive Oil," 173. Tradition has long been the subject of critical inquiry as well. Cf. Edward Shils, *Tradition* (Chicago: University of Chicago Press, 1981); Eric J. Hobsbawm and Terence O. Ranger, *The Invention of Tradition* (New York: Cambridge University Press, 1983).

25. Émile Durkheim, *Émile Durkheim: The Selected Writings*, translated by Anthony Giddens (Cambridge: Cambridge University Press, 1972), 232.

Bibliography

Abbots, Emma-Jayne, and Anna Lavis, eds. *Why We Eat, How We Eat: Contemporary Encounters between Foods and Bodies*. Burlington, VT: Ashgate, 2013.

Adamczyk, Amy. "On Thanksgiving and Collective Memory: Constructing the American Tradition." *Journal of Historical Sociology* 15, no. 3 (2002): 343–65.

Adams, J. F. *Guerrilla Gardening*. New York: Coward-McCann, 1983.

Albala, Ken. *Beans: A History*. New York: Berg, 2007.

Alkon, Alison Hope. *Black, White, and Green: Farmers Markets, Race, and the Green Economy*. Athens: University of Georgia Press, 2012.

Alkon, Alison Hope, and Julian Agyeman, eds. *Cultivating Food Justice: Race, Class, and Sustainability*. Cambridge, MA: MIT Press, 2011.

Alkon, Alison Hope, Daniel Block, Kelly Moore, Catherine Gillis, and Nicole DiNuccio. "Foodways of the Urban Poor." *Geoforum* 48 (2013): 126–35.

Alkon, Alison Hope, and Christie McCullen. "Whiteness and Farmers Markets: Performances, Perpetuations, Contestations?" *Antipode* 43, no. 4 (2010): 937–59.

Allen, Arthur. *Ripe: The Search for the Perfect Tomato*. Berkeley, CA: Counterpoint, 2010.

Allen, Will. *The Good Food Revolution: Growing Healthy Food, People, and Communities*. New York: Penguin, 2012.

Almaguer, Tomás. *Racial Fault Lines: The Historical Origins of White Supremacy in California*. Berkeley: University of California Press, 2008.

Anderson, Benedict. *Imagined Communities: Reflections on the Origin and Spread of Nationalism*. New York: Verso, 1983.

Anderson, Edgar. *Landscape Papers*. Berkeley, CA: Turtle Island Foundation, 1976.

———. *Plants, Man and Life*. Boston: Little, Brown, 1952.

Arbury, James. *Pears*. Maidstone, UK: Wells and Winter, 1997.

Avakian, Arlene Voski, and Barbara Haber. *From Betty Crocker to Feminist Food Studies: Critical Perspectives on Women and Food*. Amherst: University of Massachusetts Press, 2005.

Avieli, Nir. "Roasted Pigs and Bao Dumplings: Festive Food and Imagined Transnational Identity in Chinese-Vietnamese Festivals." *Asia Pacific Viewpoint* 46, no. 3 (2005): 281–93.

———. "Vietnamese New Year Rice Cakes: Iconic Festive Dishes and Contested National Identity." *Ethnology* 44, no. 2 (2005): 167–87.

Baker, Lauren. "Tending Cultural Landscapes and Food Citizenship in Toronto's Community Gardens," *Geographical Review* 94, no. 3 (2004): 305–25.

Barraclough, Laura R. *Making the San Fernando Valley: Rural Landscapes, Urban Development, and White Privilege.* Athens: University of Georgia Press, 2011.

Barsewisch, Bernhard von, and Torsten Foelsch. *Sieben Parks in der Prignitz: Geschichte und Zustand der Gutsparks der Gans Edlen Herren zu Putlitz.* Berlin: Bässler, 2004.

Barthel, Diane. *Historic Preservation: Collective Memory and Historical Identity.* New Brunswick, NJ: Rutgers University Press, 1996.

Barthel-Bouchier, Diane. *Cultural Heritage and the Challenge of Sustainability.* Walnut Creek, CA: Left Coast Press, 2013.

Battersby, Jane. "Urban Agriculture and Race in South Africa." In *Geographies of Race and Food: Fields, Bodies, Markets,* edited by Rachel Slocum and Arun Saldanha, 117–35. Burlington, VT: Ashgate, 2013.

Beahrs, Andrew. *Twain's Feast: Searching for America's Lost Foods in the Footsteps of Samuel Clemens.* New York: Penguin, 2010.

Becker, Howard. *Art Worlds.* Berkeley: University of California Press, 1982.

Belasco, Warren. *Appetite for Change: How the Counterculture Took on the Food Industry.* Ithaca, NY: Cornell University Press, 2006.

Bell, David, and Gill Valentine. *Consuming Geographies: We Are Where We Eat.* New York: Routledge, 1997.

Bermejo, J. Esteban Hernández, and J. León, *Neglected Crops: 1492 from a Different Perspective.* Rome: Food and Agriculture Organization of the United Nations, 1994.

Berzok, Linda Murray. *American Indian Food.* Westport, CT: Greenwood Press, 2005.

Bestor, Theodore C. *Tsukiji: The Fish Market at the Center of the World.* Berkeley: University of California Press, 2004.

Bixby, Donald E., Carolyn J. Christman, Cynthia J. Ehrman, and D. Phillip Sponenberg. *Taking Stock: The North American Livestock Census.* Blacksburg, VA: McDonald and Woodward, 1994.

Bloch-Dano, Evelyne. *La fabuleuse histoire des légumes.* Paris: Bernard Grasset, 2007.

Bobrow-Strain, Aaron. "White Bread Politics: Purity, Health, and the Triumph of Industrial Baking." In *Geographies of Race and Food: Fields, Bodies, Markets,* edited by Rachel Slocum and Arun Saldanha, 265–90. Burlington, VT: Ashgate, 2013.

Bourdieu, Pierre. *Distinction: A Social Critique of the Judgement of Taste.* Cambridge, MA: Harvard University Press, 1984.

Boutard, Anthony. *Beautiful Corn: America's Original Grain from Seed to Plate.* Gabriola Island, Canada: New Society, 2012.

Bower, Anne L., ed. *African American Foodways: Explorations of History and Culture.* Urbana: University of Illinois Press, 2007.

Brandt, Eckart. *Mein grosses Apfelbuch: Alte Apfelsorten neu entdeckt; Geschichte, Anbau, Rezepte.* Munich: Bassermann, 2008.

Braudel, Fernand, *Civilization and Capitalism, 15th–18th Century.* Vol. 1, *The Structures of Everyday Life.* 1979. Reprint, Berkeley: University of California Press, 1992.

Browning, Frank. *Apples.* New York: North Point Press, 1998.

Bryson, Bethany. "'Anything but Heavy Metal': Symbolic Exclusion and Musical Dislikes." *American Sociological Review* 61 (1996): 884–99.

Buchanan, David. *Taste, Memory: Forgotten Foods, Lost Flavors, and Why They Matter.* White River Junction, VT: Chelsea Green, 2012.

Bunker, John P. *Not Far from the Tree: A Brief History of the Apples and the Orchards of Palermo, Maine, 1804–2004.* Palermo, ME: John Bunker, 2007.

Bunyard, Edward A. *The Anatomy of Dessert: With a Few Notes on Wine.* New York: Modern Library, 2006.

———. *A Handbook of Hardy Fruits More Commonly Grown in Great Britain: Apples and Pears.* London: John Murray, 1920.

Burford, Tom. *Apples of North America: Exceptional Varieties for Gardeners, Growers, and Cooks.* Portland, OR: Timber Press, 2013.

Burger, Ann. "Food Celebrates Fall, History." *Post and Courier* (Charleston, SC), October 9, 1996.

Burger, Franziska. *Grossmutters Kochbuch: Essen und Leben vorgestern, gestern, und heute.* Linz: Denkmayr, 2004.

Bushnell, Dick. "A Pair of Big, Tasty Slicers." *Sunset Magazine* 204, no. 2 (2000): 74.

Caldwell, Melissa. "Domesticating the French Fry: McDonald's and Consumerism in Moscow." *Journal of Consumer Culture* 4, no. 1 (2004): 5–26.

Calhoun, Creighton Lee, Jr. *Old Southern Apples.* Blacksburg, VA: McDonald and Woodward, 1995.

———. *Old Southern Apples: A Comprehensive History and Description of Varieties for Collectors, Growers, and Fruit Enthusiasts.* 2nd ed., rev. and exp. White River Junction, VT: Chelsea Green, 2010.

Campbell, Susan. *A History of Kitchen Gardening.* London: Frances Lincoln, 2005.

Carmichael, Marcia. *Putting Down Roots: Gardening Insights from Wisconsin's Early Settlers.* Madison: Wisconsin Historical Society Press, 2011.

Carney, Judith A. *Black Rice: The African Origins of Rice Cultivation in the Americas.* Cambridge, MA: Harvard University Press, 2002.

———. "Fields of Survival, Foods of Memory." In *Geographies of Race and Food: Fields, Bodies, Markets*, edited by Rachel Slocum and Arun Saldanha, 61–78. Burlington, VT: Ashgate, 2013.

———. "Rice and Memory in the Age of Enslavement: Atlantic Passages to Suriname." *Slavery and Abolition* 26, no. 3 (2005): 325–47.

———. "'With Grains in Her Hair': Rice in Colonial Brazil." *Slavery and Abolition* 25, no. 1 (2004): 1–27.

Carolan, Michael S. *Embodied Food Politics*. Burlington, VT: Ashgate, 2011.

Certeau, Michel de. *The Practice of Everyday Life*. 1984. Reprint, Berkeley: University of California Press, 2011.

Charles, Jeffrey. "Searching for Gold in Guacamole: California Growers Market the Avocado, 1910–1994." In *Food Nations: Selling Taste in Consumer Societies*, edited by Warren Belasco and Philip Scranton, 131–54. New York: Routledge, 2002.

Chaskey, Scott. *Seedtime: On the History, Husbandry, Politics, and Promise of Seeds*. New York: Rodale, 2014.

Christman, Carolyn J., and Robert O. Hawes. *Birds of a Feather: Saving Rare Turkeys from Extinction*. Pittsboro, NC: American Livestock Breeds Conservancy, 1999.

Christman, Carolyn J., D. Phillip Sponenberg, and Donald E. Bixby. *A Rare Breeds Album of American Livestock*. Pittsboro, NC: American Livestock Breeds Conservancy, 1997.

Coe, Sophie D. *America's First Cuisines*. Austin: University of Texas Press, 1994.

Coleman, Leo, ed. *Food: Ethnographic Encounters*. New York: Bloomsbury, 2012.

Coleman-Jensen, Alisha, Mark Nord, and Anita Singh. *Household Food Security in the United States in 2012*. United States Department of Agriculture, Economic Research Service, Economic Research Report 155, September 2013.

Collingham, Lizzie. *Curry: A Tale of Cooks and Conquerors*. New York: Oxford University Press, 2006.

———. *The Taste of War: World War II and the Battle for Food*. New York: Penguin, 2012.

Colquhoun, Kate. *Taste: The Story of Britain through Its Cooking*. New York: Bloomsbury, 2007.

Connerton, Paul. *How Modernity Forgets*. Cambridge: Cambridge University Press, 2009.

Coulter, Lynn. *Gardening with Heirloom Seeds: Tried-and-True Flowers, Fruits, and Vegetables for a New Generation*. Chapel Hill: University of North Carolina Press, 2006.

Counihan, Carole M. *The Anthropology of Food and Body: Gender, Meaning, and Power*. New York: Routledge, 1999.

Counihan, Carole M., and P. Van Esterik. *Food and Culture: A Reader*. New York, Routledge, 2008.

Coveney, John. *Food, Morals and Meaning*. New York: Routledge, 2000.

Covey, Herbert, and Dwight Eisnach. *What the Slaves Ate: Recollections of African American Foods and Foodways from the Slave Narratives*. Santa Barbara, CA: Greenwood Press, 2009.

Creasy, Rosalind. *The Edible Heirloom Garden*. Boston: Periplus, 1999.

Crisp, Frank, and Catherine Childs Paterson, eds. *Mediaeval Gardens*. New York: Hacker Art Books, 1979.

Cronon, William. *Changes in the Land: Indians, Colonists, and the Ecology of New England*. Rev. ed. New York: Hill and Wang, 2003.

Crosby, Alfred W., Jr. *The Columbian Exchange: Biological and Cultural Consequences of 1492*. Westport, CT: Greenwood Press, 1972.

Crowden, James. *Ciderland*, Edinburgh: Birlinn, 2008.

Dahlen, Martha, and Karen Phillipps. *A Popular Guide to Chinese Vegetables*. New York: Crown, 1983.

David, Elizabeth. *French Provincial Cooking*. London: Grub Street, 2007.

Davidson, Alan. *The Oxford Companion to Food*. 2nd ed. Edited by Tom Jaine. Oxford: Oxford University Press, 2006.

DeMuth, Suzanne P., ed. *Vegetables and Fruits: A Guide to Heirloom Varieties and Community-Based Stewardship*. Vol. 1, *Annotated Bibliography*. Special Reference Brief Series, 98-05. Beltsville, MA: US Department of Agriculture, 1998.

Dennis, Gary. "A Mac, a Cortland, a . . . Burgundy?" *Union Leader* (Manchester, NH), October 1, 2003.

DeNora, Tia. "Musical Patronage and Social Change in Beethoven's Vienna." *American Journal of Sociology* 97, no. 2 (1991): 310–46.

De Roest, Kees, and Alberto Menghi. "Reconsidering 'Traditional' Food: The Case of Parmigiano Reggiano Cheese." *Sociologia Ruralis* 40, no. 4 (2000): 439–51.

DeSoucey, Michaela. "Gastronationalism: Food Traditions and Authenticity Politics in the European Union." *American Sociological Review* 75, no. 3 (2010): 432–55.

Diner, Hasia. *Hungering for America*. Cambridge, MA: Harvard University Press, 2001.

Dohner, Janet Vorwald. *The Encyclopedia of Historic and Endangered Livestock and Poultry Breeds*. New Haven, CT: Yale University Press, 2001.

Dominique, Michel, Antoine Jacobsohn, and Fabien Seignobos. *Le petit pois*. Arles: Actes Sud, 2001.

Doss, Erika. *Memorial Mania: Public Feeling in America*. Chicago: University of Chicago Press, 2012.

Douglas, Mary. "Deciphering a Meal." In *Food and Culture: A Reader*, edited by Carol Counihan and Penny Van Esterik, 36–54. 1997. Reprint, New York: Routledge, 2008.

Dreyer, Peter. *A Gardener Touched with Genius: The Life of Luther Burbank*. Berkeley: University of California Press, 1985.

Dunn, Elizabeth Cullen. "The Food of Sorrow: Humanitarian Aid to Displaced People." In *Food: Ethnographic Encounters*, edited by Leo Coleman, 139–49. New York: Bloomsbury, 2012.

———. "A Gift from the American People." *Iowa Review*, 2012. http://iowareview .uiowa.edu/?q=issue/elizabeth_cullen_dunn.

DuPuis, E. Melanie. *Nature's Perfect Food: How Milk Became America's Drink*. New York: New York University Press, 2002.

DuPuis, E. Melanie, and David Goodman. "Should We Go 'Home' to Eat? Toward a Reflexive Politics of Localism." *Journal of Rural Studies* 21 (2005): 359–71.

Durkheim, Émile. *Émile Durkheim: The Selected Writings*. Translated by Anthony Giddens. Cambridge: Cambridge University Press, 1972.

Elton, Sarah. *Consumed: Food for a Finite Planet*. Chicago: University of Chicago Press, 2013.

———. *Locavore: From Farmers' Fields to Rooftop Gardens—How Canadians Are Changing the Way We Eat*. New York: HarperCollins, 2010.

Erdrich, Heid E. *Original Local: Indigenous Foods, Stories, and Recipes from the Upper Midwest*. St. Paul: Minnesota Historical Society Press, 2013.

Estabrook, Barry. *Tomatoland: How Modern Industrial Agriculture Destroyed Our Most Alluring Fruit*. Kansas City, MO: Andrews McMeel, 2011.

Eyzaguirre, Pablo B., and Olga F. Linares. *Home Gardens and Agrobiodiversity*. Washington, DC: Smithsonian Books, 2004.

Fantasia, Rick. "Fast Food in France." *Theory and Society* 24, no. 2 (1995): 201–43.

Ferguson, Kennan. "Intensifying Taste, Intensifying Identity: Collectivity through Community Cookbooks." *Signs: Journal of Women in Culture and Society* 37, no. 3 (2012): 695–717.

———. "Mastering the Art of the Sensible: Julia Child, Nationalist." *Theory and Event* 12, no. 2 (2009).

Ferguson, Priscilla. *Accounting for Taste: The Triumph of French Cuisine*. Chicago: University of Chicago Press, 2004.

———. "A Cultural Field in the Making: Gastronomy in 19th-Century France." *American Journal of Sociology* 103, no. 3 (1998): 597–641.

———. "Trifles." *Contexts* 8, no. 4 (2004): 66–68.

Ferguson, Priscilla, and Sharon Zukin. "What's Cooking?" *Theory and Society* 24, no. 2 (1995): 193–99.

Fernald, Anya, Serena Milano, and Piero Sardo. *A World of Presidia: Food, Culture and Community*. Bra, Italy: Slow Food Editore, 2004.

Fernández-Armesto, Felipe. *Near a Thousand Tables: History of Food*. New York: Free Press, 2002.

Field, Les, and K. Tsianina Lomawaima. *Abalone Tales: Collaborative Explorations of Sovereignty and Identity in Native California*. Durham, NC: Duke University Press, 2008.

Fine, Gary Alan. *Everyday Genius: Self-Taught Art and the Culture of Authenticity*. Chicago: University of Chicago Press, 2004.

———. "The Presentation of Ethnic Authenticity: Chinese Food as a Social Accomplishment." *Sociological Quarterly* 36 (1995): 601–19.

———. "You Are What You Eat." Review essay. *Contemporary Sociology* 30, no. 3 (2001): 231–33.

Finnis, Elizabeth. "The Political Ecology of Dietary Transitions: Changing Production and Consumption Patterns in the Kolli Hills, India." *Agriculture and Human Values* 24, no. 3 (2007): 343–53.

Finucane, M., and J. Holup. "Psychosocial and Cultural Factors Affecting the Perceived Risks of Genetically Modified Food: An Overview of the Literature." *Social Science and Medicine* 60 (2005): 1603–12.

Flandrin, J. L., M. Montanari, et al. *Food: A Culinary History from Antiquity to the Present*. New York, Columbia University Press, 1999.

Flannery, Tim. *Here on Earth: A Natural History of the Planet*. New York: Harper-Collins, 2010.

Fletcher, Jane. "Apples of Our Eye." *San Francisco Chronicle*, October 10, 2001.

Foote, Kenneth E., and Maoz Azaryahu. "Toward a Geography Of Memory: Geographical Dimensions of Public Memory." *Journal of Political and Military Sociology* 35, no. 1 (2007): 125–44.

Fowler, Cary. *Shattering: Food, Politics, and the Loss of Genetic Diversity*. Tucson: University of Arizona Press, 1990.

Franz, Manfred. *Vom Streuobst zum Apfelwein*. Kreuzwertheim, Germany: Wittbach, 2005.

Fraser, Evan D. G., and Andrew Rimas. *Empires of Food: Feast, Famine, and the Rise and Fall of Civilizations*. New York: Free Press, 2010.

Freedman, Paul, ed. *Food: The History of Taste*. London: Thames and Hudson, 2007.

Freidberg, Susanne. *French Beans and Food Scares: Culture and Commerce in an Anxious Age*. New York: Oxford University Press, 2004.

Friese, Kurt Michael, Kraig Kraft, and Gary Paul Nabhan. *Chasing Chiles: Hot Spots along the Pepper Trail*. White River Junction, VT: Chelsea Green, 2011.

Fussell, Betty Harper. *The Story of Corn*. Albuquerque: University of New Mexico Press, 1992.

Geddes-Brown, Leslie. *The Walled Garden*. London: Merrell, 2007.

Gettle, Jere, and Emilee Gettle. *The Heirloom Life Gardener: The Baker Creek Way of Growing Your Own Food Easily and Naturally*. New York: Hyperion, 2011.

Gieryn, Tom. "A Space for Place in Sociology." *Annual Review of Sociology* 26 (2000): 463–96.

Glassner, Barry. *The Gospel of Food: Why We Should Stop Worrying and Enjoy What We Eat*. New York: Harper Perennial, 2008.

Goldman, Amy. *The Compleat Squash: A Passionate Grower's Guide*. New York: Artisan Books, 2004.

———. *Melons for the Passionate Grower*. New York: Artisan Books, 2002.

Goldman, Amy, and Victor Schrager. *The Heirloom Tomato: From Garden to Table; Recipes, Portraits, and History of the World's Most Beautiful Fruit*. New York: Bloomsbury, 2008.

Goldstein, Joyce. *Inside the California Food Revolution: Thirty Years that Changed Our Culinary Consciousness*. Berkeley: University of California Press, 2013.

Gollner, Adam Leith. *The Fruit Hunters: A Story of Nature, Adventure, Commerce and Obsession*. New York: Scribner, 2008.

Goodyear, Dana. *Anything that Moves: Renegade Chefs, Fearless Eaters, and the Making of a New American Food Culture*. New York: Riverhead Books, 2013.

Gray, Margaret. *Labor and the Locavore: The Making of a Comprehensive Food Ethic*. Berkeley: University of California Press, 2013.

Grazian, David. *Blue Chicago: The Search for Authenticity in Urban Blues Clubs*. Chicago: University of Chicago Press, 2003.

Grigson, Jane. *English Food*. Harmondsworth, UK: Penguin, 1999.

———. *Good Things*. Lincoln: University of Nebraska Press, 1971.

Grimes, William. *Appetite City: A Culinary History of New York*. New York: North Point Press, 2010.

Griswold, Wendy. *Cultures and Societies in a Changing World*. Thousand Oaks, CA: Pine Forge Press, 2003.

———. "A Methodological Framework for the Sociology of Culture." *Sociological Methodology* 17 (1987): 1–35.

———. "The Sociology of Culture: Four Good Arguments (and One Bad One)." *Acta Sociologica* 35 (1992): 323–28.

Guthman, Julie. *Agrarian Dreams: The Paradox of Organic Farming in California*. Berkeley: University of California Press, 2004.

———. "Can't Stomach It: How Michael Pollan et al. Made Me Want to Eat Cheetos." *Gastronomica* 7, no. 3 (2007): 75–79.

———. "Commodified Meanings, Meaningful Commodities: Re-thinking

Production-Consumption Links through the Organic System of Provision." *Sociologia Ruralis* 42, no. 2 (2002): 295–311.

———. "Fast Food/Organic Food: Reflexive Tastes and the Making of 'Yuppie Chow.'" *Social and Cultural Geography* 4, no. 1 (2003): 45–58.

———. "'If They Only Knew': Color Blindness and Universalism in California Alternative Food Institutions." *Professional Geographer* 60, no. 3 (2008): 387–97.

———. *Weighing In: Obesity, Food Justice, and the Limits of Capitalism.* Berkeley: University of California Press, 2011.

Halbwachs, Maurice. *The Collective Memory.* 1950. Reprint, New York: Harper Colophon Books, 1980.

Handler, Richard, and Eric Gable. *The New History in an Old Museum: Creating the Past at Colonial Williamsburg.* Durham, NC: Duke University Press, 1997.

Harper, Douglas, and Patrizia Faccioli. *The Italian Way: Food and Social Life.* Chicago: University of Chicago Press, 2009.

Harris, Jessica B. *Beyond Gumbo: Creole Fusion Food from the Atlantic Rim.* New York: Simon and Schuster, 2003.

———. *High on the Hog: A Culinary Journey from Africa to America.* New York: Bloomsbury USA, 2011.

———. *Iron Pots and Wooden Spoons: Africa's Gifts to New World Cooking.* New York: Simon and Schuster, 1999.

———. *Sky Juice and Flying Fish: Traditional Caribbean Cooking.* New York: Simon and Schuster, 1991.

Hartmann, Walter, and Eckhart Fritz. *Farbatlas alte Obstsorten.* Stuttgart: Eugen Ulmer, 2008.

Harvey, David. *The Condition of Postmodernity: An Enquiry into the Origins of Cultural Change.* New York: Blackwell, 1989.

Hayes-Conroy, Allison, and Jessica Hayes-Conroy. "Taking Back Taste: Feminism, Food and Visceral Politics." *Gender, Place and Culture* 15, no. 5 (2008): 471–73.

Heffner, Sarah Wolfgang. *Heirloom Country Gardens: Timeless Treasures for Today's Gardeners.* Emmaus, PA: Rodale, 2000.

Heilmeyer, Marina, Lutz Grope, Gerd Schurig, and Clemens Alexander Wimmer. *Beste Birnen bei Hofe.* Potsdamer Pomologische Geschichten. Potsdam: Vacat, 2004.

Heilmeyer, Marina, and Clemens Alexander Wimmer. *Äpfel fürs Volk.* Potsdamer Pomologische Geschichten. Potsdam: Vacat, 2007.

Heistinger, Andrea. *Handbuch Samengärtnerei: Sorten erhalten, Vielfalt vermehren, Gemüse geniessen.* Innsbruck-Bozen, Austria: Loewenzahn, 2004.

Henke, Christopher R. *Cultivating Science, Harvesting Power: Science and Industrial Agriculture in California*. Cambridge, MA: MIT Press, 2008.

Hennebo, Dieter. *Gärten des Mittelalters*. Munich: Artemis, 1987.

Hensley, Tim. "Apples of Your Eye." *Smithsonian* 33, no. 8 (2002): 111–18.

Hess, Karen. *Carolina Rice Kitchen: The African Connection*. Columbia: University of South Carolina Press, 1998.

Heynen, Nik, Hilda E. Kurtz, and Amy K. Trauger. "Food, Hunger and the City." *Geography Compass* 6 (2012): 304–11.

Hickmott, Simon. *Growing Unusual Vegetables: Weird and Wonderful Vegetables and How to Grow Them*. Bristol, UK: Eco-logic Books, 2003.

Hinrichs, Clare, Gilbert W. Gillespie, and Gail W. Feenstra. "Social Learning and Innovation at Retail Farmers' Markets." *Rural Sociology* 69, no. 1 (2004): 31–58.

Hirschfelder, Gunther. *Europäische Esskultur: Eine Geschichte der Ernährung von der Steinzeit bis heute*. Frankfurt am Main: Campus, 2005.

Hobsbawm, Eric J., and Terence O. Ranger. *The Invention of Tradition*. New York: Cambridge University Press, 1983.

Holmes, Seth. *Fresh Fruit, Broken Bodies: Migrant Farmworkers in the United States*. Berkeley: University of California Press, 2013.

Holt, Douglas. "Distinction in America? Recovering Bourdieu's Theory of Taste from Its Critics." *Poetics* 25 (1997): 931–1020.

Howard, Doreen G. *The Return of Flavor: Heirloom Vegetables, Herbs, and Fruits*. Brentwood, TN, Cool Springs Press, 2013.

Hyman, Clarissa. *Oranges: A Global History*. London: Reaktion Books, 2013.

Ilbery, Brian, et al. "Product, Process and Place: An Examination of Food Marketing and Labeling Schemes in Europe and North America." *European Urban and Regional Studies* 12, no. 2 (2005): 116–32.

Jabs, Carolyn. *The Heirloom Gardener*. San Francisco, CA: Sierra Club Books, 1984.

Jacobsen, Rowan. *American Terroir: Savoring the Flavors of Our Woods, Waters, and Fields*. New York: Bloomsbury, 2010.

Janik, Erika. *Apple: A Global History*. London: Reaktion, 2011.

Johnson, Elaine, and Laura Bonar Swezey. "Heirloom Tomatoes." *Sunset Magazine* 195 (1995): 80–84.

Johnston, Josée, and Shyon Baumann. "Democracy versus Distinction: A Study of Omnivorousness in Gourmet Food Writing." *American Journal of Sociology* 113, no. 1 (2007): 165–204.

———. *Foodies: Democracy and Distinction in the Gourmet Foodscape*. New York: Routledge, 2010.

Jones, Judith. *The Tenth Muse: My Life in Food*. New York: Anchor Books, 2008.

Jordan, Jennifer A. "Apples, Identity, and Memory in Post-1989 Germany." In *Debating German Cultural Identity since 1989*, edited by Anne Fuchs, Kathleen James-Chakraborty, and Linda Shortt, 46–64. Rochester, NY: Camden House, 2011.

———. "Elevating the Humble Dumpling: From Peasant Kitchens to Press Conferences." *Ethnology* 47, no. 2 (2008): 109–21.

———. "The Heirloom Tomato as Cultural Object." *Sociologia Ruralis* 47, no. 1 (January 2007): 20–41.

———. "Investigating the Edible: Points of Inquiry in the Study of Food, Culture, and Identity." In *Cooking, Eating, Identity: Speisen als kulturelle Codes in Zentraleuropa*, edited by Moritz Csáky and Georg-Christian Lack, 37–50. Vienna: Böhlau, 2014.

———. "Landscapes of European Memory: Biodiversity and Collective Remembrance." *History and Memory* 22, no. 2 (Fall/Winter 2010): 5–33.

———. *Structures of Memory: Understanding Urban Change in Berlin and Beyond.* Stanford, CA: Stanford University Press, 2006.

Joy, LaManda, and Teresa Gale. *Fearless Food Gardening in Chicagoland: A Month-by-Month Growing Guide for Beginners.* Chicago: Peterson Garden Project, 2013.

Kaminsky, Peter. *Pig Perfect: Encounters with Some Remarkable Swine and Some Great Ways to Cook Them.* New York: Hyperion, 2005.

Kaplan, Steven Laurence. *Good Bread Is Back.* Durham, NC: Duke University Press, 2006.

Karp, David. "A Finicky Fruit Is Sweet When Coddled." *New York Times*, September 1, 2004.

———. "Orchard of Dreams." *Gourmet Magazine*, July 2005. http://www.gourmet.com/magazine/2000s/2005/07/mariani.

Kavasch, Barrie. *Native Harvests: Recipes and Botanicals of the American Indian.* New York: Vintage, 1979.

Kawash, Samira. *Candy: A Century of Panic and Pleasure.* New York: Faber and Faber, 2013.

Kerrigan, William. "Apples on the Border: Orchards and the Contest for the Great Lakes." *Michigan Historical Review* 34, no. 1 (2008): 25–41.

Kingsolver, Barbara. *Animal, Vegetable, Miracle: Our Year of Seasonal Eating.* New York: Faber and Faber, 2010.

Kingsolver, Barbara, Steven L. Hopp, and Camille Kingsolver. *Animal, Vegetable, Miracle: A Year of Food Life.* New York: HarperCollins, 2010.

Kiple, Kenneth F. *A Movable Feast: Ten Millennia of Food Globalization.* Cambdridge: Cambridge University Press, 2007.

Kiple, Kenneth F., and Kriemhild Coneè Ornelas. *The Cambridge World History of Food*, vols. 1 and 2. Cambridge: Cambridge University Press, 2000.

Klindienst, Patricia. *The Earth Knows My Name: Food, Culture, and Sustainability in the Gardens of Ethnic Americans*. Boston: Beacon Press, 2006.

Kline, Roger A., Robert F. Becker, and Lynn Belluscio. *The Heirloom Vegetable Garden: Gardening in the 19th Century*. Ithaca, NY: Cornell University Press, 1980.

Kloppenburg, Jack, Jr. *First the Seed: The Political Economy of Plant Biotechnology*. Madison: University of Wisconsin Press, 2005.

———. "Impeding Dispossession, Enabling Repossession: Biological Open Source and the Recovery of Seed Sovereignty." *Journal of Agrarian Change* 10, no. 3 (2010): 367–88.

———, ed. *Seeds and Sovereignty: The Use and Control of Plant Genetic Resources*. Chapel Hill, NC: Duke University Press, 1988.

Koeppel, Dan. *Banana: The Fate of the Fruit That Changed the World*. New York: Plume, 2008.

Kurlansky, Mark. *The Food of a Younger Land: A Portrait of American Food*. New York: Riverhead Books, 2009.

Kurtz, Hilda E. "Linking Food Deserts and Racial Segregation: Challenges and Limitations." In *Geographies of Race and Food: Fields, Bodies, Markets*, edited by Rachel Slocum and Arun Saldanha, 247–64. Burlington, VT: Ashgate, 2013.

Ladd, Brian. *The Ghosts of Berlin: Confronting German History in the Urban Landscape*. Chicago: University of Chicago Press, 1997.

Lamont, Michel, and Annette Lareau. "Cultural Capital: Allusions, Gaps and Glissandos in Recent Theoretical Developments." *Sociological Theory* 6 (1988): 153–68.

Landsberg, Alison. *Prosthetic Memory: The Transformation of American Remembrance in the Age of Mass Culture*. New York: Columbia University Press, 2004.

Lang, James. *Notes of a Potato Watcher*. College Station: Texas A&M University Press, 2001.

Lape, Fred. *Apples and Man*. New York: Van Nostrand Reinhold, 1979.

La Pradelle, Michèle de. *Market Day in Provence*. Translated by Amy Jacobs. Chicago: University of Chicago Press, 2006.

Laszlo, Pierre. *Citrus: A History*. Chicago: University of Chicago Press, 2007.

Laudan, Rachel. *Cuisine and Empire: Cooking in World History*. Berkeley: University of California Press, 2013.

———. *The Food of Paradise: Exploring Hawaii's Culinary Heritage*. Honolulu: University of Hawai'i Press, 1996.

Lawrance, Benjamin N., and Carolyn de la Peña, eds. *Local Foods Meet Global Foodways*. New York: Routledge, 2012.

Laws, Bill. *Fifty Plants That Changed the Course of History*. Buffalo, NY: Firefly Books, 2010.

——. *Spade, Skirret and Parsnip: The Curious History of Vegetables*. Stroud, UK: History Press, 2006.

Lefebvre, Henri. *The Production of Space*. Cambridge, MA: Blackwell, 1991.

Leitch, Alison. "Slow Food and the Politics of Pork Fat: Italian Food and European Identity." *Ethnos* 68, no. 4 (2003): 437–62.

Lemoine, Élizabeth. *Les légumes d'hier et d'aujourd'hui*. Paris: Molière, 2002.

Leschziner, Vanina. "Epistemic Foundations of Cuisine: A Socio-cognitive Study of the Configuration of Cuisine in Historical Perspective." *Theory and Society* 35, no. 4 (2006): 421–43.

Levenstein, Harvey A. *Fear of Food: A History of Why We Worry about What We Eat*. Chicago: University of Chicago Press, 2012.

——. *Revolution at the Table: The Transformation of the American Diet*. New York: Oxford University Press, 1988.

Lewis, Edna. *The Taste of Country Cooking*, 30th anniversary ed. New York: Knopf, 2006.

Lewis, Edna, and Scott Peacock. *The Gift of Southern Cooking: Recipes and Revelations from Two Great American Cooks*. New York: Knopf, 2003.

Lightfoot, Kent G. *Indians, Missionaries, and Merchants: The Legacy of Colonial Encounters on the California Frontiers*. Berkeley: University of California Press, 2006.

Lin, Jan. *The Power of Urban Ethnic Places: Cultural Heritage and Urban Life*. New York: Routledge, 2011.

Littlefield, Daniel C. *Rice and Slaves: Ethnicity and the Slave Trade in Colonial South Carolina*. Urbana: University of Illinois Press, 1991.

Lockie, Stewart, Kristen Lyons, Geoffrey Lawrence, and Kerry Mummery. "Eating 'Green': Motivations Behind Organic Food Consumption in Australia." *Sociologia Ruralis* 42, no. 1 (2002): 23–40.

Lotti, Ariani. "The Commoditization of Products and Taste: Slow Food and the Conservation of Agrobiodiversity." *Agriculture and Human Values* 27, no. 1 (2010): 71–83.

Love, Bridget. "Mountain Vegetables and the Politics of Local Flavor in Japan." In *Japanese Foodways, Past and Present*, edited by Eric Rath and Stephanie Assmann, 221–42. Urbana: University of Illinois Press, 2010.

Luebbermann, Mimi. *The Heirloom Tomato Cookbook*. San Francisco, CA: Chronicle Books, 2006.

Madison, Deborah. *Vegetable Literacy: Cooking and Gardening with Twelve Families from the Edible Plant Kingdom*. Berkeley, CA: Ten Speed Press, 2013.

Mangold, Gudrun. *Most: Das Buch zu Apfel- und Birnenwein*. Tübingen: Silberburg, 2003.

Mann, Charles C. *1493: Uncovering the New World Columbus Created*. New York: Knopf, 2011.

Marcus, George, and Nancy Marcus. *Forbidden Fruits and Forgotten Vegetables: A Guide to Cooking with Ethnic, Exotic, and Neglected Produce*. New York: St. Martin's Press, 1982.

Martinez, Miranda J. *Power at the Roots: Gentrification, Community Gardens, and the Puerto Ricans of the Lower East Side*. New York: Lexington Books, 2010.

Masumoto, David Mas. *Four Seasons in Five Senses: Things Worth Savoring*. New York: W. W. Norton, 2004.

McCann, James C. *Maize and Grace: Africa's Encounter with a New World Crop, 1500-2000*. Cambridge, MA: Harvard University Press, 2005.

McCullough, David. *1776*. New York: Simon and Schuster, 2005.

McEntee, Jesse, and Julian Agyeman. "Towards the Development of a GIS Method for Identifying Rural Food Deserts: Geographic Access in Vermont, USA." *Applied Geography* 30, no. 1 (2010): 165-76.

McGee, Harold. "The Curious Cook: Stalking the Placid Apple's Untamed Kin." *New York Times*, November 21, 2007.

———. *On Food and Cooking: The Science and Lore of the Kitchen*. New York: Scribner, 2004.

McGinn, Jerry. "'Heirloom' Seeds Untouched by Science Give Adventurous Gardeners Real Taste." UPI, February 20, 1984.

McMahon, Naoimh. "Transforming Society through Purity, Solitude and Bearing Witness?" *Sociologia Ruralis* 45, no. 1/2 (2005): 98-114.

McNamee, Gregory. *Movable Feasts: The History, Science, and Lore of Food*. Westport, CT: Praeger, 2007.

McNamee, Thomas. *Alice Waters and Chez Panisse: The Romantic, Impractical, Often Eccentric, Ultimately Brilliant Making of a Food Revolution*. New York: Penguin, 2007.

McPhee, John. *Giving Good Weight*. New York: Farrar, Straus and Giroux, 1994.

McWilliams, James E. *A Revolution in Eating: How the Quest for Food Shaped America*. New York: Columbia University Press, 2007.

Meneley, Anne. "Extra Virgin Olive Oil and Slow Food." *Anthropologica* 46, no. 2 (2004): 165-76.

Miele, Mara, and Jonathan Murdoch. "The Practical Aesthetics of Traditional Cuisines: Slow Food in Tuscany." *Sociologia Ruralis* 42, no. 4 (2002): 312-28.

Miller, Adrian. *Soul Food: The Surprising Story of an American Cuisine One Plate at a Time*. Chapel Hill: University of North Carolina Press, 2013.

Milligan, Melinda. "Buildings as History: The Place of Collective Memory in the Study of Historic Preservation." *Symbolic Interaction* 30, no. 1 (2007): 105-23.

Minkoff-Zern, Laura-Anne. "Pushing the Boundaries of Indigeneity and Agricultural Knowledge: Oaxacan Immigrant Gardening in California." *Agriculture and Human Values* 29 (2012): 381-92.

Mintz, Sidney W. *Sweetness and Power: The Place of Sugar in Modern History*. New York: Penguin Books, 1986.

Mitchell, Don. "'The Issue Is Basically One of Race': Braceros, the Labor Process, and the Making of the Agro-industrial Landscape of Mid-Twentieth Century California." In *Geographies of Race and Food: Fields, Bodies, Markets*, edited by Rachel Slocum and Arun Saldanha, 79-96. Burlington, VT: Ashgate, 2013.

——. *They Saved the Crops: Labor, Landscape, and the Struggle over Industrial Farming in Bracero-Era California*. Athens: University of Georgia Press, 2012.

Moberg, Mark. *Citrus, Strategy, and Class: The Politics of Development in Southern Belize*. Iowa City: University of Iowa Press, 1992.

——. *Myths of Ethnicity and Nation: Immigration, Work, and Identity in the Belize Banana Industry*. Knoxville: University of Tennessee Press, 1997.

——. *Slipping Away: Banana Politics and Fair Trade in the Eastern Caribbean*. Dislocations, vol. 4. Oxford, NY: Berghahn Books, 2008.

Morgan, Joan, Alison Richards, and Brogdale Horticultural Trust. *The Book of Apples*. London: Ebury Press, 1993.

Morgan, Kevin, Terry Marsden, and Jonathan Murdoch. *Worlds of Food: Place, Power, and Provenance in the Food Chain*. Oxford: Oxford University Press, 2006.

Moss, Michael. *Salt, Sugar, Fat: How the Food Giants Hooked Us*. New York: Random House, 2013.

Mueller, Tom. *Extra Virginity: The Sublime and Scandalous World of Olive Oil*. New York: W. W. Norton, 2011.

Nabhan, Gary Paul. *Coming Home to Eat: The Pleasures and Politics of Local Foods*. New York: Norton, 2002.

——. *The Desert Smells like Rain*. Tucson: University of Arizona Press, 2002.

——. *Enduring Seeds: Native American Agriculture and Wild Plant Conservation*. Tucson: University of Arizona Press, 2002.

——. *Where Our Food Comes From: Retracing Nikolay Vavilov's Quest to End Famine*. Washington, DC: Island Press/Shearwater Books, 2009.

Nabhan, Gary Paul, Ashley Rood, and Deborah Madison. *Renewing America's Food Traditions: Saving and Savoring the Continent's Most Endangered Foods*. White River Junction, VT: Chelsea Green, 2008.

Nazarea, Virginia D. *Cultural Memory and Biodiversity*. Tucson: University of Arizona Press, 1998.

———. *Heirloom Seeds and Their Keepers: Marginality and Memory in the Conservation of Biological Diversity*. Tucson: University of Arizona Press, 2005.

———. "Memory in Biodiversity Conservation." *Annual Review of Anthropology* 35 (2006): 317–35.

Nestle, Marion. *Food Politics: How the Food Industry Influences Nutrition and Health*. 3rd ed. Berkeley: University of California Press, 2013.

Nicolaides, Becky M. *My Blue Heaven: Life and Politics in the Working-Class Suburbs of Los Angeles, 1920–1965*. Chicago: University of Chicago Press, 2002.

Nora, Pierre, Lawrence D. Kritzman, and Arthur Goldhammer. *Realms of Memory: Rethinking the French Past*. New York: Columbia University Press, 1996.

Nuckols, Carol. "Seeds of Change Offers the Uncommon, the Unusual." *Post and Courier* (Charleston, SC), June 25, 1995.

Olick, Jeffrey, and Joyce Robbins. "Social Memory Studies: From 'Collective Memory' to the Historical Sociology of Mnemonic Practices." *Annual Review of Sociology* 24, no. 1 (1998): 105–41.

Opie, Frederick Douglass. *Hog and Hominy: Soul Food from Africa to America; Arts and Traditions of the Table*. New York: Columbia University Press, 2008.

Palmer, Carol. "Milk and Cereals: Identifying Food and Food Identity among Fallahin and Bedouin in Jordan." *Levant* 34 (2002): 173–95.

Patel, Raj. *Stuffed and Starved: The Hidden Battle for the World Food System*. New York: Melville House, 2007.

Paulson, Susan. "Sensations of Food: Growing for the Nation and Eating with the Hand in Bahia, Brazil." In *Geographies of Race and Food: Fields, Bodies, Markets*, edited by Rachel Slocum and Arun Saldanha, 97–115. Burlington, VT: Ashgate, 2013.

Pearlman, Alison. *Smart Casual: The Transformation of Gourmet Restaurant Style in America*. Chicago: University of Chicago Press, 2013.

Perry, Luddene, and Dan Schultz. *A Field Guide to Buying Organic*. New York: Bantam Dell, 2005.

Peterson, Richard A. *Creating Country Music: Fabricating Authenticity*. Chicago: University of Chicago Press, 1997.

Peterson, T. Sarah. *Acquired Taste: The French Origins of Modern Cooking*. Ithaca, NY: Cornell University Press, 1994.

Petrini, Carlo. *Slow Food: The Case for Taste*. New York: Columbia University Press, 2004.

Pietrykowski, Bruce. "You Are What You Eat: The Social Economy of the Slow Food Movement." *Review of Social Economy* 62, no. 3 (2004): 307–21.

Pilcher, Jeffrey. *Que vivan los tamales!: Food and the Making of Mexican Identity*. Albuquerque: University of New Mexico Press, 1998.

Pirc, Helmut. *Wildobst im eigenen Garten*. Graz, Austria: Stocker, 2002.

Planck, Nina. "How New York's Greenmarket Went Stale." *New York Times*, April 24, 2004, 17.

Pollan, Michael. *The Botany of Desire: A Plant's Eye View of the World*. New York: Random House, 2001.

———. *Cooked: A Natural History of Transformation*. New York: Penguin, 2013.

———. *The Omnivore's Dilemma: A Natural History of Four Meals*. New York: Penguin, 2006.

———. *Second Nature: A Gardener's Education*. New York: Atlantic Monthly Press, 1991.

Pratt, Jeff. "Food Values: The Local and the Authentic." *Critique of Anthropology* 27, no. 3 (2007): 285–300.

Prescott, John. *Taste Matters: Why We Like the Foods We Do*. London: Reaktion Books, 2012.

Price, Susan Davis. *Growing Home: Stories of Ethnic Gardening*. Minneapolis: University of Minnesota Press, 2000.

Probyn, Elspeth. *Carnal Appetites: Food, Sex, Identities*. New York: Routledge, 2000.

Quest-Riston, Charles. *The English Garden: A Social History*. New York: Penguin, 2003.

Rao, Hayagreeva, Philippe Monin, and Rodolphe Durand. "Border Crossing: Bricolage and the Erosion of Categorical Boundaries in French Gastronomy." *American Sociological Review* 70, no. 6 (2005): 968–91.

Rath, Eric. *Food and Fantasy in Early Modern Japan*. Berkeley: University of California Press, 2010.

Ray, Janisse. *The Seed Underground: A Growing Revolution to Save Food*. White River Junction, VT: Chelsea Green, 2012.

Ray, Krishnendu. *The Migrant's Table: Meals and Memories in Bengali-American Households*. Philadelphia: Temple University Press, 2004.

Ricoeur, Paul. *History, Memory, Forgetting*. Translated by Kathleen Blamey and David Pellauer. Chicago: University of Chicago Press, 2004.

Robinson, Jo. *Eating on the Wild Side: The Missing Link to Optimum Health*. New York: Little, Brown, 2013.

Roe, Emma J. 2006. "Things Becoming Food and the Embodied, Material Practices of an Organic Food Consumer." *Sociologia Ruralis* 46, no. 2 (2006): 104–21.

Roseberry, William. "The Rise of Yuppie Coffees and the Reimagination of Class in the United States." *American Anthropologist*, n.s., 98, no. 4 (1996): 762–75.

Rosenblatt, Lucas, and Edith Beckmann. *Das goldene Buch der Kartoffel*. Weil der Stadt, Germany: Hädecke, 2013.

Roy, Parama. *Alimentary Tracts: Appetites, Aversions and the Postcolonial*. Durham, NC: Duke University Press, 2010.

Russell, James. *Man-Made Eden: Historic Orchards in Somerset and Gloucestershire*. Bristol, UK: Redcliffe, 2007.

Saleh, Elizabeth. "Eating and Drinking Kefraya: The Karam in the Vineyards." In *Why We Eat, How We Eat: Contemporary Encounters between Foods and Bodies*, edited by Emma-Jayne Abbots and Anna Lavis, 103–18. Burlington, VT: Ashgate, 2013.

Salmón, Enrique. *Eating the Landscape: American Indian Stories of Food, Identity, and Resilience*. Tucson: University of Arizona Press, 2012.

Sando, Steve. *The Rancho Gordo Heirloom Bean Grower's Guide: Steve Sando's 50 Favorite Varieties*. Portland, OR: Timber Press, 2011.

Saul, Nick, and Andrea Curtis. *The Stop: How the Fight for Good Food Transformed a Community and Inspired a Movement*. Brooklyn, NY: Melville House, 2013.

Scarpellini, Emanuela. *Material Nation: A Consumer's History of Modern Italy*. New York: Oxford University Press, 2011.

Scheffler, Ute. *Alles Soljanka, oder wie? Das ultimative DDR Kochbuch, 1949–1989*. Leipzig: Buchverlag für die Frau, 2008.

Schermaul, Erika. *Pardiesapfel und Pastorenbirne: Bilder und Geschichten von alten Obstsorten*. Ostfildern, Germany: Thorbecke, 2005.

Schlosser, Eric. *Fast Food Nation: The Dark Side of the All-American Meal*. New York: Mariner Books, 2012.

Schneider, Elizabeth. *Uncommon Fruits and Vegetables: A Commonsense Guide*. New York: Harper and Row, 1986.

Schurman, Rachel, and William A. Munro. *Fighting for the Future of Food: Activists versus Agribusiness in the Struggle over Biotechnology*. Minneapolis: University of Minnesota Press, 2010.

Schwartz, Barry. *Abraham Lincoln and the Forge of National Memory*. Chicago: University of Chicago Press, 2000.

Seabrook, John. "The Fruit Detective." *New Yorker* 78, no. 24 (2002): 70.

Sen, Arijit. "From Curry Mahals to Chaat Cafes: Spatialities of the South Asian Culinary Landscape." In *Curried Cultures*, edited by Tulasi Srinivasan and Krishnendu Ray, 196–218. Berkeley: University of California Press, 2012.

Shapiro, Laura. *Perfection Salad: Women and Cooking at the Turn of the Century*. Berkeley: University of California Press, 2008.

Sheller, Mimi. "Skinning the Banana Trade: Racial Erotics and Ethical Consumption." In *Geographies of Race and Food: Fields, Bodies, Markets*, edited by Rachel Slocum and Arun Saldanha, 291–311. Burlington, VT: Ashgate, 2013.

Shepherd, Gordon M. *Neurogastronomy: How the Brain Creates Flavor and Why It Matters*. New York: Columbia University Press, 2012.

Shils, Edward. *Tradition*. Chicago: University of Chicago Press, 1981.

Shiva, Vandana. *Stolen Harvest: The Hijacking of the Global Food Supply*. Cambridge, MA: South End Press, 2000.

Simader, Ernst. *Mostland Oberösterreich*. Linz, Austria: Trauner, 2006.

Simmel, Georg. "The Meal." In *Simmel on Culture: Selected Writings*, edited by David Frisby and Mike Featherstone, 130–35. Thousand Oaks, CA: Sage, 1997.

Slater, Nigel. *Ripe: A Cook in the Orchard*. Berkeley, CA: Ten Speed Press, 2012.

Slocum, Rachel. "Race in the Study of Food." In *Geographies of Race and Food: Fields, Bodies, Markets*, edited by Rachel Slocum and Arun Saldanha, 25–57. Burlington, VT: Ashgate, 2013.

———. "Thinking Race through Corporeal Feminist Theory: Divisions and Intimacies at the Minneapolis Farmers' Market." *Social and Cultural Geography* 9, no. 8 (2008): 849–69.

Slocum, Rachel, and Arun Saldanha, eds. *Geographies of Race and Food: Fields, Bodies, Markets*. Burlington, VT: Ashgate, 2013.

Smith, Andrew F. *Eating History: 30 Turning Points in the Making of American Cuisine*. New York: Columbia University Press, 2009.

———. *Potato: A Global History*. London: Reaktion Books, 2011.

———. *The Tomato in America: Early History, Culture, and Cookery*. Columbia: University of South Carolina Press, 1994.

———. *The Turkey: An American Story*. Urbana: University of Illinois Press, 2006.

———, ed. *The Oxford Companion to American Food and Drink*. New York: Oxford University Press, 2007.

Smith, Jane S. *The Garden of Invention: Luther Burbank and the Business of Breeding Plants*. New York: Penguin, 2009.

Sokolov, Raymond. *Why We Eat What We Eat: How the Encounter between the New World and the Old Changed the Way Everyone on the Planet Eats*. New York: Summit Books, 1991.

Sonneman, Toby. *Lemon: A Global History*. London: Reaktion Books, 2012.

Sonnino, Roberta. "For a 'Piece of Bread'?: Interpreting Sustainable Development through Agritourism in Southern Tuscany." *Sociologia Ruralis* 44, no. 3 (2004): 285–300.

Spillman, Lyn, and Brian Conway. "Texts, Bodies, and the Memory of Bloody Sunday." *Symbolic Interaction* 30, no. 1 (2007): 79–103.

Standage, Tom. *An Edible History of Humanity*. New York: Walker, 2009.

Stanley, Tim. *The Last of the Prune Pickers: A Pre-Silicon Valley Story*. Irvine, CA: 2 Timothy Publishing, 2009.

Stark, Tim. *Heirloom: Notes from an Accidental Tomato Farmer*. New York: Broadway Books, 2008.

Staub, Jack. *Alluring Lettuces*. Layton, UT: Gibbs Smith, 2010.

Steele, Romney. *Plum Gorgeous: Recipes and Memories from the Orchard*. Kansas City, MO: Andrews McMeel, 2011.

Stewart, Amy. *The Drunken Botanist: The Plants That Create the World's Great Drinks*. Chapel Hill, NC: Algonquin, 2013.

Stickland, Sue, and David Cavagnaro. *Heirloom Vegetables: A Home Gardener's Guide to Finding and Growing Vegetables from the Past*. New York: Fireside Books, 1998.

Stilphen, George Albert, ed. *The Apples of Maine: A Compilation of the History, Physical and Cultural Characteristics of All the Varieties of Apples Known to Have Been Grown in the State of Maine*. Adapted from a thesis submitted by Frederick Charles Bradford to the University of Maine at Orono, 1911. Otisfield, ME: Stilphen's Crooked River Farm, 1933.

Stocks, Christopher. *Forgotten Fruits: The Stories behind Britain's Traditional Fruit and Vegetables*. London: Windmill, 2009.

Strank, Karl Josef, and Jutta Meurers-Balke, eds. *Obst, Gemüse und Kräuter Karls des Grossen: ". . . dass man im Garten alle Kräuter habe . . ."* Mainz am Rhein: Philipp von Zabern, 2008.

Striffler, Steve, and Mark Moberg, eds. *Banana Wars: Power, Production and History in the Americas*. Durham, NC: Duke University Press, 2003.

Stuckey, Barb. *Taste What You're Missing: The Passionate Eater's Guide to Why Good Food Tastes Good*. New York: Free Press, 2012.

Sturken, Marita. *Tourists of History: Memory, Kitsch, and Consumerism from Oklahoma City to Ground Zero*. Durham, NC: Duke University Press, 2007.

Sutton, David E. *Remembrance of Repasts: An Anthropology of Food and Memory*. New York: Berg, 2001.

Symons, Michael. *The Pudding That Took a Thousand Cooks: The Story of Cooking in Civilisation and Daily Life*. New York: Viking, 1998.

Tannahill, Reay. *Food in History*. New York: Stein and Day, 1973.

Tellström, Richard, Inga-Britt Gustafsson, and Lena Mossberg. "Local Food Cultures in the Swedish Rural Economy." *Sociologia Ruralis* 45, no. 4 (2005): 346–59.

Terry, Bryant. *Afro-Vegan: Farm-Fresh African, Caribbean, and Southern Flavors*. Berkeley, CA: Ten Speed Press, 2014.

———. *Vegan Soul Kitchen: Fresh, Healthy, and Creative African-American Cuisine*. Boston: Da Capo Press, 2009.

Thieme, Evelyn, Jutta Schneider, and Michael Will. *Streuobstwiesen: Alte Obstsorten neu entdeckt*. Ostfildern, Germany: Thorbecke, 2008.

Thoreau, Henry David. *"Wild Apples" and Other Natural History Essays*. Athens: University of Georgia Press, 2002.

Thorness, Bill. *Edible Heirlooms: Heritage Vegetables for the Maritime Garden.* Seattle: Skipstone, 2009.

Till, Karen. *The New Berlin: Memory, Politics, Place.* Minneapolis: University of Minnesota Press, 2005.

Toussaint-Samat, Maguelonne. *A History of Food.* 2d ed. New York: Wiley-Blackwell, 2008.

Tregear, Angela. "From Stilton to Vimto: Using Food History to Re-think Typical Products in Rural Development." *Sociologia Ruralis* 43, no. 2 (2003): 91–107.

Trubek, Amy. *The Taste of Place: A Cultural Journey into Terroir.* Berkeley: University of California Press, 2008.

Tuana, Nancy. "Coming to Understand: Orgasm and the Epistemology of Ignorance." *Hypatia* 19, no. 1 (2004): 194–232.

Veteto, James Robert. "The History and Survival of Traditional Heirloom Vegetable Varieties and Strategies for the Conservation of Crop Biodiversity in the Southern Appalachian Mountains of Western North Carolina: A Thesis." PhD diss., Appalachian State University, 2005.

———. "The History and Survival of Traditional Heirloom Vegetable Varieties in the Southern Appalachian Mountains of Western North Carolina." *Agriculture and Human Values* 25, no. 1 (2008): 121.

Viard, Michel. *Légumes d'autrefois: Histoire, variétés insolites, recettes gourmandes.* Paris: Maison Rustique, 2005.

Von Bremzen, Anya. *Mastering the Art of Soviet Cooking: A Memoire of Food and Longing.* New York: Crown, 2013.

Votteler, Willi. *Altbewährte Apfel- und Birnensorten.* Munich: Obst- und Gartenbauverlag des Bayerischen Landesverbandes für Gartenbau und Landespflege, 2008.

Wagner, Christoph, and Lois Lammerhuber. *Most.* Vienna: Pichler, 1999.

Wagner-Pacifici, Robin, and Barry Schwartz. "The Vietnam Veteran's Memorial: Commemorating a Difficult Past." *American Journal of Sociology* 97, no. 2 (1991): 376–420.

Walker, Richard A. *The Conquest of Bread: 150 Years of Agribusiness in California.* New York: New Press, 2004.

Warnes, Andrew. *Savage Barbecue: Race, Culture, and the Invention of America's First Food.* Athens: University of Georgia Press, 2010.

Waters, Alice. *The Art of Simple Food: Notes, Lessons, and Recipes from a Delicious Revolution.* New York: Random House, 2010.

Watson, Ben. *Cider, Hard and Sweet: History, Traditions, and Making Your Own.* Woodstock, VT: Countryman Press, 2008.

Watson, Benjamin A. *Taylor's Guide to Heirloom Vegetables.* Boston: Houghton Mifflin, 1996.

Watson, James L., and Melissa L. Caldwell. *The Cultural Politics of Food and Eating: A Reader*. New York: Blackwell, 2005.

Weaver, William Woys. *Heirloom Vegetable Gardening: A Master Gardener's Guide to Planting, Seed Saving, and Cultural History*. New York: Henry Holt, 1997.

———. *100 Vegetables and Where They Came From*. Chapel Hill, NC: Algonquin Books of Chapel Hill, 2000.

Weber, Klaus, Kathryn Heinze, and Michaela Desoucey. "Forage for Thought: Mobilizing Codes in the Movement for Grass-Fed Meat and Dairy Products." *Administrative Science Quarterly* 53, no. 3 (2008): 529–67.

Weber, Max. "Class, Status, Party." In *From Max Weber*. Translated by H. H. Gerth and C. W. Mills, 180–95. New York: Oxford University Press, 1946.

Weiss, Brad. "Configuring the Authentic Value of Real Food: Farm-to-Fork, Snout-to-Tail, and Local Food Movements." *American Ethnologist* 39, no. 3 (2012): 614–26.

Welborn, Jane. "Apple Sleuths Hungry for Bites of History." *News and Record* (Greensboro, NC), October 6, 1999.

Whealy, Diane Ott. *Gathering: Memoir of a Seed Saver*. Oakland, CA: Wilsted and Taylor, 2011.

Winskie, Jonathan, and Jessica Murray. "Heirloom Seed and Story Keepers: Growing Community and Sustainability through Arts-Based Research." *Papers and Publications: Interdisciplinary Journal of Undergraduate Research* 2, no. 1 (2013): art. 10.

Winter, Jay. *Remembering War: The Great War between Memory and History in the Twentieth Century*. New Haven, CT: Yale University Press, 2006.

Witt, Doris. *Black Hunger: Soul Food and America*. Minneapolis: University of Minnesota Press, 2004.

Wolff, Franziska. "Industrial Transformation and Agriculture: Agrobiodiversity Loss as Sustainability Problem." In *Governance for Industrial Transformation*, edited by Klaus Jacob, Manfred Binder, and Anna Wieczorek, 338–55. Proceedings of the 2003 Berlin Conference on the Human Dimensions of Global Environmental Policy Research Centre, Berlin.

Wynne, Peter. *Apples*. New York: Hawthorn Books, 1975.

Yepsen, Roger B. *Apples*. New York: W. W. Norton, 1994.

———. *A Celebration of Heirloom Vegetables: Growing and Cooking Old-Time Varieties*. New York: Artisan, 1998.

Yotova, Maria. "'The Bacillus That Makes Our Milk': Ethnocentric Perceptions of Yogurt in Postsocialist Bulgaria." In *Why We Eat, How We Eat: Contemporary Encounters between Foods and Bodies*, edited by Emma-Jayne Abbots and Anna Lavis, 169–85. Burlington, VT: Ashgate, 2013.

Young, James. *At Memory's Edge: After-Images of the Holocaust in Contemporary Art and Architecture*. New Haven, CT: Yale University Press, 2000.

Zirfas, Jörg. *Apfel: Eine kleine kulinarische Anthologie*. Stuttgart: Reclam, 1998.

Zola, Émile. *The Belly of Paris*. Translated by Brian Nelson. New York: Oxford University Press, 2007.

Zukin, Sharon. *Naked City: The Death and Life of Authentic Urban Places*. New York: Oxford University Press, 2011.

———. *Point of Purchase: How Shopping Changed American Culture*. New York: Routledge, 2005.

Index

Abbots, Emma-Jayne, 225n7

achocha, 265n56

Adams Morgan farmers' market (Washington, DC), 96

AeppelTreow Winery (WI), 109

African American farmers, 225n9

African American food, 150–56, 273–74nn87–88, 274n97, 274n102, 275n106

African food, 136, 138; cassava, 139, 268–69nn14–16; in Southern US cooking, 150–56, 273–74nn87–88, 274n97, 274n102, 275n106

agrobiodiversity, 223n2 (ch. 1), 224n4

Albemarle Pippin apple, 104–5

Alexanders, 163

Alice's Garden (Milwaukee), 130

Alinea (Chicago), 21

Alkon, Alison Hope, 246n104, 257n116

Allen, Will, 229n32

American food, 136, 146–56; African American food, 150–56, 273–74nn87–88, 274n97, 274n102, 275n106; Appalachian food, 275n106; beans, 140–41; bread, 275n109; culinary cosmopolitanism in, 272n76; foraging and, 150–51; gardening and, 150; immigrant sources of, 147–50, 156–57, 177–79, 271–72nn65–67, 272n70, 272n76, 275n110; indigenous fruits, 187–88, 194–95, 278n20; regionalism and multiculturalism in, 150–51; shifting trends in, 148–49. See also Native Americans

American Livestock Breeds Conservancy, 58, 242n81

American Mother apples, 252n49

American Pomological Society, 85, 93

American Terroir (Jacobsen), 85

Anatomy of Dessert, The (Bunyard), 76, 98–99

Anderson, Benedict, 257n119

Andes tomatoes, 45

Andoh, Elizabeth, 266n86

Angels' Kitchen, The (Murillo), 46

Animal, Vegetable, Miracle (Kingsolver), 27

Anson Mills grits, 152

antique varieties, 223n2 (prologue). *See also* heirloom varieties

applejack, 109, 150

apple pie, 101

apples, 73–112, 209, 216; appearance of, 89–90, 98; biodiversity of, 83–91; breeding of, 81–82, 84, 249nn4–5, 250n14, 252n47, 253n65; cider from, 74, 84–85, 86, 108–11, 248n2; classification and pomology of, 82–83, 85–86, 91, 101; commercial standardization of, 88–91, 96–97, 256n94; dwarf rootstock and, 89–90; flavor preferences for, 75–76, 80; forgotten varieties of, 89–90, 103, 106–8, 111–12, 254n69, 255n89; grafting of, 79, 81, 85, 86–87, 89–90, 94, 250n14, 260n147; growing from seed of, 84–85, 86, 250n14; in heirloom orchards and open-air museums,

farmers' markets, 68–70; of farms
and gardens, 70–72, 132–34; of
heirloom orchards and open-air
museums, 9, 49, 70–71, 91, 102–6,
132–34; of the human body, 67;
imagined communities as, 100,
257n119; of public edible gardens,
63, 132–33. *See also* identity of place;
mobility of food
social transformation of food. *See*
memory shaping materiality
Sonoma Antique Apple Nursery, 95
sorrel, 164
soursop, 183
Southern (soul) food, 138, 150–56,
273–74nn87–88, 274n97, 274n102,
275n106
Southern Foodways Alliance, 152
Southern Seed Legacy, 54, 56–57, 152,
242n77
Spanish paprika, 139
spice trade, 159
spinach, 127, 263n24
squash, 121, 135, 262n19, 263n24,
264n34, 268n12
Standage, Tom, 144–45
Stark, Tim, 43–45
status symbols. *See* culinary status
symbols
Stekovics, Erich, 57
Stewart, Martha: heirloom food movement and, 10, 22, 42–43, 62, 142,
235n5, 243n87; satire of, 193, 282n92
Stickley, Gustav, 247n117
Stocks, Christopher: on apples, 81; on
cabbages, 122; on cherries, 192; on
English varieties, 99; on jam, 189;
on landscapes of culinary memory, 106–7; on leeks, 163; on plums,

277n9; on raspberries, 194; on rhubarb, 205–6; on strawberries, 195;
on turnips and carrots, 124–25
stone fruits, 167–76; distilling/bran-
dies and liqueurs, 168, 189, 190;
espalier techniques for, 193; grafting of, 172–73; microclimates supporting, 167–68, 176; out-of-season
dried varieties of, 115; ripening of,
174; time investment/care/pruning
of trees, 176; transport/mobility of,
174–75
strawberries, 125, 187, 194–95,
282n104; wild, 194–95
sugar, 159
sugar apples, 183
sugarcane, 137
Sun Crest peaches, 193
supermarkets, 66–67, 69
Svalbard Global Seed Vault (Norway),
16, 34
swedes, 125
sweet potatoes, 263n24
Swiss chard, 128, 157–58, 263n24

taro, 268n14
taste (aesthetics): Bourdieu on habitus and, 65, 99, 257n119; formation of, 278n10; function in space
of, 247n112; national identity and,
98–102, 257–58nn115–16; social
qualities of, 65–72, 99–100, 216,
240n71, 242n81, 242n83, 244n95,
246nn109–10
taste (flavor). *See* flavor
Tavernier, Jean-Baptiste, 126
Taylor's Guide to Heirloom Vegetables,
52, 62
tepary beans, 140–41